Copyright © 2020 National Fire Protection Association® and the Ameri(

NFPA® 54

ANSI Z223.1–2021

National Fuel Gas Code

2021 Edition

This edition of NFPA 54/ANSI Z223.1, *National Fuel Gas Code*, was prepared by the Technical Committee on National Fuel Gas Code. It was issued by the Standards Council on March 15, 2020, with an effective date of April 4, 2020, and supersedes all previous editions.

This edition of NFPA 54/ANSI Z223.1 was approved as an American National Standard on April 4, 2020. The ANSI designation, Z223.1-2021, was approved on April 2, 2020. The NFPA designation is NFPA 54-2021.

Origin and Development of NFPA 54/ANSI Z223.1

This code offers criteria for the installation and operation of gas piping and gas equipment on consumers' premises. It is the cumulative result of years of experience of many individuals and many organizations acquainted with the installation of gas piping and equipment designed for utilization of gaseous fuels. It is intended to promote public safety by providing requirements for the safe and satisfactory utilization of gas.

Changes in this code can become necessary from time to time. When any revision is deemed advisable, recommendations should be forwarded to the Secretary, Accredited Standards Committee Z223, 400 N. Capitol St. NW, Washington, DC 20001, and the Secretary, Standards Council, National Fire Protection Association, 1 Batterymarch Park, Quincy, MA 02169-7471.

Prior to 1974, the following three codes covered the installation of gas piping and appliances:

(1) *American National Standard Installation of Gas Appliances and Gas Piping*, ANSI Z21.30 (NFPA 54)
(2) *Installation of Gas Piping and Gas Equipment on Industrial Premises and Certain Other Premises*, ANSI Z83.1 (NFPA 54A)
(3) *Fuel Gas Piping*, ASME B31.2

The first edition of the code was issued in 1974. It combined the requirements of the three predecessor documents. The American Gas Association and the National Fire Protection Association have continued co-sponsorship of the code following the first edition.

The second edition of the code, incorporating pertinent portions of B31.2, was issued in 1980 and reorganized the code to the current format. Subsequent editions were issued in 1984, 1988, 1992, 1996, 1999, and 2002, respectively. The scope of the code was expanded in 1988 to include piping systems up to and including 125 psi (862 kPa). Revision highlights from subsequent editions include the following:

The 2006 edition incorporated expanded steel, copper, and polyethylene pipe sizing tables. Requirements for appliance shutoff valves were revised to allow manifold systems with all shutoff valves in one location up to 50 ft (15 m) from the most remote appliance, and the chapters were reorganized by application.

The 2009 edition included allowing press-connect fittings for gas tubing systems, new requirements for bonding of CSST piping systems, expanded CSST sizing tables to recognize additional available sizes, new coverage of outdoor decorative appliances, and a new requirement to seal the annular space around the side wall vent penetrations.

The 2012 edition included revised fuel gas piping purging procedures that require outdoor purging of piping with larger pipe sizes or higher operating pressures and allows smaller or lower operating pressure piping to be purged indoors under specific conditions.

The 2015 edition revised the bonding requirements for CSST so that the bonding connection can be placed on any metallic fitting in the piping system as long as the bonding jumper does not exceed 75 ft (22 m) in length. Overpressure protection requirements were rewritten and overpressure protection is required on any system containing an appliance with a maximum inlet pressure of 14 in. w.c. (3.5 kPa) that is supplied with gas at the point of delivery at a pressure greater than 2 psig (14 kPa). Annex G, Recommended Procedure for Safety Inspection of an Existing Appliance Installation, was expanded and revised to reflect modern appliances and test methods.

In the 2018 edition, revisions to piping included allowing listed arc-resistant jacket or coated CSST to use the appliance's electrical grounding connector as the bonding means and recognizing stainless steel smooth wall pipe and tubing products as acceptable piping materials. The minimum allowed wall thickness of carbon and stainless steel pipe was revised to Schedule 10, but joints on Schedule 10 pipe cannot be made with screwed fittings. Press-connect fittings were added as an acceptable joining method for pipe.

Revisions to the venting requirements included requiring listing to the appropriate UL standards for plastic venting materials, factory-built chimneys, Type B and BW vents, chimney lining systems, and special gas vents. Direct vent clearances to building openings for appliances with an input above 150,000 Btu (44 kW) are to be in accordance with the appliance manufacturer's installation instructions.

Finally, in Chapter 9 a requirement was added that an existing gas appliance installation be inspected for combustion air and venting code compliance when the building structure that it is installed in is modified with specific air infiltration-reducing changes.

The 2021 edition includes revisions in Chapter 10 that now require appliances to be listed to and in compliance with the appropriate ANSI/CSA appliance listing standard, thereby providing an increased level of safety. Installation requirements for unlisted appliances have been removed, and they will now have to be evaluated through the application of equivalency.

A table for through the wall vent terminal clearances has been added to Chapter 12, along with an associated annex figure that coordinates this code with the clearances in ANSI product standards. Engineering methods are now defined in Chapter 4 to provide guidance to authorities having jurisdiction on acceptable engineering methods that will eliminate the need to approve individually all engineering methods used.

Finally, electric isolation requirements for gas piping installation have been revised and reorganized to better reflect where the dielectric union is to be installed in the system and what it is protecting.

Technical Committee on National Fuel Gas Code
Joint Listing of NFPA 54 and ASC Z223 Committee

Frank J. Mortimer, *Chair*
EMC Insurance Company, IA [I/I]
Rep. Property Casualty Insurers Association of America

Paul W. Cabot, *Nonvoting Secretary*
American Gas Association, DC [IM]
Rep. American Gas Association

Dmitry Antonov, Intertek, NY [RT/AR-TL]
Eric Adiar†, Hearth, Patio & Barbecue Association, VA [M]
Thomas Andrews, Michigan Technical Education Center, MI [SE/SE]
David Berning†, Product Design Engineering, SC [M]
Jonathan Brania, UL LLC, NC [RT/AR-TL]
James P. Brewer, Magic Sweep Corporation, VA [IM/I-M]
  Rep. National Chimney Sweep Guild
Chris Dale Byers, Piedmont Natural Gas, SC [U/ES]
Thomas R. Crane, Crane Engineering, MN [SE/SE]
Gerald G. Davis*, Williams Meter Company, MD [IM]
Mike Deegan, Clearwater Gas System, FL [U/ES]
  Rep. American Public Gas Association
Mark Fasel, Viega LLC, IN [M/M]]
Alberto Jose Fossa*, NEWEN Creative Engineering, Brazil [SE]
  Rep. NFPA Latin American Section
Richard L. Gilbert*, Texas Propane Gas Association, TX [IM]
Enrique Trejo Gonzalez, International Association of Plumbing & Mechanical Officials (IAPMO), CA [E/EA]
  Rep. International Association of Plumbing & Mechanical Officials
Mike Gorham, Northwest Gas Company, MN [IM/ES]
  Rep. National Propane Gas Association
Gregg A. Gress, International Code Council, IL [E/EA]
Roger W. Griffith*, Griffith Engineering, TN [U]
Steen Hagensen, ENERVEX, GA [M/M]
William T. Hamilton*, UGI Utilities Inc., PA [IM]
  Rep. American Gas Association
Peter T. Holmes*, Maine Fuel Board, ME [E]
Diane Jakobs, Rheem, AR [M/M]
  Rep. Air-Conditioning, Heating, & Refrigeration Institute

James Kendzel*, American Supply Association, IL [U]
Jeff Kleiss, Lochinvar, TN [M/M]
  Rep. Air-Conditioning, Heating, & Refrigeration Institute
Vladimir Kochkin†, National Association of Home Builders, DC [I-M]
Marek Kulik*, Technical Standards and Safety Authority, Canada [E]
Theodore C. Lemoff, Naples, FL [SE/SE]
Timothy McNulty*, RM Manifold Group Inc., dba US Draft Company, TX [M]
William J Murray*, Corning Incorporated, NY [U]
Tung Nguyen*, Emerson Automation Solution, TX [M]
Andrea Lanier Papageorge, Southern Company Gas, GA [IM/ES]
  Rep. American Gas Association
Dale L. Powell, Copper Development Association, Inc., PA [M/M]
  Rep. Copper Development Association Inc.
Phillip H. Ribbs*, PHR Consultants, CA [L]
  Rep. California State Pipe Trades Council
April Dawn Richardson, Railroad Commission of Texas, TX [E/EA]
Brian Ryglewicz*, Chimney Design Solutions Inc., NJ [M]
Eric C. Smith, State of Nevada, NV [E/EA]
  Rep. International Fire Marshals Association
Jason Stanek, Metropolitan Utilities District (MUD), NE [IM/ES]
  Rep. American Gas Association
Peter C. Swim*, Whirlpool Corporation, MI [M]
Franklin R. Switzer, Jr., S-afe, Inc., NY [SE/SE]
Mathew Williams†, Association of Home Appliance Manufacturers, DC [M]

Alternates

Hugo Aguilar, International Association of Plumbing & Mechanical Officials (IAPMO), CA [E/EA]
  (Alt. to Enrique Trejo Gonzalez)
Jeremy R. Conjura*, Corning Incorporated, NY [U]
  (Alt. to William J Murray)
Kody N. Daniel, EMC Insurance Companies, IA [I/I]
  (Alt. to Frank J. Mortimer)
John P. Doucette, State of CT Department of Administrative Services, CT [E/EA]
  (Alt. to Peter T. Holmes)
Craig Drumheller†, National Association of Home Builders, DC [I-M]
  (Alt. to Vladimir Kochkin)
Ralph Euchner, PSNC Energy, NC [IM/ES]
  (Alt. to Andrea Lanier Papageorge)
Pennie L. Feehan, Pennie L. Feehan Consulting, CA [M/M]
  (Alt. to Dale L. Powell)

Fred Grable, International Code Council, IL [E/EA]
  (Alt. to Gregg A. Gress)
Paul Gugliotta†, National Grid, NY [ES]
  (Alt. to Jason Stanek)
Travis F. Hardin*, UL LLC, NC [RT]
  (Alt. to Jonathan Brania)
John Kory, CSA America, Inc., OH [RT/AR-TL]
  (Voting Alt.)
Donald J. MacBride, Dominion East Ohio Gas, OH [IM/ES]
  (Alt. to William T. Hamilton)
Jean L. McDowell*, McDowell Owens Engineering Inc., TX [IM]
  (Alt. to Richard L. Gilbert)
John R. Puskar, Prescient Technical Services LLC, OH [SE/SE]
  (Alt. to Theodore C. Lemoff)
Phillip W. Stephens, Weil Mclain, IN [M/M]
  (Alt. to Jeff Kleiss)
Bruce J. Swiecicki, National Propane Gas Association, IL [IM/ES]
  (Alt. to Mike Gorham)

Andy John Thielen, Crane Engineering, MN [SE/SE]
(Alt. to Thomas R. Crane)

Kent Lowery Thompson*, Railroad Commission of Texas, TX [E]
(Alt. to April Dawn Richardson)

Alex Ing, NFPA Staff Liaison

Robert Torbin, Omega Flex, Inc., MA [M/M]
(Alt. to Diane Jakobs)

*NFPA 54 Committee only. †Z223 Committee only. [NFPA Interest Category/ASC Z223 Interest Category]

This list represents the membership at the time the Committee was balloted on the final text of this edition. Since that time, changes in the membership may have occurred. A key to classifications is found at the back of the document.

NOTE: Membership on a committee shall not in and of itself constitute an endorsement of the Association or any document developed by the committee on which the member serves.

The National Fuel Gas Code Committee is a committee functioning jointly under American National Standards Institute Accredited Standard Committee Z223 procedures and the National Fire Protection Association and, accordingly, the National Fuel Gas Code bears two designations, ANSI Z223.1 and NFPA 54. In the ANSI context, the code is prepared by the Accredited Standards Committee on National Fuel Gas Code, Z223, sponsored by the American Gas Association (Administrative Secretariat). In the NFPA context, the committee is an NFPA Technical Committee submitted to ANSI under NFPA audited designation.

Committee Scope: This Committee shall have primary responsibility for documents on safety code for gas piping systems on consumers' premises and the installation of gas utilization equipment and accessories for use with fuel gases such as natural gas, manufactured gas, liquefied petroleum gas in the vapor phase, liquefied petroleum gas-air mixtures, or mixtures of these gases, including: a. The design, fabrication, installation, testing, operation, and maintenance of gas piping systems from the point of delivery to the connections with each gas utilization device. Piping systems covered by this Code are limited to a maximum operating pressure of 125 psig. For purposes of this Code, the point of delivery is defined as the outlet of the meter set assembly, or the outlet of the service regulator or service shutoff valve where no meter is provided. b. The installation of gas utilization equipment, related accessories, and their ventilation and venting systems.

Contents

Chapter 1	Administration	54–7
1.1	Scope.	54–7
1.2	Purpose.	54–7
1.3	Retroactivity.	54–8
1.4	Equivalency.	54–8
1.5	Enforcement.	54–8

Chapter 2	Referenced Publications	54–8
2.1	General.	54–8
2.2	NFPA Publications.	54–8
2.3	Other Publications.	54–8
2.4	References for Extracts in Mandatory Sections.	54–10

Chapter 3	Definitions	54–10
3.1	General.	54–10
3.2	NFPA Official Definitions.	54–10
3.3	General Definitions.	54–10

Chapter 4	General	54–17
4.1	Qualified Agency.	54–17
4.2	Interruption of Service.	54–17
4.3	Prevention of Accidental Ignition.	54–17
4.4	Noncombustible Material.	54–18
4.5	Engineering Methods.	54–18

Chapter 5	Gas Piping System Design, Materials, and Components	54–18
5.1	Piping Plan.	54–18
5.2	Interconnections Between Gas Piping Systems.	54–18
5.3	Sizing of Gas Piping Systems.	54–18
5.4	Operating Pressure.	54–18
5.5	Piping Materials and Joining Methods.	54–19
5.6	Gas Meters.	54–21
5.7	Gas Pressure Regulators.	54–22
5.8	Overpressure Protection Devices.	54–22
5.9	Back Pressure Protection.	54–23
5.10	Low-Pressure Protection.	54–23
5.11	Shutoff Valves.	54–23
5.12	Excess Flow Valve(s).	54–23
5.13	Expansion and Flexibility.	54–23
5.14	Pressure Regulator and Pressure Control Venting.	54–23

Chapter 6	Pipe Sizing	54–24
6.1	Pipe Sizing Methods.	54–24
6.2	Sizing Natural Gas Piping Systems.	54–24
6.3	Sizing Propane Piping Systems.	54–24
6.4	Sizing Equations.	54–24

Chapter 7	Gas Piping Installation	54–62
7.1	Installation of Underground Piping.	54–62
7.2	Installation of Aboveground Piping.	54–63
7.3	Concealed Piping in Buildings.	54–64
7.4	Piping in Vertical Chases.	54–64
7.5	Gas Pipe Turns.	54–64
7.6	Drips and Sediment Traps.	54–65
7.7	Outlets.	54–65
7.8	Manual Gas Shutoff Valves.	54–65
7.9	Prohibited Devices.	54–65
7.10	Systems Containing Gas–Air Mixtures Outside the Flammable Range.	54–65
7.11	Systems Containing Flammable Gas–Air Mixtures.	54–65
7.12	Electrical Bonding and Grounding.	54–66
7.13	Electrical Circuits.	54–67
7.14	Electrical Connections.	54–67

Chapter 8	Inspection, Testing, and Purging	54–67
8.1	Pressure Testing and Inspection.	54–67
8.2	Piping System Leak Check.	54–68
8.3	Purging Requirements.	54–68

Chapter 9	Appliance, Equipment, and Accessory Installation	54–69
9.1	General.	54–69
9.2	Accessibility and Clearance.	54–70
9.3	Air for Combustion and Ventilation.	54–71
9.4	Appliances on Roofs.	54–72
9.5	Appliances in Attics.	54–73
9.6	Appliance and Equipment Connections to Building Piping.	54–73
9.7	Electrical.	54–75
9.8	Room Temperature Thermostats.	54–75

Chapter 10	Installation of Specific Appliances	54–75
10.1	General.	54–75
10.2	Air-Conditioning Appliances.	54–75
10.3	Central Heating Boilers and Furnaces.	54–77
10.4	Clothes Dryers.	54–79
10.5	Conversion Burners.	54–80
10.6	Decorative Appliances for Installation in Vented Fireplaces.	54–80
10.7	Gas Fireplaces, Vented.	54–80
10.8	Direct Gas-Fired Heating and Forced Ventilation Appliances.	54–80
10.9	Duct Furnaces.	54–81
10.10	Floor Furnaces.	54–81
10.11	Food Service Appliance, Floor-Mounted.	54–82
10.12	Food Service Appliances, Counter Appliances.	54–83
10.13	Household Cooking Appliances.	54–83
10.14	Illuminating Appliances.	54–83
10.15	Incinerators, Commercial-Industrial.	54–84
10.16	Infrared Heaters.	54–84
10.17	Open-Top Broiler Units.	54–84
10.18	Outdoor Cooking Appliances.	54–84
10.19	Pool Heaters.	54–84
10.20	Refrigerators.	54–85
10.21	Room Heaters.	54–85
10.22	Stationary Gas Engines.	54–85
10.23	Gas-Fired Toilets.	54–85
10.24	Unit Heaters.	54–85
10.25	Wall Furnaces.	54–86
10.26	Water Heaters.	54–86
10.27	Compressed Natural Gas (CNG) Vehicular Fuel Systems.	54–87
10.28	Appliances for Installation in Manufactured Housing.	54–87
10.29	Fuel Cell Power Plants.	54–87
10.30	Outdoor Open Flame Decorative Appliances.	54–87
10.31	Outdoor Infrared Heaters.	54–87

Chapter 11	Procedures to Be Followed to Place Appliance in Operation	54–87
11.1	Adjusting the Burner Input.	54–87
11.2	Primary Air Adjustment.	54–87
11.3	Safety Shutoff Devices.	54–87
11.4	Automatic Ignition.	54–87
11.5	Protective Devices.	54–87
11.6	Checking the Draft.	54–88
11.7	Operating Instructions.	54–88

Chapter 12	Venting of Appliances	54–88
12.1	Minimum Safe Performance.	54–88

2021 Edition

12.2	General.	54-88
12.3	Specification for Venting.	54-88
12.4	Design and Construction.	54-88
12.5	Type of Venting System to Be Used.	54-89
12.6	Masonry, Metal, and Factory-Built Chimneys.	54-89
12.7	Gas Vents.	54-91
12.8	Single-Wall Metal Pipe.	54-92
12.9	Through-the-Wall Vent Termination.	54-93
12.10	Condensation Drain.	54-94
12.11	Vent Connectors for Category I Appliances.	54-94
12.12	Vent Connectors for Category II, Category III, and Category IV Appliances.	54-97
12.13	Draft Hoods and Draft Controls.	54-97
12.14	Manually Operated Dampers.	54-97
12.15	Automatically Operated Vent Dampers.	54-97
12.16	Obstructions.	54-97
Chapter 13	Sizing of Category I Venting Systems	54-97
13.1	Additional Requirements to Single Appliance Vent.	54-97
13.2	Additional Requirements to Multiple-Appliance Vent.	54-106
Annex A	Explanatory Material	54-117
Annex B	Sizing and Capacities of Gas Piping	54-129
Annex C	Suggested Method of Checking for Leakage	54-138
Annex D	Suggested Emergency Procedure for Gas Leaks	54-139
Annex E	Flow of Gas Through Fixed Orifices	54-139
Annex F	Sizing of Venting Systems Serving Appliances Equipped with Draft Hoods, Category I Appliances, and Appliances Listed for Use with Type B Vents	54-145
Annex G	Recommended Procedure for Safety Inspection of an Existing Appliance Installation	54-153
Annex H	Indoor Combustion Air Calculation Examples	54-158
Annex I	Example of Combination of Indoor and Outdoor Combustion and Ventilation Opening Design	54-159
Annex J	Enforcement	54-160
Annex K	Informational References	54-161
Index		54-164

NFPA 54

ANSI Z223.1–2021

National Fuel Gas Code

2021 Edition

IMPORTANT NOTE: This AGA and NFPA document is made available for use subject to important notices and legal disclaimers. These notices and disclaimers appear in all publications containing this document and may be found under the heading "Important Notices and Disclaimers Concerning AGA and NFPA Standards." They can also be obtained on request from NFPA or viewed at www.nfpa.org/disclaimersAGA.

UPDATES, ALERTS, AND FUTURE EDITIONS: New editions of NFPA codes, standards, recommended practices, and guides (i.e., NFPA Standards) are released on scheduled revision cycles. This edition may be superseded by a later one, or it may be amended outside of its scheduled revision cycle through the issuance of Tentative Interim Amendments (TIAs). An official NFPA Standard at any point in time consists of the current edition of the document, together with all TIAs and Errata in effect. To verify that this document is the current edition or to determine if it has been amended by TIAs or Errata, please consult the National Fire Codes® Subscription Service or the "List of NFPA Codes & Standards" at www.nfpa.org/docinfo. In addition to TIAs and Errata, the document information pages also include the option to sign up for alerts for individual documents and to be involved in the development of the next edition.

NOTICE: An asterisk (*) following the number or letter designating a paragraph indicates that explanatory material on the paragraph can be found in Annex A.

A reference in brackets [ ] following a section or paragraph indicates material that has been extracted from another NFPA document. Extracted text may be edited for consistency and style and may include the revision of internal paragraph references and other references as appropriate. Requests for interpretations or revisions of extracted text shall be sent to the technical committee responsible for the source document.

Information on referenced publications can be found in Chapter 2 and Annex K.

All pressures used in this code are gauge pressure unless otherwise indicated.

Chapter 1 Administration

1.1 Scope.

1.1.1 Applicability.

1.1.1.1 This code is a safety code that shall apply to the installation of fuel gas piping systems, appliances, equipment, and related accessories as shown in 1.1.1.1(A) through 1.1.1.1(F).

(A)* Coverage of piping systems shall extend from the point of delivery to the appliance connections. For other than undiluted liquefied petroleum gas (LP-Gas) systems, the point of delivery shall be the outlet of the service meter assembly or the outlet of the service regulator or service shutoff valve where no meter is provided. For undiluted LP-Gas systems, the point of delivery shall be considered to be the outlet of the final pressure regulator, exclusive of line gas regulators where no meter is installed. Where a meter is installed, the point of delivery shall be the outlet of the meter.

(B) This code shall apply to natural gas systems operating at a pressure of 125 psi (862 kPa) or less.

(C) This code shall apply to LP-Gas systems operating at a pressure of 50 psi (345 kPa) or less.

(D) This code shall apply to gas–air mixture systems operating within the flammable range at a pressure of 10 psi (69 kPa) or less.

(E) Requirements for piping systems shall include design, materials, components, fabrication, assembly, installation, testing, inspection, operation, and maintenance.

(F) Requirements for appliances, equipment, and related accessories shall include installation, combustion, and ventilation air and venting.

1.1.1.2 This code shall not apply to the following items:

(1) Portable LP-Gas appliances and equipment of all types that are not connected to a fixed fuel piping system
(2) Installation of appliances such as brooders, dehydrators, dryers, and irrigation equipment used for agricultural purposes
(3) Raw material (feedstock) applications except for piping to special atmosphere generators
(4) Oxygen–fuel gas cutting and welding systems
(5) Industrial gas applications using such gases as acetylene and acetylenic compounds, hydrogen, ammonia, carbon monoxide, oxygen, and nitrogen
(6) Petroleum refineries, pipeline compressor or pumping stations, loading terminals, compounding plants, refinery tank farms, and natural gas processing plants
(7) Large integrated chemical plants or portions of such plants where flammable or combustible liquids or gases are produced by chemical reactions or used in chemical reactions
(8) LP-Gas installations at utility gas plants
(9) Liquefied natural gas (LNG) installations
(10) Fuel gas piping in electric utility power plants
(11) Proprietary items of equipment, apparatus, or instruments such as gas generating sets, compressors, and calorimeters
(12) LP-Gas equipment for vaporization, gas mixing, and gas manufacturing
(13) LP-Gas piping for buildings under construction or renovations that is not to become part of the permanent building piping system — that is, temporary fixed piping for building heat
(14) Installation of LP-Gas systems for railroad switch heating
(15) Installation of LP-Gas and compressed natural gas (CNG) systems on vehicles
(16) Gas piping, meters, gas pressure regulators, and other appurtenances used by the serving gas supplier in distribution of gas, other than undiluted LP-Gas
(17) Building design and construction, except as specified herein
(18) Fuel gas systems on recreational vehicles manufactured in accordance with NFPA 1192
(19) Fuel gas systems using hydrogen as a fuel
(20) Construction of appliances

1.1.2 Other Standards. In applying this code, reference shall also be made to the manufacturers' instructions and the serving gas supplier regulations.

1.2 Purpose. (Reserved)

1.3 Retroactivity. Unless otherwise stated, the provisions of this code shall not be applied retroactively to existing systems that were in compliance with the provisions of the code in effect at the time of installation.

1.4 Equivalency. The provisions of this code are not intended to prevent the use of any material, appliance, equipment, method of construction, or installation procedure, provided that any such alternative is acceptable to the authority having jurisdiction. The authority having jurisdiction shall require that sufficient evidence be submitted to substantiate any claims made regarding the safety of such alternatives.

1.5 Enforcement. This code shall be administered and enforced by the authority having jurisdiction designated by the governing authority.

Chapter 2 Referenced Publications

2.1 General. The documents or portions thereof listed in this chapter are referenced within this code and shall be considered part of the requirements of this document.

2.2 NFPA Publications. National Fire Protection Association, 1 Batterymarch Park, Quincy, MA 02169-7471.

NFPA 30A, *Code for Motor Fuel Dispensing Facilities and Repair Garages*, 2021 edition.
NFPA 37, *Standard for the Installation and Use of Stationary Combustion Engines and Gas Turbines*, 2018 edition.
NFPA 51, *Standard for the Design and Installation of Oxygen–Fuel Gas Systems for Welding, Cutting, and Allied Processes*, 2018 edition.
NFPA 52, *Vehicular Natural Gas Fuel Systems Code*, 2019 edition.
NFPA 58, *Liquefied Petroleum Gas Code*, 2020 edition.
NFPA 70®, *National Electrical Code®*, 2020 edition.
NFPA 82, *Standard on Incinerators and Waste and Linen Handling Systems and Equipment*, 2019 edition.
NFPA 88A, *Standard for Parking Structures*, 2019 edition.
NFPA 90A, *Standard for the Installation of Air-Conditioning and Ventilating Systems*, 2021 edition.
NFPA 90B, *Standard for the Installation of Warm Air Heating and Air-Conditioning Systems*, 2021 edition.
NFPA 96, *Standard for Ventilation Control and Fire Protection of Commercial Cooking Operations*, 2021 edition.
NFPA 211, *Standard for Chimneys, Fireplaces, Vents, and Solid Fuel–Burning Appliances*, 2019 edition.
NFPA 409, *Standard on Aircraft Hangars*, 2016 edition.
NFPA 780, *Standard for the Installation of Lightning Protection Systems*, 2020 edition.
NFPA 853, *Standard for the Installation of Stationary Fuel Cell Power Systems*, 2020 edition.
NFPA 1192, *Standard on Recreational Vehicles*, 2021 edition.

2.3 Other Publications.

2.3.1 ASME Publications. American Society of Mechanical Engineers, Two Park Avenue, New York, NY 10016-5990, (800) 843-2763. www.asme.org

ANSI/ASME B1.20.1, *Pipe Threads, General Purpose, Inch*, 2013.

ANSI/ASME B16.1, *Gray Iron Pipe Flanges and Flanged Fittings: Classes 25, 125, and 250*, 2015.

ANSI/ASME B16.5, *Pipe Flanges and Flanged Fittings: NPS ½ through NPS 24 Metric/Inch Standard*, 2017.

ANSI/ASME B16.20, *Metallic Gaskets for Pipe Flanges: Ring-Joint, Spiral-Wound and Jacketed*, 2017.

ANSI/ASME B16.21, *Nonmetallic Flat Gaskets for Pipe Flanges*, 2016.

ANSI/ASME B16.24, *Cast Copper Alloy Pipe Flanges and Flanged Fittings: Classes 150, 300, 600, 900, 1500, and 2500*, 2016.

ANSI/ASME B16.33, *Manually Operated Metallic Gas Valves for Use in Gas Piping Systems up to 175 psi (Sizes NPS 1/2 through NPS 2)*, 2012.

ANSI/ASME B16.42, *Ductile Iron Pipe Flanges and Flanged Fittings: Classes 150 and 300*, 2016.

ANSI/ASME B16.44, *Manually Operated Metallix Gas Valves for Use in Above Ground Piping Systems up to 5 psi*, 2012 (R2017).

ANSI/ASME B16.47, *Large Diameter Steel Flanges: NPS 26 through NPS 60 Metric/Inch Standard*, 2017.

ANSI/ASME B36.10M, *Welded and Seamless Wrought Steel Pipe*, 2018.

2.3.2 ASTM Publications. ASTM International, 100 Barr Harbor Drive, P.O. Box C700, West Conshohocken, PA 19428-2959, (610) 832-9585. www.astm.org

ASTM A53, *Standard Specification for Pipe, Steel, Black and Hot-Dipped, Zinc-Coated Welded and Seamless*, 2018.

ASTM A106, *Standard Specification for Seamless Carbon Steel Pipe for High-Temperature Service*, 2019.

ASTM A254, *Standard Specification for Copper-Brazed Steel Tubing*, 2012.

ASTM A268, *Standard Specification for Seamless and Welded Ferritic and Martensitic Stainless Steel Tubing for General Service*, 2010, reaffirmed 2016.

ASTM A269, *Standard Specification for Seamless and Welded Austenitic Stainless Steel Tubing for General Service*, 2015a.

ASTM A312, *Standard Specification for Seamless, Welded, and Heavily Cold Worked Austenitic Stainless Steel Pipes*, 2018a.

ASTM B88, *Standard Specification for Seamless Copper Water Tube*, 2016.

ASTM B210, *Standard Specification for Aluminum and Aluminum-Alloy Drawn Seamless Tubes*, 2019.

ASTM B241, *Standard Specification for Aluminum and Aluminum-Alloy Seamless Pipe and Seamless Extruded Tube*, 2016.

ASTM B280, *Standard Specification for Seamless Copper Tube for Air Conditioning and Refrigeration Field Service*, 2018.

ASTM D2513, *Standard Specification for Polyethylene (PE) Gas Pressure Pipe, Tubing, and Fittings*, 2018a.

ASTM E136, *Standard Test Method for Behavior of Materials in a Vertical Tube Furnace at 750°C*, 2019.

ASTM E2652, *Standard Test Method for Behavior of Materials in a Tube Furnace with a Cone-shaped Airflow Stabilizer, at 750°C*, 2018.

ASTM F1973, *Standard Specification for Factory Assembled Anodeless Risers and Transition Fittings in Polyethylene (PE) and Polyamide 11 (PA11) and Polyamide 12 (PA12) Fuel Gas Distribution Systems*, 2013, reaffirmed 2018.

ASTM F2509, *Standard Specification for Field-Assembled Anodeless Riser Kits for Use on Outside Diameter Controlled Polyethylene Gas Distribution Pipe and Tubing*, 2015.

ASTM F2945, *Standard Specification for Polyamide 11 Gas Pressure Pipe, Tubing, and Fittings*, 2018.

2.3.3 CSA Group Publications. CSA Group, 178 Rexdale Boulevard, Toronto, ON M9W 1R3, Canada, (216) 524-4990. www.csagroup.org

ANSI/CSA FC 1, *Fuel Cell Technologies — Part 3-100: Stationary Fuel Cell Power Systems — Safety*, 2014, reaffirmed 2018.

ANSI/CSA NGV 5.1, *Residential Fueling Appliances*, 2016.

ANSI/CSA NVG 5.2, *Vehicle Fueling Appliances (VFA)*, 2017.

ANSI LC 1/CSA 6.26, *Fuel Gas Piping Systems Using Corrugated Stainless Steel Tubing (CSST)*, 2018.

ANSI LC 4/CSA 6.32, *Press-Connect Metallic Fittings for Use in Fuel Gas Distribution Systems*, 2012, reaffirmed 2016.

ANSI Z21.1/CSA 1.1, *Household Cooking Gas Appliances*, 2018.

ANSI Z21.5.1/CSA 7.1, *Gas Clothes Dryers, Volume I, Type 1 Clothes Dryers*, 2017.

ANSI Z21.5.2/CSA 7.2, *Gas Clothes Dryers, Volume II, Type 2 Clothes Dryers*, 2016.

ANSI Z21.8, *Installation of Domestic Gas Conversion Burners*, 1994, reaffirmed 2017.

ANSI Z21.10.1/CSA 4.1, *Gas Water Heaters, Volume I, Storage Water Heaters with Input Ratings of 75,000 Btu per Hour or Less*, 2017.

ANSI Z21.10.3/CSA 4.3, *Gas Water Heaters, Volume III, Storage Water Heaters with Input Ratings Above 75,000 Btu per Hour, Circulating or Instantaneous*, 2017.

ANSI Z21.11.2, *Gas-Fired Room Heaters — Volume II, Unvented Room Heaters*, 2016.

ANSI Z21.13/CSA 4.9, *Gas-Fired Low-Pressure Steam and Hot Water Boilers*, 2017.

ANSI Z21.15/CSA 9.1, *Manually operated gas valves for appliances, appliance connector valves and hose end valves*, 2009, reaffirmed 2014.

ANSI Z21.18/CSA 6.3, *Gas Appliance Pressure Regulators*, 2007, reaffirmed 2016.

ANSI Z21.19/CSA 1.4, *Refrigerators Using Gas Fuel*, 2014.

ANSI Z21.22/CSA 4.4, *Relief Valves for Hot Water Supply Systems*, 2015.

ANSI Z21.24/CSA 6.10, *Connectors for Gas Appliances*, 2015.

ANSI Z21.40.1/CSA 2.91, *Gas-Fired Heat Activated Air Conditioning and Heat Pump Appliances*, 1996, reaffirmed 2017.

ANSI Z21.40.2/CSA 2.92, *Air Conditioning and Heat Pump Appliances (Internal Combustion)*, 1996, reaffirmed 2017.

ANSI Z21.41/CSA 6.9, *Quick-Disconnect Devices for Use with Gas Fuel Appliances*, 2014.

ANSI Z21.47/CSA 2.3, *Gas-Fired Central Furnaces*, 2016.

ANSI Z21.50/CSA 2.22, *Vented Decorative Gas Appliances*, 2019.

ANSI Z21.54/CSA 8.4, *Gas Hose Connectors for Portable Outdoor Gas-Fired Appliances*, 2019.

ANSI Z21.56/CSA 4.7, *Gas-Fired Pool Heaters*, 2017.

ANSI Z21.60/CSA 2.26, *Decorative Gas Appliances for Installation in Solid-Fuel Burning Fireplaces*, 2017.

ANSI Z21.69/CSA 6.16, *Connectors for Movable Gas Appliances*, 2015.

ANSI Z21.75/CSA 6.27, *Connectors for Outdoor Gas Appliances and Manufactured Homes*, 2016.

ANSI Z21.80/CSA 6.22, *Line Pressure Regulators*, 2019.

ANSI Z21.86/CSA 2.32, *Vented Gas-Fired Space Heating Appliances*, 2016.

ANSI Z21.90/CSA 6.24, *Gas Convenience Outlets and Optional Enclosures*, 2015.

ANSI Z21.93/CSA 6.30, *Excess Flow Valves for Natural and LP-Gas with Pressures Up to 5 psig*, 2017.

ANSI Z21.97/CSA 2.41, *Outdoor Decorative Gas Appliances*, 2017.

ANSI Z83.4/CSA 3.7, *Non-Recirculating Direct Gas-Fired Heating and Forced Ventilation Appliances for Commercial and Industrial Application*, 2017.

ANSI Z83.8/CSA 2.6, *Gas Unit Heaters, as Packaged Heaters, Gas Utility Heaters, and Gas-Fired Duct Furnaces*, 2016.

ANSI Z83.11/CSA 1.8, *Gas Food Service Equipment*, 2016.

ANSI Z83.18, *Recirculating Direct Gas-Fired Heating and Forced Ventilation Appliances for Commercial and Industrial Application*, 2017.

ANSI Z83.19/CSA 2.35, *Gas-Fired High-Intensity Infrared Heaters*, 2017.

ANSI Z83.20/CSA 2.34, *Gas-Fired Tubular and Low-Intensity Infrared Heaters*, 2016.

ANSI Z83.26/CSA 2.27, *Gas-Fired Outdoor Infrared Patio Heaters*, 2014.

2.3.4 MSS Publications. Manufacturers Standardization Society of the Valve and Fittings Industry, 127 Park Street, NE, Vienna, VA 22180-4602, (703) 281-6613. www.msshq.org

ANSI/MSS SP-58, *Pipe Hangers and Supports — Materials, Design, Manufacture, Selection, Application, and Installation*, 2018.

2.3.5 UL Publications. Underwriters Laboratories Inc., 333 Pfingsten Road, Northbrook, IL 60062-2096. www.ul.com

UL 103, *Chimneys, Factory-Built, Residential Type and Building Heating Appliances*, 2010, revised 2017.

UL 441, *Gas Vents*, 2016.

UL 467, *Grounding and Bonding Equipment*, 2013.

UL 641, *Type L Low-Temperature Venting Systems*, 2010, revised 2018.

UL 651, *Schedule 40 and 80 Rigid PVC Conduit and Fittings*, 2011, revised 2018.

UL 959, *Medium Heat Appliance Factory-Built Chimneys*, 2010, revised 2014.

UL 1738, *Venting Systems for Gas Burning Appliances, Categories II, III and IV*, 2010, revised 2014.

UL 1777, *Chimney Liners*, 2015, revised 2019.

UL 2158A, *Clothes Dryer Transition Ducts*, 2013, revised 2017.

UL 2561, *1400 Degree Fahrenheit Factory-Built Chimneys*, 2016, revised 2018.

UL 378, *Draft Equipment*, 2006, revised 2013.

2.3.6 US Government Publications. US Government Publishing Office, 732 North Capitol Street, NW, Washington, DC 20401-0001. www.gpo.gov

Title 49, Code of Federal Regulations, Part 192, "Transportation of Natural and Other Gas by Pipeline: Minimum Federal Standards."

2.3.7 Other Publications.

Merriam-Webster's Collegiate Dictionary, 11th edition, Merriam-Webster, Inc., Springfield, MA, 2003.

2.4 References for Extracts in Mandatory Sections.

NFPA 31, *Standard for the Installation of Oil-Burning Equipment*, 2016 edition.
NFPA 70®, *National Electrical Code*®, 2017 edition.
NFPA 88A, *Standard for Parking Structures*, 2019 edition.
NFPA 90A, *Standard for the Installation of Air-Conditioning and Ventilating Systems*, 2018 edition.
NFPA *101*®, *Life Safety Code*®, 2018 edition.
NFPA 501, *Standard on Manufactured Housing*, 2017 edition.
NFPA *5000*®, *Building Construction and Safety Code*®, 2018 edition.

Chapter 3 Definitions

3.1 General. The definitions contained in this chapter shall apply to the terms used in this code. Where terms are not defined in this chapter or within another chapter, they shall be defined using their ordinarily accepted meanings within the context in which they are used. *Merriam-Webster's Collegiate Dictionary*, 11th edition, shall be the source for the ordinarily accepted meaning.

3.2 NFPA Official Definitions.

3.2.1* Approved. Acceptable to the authority having jurisdiction.

3.2.2* Authority Having Jurisdiction (AHJ). An organization, office, or individual responsible for enforcing the requirements of a code or standard, or for approving equipment, materials, an installation, or a procedure.

3.2.3* Code. A standard that is an extensive compilation of provisions covering broad subject matter or that is suitable for adoption into law independently of other codes and standards.

3.2.4 Labeled. Equipment or materials to which has been attached a label, symbol, or other identifying mark of an organization that is acceptable to the authority having jurisdiction and concerned with product evaluation, that maintains periodic inspection of production of labeled equipment or materials, and by whose labeling the manufacturer indicates compliance with appropriate standards or performance in a specified manner.

3.2.5* Listed. Equipment, materials, or services included in a list published by an organization that is acceptable to the authority having jurisdiction and concerned with evaluation of products or services, that maintains periodic inspection of production of listed equipment or materials or periodic evaluation of services, and whose listing states that either the equipment, material, or service meets appropriate designated standards or has been tested and found suitable for a specified purpose.

3.2.6 Shall. Indicates a mandatory requirement.

3.3 General Definitions.

3.3.1 Accessible. Having access to but which first requires the removal of a panel, door, or similar covering of the item described.

3.3.1.1 *Readily Accessible.* Having direct access without the need of removing or moving any panel, door, or similar covering of the item described.

3.3.2 Air.

3.3.2.1 *Circulating Air.* Air for cooling, heating, or ventilation distributed to habitable spaces.

3.3.2.2 *Dilution Air.* Air that enters a draft hood or draft regulator and mixes with the flue gases.

3.3.2.3 *Excess Air.* Air that passes through the combustion chamber and the appliance flues in excess of that which is theoretically required for complete combustion.

3.3.2.4 *Primary Air.* The air introduced into a burner that mixes with the gas before it reaches the port or ports.

3.3.3 Anodeless Riser. An assembly of steel-cased plastic pipe used to make the transition between plastic piping installed underground and metallic piping installed aboveground.

3.3.4 Appliance. Any device that utilizes a fuel to produce light, heat, power, refrigeration, or air conditioning, or any device that compresses fuel gas.

3.3.4.1 *Decorative Appliance for Installation in a Vented Fireplace.* A self-contained, freestanding, fuel gas–burning appliance designed for installation only in a vented fireplace and whose primary function lies in the aesthetic effect of the flame.

3.3.4.2 *Direct Vent Appliances.* Appliances that are constructed and installed so that all air for combustion is derived directly from the outdoors and all flue gases are discharged to the outdoors.

3.3.4.3 *Fan-Assisted Combustion Appliance.* An appliance equipped with an integral mechanical means to either draw or force products of combustion through the combustion chamber or heat exchanger.

3.3.4.4 *Food Service Appliance.*

3.3.4.4.1 *Baking and Roasting Oven.* An oven primarily intended for volume food preparation that is composed of one or more sections or units of the following types: (1) cabinet oven, an oven having one or more cavities heated by a single burner or group of burners; (2) reel-type oven, an oven employing trays that are moved by mechanical means; or (3) sectional oven, an oven composed of one or more independently heated cavities.

3.3.4.4.2 *Gas Counter Appliance.* An appliance such as a gas coffee brewer and coffee urn and any appurtenant water heating appliance, food and dish warmer, hot plate, and griddle.

3.3.4.4.3 *Gas Deep Fat Fryer.* An appliance, including a cooking vessel in which oils or fats are placed to such a depth that the cooking food is essentially supported by displacement of the cooking fluid or a perforated container immersed in the cooking fluid rather than by the bottom of the vessel, designed primarily for use in hotels, restaurants, clubs, and similar institutions.

3.3.4.4.4 *Kettle.* An appliance with a cooking chamber that is heated either by a steam jacket in which steam is generated by gas heat or by direct gas heat applied to the cooking chamber.

3.3.4.4.5 *Steam Cooker.* An appliance that cooks, defrosts, or reconstitutes food by direct contact with steam.

3.3.4.4.6 *Steam Generator.* A separate appliance primarily intended to supply steam for use with food service appliances.

3.3.4.5 *Gas Counter Appliances.* See 3.3.4.4.2.

3.3.4.6 *Household Cooking Appliance.* An appliance for domestic food preparation, providing at least one function of (1) top or surface cooking, (2) oven cooking, or (3) broiling.

3.3.4.6.1 *Household Broiler Cooking Appliance.* A unit that cooks primarily by radiated heat.

3.3.4.6.2 *Household Built-In Unit Cooking Appliance.* A unit designed to be recessed into, placed upon, or attached to the construction of a building, but not for installation on the floor.

3.3.4.7 *Low-Heat Appliance.* An appliance needing a chimney capable of withstanding a continuous flue gas temperature not exceeding 1000°F (538°C).

3.3.4.8 *Medium-Heat Appliance.* An appliance needing a chimney capable of withstanding a continuous flue gas temperature not exceeding 1800°F (982°C).

3.3.4.9 *Outdoor Cooking Appliance.* A gas-fired cooking appliance for outdoor use only that is provided with a means of support by the manufacturer and is connected to a fixed gas piping system.

3.3.4.10 *Vented Appliance.*

3.3.4.10.1* *Category I Vented Appliance.* An appliance that operates with a nonpositive vent static pressure and with a vent gas temperature that avoids excessive condensate production in the vent.

3.3.4.10.2 *Category II Vented Appliance.* An appliance that operates with a nonpositive vent static pressure and with a vent gas temperature that can cause excessive condensate production in the vent.

3.3.4.10.3 *Category III Vented Appliance.* An appliance that operates with a positive vent static pressure and with a vent gas temperature that avoids excessive condensate production in the vent.

3.3.4.10.4 *Category IV Vented Appliance.* An appliance that operates with a positive vent static pressure and with a vent gas temperature that can cause excessive condensate production in the vent.

3.3.5 Appliance Categorized Vent Diameter/Area. The minimum vent diameter/area permissible for Category I appliances to maintain a nonpositive vent static pressure when tested in accordance with nationally recognized standards.

3.3.6 Automatic Firecheck. A device for stopping the progress of a flame front in burner mixture lines (flashback) and for automatically shutting off the fuel–air mixture.

3.3.7 Automatic Vent Damper. A device that is intended for installation in the venting system, in the outlet of or downstream of the appliance draft hood, of an individual automatically operated appliance and that is designed to automatically open the venting system when the appliance is in operation and to automatically close off the venting system when the appliance is in a standby or shutdown condition.

3.3.8 Backfire Preventer. See 3.3.86, Safety Blowout.

3.3.9 Baffle. An object placed in an appliance to change the direction of or retard the flow of air, air–gas mixtures, or flue gases.

3.3.10 Boiler.

3.3.10.1 *Hot Water Heating Boiler.* A boiler designed to heat water for circulation through an external space heating system.

3.3.10.2 *Hot Water Supply Boiler.* A boiler used to heat water for purposes other than space heating.

3.3.10.3 *Low Pressure Boiler.* A boiler for generating steam at gauge pressures not in excess of 15 psi (gauge pressure of 103 kPa) or for furnishing water at a maximum temperature of 250°F (121°C) at a maximum gauge pressure of 160 psi (gauge pressure of 1100 kPa). [31, 2016]

3.3.10.4 *Steam Boiler.* A boiler designed to convert water into steam that is supplied to an external system.

3.3.11 Bonding Jumper. A reliable conductor to ensure the required electrical conductivity between metal parts required to be electrically connected. [70:100]

3.3.12 Branch Line. Gas piping that conveys gas from a supply line to the appliance.

3.3.13 Breeching. See 3.3.100, Vent Connector.

3.3.14 Broiler. A general term including broilers, salamanders, barbecues, and other devices cooking primarily by radiated heat, excepting toasters.

3.3.14.1 *Unit Broiler.* A broiler constructed as a separate appliance.

3.3.15 Btu. Abbreviation for British thermal unit, which is the quantity of heat required to raise the temperature of 1 pound of water 1 degree Fahrenheit (equivalent to 1055 joules).

3.3.16 Burner. A device for the final conveyance of gas, or a mixture of gas and air, to the combustion zone.

3.3.16.1 *Forced-Draft Burner.* See 3.3.16.5, Power Burner.

3.3.16.2 *Gas Conversion Burner.* A unit consisting of a burner and its controls utilizing gaseous fuel for installation in an appliance originally utilizing another fuel.

3.3.16.3 *Injection- (Bunsen-) Type Burner.* A burner employing the energy of a jet of gas to inject air for combustion into the burner and mix it with the gas.

3.3.16.4 *Main Burner.* A device or group of devices essentially forming an integral unit for the final conveyance of gas or a mixture of gas and air to the combustion zone and on which combustion takes place to accomplish the function for which the appliance is designed.

3.3.16.5 *Power Burner.* A burner in which either gas or air, or both, are supplied at a pressure exceeding, for gas, the line pressure, and for air, atmospheric pressure; this added pressure being applied at the burner. A burner for which air for combustion is supplied by a fan ahead of the appliance is commonly designated as a forced-draft burner.

3.3.16.5.1 *Fan-Assisted Power Burner.* A burner that uses either induced or forced draft.

3.3.17 Chimney. One or more passageways, vertical or nearly so, for conveying flue or vent gases to the outdoors.

3.3.17.1 *Exterior Masonry Chimneys.* Masonry chimneys exposed to the outdoors on one or more sides below the roof line.

3.3.17.2 *Factory-Built Chimney.* A chimney composed of listed factory-built components assembled in accordance with the manufacturer's installation instructions to form the completed chimney.

3.3.17.3 *Masonry Chimney.* A field-constructed chimney of solid masonry units, bricks, stones, listed masonry chimney units, or reinforced Portland cement concrete, lined with suitable chimney flue liners.

3.3.17.4 *Metal Chimney.* A field-constructed chimney of metal.

3.3.18 Clothes Dryer. An appliance used to dry wet laundry by means of heat.

3.3.18.1 *Type 1 Clothes Dryer.* Primarily used in family living environment. May or may not be coin-operated for public use.

3.3.18.2 *Type 2 Clothes Dryer.* Used in business with direct intercourse of the function with the public. May or may not be operated by public or hired attendant. May or may not be coin-operated.

3.3.19 Combustion. A chemical process of oxidation that occurs at a rate fast enough to produce heat and usually light in the form of either a glow or flame. [**5000,** 2018]

3.3.20 Combustion Chamber. The portion of an appliance within which combustion occurs.

3.3.21 Combustion Products. Constituents resulting from the combustion of a fuel with the oxygen of the air, including the inert but excluding excess air.

3.3.22 Condensate. The liquid that separates from a gas because of a reduction in temperature or an increase in pressure.

3.3.23 Controls. Devices designed to regulate the gas, air, water, or electrical supply to an appliance, either manually or automatically.

3.3.23.1 *Limit Control.* A device responsive to changes in pressure, temperature, or liquid level for turning on, shutting off, or throttling the gas supply to an appliance.

3.3.24 Copper Alloy. A homogenous mixture of two or more metals in which copper is the primary component, such as brass and bronze.

3.3.25 Cubic Foot (ft^3) of Gas. The amount of gas that would occupy 1 ft^3 (0.03 m^3) when at a temperature of 60°F (16°C), saturated with water vapor and under a pressure equivalent to that of 30 in. mercury (101 kPa).

3.3.26 Deep Fat Fryer. See 3.3.4.4.3, Gas Deep Fat Fryer.

3.3.27 Device.

3.3.27.1 *Automatic Gas Shutoff Device.* A device constructed so that the attainment of a water temperature in a hot water supply system in excess of some predetermined limit acts in such a way as to cause the gas to the system to be shut off.

3.3.27.2 *Pressure Limiting Device.* Equipment that under abnormal conditions will act to reduce, restrict, or shut off the supply of gas flowing into a system in order to prevent the gas pressure in that system from exceeding a predetermined value.

3.3.27.3 *Quick-Disconnect Device.* A hand-operated device that provides a means for connecting and disconnecting an appliance or an appliance connector to a gas supply and that is equipped with an automatic means to shut off the gas supply when the device is disconnected.

3.3.27.4 *Safety Shutoff Device.* A device that will shut off the gas supply to the controlled burner(s) in the event the source of ignition fails. This device can interrupt the flow of gas to main burner(s) only or to pilot(s) and main burner(s) under its supervision.

3.3.28 Diversity Factor. Ratio of the maximum probable demand to the maximum possible demand.

3.3.29 Draft. A pressure difference that causes gases or air to flow through a chimney, vent, flue, or appliance.

3.3.29.1 *Mechanical Draft.* Draft produced by a fan or an air or steam jet. When a fan is located so as to push the flue gases through the chimney or vent, the draft is forced. When the fan is located so as to pull the flue gases through the chimney or vent, the draft is induced.

3.3.29.2 *Natural Draft.* Draft produced by the difference in the weight of a column of flue gases within a chimney or vent system and a corresponding column of air of equal dimension outside the chimney or venting system. [**31,** 2016]

3.3.30 Draft Hood. A nonadjustable device built into an appliance, or made a part of the vent connector from an appliance, that is designed to (1) provide for the ready escape of the flue gases from the appliance in the event of no draft, backdraft, or stoppage beyond the draft hood, (2) prevent a backdraft from entering the appliance, and (3) neutralize the effect of stack action of the chimney or gas vent upon the operation of the appliance.

3.3.31 Drip. The container placed at a low point in a system of piping to collect condensate and from which it may be removed.

3.3.32 Dry Gas. A gas having a moisture and hydrocarbon dew point below any normal temperature to which the gas piping is exposed.

3.3.33 Effective Ground-Fault Current Path. An intentionally constructed, low impedance electrically conductive path designed and intended to carry current under ground-fault conditions from the point of a ground fault on a wiring system to the electrical supply source and that facilitates the operation of the overcurrent protective device or ground-fault detectors. [70:100]

3.3.34 Engineering Methods. Design methods that rely on the application of mathematics, sciences, empirical evidence, and engineering principles.

3.3.35 Equipment. Devices other than appliances.

3.3.36 Explosion Heads (Soft Heads or Rupture Discs). A protective device for relieving excessive pressure in a premix system by bursting of a rupturable disc.

3.3.37 FAN Max. The maximum input rating of a Category I, fan-assisted appliance attached to a vent or connector.

3.3.38 FAN Min. The minimum input rating of a Category I, fan-assisted appliance attached to a vent or connector.

3.3.39 FAN+FAN. The maximum combined appliance input rating of two or more Category I, fan-assisted appliances attached to the common vent.

3.3.40 FAN+NAT. The maximum combined appliance input rating of one or more Category I, fan-assisted appliances and one or more Category I, draft hood–equipped appliances attached to the common vent.

3.3.41 Fireplace. A fire chamber and hearth constructed of noncombustible material for use with solid fuels and provided with a chimney.

  3.3.41.1 *Gas Fireplace.*

  3.3.41.1.1 *Direct Vent Gas Fireplace.* A system consisting of (1) an appliance for indoor installation that allows the view of flames and provides the simulation of a solid fuel fireplace, (2) combustion air connections between the appliance and the vent air intake terminal, (3) flue-gas connections between the appliance and the vent-air intake terminal, and (4) a vent air intake terminal for installation outdoors, constructed such that all air for combustion is obtained from the outdoor atmosphere and all flue gases are discharged to the outdoor atmosphere.

  3.3.41.1.2 *Vented Gas Fireplace.* A vented appliance that allows the view of flames and provides the simulation of a solid fuel fireplace.

3.3.42 Flame Arrester. A nonvalve device for use in a gas–air mixture line containing a means for temporarily stopping the progress of a flame front (flashback).

3.3.43 Flue.

  3.3.43.1 *Appliance Flue.* The passage(s) within an appliance through which combustion products pass from the combustion chamber of the appliance to the draft hood inlet opening on an appliance equipped with a draft hood or to the outlet of the appliance on an appliance not equipped with a draft hood.

  3.3.43.2 *Chimney Flue.* The passage(s) in a chimney for conveying the flue or vent gases to the outdoors.

3.3.44 Flue Collar. That portion of an appliance designed for the attachment of a draft hood, vent connector, or venting system.

3.3.45 Furnace.

  3.3.45.1 *Central Furnace.* A self-contained appliance for heating air by transfer of heat of combustion through metal to the air and designed to supply heated air through ducts to spaces remote from or adjacent to the appliance location.

  3.3.45.2 *Direct Vent Wall Furnace.* A system consisting of an appliance, combustion air, and flue gas connections between the appliance and the outdoor atmosphere, and a vent cap supplied by the manufacturer and constructed so that all air for combustion is obtained from the outdoor atmosphere and all flue gases are discharged to the outdoor atmosphere.

  3.3.45.3 *Duct Furnace.* A furnace normally installed in distribution ducts of air-conditioning systems to supply warm air for heating. This definition applies only to an appliance that, for air circulation, depends on a blower not furnished as part of the furnace.

  3.3.45.4 *Enclosed Furnace.* A specific heating, or heating and ventilating, furnace incorporating an integral total enclosure and using only outdoor air for combustion.

  3.3.45.5 *Floor Furnace.* A completely self-contained unit furnace suspended from the floor of the space being heated, taking air for combustion from outside this space.

  3.3.45.6 *Forced-Air Furnace.* A furnace equipped with a fan or blower that provides the primary means for circulation of air.

  3.3.45.7 *Vented Wall Furnace.* A self-contained, vented, fuel gas–burning appliance complete with grilles or equivalent, designed for incorporation in or permanent attachment to the structure of a building and furnishing heated air, circulated by gravity or by a fan, directly into the space to be heated through openings in the casing.

3.3.46 Furnace Plenum. A compartment or chamber that is supplied with the furnace or constructed of ductwork that is attached to the inlet or outlet of a furnace or air-handling unit and has one or more circulating air ducts connected to it.

3.3.47 Garage.

  3.3.47.1 *Repair Garage.* A building, structure, or portions thereof wherein major repair, painting, or body and fender work is performed on motorized vehicles or automobiles, and includes associated floor space used for offices, parking, and showrooms.

3.3.47.2 *Residential Garage.* A building or room in which self-propelled passenger vehicles are or can be stored and that will not normally be used for other than minor service or repair operations on such stored vehicles.

3.3.48 Gas Convenience Outlet. A permanently mounted, hand-operated device providing a means for connecting and disconnecting an appliance or an appliance connector to the gas supply piping.

3.3.49 Gases. Include natural gas, manufactured gas, liquefied petroleum (LP) gas in the vapor phase only, liquefied petroleum gas–air mixtures, and mixtures of these gases, plus gas–air mixtures within the flammable range, with the fuel gas or the flammable component of a mixture being a commercially distributed product.

3.3.49.1 *Flue Gases.* Products of combustion plus excess air in appliance flues or heat exchangers.

3.3.49.2 *Utility Gases.* Natural gas, manufactured gas, liquefied petroleum gas–air mixtures, or mixtures of any of these gases.

3.3.49.3 *Vent Gases.* Products of combustion from appliances plus excess air, plus dilution air in the venting system above the draft hood or draft regulator.

3.3.50 Gas-Fired Air Conditioner. An automatically operated appliance for supplying cooled and/or dehumidified air or chilled liquid.

3.3.51 Gas-Fired Heat Pump. An automatically operated appliance utilizing a refrigeration system for supplying either heated air or liquid or heated and/or cooled air or liquid.

3.3.52 Gas-Mixing Machine. Any combination of automatic proportioning control devices, blowers, or compressors that supply mixtures of gas and air to multiple burner installations where control devices or other accessories are installed between the mixing device and burner.

3.3.53* Gas Vent. A passageway composed of listed factory-built components assembled in accordance with the manufacturer's installation instructions for conveying vent gases from appliances or their vent connectors to the outdoors.

3.3.53.1 *Common Vent.* That portion of a vent or chimney system that conveys vent gases from more than one appliance.

3.3.53.2 *Special-Type Gas Vent.* Gas vents for venting listed Category II, III, and IV appliances.

3.3.53.3 *Type B Gas Vent.* A gas vent for venting listed gas appliances with draft hoods and other Category I appliances listed for use with Type B gas vents.

3.3.53.4 *Type B-W Gas Vent.* A gas vent for venting listed wall furnaces.

3.3.53.5 *Type L Gas Vent.* A gas vent for venting appliances listed for use with Type L vents and appliances listed for use with Type B gas vents.

3.3.54 Gravity. See 3.3.91, Specific Gravity.

3.3.55 Grounding Electrode. A conducting object through which a direct connection to earth is established. [70:100]

3.3.56 Heater.

3.3.56.1 *Infrared Heater.* A heater that directs a substantial amount of its energy output in the form of infrared energy into the area to be heated. Such heaters may be of either the vented or unvented type.

3.3.56.2 *Nonrecirculating Direct Gas-Fired Heating and Forced Ventilation Appliances for Commercial and Industrial Application.* A nonrecirculating direct gas-fired heating and forced ventilation appliance in which all the products of combustion generated by the appliance are released into the outdoor airstream being heated.

3.3.56.3 *Pool Heater.* An appliance designed for heating nonpotable water stored at atmospheric pressure, such as water in swimming pools, therapeutic pools, and similar applications.

3.3.56.4 *Recirculating Direct Gas-Fired Heating and Forced Ventilation Appliances for Commercial and Industrial Application.* A recirculating direct gas-fired heating and forced ventilation appliance in which all of the products of combustion generated by the appliance are released into the airstream being heated.

3.3.56.5 *Unit Heater.* A self-contained, automatically controlled, vented, fuel gas–burning, space-heating appliance intended for installation in the space to be heated without the use of ducts, having integral means for circulation of air.

3.3.56.6 *Unvented Room Heater.* An unvented, self-contained, freestanding, nonrecessed, fuel gas–burning appliance for furnishing warm air by gravity or fan circulation to the space in which installed, directly from the heater without duct connection.

3.3.56.7 *Water Heater.* An appliance for supplying hot water for domestic or commercial purposes.

3.3.57 Heating Value (Total). The number of British thermal units produced by the combustion, at constant pressure, of 1 ft^3 (0.03 m^3) of gas when the products of combustion are cooled to the initial temperature of the gas and air, when the water vapor formed during combustion is condensed, and when all the necessary corrections have been applied.

3.3.58 Hot Plate. See 3.3.4.4.2, Gas Counter Appliance.

3.3.58.1 *Domestic Hot Plate.* A fuel gas–burning appliance consisting of one or more open-top-type burners installed on short legs or a base.

3.3.59 Ignition.

3.3.59.1 *Automatic Ignition.* Ignition of gas at the burner(s) when the gas-controlling device is turned on, including re-ignition if the flames on the burner(s) have been extinguished by means other than by the closing of the gas-controlling device.

3.3.59.2 *Sources of Ignition.* Appliances or equipment that, because of their intended modes of use or operation, are capable of providing sufficient thermal energy to ignite flammable gas–air mixtures.

3.3.60 Insulating Millboard. A factory-fabricated board formed with noncombustible materials, normally fibers, and having a thermal conductivity in the range of 1 Btu/in./ft^2/°F/hr (0.14 W/m/°K).

3.3.61 Kettle. See 3.3.4.4.4.

3.3.62 Manifold.

3.3.62.1 *Common Vent Manifold.* A horizontal extension of the common vent within the room in which the appliances are installed.

3.3.62.2 *Gas Manifold.* The conduit of an appliance that supplies gas to the individual burners.

3.3.63 Manufactured Home. A structure, transportable in one or more sections, that, in the traveling mode, is 8 body-ft (2.4 m) or more in width or 40 body-ft (12.2 m) or more in length or, that on site is 320 ft^2 (29.7 m^2) or more, is built on a permanent chassis, is designed to be used as a dwelling with or without a permanent foundation, whether or not connected to the utilities, and includes plumbing, heating, air-conditioning, and electrical systems contained therein. Such terms shall include any structure that meets all the requirements of this paragraph except the size requirements and with respect to which the manufacturer voluntarily files a certification required by the regulatory agency. Calculations used to determine the number of square feet in a structure are based on the structure's exterior dimensions, include all expandable rooms, cabinets, and other projections containing interior space, but do not include bay windows. [501, 2017]

3.3.64 Material.

3.3.64.1* *Combustible (Material).* A material that, in the form in which it is used and under the conditions anticipated, will ignite and burn; a material that does not meet the definition of noncombustible. [101, 2015]

3.3.64.2 *Noncombustible Material.* A material that, in the form in which it is used and under the conditions anticipated, will not ignite, burn, support combustion, or release flammable vapors when subjected to fire or heat.

3.3.65 Meter. An instrument installed to measure the volume of gas delivered through it.

3.3.66 Mixing Blower. A motor-driven blower to produce gas–air mixtures for combustion.

3.3.67 NA. Vent configuration that is not allowed due to potential for condensate formation or pressurization of the venting system or that is not applicable due to physical or geometric restraints.

3.3.68 NAT Max. The maximum input rating of a Category I, draft hood–equipped appliance attached to a vent or connector.

3.3.69 NAT+NAT. The maximum combined appliance input rating of two or more Category I, draft hood–equipped appliances attached to the common vent.

3.3.70 Occupancy.

3.3.70.1 *Health Care Occupancy.* An occupancy used to provide medical or other treatment or care simultaneously to four or more patients on an inpatient basis, where such patients are mostly incapable of self-preservation due to age, physical or mental disability, or because of security measures not under the occupants' control. [5000, 2018]

3.3.70.2 *Residential Board and Care Occupancy.* An occupancy used for lodging and boarding of four or more residents, not related by blood or marriage to the owners or operators, for the purpose of providing personal care services. [5000, 2018]

3.3.71 Orifice. The opening in a cap, spud, or other device whereby the flow of gas is limited and through which the gas is discharged to the burner.

3.3.72 Oven, Baking and Roasting. See 3.3.4.4.1, Baking and Roasting Oven.

3.3.73 Parking Structure. A building, structure, or portion thereof used for the parking, storage, or both, of motor vehicles. [88A, 2019]

3.3.73.1 *Basement or Underground Parking Structure.* A parking structure or portion thereof located below finished ground level.

3.3.73.2 *Enclosed Parking Structure.* Having exterior enclosing walls that have less than 25 percent of the total wall area open to atmosphere at each level using at least two sides of the structure.

3.3.74 Pilot. A small flame that is utilized to ignite the gas at the main burner or burners.

3.3.75 Pipe. Rigid conduit used to convey fuel gas or other fluids.

3.3.75.1 *Equivalent Length Pipe.* The resistance of valves, controls, and fittings to gas flow expressed as equivalent length of straight pipe for convenience in calculating pipe sizes.

3.3.76 Piping. Pipe or tubing.

3.3.76.1 *Concealed Gas Piping.* Gas piping that, when in place in a finished building, would require removal of permanent construction to gain access to the piping.

3.3.76.2 *Control Piping.* All piping, valves, and fittings used to interconnect air, gas, or hydraulically operated control apparatus or instrument transmitters and receivers.

3.3.77 Plenum. A compartment or chamber to which one or more ducts are connected and that forms part of the air distribution system. [90A, 2018]

3.3.78 Point of Delivery. The location point where the customer-owned fuel gas piping begins *[see 1.1.1.1(A)]*.

3.3.79 Pressure. Unless otherwise stated, a measurement expressed in pounds per square inch above atmospheric pressure.

3.3.79.1 *Atmospheric Pressure.* The pressure of the weight of air on the surface of the earth, approximately 14.7 pounds per square inch (psia) (101 kPa absolute) at sea level.

3.3.79.2 *Back Pressure.* Pressure against which a fluid is flowing, resulting from friction in lines, restrictions in pipes or valves, pressure in vessel to which fluid is flowing, hydrostatic head, or other impediment that causes resistance to fluid flow.

3.3.79.3 *Design Pressure.* The maximum operating pressure permitted by this code, as determined by the design procedures applicable to the materials involved.

3.3.79.4 *Maximum Working Pressure.* The maximum pressure at which a piping system can be operated in accordance with the provisions of this code.

3.3.79.5 *Supply Pressure.* The gas pressure measured at the inlet to the appliance.

3.3.80 Pressure Drop. The loss in pressure due to friction or obstruction in pipes, valves, fittings, regulators, and burners.

3.3.81 Purge. To free a gas conduit of air or gas, or a mixture of gas and air.

3.3.82 Qualified Agency. Any individual, firm, corporation, or company that either in person or through a representative is engaged in and is responsible for (1) the design, installation, testing, or replacement of gas piping or (2) the connection, installation, testing, repair, or servicing of appliances and equipment; that is experienced in such work; that is familiar with all precautions required; and that has complied with all the requirements of the authority having jurisdiction.

3.3.83 Refrigerator (Using Gas Fuel). An appliance that is designed to extract heat from a suitable chamber.

3.3.84 Regulator.

3.3.84.1 *Draft Regulator.* A device that functions to maintain a desired draft in the appliance by automatically reducing the draft to the desired value.

3.3.84.1.1 *Barometric Draft Regulator.* A balanced damper device attached to a chimney, vent connector, breeching, or flue gas manifold to control chimney draft.

3.3.84.2 *Gas Appliance Pressure Regulator.* A pressure regulator for controlling pressure to the appliance manifold.

3.3.84.3 *Line Pressure Regulator.* A pressure regulator placed in a gas line between the service regulator and the appliance regulator.

3.3.84.4* *Monitor Regulator.* A pressure regulator that is installed in series with another pressure regulator for the purpose of preventing an overpressure in the downstream piping system.

3.3.84.5 *Pressure Regulator.* Equipment placed in a gas line for reducing, controlling, and maintaining the pressure in that portion of the piping system downstream of the equipment.

3.3.84.6 *Regulator Vent.* The opening in the atmospheric side of the regulator housing permitting the in and out movement of air to compensate for the movement of the regulator diaphragm.

3.3.84.7 *Series Regulator.* A pressure regulator in series with one or more other pressure regulators.

3.3.84.8 *Service Regulator.* A pressure regulator installed by the serving gas supplier to reduce and limit the service line gas pressure to delivery pressure.

3.3.85 Relief Opening. The opening provided in a draft hood to permit the ready escape to the atmosphere of the flue products from the draft hood in the event of no draft, backdraft, or stoppage beyond the draft hood and to permit inspiration of air into the draft hood in the event of a strong chimney updraft.

3.3.86 Safety Blowout (Backfire Preventer). A protective device incorporating a bursting disc for excessive pressure release, means for stopping a flame front, and an electric switch or other release mechanism for actuating a built-in or separate safety shutoff.

3.3.87 Service Head Adapter. A transition fitting for use with plastic piping (which is encased in non-pressure-carrying metal pipe) that connects the metal pipe casing and plastic pipe and tubing to the remainder of the piping system.

3.3.88 Service Meter Assembly. The meter, valves, piping, fittings, and equipment installed by the serving gas supplier to connect the gas supply to the customer's house or yard piping.

3.3.89 Service Regulator. See 3.3.84.5, Pressure Regulator; and 3.3.84.8, Service Regulator.

3.3.90 Shutoff. See 3.3.98, Valve.

3.3.91 Specific Gravity. As applied to gas, the ratio of the weight of a given volume to that of the same volume of air, both measured under the same conditions.

3.3.92 Steam Cooker. See 3.3.4.4.5, Steam Cooker.

3.3.93 Steam Generator. See 3.3.4.4.6, Steam Generator.

3.3.94 Stress. The resultant internal force that resists change in the size or shape of a body acted on by external forces. In this code, the term *stress* is often used as being synonymous with unit stress, which is the stress per unit area (psi).

3.3.94.1 *Hoop Stress.* The stress in a pipe wall, acting circumferentially in a plane perpendicular to the longitudinal axis of the pipe and produced by the pressure of the fluid in the pipe.

3.3.95 System.

3.3.95.1 *Central Premix System.* A system that distributes flammable gas–air mixtures to two or more remote stations.

3.3.95.2 *Fan-Assisted Combustion System.* An appliance equipped with an integral mechanical means to either draw or force products of combustion through the combustion chamber or heat exchanger.

3.3.95.3 *Hybrid Pressure System.* A piping system in which the pressure at the point of delivery is reduced by one or more line pressure regulators prior to the appliance connection.

3.3.95.4 *Mechanical Exhaust System.* Equipment installed in and made a part of the vent to provide the required flow of gases through the vent.

3.3.95.5 *Natural Draft Venting System.* A venting system that relies on natural draft to convey the products of combustion.

3.3.95.6 *Piping System.* All pipe, tubing, valves, and fittings from the point of delivery to the outlets of the appliance shutoff valves.

3.3.95.7* *Venting System.* A continuous open passageway from the flue collar or draft hood of an appliance to the outdoors for the purpose of removing flue or vent gases.

3.3.95.7.1 *Mechanical Draft Venting System.* A venting system designed to remove flue or vent gases by mechanical means, which can consist of an induced draft portion under nonpositive static pressure or a forced draft portion under positive static pressure.

3.3.96 Tensile Strength. The highest unit tensile stress (referred to the original cross section) a material can sustain before failure (psi).

3.3.97 Tubing. Semirigid conduit of copper, steel, aluminum, corrugated stainless steel tubing (CSST), or plastic.

3.3.98 Valve.

3.3.98.1 *Appliance Shutoff Valve.* A valve used to shut off the fuel gas to an individual appliance.

3.3.98.2 *Automatic Valve.* An automatic or semiautomatic device consisting essentially of a valve and operator that control the gas supply to the burner(s) during operation of an appliance.

3.3.98.3 *Excess Flow Valve (EFV).* A valve designed to activate when the fuel gas passing through it exceeds a prescribed flow rate.

3.3.98.4 *Manual Reset Valve.* An automatic shutoff valve installed in the gas supply piping and set to shut off when unsafe conditions occur. The device remains closed until manually reopened.

3.3.98.5 *Relief Valve.* A safety valve designed to forestall the development of a dangerous condition by relieving either pressure, temperature, or vacuum in a hot water supply system.

3.3.98.5.1 *Pressure Relief Valve.* A valve that automatically opens and closes a relief vent, depending on whether the pressure is above or below a predetermined value.

3.3.98.5.2 *Temperature Relief Valve.* A valve that automatically opens and automatically closes a relief vent, depending on whether the temperature is above or below a predetermined value.

3.3.98.5.3 *Vacuum Relief Valve.* A valve that automatically opens and closes a vent for relieving a vacuum within the hot water supply system, depending on whether the vacuum is above or below a predetermined value.

3.3.98.6 *Service Shutoff Valve.* A valve, installed by the serving gas supplier between the source of supply and the customer piping system, to shut off the fuel gas to the entire piping system.

3.3.98.7 *System Shutoff Valve.* A valve installed after the point of delivery to shut off the fuel gas to the entire piping system.

3.3.99 Valve Member. That part of a gas valve rotating within or in respect to the valve body that, by its position with respect to the valve body, controls the flow of gas.

3.3.99.1 *Nondisplaceable Valve Member.* A valve member that cannot be moved from its seat by a force applied to the handle or to any exterior portion of the valve.

3.3.100 Vent Connector. The pipe or duct that connects a fuel gas–burning appliance to a vent or chimney.

3.3.101 Vent Offset. An arrangement of two or more fittings and pipe installed for the purpose of locating a vertical section of vent pipe in a different but parallel plane with respect to an adjacent section of vertical vent pipe.

3.3.102 Venting. The conveyance of combustion products to the outdoors.

3.3.103 Wall Head Adapter. A transition fitting for terminating plastic pipe inside of buildings at the building wall.

3.3.104 Zero Governor. A regulating device that is normally adjusted to deliver gas at atmospheric pressure within its flow rating.

Chapter 4   General

4.1 Qualified Agency. The following shall be performed only by a qualified agency:

(1) The design, installation, testing, purging, and replacement of gas piping, appliances, equipment, and accessories
(2) The repair and servicing of appliances and equipment

4.2 Interruption of Service.

4.2.1 Notification of Interrupted Service. When the gas supply is to be turned off, it shall be the duty of the qualified agency to notify all affected users. Where two or more users are served from the same supply system, precautions shall be exercised to ensure that service only to the proper user is turned off.

Exception: In cases of emergency, affected users shall be notified as soon as possible of the actions taken by the qualified agency.

4.2.2 Work Interruptions. When interruptions in work occur while repairs or alterations are being made to an existing piping system, the system shall be left in a safe condition.

4.3 Prevention of Accidental Ignition.

4.3.1 Potential Ignition Sources. Where work is being performed on piping that contains or has contained gas, the following shall apply:

(1) Provisions for electrical continuity shall be made before alterations are made in a metallic piping system.
(2) Smoking, open flames, lanterns, welding, or other sources of ignition shall not be permitted.
(3) A metallic electrical bond shall be installed around the location of cuts in metallic gas pipes made by other than cutting torches. Where cutting torches, welding, or other sources of ignition are to be used, it shall be determined that all sources of gas or gas–air mixtures have been secured and that all flammable gas or liquids have been cleared from the area. Piping shall be purged as required in Section 8.3 before welding or cutting with a torch is attempted.
(4) Artificial illumination shall be restricted to listed safety-type flashlights and safety lamps. Electric switches shall not be turned on or turned off.

4.3.2 Handling of Flammable Liquids.

4.3.2.1* *Drip Liquids.* Liquid that is removed from a drip in existing gas piping shall be handled to avoid spillage or ignition.

4.3.2.2 Other Flammable Liquids. Flammable liquids used by the installer shall be handled with precaution and shall not be left within the premises from the end of one working day to the beginning of the next.

4.4* Noncombustible Material. A material that complies with any of the following shall be considered a noncombustible material:

(1) A material that, in the form in which it is used and under the conditions anticipated, will not ignite, burn, support combustion, or release flammable vapors when subjected to fire or heat
(2) A material that is reported as passing ASTM E136, *Standard Test Method for Behavior of Materials in a Vertical Tube Furnace at 750°C*
(3) A material that is reported as complying with the pass/fail criteria of ASTM E136 when tested in accordance with the test method and procedure in ASTM E2652, *Standard Test Method for Behavior of Materials in a Tube Furnace with a Cone-shaped Airflow Stabilizer, at 750°C*

4.5 Engineering Methods. Where an engineering method is used to calculate flow of air or gas, or to determine the size of gas pipe or a gas vent, the authority having jurisdiction shall be permitted to require submittal of any or all of the following:

(1) Calculations including documentation that the method used is published and recognized as being valid for the calculations provided
(2) The name of any software used, input and output developed, and documentation that the software is recognized as being valid for the calculations provided
(3)* The name of the person that performed the calculation or design, along with their qualifications to perform the calculation or design

Chapter 5   Gas Piping System Design, Materials, and Components

5.1 Piping Plan.

5.1.1 Installation of Piping System. Where required by the authority having jurisdiction, a piping sketch or plan shall be prepared before proceeding with the installation. The plan shall show the proposed location of piping, the size of different branches, the various load demands, and the location of the point of delivery.

5.1.2 Addition to Existing System. When additional appliances are being connected to a gas piping system, the existing piping shall be checked to determine whether it has adequate capacity. If the capacity of the system is determined to be inadequate for the additional appliances, the existing system shall be enlarged as required, or separate gas piping of adequate capacity shall be provided.

5.2 Interconnections Between Gas Piping Systems.

5.2.1 Interconnections Supplying Separate Users. Where two or more meters, or two or more service regulators where meters are not provided, are located on the same premises and supply separate users, the gas piping systems shall not be interconnected on the outlet side of the meters or service regulators.

5.2.2 Interconnections for Standby Fuels.

5.2.2.1 Where a supplementary gas for standby use is connected downstream from a meter or a service regulator where a meter is not provided, equipment to prevent backflow shall be installed.

5.2.2.2 A three-way valve installed to admit the standby supply and at the same time shut off the regular supply shall be permitted to be used for this purpose.

5.3 Sizing of Gas Piping Systems.

5.3.1* General Considerations. Gas piping systems shall be of such size and so installed as to provide a supply of gas sufficient to meet the maximum demand and supply gas to each appliance inlet at not less than the minimum supply pressure required by the appliance.

5.3.2* Maximum Gas Demand.

5.3.2.1* The volumetric flow rate of gas to be provided shall be the sum of the maximum input of the appliances served.

5.3.2.2 The volumetric flow rate of gas to be provided shall be adjusted for altitude where the installation is above 2,000 ft (609.6 m).

5.3.2.3 The total connected hourly load shall be used as the basis for piping sizing, assuming all appliances are operating at full capacity simultaneously.

Exception: Sizing shall be permitted to be based upon established load diversity factors.

5.3.3* Sizing Methods. Gas piping shall be sized in accordance with one of the following:

(1) Pipe sizing tables or sizing equations in Chapter 6
(2) Sizing tables included in a listed piping system manufacturer's installation instructions
(3) Engineering methods

5.3.4 Allowable Pressure Drop. The design pressure loss in a piping system from the point of delivery to the inlet connection of all appliances served shall be such that the supply pressure at each appliance inlet is greater than or equal to the minimum pressure required by the appliance.

5.4 Operating Pressure.

5.4.1 Piping System Operating Pressure Limitations. The maximum operating pressure for any piping system shall not exceed 125 psi (862 kPa).

5.4.2 Flammable Gas–Air Mixtures. The maximum operating pressure for piping systems for gas–air mixtures within the flammable range shall be 10 psi (69 kPa).

5.4.3 LP-Gas Piping Systems. The maximum operating pressure for LP-Gas piping systems shall be 20 psi (140 kPa), except as provided in 5.4.4(8).

5.4.4 Maximum Operating Pressure in Buildings. The maximum operating pressure for any piping systems located inside buildings shall not exceed 5 psi (34 kPa) unless one or more of the following conditions are met:

(1)* The piping joints are welded or brazed.
(2) The piping is joined by fittings listed to ANSI LC 4/CSA 6.32, *Press-Connect Metallic Fittings for Use in Fuel Gas Distri-*

bution Systems, and installed according to the manufacturer's installation instructions.

(3) The piping joints are flanged and all pipe-to-flange connections are made by welding or brazing.

(4) The piping is located in a ventilated chase or otherwise enclosed for protection against accidental gas accumulation.

(5) The piping is located inside buildings or separate areas of buildings used exclusively for one of the following:

    (a) Industrial processing or heating
    (b) Research
    (c) Warehousing
    (d) Boiler or mechanical rooms

(6) The piping is a temporary installation for buildings under construction.

(7) The piping serves appliances or equipment used for agricultural purposes.

(8) The piping system is an LP-Gas piping system with an operating pressure greater than 20 psi (138 kPa) and complies with NFPA 58.

5.4.5 LP-Gas Systems Operating Below −5°F (−21°C). LP-Gas systems designed to operate below −5°F (−21°C) or with butane or a propane-butane mix shall be designed to either accommodate liquid LP-Gas or to prevent LP-Gas vapor from condensing back into a liquid.

5.5 Piping Materials and Joining Methods.

5.5.1 General.

5.5.1.1 Acceptable Materials. Materials used for piping systems shall either comply with the requirements of this chapter or be acceptable to the authority having jurisdiction.

5.5.1.2 Used Materials. Pipe, fittings, valves, or other materials shall not be used again unless they are free of foreign materials and have been ascertained to be adequate for the service intended.

5.5.2 Metallic Pipe.

5.5.2.1 Cast Iron. Cast-iron pipe shall not be used.

5.5.2.2 Steel, Stainless Steel, and Wrought Iron. Steel, stainless steel, and wrought-iron pipe shall be at least Schedule 10 and shall comply with the dimensional standards of ANSI/ASME B36.10M, *Welded and Seamless Wrought Steel Pipe*, and one of the following:

(1) ASTM A53, *Standard Specification for Pipe, Steel, Black and Hot-Dipped, Zinc-Coated Welded and Seamless*

(2) ASTM A106, *Standard Specification for Seamless Carbon Steel Pipe for High-Temperature Service*

(3) ASTM A312, *Standard Specification for Seamless, Welded, and Heavily Cold Worked Austenitic Stainless Steel Pipes*

5.5.2.3* Copper and Copper Alloy. Copper and copper alloy pipe shall not be used if the gas contains more than an average of 0.3 grains of hydrogen sulfide per 100 scf of gas (0.7 mg/100 L).

5.5.2.4 Threaded Copper, Copper Alloy, and Aluminum. Threaded copper, copper alloy, or aluminum alloy pipe shall not be used with gases corrosive to such material.

5.5.2.5 Aluminum Alloy. Aluminum alloy pipe shall comply with ASTM B241, *Standard Specification for Aluminum and Aluminum-Alloy Seamless Pipe and Seamless Extruded Tube* (except that the use of alloy 5456 is prohibited), and shall be marked at each end of each length indicating compliance. Aluminum alloy pipe shall be coated to protect against external corrosion where it is in contact with masonry, plaster, or insulation or is subject to repeated wettings by such liquids as water, detergents, or sewage.

5.5.2.6 Aluminum Installation. Aluminum alloy pipe shall not be used in exterior locations or underground.

5.5.3 Metallic Tubing.

5.5.3.1 Tubing shall not be used with gases corrosive to the tubing material.

5.5.3.2 Steel. Steel tubing shall comply with ASTM A254, *Standard Specification for Copper-Brazed Steel Tubing*.

5.5.3.3 Stainless Steel. Stainless steel tubing shall comply with one of the following:

(1) ASTM A268, *Standard Specification for Seamless and Welded Ferritic and Martensitic Stainless Steel Tubing for General Service*

(2) ASTM A269, *Standard Specification for Seamless and Welded Austenitic Stainless Steel Tubing for General Service*

5.5.3.4* Copper and Copper Alloy. Copper and copper alloy tubing shall not be used if the gas contains more than an average of 0.3 grains of hydrogen sulfide per 100 scf of gas (0.7 mg/100 L). Copper tubing shall comply with standard Type K or Type L of ASTM B88, *Standard Specification for Seamless Copper Water Tube*, or ASTM B280, *Standard Specification for Seamless Copper Tube for Air Conditioning and Refrigeration Field Service*.

5.5.3.5 Aluminum. Aluminum alloy tubing shall comply with ASTM B210, *Standard Specification for Aluminum and Aluminum-Alloy Drawn Seamless Tubes*, or ASTM B241, *Standard Specification for Aluminum and Aluminum-Alloy Seamless Pipe and Seamless Extruded Tube*. Aluminum alloy tubing shall be coated to protect against external corrosion where it is in contact with masonry, plaster, or insulation or is subject to repeated wettings by such liquids as water, detergent, or sewage. Aluminum alloy tubing shall not be used in exterior locations or underground.

5.5.3.6 Corrugated Stainless Steel. Corrugated stainless steel tubing shall be listed in accordance with ANSI LC 1/CSA 6.26, *Fuel Gas Piping Systems Using Corrugated Stainless Steel Tubing*.

5.5.4 Plastic Pipe, Tubing, and Fittings.

5.5.4.1 Standard and Marking.

5.5.4.1.1 Polyethylene plastic pipe, tubing, and fittings used to supply fuel gas shall conform to ASTM D2513, *Standard Specification for Polyethylene (PE) Gas Pressure Pipe, Tubing, and Fittings*. Pipe to be used shall be marked "gas" and "ASTM D2513."

5.5.4.1.2 Polyamide pipe, tubing, and fittings shall be identified in and conform to ASTM F2945, *Standard Specification for Polyamide 11 Gas Pressure Pipe, Tubing, and Fittings*. Pipe to be used shall be marked "gas" and "ASTM F2945."

5.5.4.1.3 Polyvinyl chloride (PVC) and chlorinated polyvinyl chloride (CPVC) plastic pipe, tubing, and fittings shall not be used to supply fuel gas.

5.5.4.2* Regulator Vent Piping. Plastic pipe and fittings used to connect regulator vents to remote vent terminations shall be PVC conforming to UL 651, *Schedule 40 and 80 Rigid PVC*

Conduit and Fittings. PVC vent piping shall not be installed indoors.

5.5.4.3 Anodeless Risers. Anodeless risers shall comply with the following:

(1) Factory-assembled anodeless risers shall be recommended by the manufacturer for the gas used and shall be leak tested by the manufacturer in accordance with written procedures.
(2) Service head adapters and field-assembled anodeless risers incorporating service head adapters shall be recommended by the manufacturer for the gas used and shall be design-certified to meet the requirements of Category I of ASTM D2513, *Standard Specification for Polyethylene (PE) Gas Pressure Pipe, Tubing, and Fittings,* and 49 CFR 192.281(e). The manufacturer shall provide the user qualified installation instructions as prescribed by 49 CFR 192.283(b).
(3) The use of plastic pipe, tubing, and fittings in undiluted LP-Gas piping systems shall be in accordance with NFPA 58.

5.5.5 Workmanship and Defects. Gas pipe, tubing, and fittings shall be clear and free from cutting burrs and defects in structure or threading and shall be thoroughly brushed and chip and scale blown. Defects in pipe, tubing, and fittings shall not be repaired. Defective pipe, tubing, and fittings shall be replaced.

5.5.6 Metallic Pipe Threads.

5.5.6.1 Specifications for Pipe Threads. Metallic pipe and fitting threads shall be taper pipe threads and shall comply with ANSI/ASME B1.20.1, *Pipe Threads, General Purpose, Inch.*

5.5.6.2 Damaged Threads. Pipe with threads that are stripped, chipped, corroded, or otherwise damaged shall not be used. Where a weld opens during the operation of cutting or threading, that portion of the pipe shall not be used.

5.5.6.3 Number of Threads. Field threading of metallic pipe shall be in accordance with Table 5.5.6.3.

5.5.6.4* Thread Joint Sealing.

5.5.6.4.1 Threaded joints shall be made using a thread joint sealing material.

Table 5.5.6.3 Specifications for Threading Metallic Pipe

Iron Pipe Size (in.)	Approximate Length of Threaded Portion (in.)	Approximate No. of Threads to Be Cut
½	¾	10
¾	¾	10
1	⅞	10
1¼	1	11
1½	1	11
2	1	11
2½	1½	12
3	1½	12
4	1⅝	13

For SI units, 1 in. = 25.4 mm.

5.5.6.4.2 Thread joint sealing materials shall be compatible with the pipe and fitting material on which the compounds are used.

5.5.6.4.3 Thread joint sealing materials shall be non-hardening and shall be resistant to the chemical constituents of the gases to be conducted through the piping.

5.5.7 Metallic Piping Joints and Fittings. The type of piping joint used shall be suitable for the pressure and temperature conditions and shall be selected giving consideration to joint tightness and mechanical strength under the service conditions. The joint shall be able to sustain the maximum end force due to the internal pressure and any additional forces due to temperature expansion or contraction, vibration, fatigue, or the weight of the pipe and its contents.

5.5.7.1* Pipe Joints. Schedule 40 and heavier pipe joints shall be threaded, flanged, brazed, welded, or assembled with press-connect fittings listed to ANSI LC 4/CSA 6.32, *Press-Connect Metallic Fittings for Use in Fuel Gas Distribution Systems.*

(A) Pipe lighter than Schedule 40 shall be connected using press-connect fittings, flanges, brazing, or welding.

(B) Where nonferrous pipe is brazed, the brazing materials shall have a melting point in excess of 1000°F (538°C).

(C) Brazing alloys shall not contain more than 0.05 percent phosphorus.

5.5.7.2 Copper Tubing Joints. Copper tubing joints shall be assembled with approved gas tubing fittings, shall be brazed with a material having a melting point in excess of 1000°F (538°C), or shall be assembled with press-connect fittings listed to ANSI LC 4/CSA 6.32, *Press-Connect Metallic Fittings for Use in Fuel Gas Distribution Systems.* Brazing alloys shall not contain more than 0.05 percent phosphorus.

5.5.7.3 Stainless Steel Tubing Joints. Stainless steel joints shall be welded, assembled with approved tubing fittings, brazed with a material having a melting point in excess of 1000°F (538°C), or assembled with press-connect fittings listed to ANSI LC 4/CSA 6.32, *Press-Connect Metallic Fittings for Use in Fuel Gas Distribution Systems.* Brazing alloys and fluxes shall be recommended by the manufacturer for use on stainless steel alloys.

5.5.7.4 Flared Joints. Flared joints shall be used only in systems constructed from nonferrous pipe and tubing where experience or tests have demonstrated that the joint is suitable for the conditions and where provisions are made in the design to prevent separation of the joints.

5.5.7.5 Metallic Pipe Fittings. Metallic fittings shall comply with the following:

(1) Threaded fittings in sizes larger than 4 in. (100 mm) shall not be used.
(2) Fittings used with steel, stainless steel, or wrought-iron pipe shall be steel, stainless steel, copper alloy, malleable iron, or cast iron.
(3) Fittings used with copper or copper alloy pipe shall be copper or copper alloy.
(4) Fittings used with aluminum alloy pipe shall be aluminum alloy.
(5) *Cast-Iron Fittings.* Cast-iron fittings shall comply with the following:
   (a) Flanges shall be permitted.
   (b) Bushings shall not be used.

(c) Fittings shall not be used in systems containing flammable gas–air mixtures.
(d) Fittings in sizes 4 in. (100 mm) and larger shall not be used indoors unless approved by the authority having jurisdiction.
(e) Fittings in sizes 6 in. (150 mm) and larger shall not be used unless approved by the authority having jurisdiction.

(6) *Aluminum Alloy Fittings.* Threads shall not form the joint seal.

(7) *Zinc–Aluminum Alloy Fittings.* Fittings shall not be used in systems containing flammable gas–air mixtures.

(8) *Special Fittings.* Fittings such as couplings, proprietary-type joints, saddle tees, gland-type compression fittings, and flared, flareless, or compression-type tubing fittings shall be as follows:
(a) Used within the fitting manufacturer's pressure–temperature recommendations
(b) Used within the service conditions anticipated with respect to vibration, fatigue, thermal expansion, or contraction
(c) Acceptable to the authority having jurisdiction

(9) When pipe fittings are drilled and tapped in the field, the operation shall be in accordance with the following:
(a) The operation shall be performed on systems having operating pressures of 5 psi (34 kPa) or less.
(b) The operation shall be performed by the gas supplier or their designated representative.
(c) The drilling and tapping operation shall be performed in accordance with written procedures prepared by the gas supplier.
(d) The fittings shall be located outdoors.
(e) The tapped fitting assembly shall be inspected and proven to be free of leaks.

5.5.8 Plastic Piping Joints and Fittings. Plastic pipe, tubing, and fittings shall be joined in accordance with the manufacturers' instructions. The following shall be observed when making such joints:

(1) The joint shall be designed and installed so that the longitudinal pullout resistance of the joint will be at least equal to the tensile strength of the plastic piping material.
(2) Heat fusion joints shall be made in accordance with qualified procedures that have been established and proven by test to produce gastight joints at least as strong as the pipe or tubing being joined. Joints shall be made with the joining method recommended by the pipe manufacturer. Polyethylene heat fusion fittings shall be marked "ASTM D2513." Polyamide heat fusion fittings shall be marked "ASTM F2945."
(3) Where compression-type mechanical joints are used, the gasket material in the fitting shall be compatible with the plastic piping and with the gas distributed by the system. An internal tubular rigid stiffener shall be used in conjunction with the fitting. The stiffener shall be flush with the end of the pipe or tubing and shall extend at least to the outside end of the compression fitting when installed. The stiffener shall be free of rough or sharp edges and shall not be a force fit in the plastic. Split tubular stiffeners shall not be used.
(4) Plastic piping joints and fittings for use in LP-Gas piping systems shall be in accordance with NFPA 58.

5.5.9 Flanges.

5.5.9.1 Flange Specifications.

5.5.9.1.1 Cast iron flanges shall be in accordance with ANSI/ASME B16.1, *Gray Iron Pipe Flanges and Flanged Fittings: Classes 25, 125, and 250.*

5.5.9.1.2 Steel flanges shall be in accordance with the following: ANSI/ASME B16.5, *Pipe Flanges and Flanged Fittings: NPS ½ through NPS 24 Metric/Inch Standard,* or ANSI/ASME B16.47, *Large Diameter Steel Flanges: NPS 26 through NPS 60 Metric/Inch Standard.*

5.5.9.1.3 Non-ferrous flanges shall be in accordance with ANSI/ASME B16.24, *Cast Copper Alloy Pipe Flanges and Flanged Fittings: Classes 150, 300, 600, 900, 1500, and 2500.*

5.5.9.1.4 Ductile iron flanges shall be in accordance with ANSI/ASME B16.42, *Ductile Iron Pipe Flanges and Flanged Fittings, Classes 150 and 300.*

5.5.9.2 Dissimilar Flange Connections. Raised-face flanges shall not be joined to flat-faced cast iron, ductile iron or non-ferrous material flanges.

5.5.9.3 Flange Facings. Standard facings shall be permitted for use under this code. Where 150 psi (1034 kPa) steel flanges are bolted to Class 125 cast-iron flanges, the raised face on the steel flange shall be removed.

5.5.9.4 Lapped Flanges. Lapped flanges shall be used only aboveground or in exposed locations accessible for inspection.

5.5.10 Flange Gaskets. The material for gaskets shall be capable of withstanding the design temperature and pressure of the piping system and the chemical constituents of the gas being conducted without change to its chemical and physical properties. The effects of fire exposure to the joint shall be considered in choosing the material.

5.5.10.1 Acceptable materials shall include the following:
(1) Metal (plain or corrugated)
(2) Composition
(3) Aluminum "O" rings
(4) Spiral-wound metal gaskets
(5) Rubber-faced phenolic
(6) Elastomeric

5.5.10.2 Gasket Specifications.

5.5.10.2.1 Metallic flange gaskets shall be in accordance with ANSI/ASME B16.20, *Metallic Gaskets for Pipe Flanges: Ring-Joint, Spiral-Wound and Jacketed.*

5.5.10.2.2 Non-metallic flange gaskets shall be in accordance with ANSI/ASME B16.21, *Nonmetallic Flat Gaskets for Pipe Flanges.*

5.5.10.3 Full-face flange gaskets shall be used with all non-steel flanges.

5.5.10.4 When a flanged joint is separated, the gasket shall be replaced.

5.6* Gas Meters.

5.6.1 Capacity. Gas meters shall be selected for the maximum expected pressure and permissible pressure drop.

5.6.2 Location.

5.6.2.1 Gas meters shall be located in ventilated spaces readily accessible for examination, reading, replacement, or necessary maintenance.

5.6.2.2 Gas meters shall not be placed where they will be subjected to damage, such as adjacent to a driveway, under a fire escape, in public passages, halls, or where they will be subject to excessive corrosion or vibration.

5.6.2.3 Gas meters shall not be located where they will be subjected to extreme temperatures or sudden extreme changes in temperature or in areas where they are subjected to temperatures beyond those recommended by the manufacturer.

5.6.3 Supports. Gas meters shall be supported or connected to rigid piping so as not to exert a strain on the meters. Where flexible connectors are used to connect a gas meter to downstream piping at mobile homes in mobile home parks, the meter shall be supported by a post or bracket placed in a firm footing or by other means providing equivalent support.

5.6.4 Meter Protection. Meters shall be protected against overpressure, back pressure, and vacuum.

5.6.5 Identification. Gas piping at multiple meter installations shall be marked by a metal tag or other permanent means designating the building or the part of the building being supplied and attached by the installing agency.

5.7* Gas Pressure Regulators.

5.7.1 Where Required. A line pressure regulator shall be installed where the gas supply pressure exceeds the maximum allowable inlet pressure of the appliance served.

5.7.2 Listing. Line pressure regulators shall be listed in accordance with ANSI Z21.80/CSA 6.22, *Line Pressure Regulators*, where the outlet pressure is set to 2 psi or less.

5.7.3 Location. The gas pressure regulator shall be accessible for servicing.

5.7.4 Regulator Protection. Pressure regulators shall be protected against physical damage.

5.7.5 Regulator Vents. Regulator vents shall be in accordance with Section 5.14.

5.7.6 Identification. Line pressure regulators at multiple regulator installations shall be marked by a metal tag or other permanent means designating the building or the part of the building being supplied.

5.8 Overpressure Protection Devices.

5.8.1 Where Required. Where the serving gas supplier delivers gas at a pressure greater than 2 psi (14 kPa) for piping systems serving appliances designed to operate at a gas pressure of 14 in. w.c. (3.4 kPa) or less, overpressure protection devices shall be installed. Piping systems serving equipment designed to operate at inlet pressures greater than 14 in. w.c. (3.4 kPa) shall be equipped with overpressure protection devices as required by the appliance manufacturer's installation instructions.

5.8.2 Pressure Limitation Requirements.

5.8.2.1 Where piping systems serving appliances designed to operate with a gas supply pressure of 14 in. w.c. (3.4 kPa) or less are required to be equipped with overpressure protection by 5.8.1, each overpressure protection device shall be adjusted to limit the gas pressure to each connected appliance to 2 psi (14 kPa) or less upon a failure of the line pressure regulator.

5.8.2.2 Where piping systems serving appliances designed to operate with a gas supply pressure greater than 14 in. w.c. (3.4 kPa) are required to be equipped with overpressure protection by 5.8.1, each overpressure protection device shall be adjusted to limit the gas pressure to each connected appliance as required by the appliance manufacturer's installation instructions.

5.8.2.3 Each overpressure protection device installed to meet the requirements of this section shall be capable of limiting the pressure to its connected appliance(s) as required by this section independently of any other pressure control equipment in the piping system.

5.8.2.4 Each gas piping system for which an overpressure protection device is required by this section shall be designed and installed so that a failure of the primary pressure control device(s) is detectable.

5.8.2.5 If a pressure relief valve is used to meet the requirements of this section, it shall have a flow capacity such that the pressure in the protected system is maintained at or below the limits specified in 5.8.2.1 under the following conditions:

(1) The line pressure regulator for which the relief valve is providing overpressure protection has failed wide open.
(2) The gas pressure at the inlet of the line pressure regulator for which the relief valve is providing overpressure protection is not less than the regulator's normal operating inlet pressure.

5.8.3 Overpressure Protection Devices.

5.8.3.1 Overpressure protection devices shall be one of the following:

(1) Pressure relief valve.
(2) Monitor regulator.
(3) Series regulator installed upstream from the line regulator and set to continuously limit the pressure on the inlet of the line regulator to the maximum values specified by 5.8.2.1 or less.
(4) Automatic shutoff device installed in series with the line pressure regulator and set to shut off when the pressure on the downstream piping system reaches the maximum values specified by 5.8.2.1 or less. This device shall be designed so that it will remain closed until manually reset.

5.8.3.2 The devices in 5.8.3.1 shall be installed either as an integral part of the service or line pressure regulator or as separate units. Where separate overpressure protection devices are installed, they shall comply with 5.8.4 through 5.8.9.

5.8.4 Construction and Installation. All overpressure protection devices shall meet the following requirements:

(1) Be constructed of materials so that the operation of the device is not impaired by corrosion of external parts by the atmosphere or of internal parts by the gas.
(2) Be designed and installed so they can be operated to determine whether the valve is free. The devices shall also be designed and installed so they can be tested to determine the pressure at which they operate and be examined for leakage when in the closed position.

5.8.5 External Control Piping. External control piping shall be designed and installed so that damage to the control piping of one device does not render both the regulator and the overpressure protective device inoperative.

5.8.6 Setting. Each pressure limiting or pressure relieving device shall be set so that the gas pressure supplied to the connected appliance(s) does not exceed the limits specified in 5.8.2.1 and 5.8.2.2.

5.8.7 Unauthorized Operation. Where unauthorized operation of any shutoff valve could render a pressure relieving valve or pressure limiting device inoperative, one of the following shall be accomplished:

(1) The valve shall be locked in the open position. Instruct authorized personnel in the importance of leaving the shutoff valve open and of being present while the shutoff valve is closed so that it can be locked in the open position before leaving the premises.
(2) Duplicate relief valves shall be installed, each having adequate capacity to protect the system, and arrange the isolating valves or three-way valve so that only one relief valve can be rendered inoperative at a time.

5.8.8 Vents.

5.8.8.1 The discharge stacks, vents, or outlet parts of all pressure relieving and pressure limiting devices shall be located so that gas is safely discharged to the outdoors. Discharge stacks or vents shall be designed to prevent the entry of water, insects, or other foreign material that could cause blockage.

5.8.8.2 The discharge stack or vent line shall be at least the same size as the outlet of the pressure relieving device.

5.8.9 Size of Fittings, Pipe, and Openings. The fittings, pipe, and openings located between the system to be protected and the pressure relieving device shall be sized to prevent hammering of the valve and to prevent impairment of relief capacity.

5.9 Back Pressure Protection.

5.9.1 Where to Install.

5.9.1.1 Protective devices shall be installed as close to the equipment as practical where the design of equipment connected is such that air, oxygen, or standby gases could be forced into the gas supply system.

5.9.1.2 Gas and air combustion mixers incorporating double diaphragm "zero" or "atmosphere" governors or regulators shall require no further protection unless connected directly to compressed air or oxygen at pressures of 5 psi (34 kPa) or more.

5.9.2 Protective Devices. Protective devices shall include but not be limited to the following:

(1) Check valves
(2) Three-way valves (of the type that completely closes one side before starting to open the other side)
(3) Reverse flow indicators controlling positive shutoff valves
(4) Normally closed air-actuated positive shutoff pressure regulators

5.10* Low-Pressure Protection. A protective device shall be installed between the meter and the appliance or equipment if the operation of the appliance or equipment is such that it could produce a vacuum or a dangerous reduction in gas pressure at the meter. Such protective devices include, but are not limited to, mechanical, diaphragm-operated, or electrically operated low-pressure shutoff valves.

5.11 Shutoff Valves. Shutoff valves shall be selected in accordance with Table 5.11. Shutoff valves of size 1 in. (25 mm) National Pipe Thread and smaller shall be listed and labeled. Where used outdoors, such use shall be in accordance with the manufacturer's recommendation.

Table 5.11 Manual Gas Valve Standards

Shutoff Valve Application	Valve Meeting the Following Standards
Appliance shutoff valve up to ½ psi	ANSI Z21.15/CSA 9.1 ANSI/ASME B16.44 ANSI/ASME B16.33 marked 125 G ANSI LC 4/CSA 6.32
Valve up to ½ psi	ANSI/ASME B16.44 ANSI/ASME B16.33 marked 125 G ANSI LC 4/CSA 6.32
Valve up to 2 psi	ANSI/ASME B16.44 labeled 2G ANSI/ASME B16.33 marked 125 G ANSI LC 4/CSA 6.32 with ANSI/ASME B16.44 labeled 2G or labeled 5G ANSI LC 4/CSA 6.32 with ANSI/ASME B16.33 marked 125 G
Valve up to 5 psi	ANSI/ASME B16.44 labeled 5G ANSI/ASME B16.33 ANSI LC 4/CSA 6.32 with ANSI/ASME B16.44 marked 5G ANSI LC 4/CSA 6.32 with ANSI/ASME B16.33 marked 125 G
Valve up to 125 psi	ANSI/ASME B16.33 marked 125 G ANSI LC 4/CSA 6.32 with ANSI/ASME B16.33 marked 125 G

For SI units, 1 psi gauge = 6.895 kPa.

5.12 Excess Flow Valve(s). Where automatic excess flow valves are installed, they shall be listed in accordance with ANSI Z21.93/CSA 6.30, *Excess Flow Valves for Natural and LP-Gas with Pressures Up to 5 psig*, and shall be sized and installed in accordance with the manufacturers' instructions.

5.13 Expansion and Flexibility.

5.13.1 Design. Piping systems shall be designed to prevent failure from thermal expansion or contraction.

5.13.2 Special Local Conditions. Where local conditions include earthquake, tornado, unstable ground, or flood hazards, special consideration shall be given to increased strength and flexibility of piping supports and connections.

5.14 Pressure Regulator and Pressure Control Venting. The venting of the atmospheric side of diaphragms in line pressure regulators, gas appliance regulators, and gas pressure limit controls shall be in accordance with all of the following:

(1) An independent vent pipe to the outdoors, sized in accordance with the device manufacturer's instructions, shall be provided where the location of a device is such

that a discharge of fuel gas will cause a hazard. For devices other than appliance regulators, vents are not required to be independent where the vents are connected to a common manifold designed in accordance with engineering methods to minimize backpressure in the event of diaphragm failure and such design is approved.

Exception No. 1: A regulator and vent limiting means combination listed as complying with ANSI Z21.80/CSA 6.22, Line Pressure Regulators, shall not be required to be vented to the outdoors.

Exception No. 2: A listed gas appliance regulator factory equipped with a vent limiting device is not required to be vented to the outdoors.

(2) Materials for vent piping shall be in accordance with Section 5.5.
(3) The vent terminus shall be designed to prevent the entry of water, insects, and other foreign matter that could cause blockage.
(4) Vent piping shall be installed to minimize static loads and bending moments placed on the regulators and gas pressure control devices.
(5) Vents shall terminate not less than 3 ft (0.9 m) from a possible source of ignition.
(6) At locations where a vent termination could be submerged during floods or snow accumulations, an antiflood-type breather vent fitting shall be installed, or the vent terminal shall be located above the height of the expected flood waters or snow.
(7) Vent piping from pressure regulators and gas pressure controls shall not be connected to a common manifold that serves a bleed line from a diaphragm-type gas valve.

Chapter 6 Pipe Sizing

6.1* Pipe Sizing Methods. Where the pipe size is to be determined using any of the methods in 6.1.1 through 6.1.3, the diameter of each pipe segment shall be obtained from the pipe sizing tables in Section 6.2 or Section 6.3 or from the sizing equations in Section 6.4. For SI units, 1 ft³ = 0.028 m³, 1 ft = 0.305 m, 1 in. w.c. = 0.249 kPa, 1 psi = 6.894 kPa, 1000 Btu/hr = 0.293 kW.

6.1.1* Longest Length Method. The pipe size of each section of gas piping shall be determined using the longest length of piping from the point of delivery to the most remote outlet and the load of the section.

6.1.2* Branch Length Method. Pipe shall be sized as follows:

(1) Pipe size of each section of the longest pipe run from the point of delivery to the most remote outlet shall be determined using the longest run of piping and the load of the section.
(2) The pipe size of each section of branch piping not previously sized shall be determined using the length of piping from the point of delivery to the most remote outlet in each branch and the load of the section.

6.1.3 Hybrid Pressure. The pipe size for each section of higher pressure gas piping shall be determined using the longest length of piping from the point of delivery to the most remote line pressure regulator. The pipe size from the line pressure regulator to each outlet shall be determined using the length of piping from the regulator to the most remote outlet served by the regulator.

6.2 Sizing Natural Gas Piping Systems. Sizing of piping systems shall be in accordance with 6.2.1 or 6.2.2.

6.2.1 Table 6.2.1(a) through Table 6.2.1(x) shall be used in conjunction with one of the methods described in 6.1.1 through 6.1.3 for piping materials other than non-corrugated stainless steel tubing.

6.2.2 Section 6.4 shall be used in conjunction with one of the methods described in 6.1.1 through 6.1.3 for non-corrugated stainless steel tubing.

6.3 Sizing Propane Piping Systems. Sizing of piping systems shall be in accordance with 6.3.1 or 6.3.2.

6.3.1 Table 6.3.1(a) through Table 6.3.1(m) shall be used in conjunction with one of the methods described in 6.1.1 through 6.1.3 for piping materials other than non-corrugated stainless steel tubing.

6.3.2 Section 6.4 shall be used in conjunction with one of the methods described in 6.1.1 through 6.1.3 for non-corrugated stainless steel tubing.

6.4 Sizing Equations. The inside diameter of smooth wall pipe or tubing shall be determined by the sizing equations in 6.4.1 and 6.4.2 using the equivalent pipe length determined by the methods in 6.1.1 through 6.1.3.

6.4.1* Low-Pressure Gas Formula. Less than 1.5 psi (10.3 kPa):

$$D = \frac{Q^{0.381}}{19.17 \left(\dfrac{\Delta H}{Cr \times L} \right)^{0.206}} \quad [6.4.1]$$

where:
D = inside diameter of pipe (in.)
Q = input rate appliance(s) (cubic feet per hour at 60°F and 30 in. mercury column)
ΔH = pressure drop [in. w.c. (27.7 in. H₂O = 1 psi)]
L = equivalent length of pipe (ft)
See Table 6.4.2 for values of Cr.

6.4.2* High-Pressure Gas Formula. 1.5 psi (10.3 kPa) and above:

$$D = \frac{Q^{0.381}}{18.93 \left[\dfrac{(P_1^2 - P_2^2) \cdot Y}{Cr \times L} \right]^{0.206}} \quad [6.4.2]$$

where:
D = inside diameter of pipe (in.)
Q = input rate appliance(s) (cubic feet per hour at 60°F and 30 in. mercury column)
P_1 = upstream pressure [psia (P_1 + 14.7)]
P_2 = downstream pressure [psia (P_2 + 14.7)]
L = equivalent length of pipe (ft)
See Table 6.4.2 for values of Cr and Y.

Table 6.2.1(a) Schedule 40 Metallic Pipe

														Gas:	Natural
														Inlet Pressure:	Less than 2 psi
														Pressure Drop:	0.3 in. w.c.
														Specific Gravity:	0.60

	Pipe Size (in.)													
Nominal:	½	¾	1	1¼	1½	2	2½	3	4	5	6	8	10	12
Actual ID:	0.622	0.824	1.049	1.380	1.610	2.067	2.469	3.068	4.026	5.047	6.065	7.981	10.020	11.938
Length (ft)	Capacity in Cubic Feet of Gas per Hour													
10	131	273	514	1,060	1,580	3,050	4,860	8,580	17,500	31,700	51,300	105,000	191,000	303,000
20	90	188	353	726	1,090	2,090	3,340	5,900	12,000	21,800	35,300	72,400	132,000	208,000
30	72	151	284	583	873	1,680	2,680	4,740	9,660	17,500	28,300	58,200	106,000	167,000
40	62	129	243	499	747	1,440	2,290	4,050	8,270	15,000	24,200	49,800	90,400	143,000
50	55	114	215	442	662	1,280	2,030	3,590	7,330	13,300	21,500	44,100	80,100	127,000
60	50	104	195	400	600	1,160	1,840	3,260	6,640	12,000	19,500	40,000	72,600	115,000
70	46	95	179	368	552	1,060	1,690	3,000	6,110	11,100	17,900	36,800	66,800	106,000
80	42	89	167	343	514	989	1,580	2,790	5,680	10,300	16,700	34,200	62,100	98,400
90	40	83	157	322	482	928	1,480	2,610	5,330	9,650	15,600	32,100	58,300	92,300
100	38	79	148	304	455	877	1,400	2,470	5,040	9,110	14,800	30,300	55,100	87,200
125	33	70	131	269	403	777	1,240	2,190	4,460	8,080	13,100	26,900	48,800	77,300
150	30	63	119	244	366	704	1,120	1,980	4,050	7,320	11,900	24,300	44,200	70,000
175	28	58	109	224	336	648	1,030	1,820	3,720	6,730	10,900	22,400	40,700	64,400
200	26	54	102	209	313	602	960	1,700	3,460	6,260	10,100	20,800	37,900	59,900
250	23	48	90	185	277	534	851	1,500	3,070	5,550	8,990	18,500	33,500	53,100
300	21	43	82	168	251	484	771	1,360	2,780	5,030	8,150	16,700	30,400	48,100
350	19	40	75	154	231	445	709	1,250	2,560	4,630	7,490	15,400	28,000	44,300
400	18	37	70	143	215	414	660	1,170	2,380	4,310	6,970	14,300	26,000	41,200
450	17	35	66	135	202	389	619	1,090	2,230	4,040	6,540	13,400	24,400	38,600
500	16	33	62	127	191	367	585	1,030	2,110	3,820	6,180	12,700	23,100	36,500
550	15	31	59	121	181	349	556	982	2,000	3,620	5,870	12,100	21,900	34,700
600	14	30	56	115	173	333	530	937	1,910	3,460	5,600	11,500	20,900	33,100
650	14	29	54	110	165	318	508	897	1,830	3,310	5,360	11,000	20,000	31,700
700	13	27	52	106	159	306	488	862	1,760	3,180	5,150	10,600	19,200	30,400
750	13	26	50	102	153	295	470	830	1,690	3,060	4,960	10,200	18,500	29,300
800	12	26	48	99	148	285	454	802	1,640	2,960	4,790	9,840	17,900	28,300
850	12	25	46	95	143	275	439	776	1,580	2,860	4,640	9,530	17,300	27,400
900	11	24	45	93	139	267	426	752	1,530	2,780	4,500	9,240	16,800	26,600
950	11	23	44	90	135	259	413	731	1,490	2,700	4,370	8,970	16,300	25,800
1,000	11	23	43	87	131	252	402	711	1,450	2,620	4,250	8,720	15,800	25,100
1,100	10	21	40	83	124	240	382	675	1,380	2,490	4,030	8,290	15,100	23,800
1,200	NA	20	39	79	119	229	364	644	1,310	2,380	3,850	7,910	14,400	22,700
1,300	NA	20	37	76	114	219	349	617	1,260	2,280	3,680	7,570	13,700	21,800
1,400	NA	19	35	73	109	210	335	592	1,210	2,190	3,540	7,270	13,200	20,900
1,500	NA	18	34	70	105	203	323	571	1,160	2,110	3,410	7,010	12,700	20,100
1,600	NA	18	33	68	102	196	312	551	1,120	2,030	3,290	6,770	12,300	19,500
1,700	NA	17	32	66	98	189	302	533	1,090	1,970	3,190	6,550	11,900	18,800
1,800	NA	16	31	64	95	184	293	517	1,050	1,910	3,090	6,350	11,500	18,300
1,900	NA	16	30	62	93	178	284	502	1,020	1,850	3,000	6,170	11,200	17,700
2,000	NA	16	29	60	90	173	276	488	1,000	1,800	2,920	6,000	10,900	17,200

NA: A flow of less than 10 cfh.
Note: All table entries are rounded to 3 significant digits.

Table 6.2.1(b) Schedule 40 Metallic Pipe

												Gas:	Natural
												Inlet Pressure:	Less than 2 psi
												Pressure Drop:	0.5 in. w.c.
												Specific Gravity:	0.60

	Pipe Size (in.)												
Nominal:	½	¾	1	1¼	1½	2	2½	3	4	5	6	8	10	12
Actual ID:	0.622	0.824	1.049	1.380	1.610	2.067	2.469	3.068	4.026	5.047	6.065	7.981	10.020	11.938
Length (ft)	Capacity in Cubic Feet of Gas per Hour												
10	172	360	678	1,390	2,090	4,020	6,400	11,300	23,100	41,800	67,600	139,000	252,000	399,000
20	118	247	466	957	1,430	2,760	4,400	7,780	15,900	28,700	46,500	95,500	173,000	275,000
30	95	199	374	768	1,150	2,220	3,530	6,250	12,700	23,000	37,300	76,700	139,000	220,000
40	81	170	320	657	985	1,900	3,020	5,350	10,900	19,700	31,900	65,600	119,000	189,000
50	72	151	284	583	873	1,680	2,680	4,740	9,660	17,500	28,300	58,200	106,000	167,000
60	65	137	257	528	791	1,520	2,430	4,290	8,760	15,800	25,600	52,700	95,700	152,000
70	60	126	237	486	728	1,400	2,230	3,950	8,050	14,600	23,600	48,500	88,100	139,000
80	56	117	220	452	677	1,300	2,080	3,670	7,490	13,600	22,000	45,100	81,900	130,000
90	52	110	207	424	635	1,220	1,950	3,450	7,030	12,700	20,600	42,300	76,900	122,000
100	50	104	195	400	600	1,160	1,840	3,260	6,640	12,000	19,500	40,000	72,600	115,000
125	44	92	173	355	532	1,020	1,630	2,890	5,890	10,600	17,200	35,400	64,300	102,000
150	40	83	157	322	482	928	1,480	2,610	5,330	9,650	15,600	32,100	58,300	92,300
175	37	77	144	296	443	854	1,360	2,410	4,910	8,880	14,400	29,500	53,600	84,900
200	34	71	134	275	412	794	1,270	2,240	4,560	8,260	13,400	27,500	49,900	79,000
250	30	63	119	244	366	704	1,120	1,980	4,050	7,320	11,900	24,300	44,200	70,000
300	27	57	108	221	331	638	1,020	1,800	3,670	6,630	10,700	22,100	40,100	63,400
350	25	53	99	203	305	587	935	1,650	3,370	6,100	9,880	20,300	36,900	58,400
400	23	49	92	189	283	546	870	1,540	3,140	5,680	9,190	18,900	34,300	54,300
450	22	46	86	177	266	512	816	1,440	2,940	5,330	8,620	17,700	32,200	50,900
500	21	43	82	168	251	484	771	1,360	2,780	5,030	8,150	16,700	30,400	48,100
550	20	41	78	159	239	459	732	1,290	2,640	4,780	7,740	15,900	28,900	45,700
600	19	39	74	152	228	438	699	1,240	2,520	4,560	7,380	15,200	27,500	43,600
650	18	38	71	145	218	420	669	1,180	2,410	4,360	7,070	14,500	26,400	41,800
700	17	36	68	140	209	403	643	1,140	2,320	4,190	6,790	14,000	25,300	40,100
750	17	35	66	135	202	389	619	1,090	2,230	4,040	6,540	13,400	24,400	38,600
800	16	34	63	130	195	375	598	1,060	2,160	3,900	6,320	13,000	23,600	37,300
850	16	33	61	126	189	363	579	1,020	2,090	3,780	6,110	12,600	22,800	36,100
900	15	32	59	122	183	352	561	992	2,020	3,660	5,930	12,200	22,100	35,000
950	15	31	58	118	178	342	545	963	1,960	3,550	5,760	11,800	21,500	34,000
1,000	14	30	56	115	173	333	530	937	1,910	3,460	5,600	11,500	20,900	33,100
1,100	14	28	53	109	164	316	503	890	1,810	3,280	5,320	10,900	19,800	31,400
1,200	13	27	51	104	156	301	480	849	1,730	3,130	5,070	10,400	18,900	30,000
1,300	12	26	49	100	150	289	460	813	1,660	3,000	4,860	9,980	18,100	28,700
1,400	12	25	47	96	144	277	442	781	1,590	2,880	4,670	9,590	17,400	27,600
1,500	11	24	45	93	139	267	426	752	1,530	2,780	4,500	9,240	16,800	26,600
1,600	11	23	44	89	134	258	411	727	1,480	2,680	4,340	8,920	16,200	25,600
1,700	11	22	42	86	130	250	398	703	1,430	2,590	4,200	8,630	15,700	24,800
1,800	10	22	41	84	126	242	386	682	1,390	2,520	4,070	8,370	15,200	24,100
1,900	10	21	40	81	122	235	375	662	1,350	2,440	3,960	8,130	14,800	23,400
2,000	NA	20	39	79	119	229	364	644	1,310	2,380	3,850	7,910	14,400	22,700

NA: A flow of less than 10 cfh.
Note: All table entries are rounded to 3 significant digits.

Table 6.2.1(c) Schedule 40 Metallic Pipe

						Gas:	Natural
						Inlet Pressure:	Less than 2 psi
						Pressure Drop:	3.0 in. w.c.
						Specific Gravity:	0.60

INTENDED USE: Initial supply pressure of 8.0 in. w.c. or greater

	Pipe Size (in.)								
Nominal:	½	¾	1	1¼	1½	2	2½	3	4
Actual ID:	0.622	0.824	1.049	1.380	1.610	2.067	2.469	3.068	4.026
Length (ft)	Capacity in Thousands of Btu per Hour								
10	454	949	1,790	3,670	5,500	10,600	16,900	29,800	60,800
20	312	652	1,230	2,520	3,780	7,280	11,600	20,500	41,800
30	250	524	986	2,030	3,030	5,840	9,310	16,500	33,600
40	214	448	844	1,730	2,600	5,000	7,970	14,100	28,700
50	190	397	748	1,540	2,300	4,430	7,060	12,500	25,500
60	172	360	678	1,390	2,090	4,020	6,400	11,300	23,100
70	158	331	624	1,280	1,920	3,690	5,890	10,400	21,200
80	147	308	580	1,190	1,790	3,440	5,480	9,690	19,800
90	138	289	544	1,120	1,670	3,230	5,140	9,090	18,500
100	131	273	514	1,060	1,580	3,050	4,860	8,580	17,500
125	116	242	456	936	1,400	2,700	4,300	7,610	15,500
150	105	219	413	848	1,270	2,450	3,900	6,890	14,100
175	96	202	380	780	1,170	2,250	3,590	6,340	12,900
200	90	188	353	726	1,090	2,090	3,340	5,900	12,000
250	80	166	313	643	964	1,860	2,960	5,230	10,700
300	72	151	284	583	873	1,680	2,680	4,740	9,660
350	66	139	261	536	803	1,550	2,470	4,360	8,890
400	62	129	243	499	747	1,440	2,290	4,050	8,270
450	58	121	228	468	701	1,350	2,150	3,800	7,760
500	55	114	215	442	662	1,280	2,030	3,590	7,330
550	52	109	204	420	629	1,210	1,930	3,410	6,960
600	50	104	195	400	600	1,160	1,840	3,260	6,640
650	47	99	187	384	575	1,110	1,760	3,120	6,360
700	46	95	179	368	552	1,060	1,690	3,000	6,110
750	44	92	173	355	532	1,020	1,630	2,890	5,890
800	42	89	167	343	514	989	1,580	2,790	5,680
850	41	86	162	332	497	957	1,530	2,700	5,500
900	40	83	157	322	482	928	1,480	2,610	5,330
950	39	81	152	312	468	901	1,440	2,540	5,180
1000	38	79	148	304	455	877	1,400	2,470	5,040
1100	36	75	141	289	432	833	1,330	2,350	4,780
1200	34	71	134	275	412	794	1,270	2,240	4,560
1300	33	68	128	264	395	761	1,210	2,140	4,370
1400	31	65	123	253	379	731	1,160	2,060	4,200
1500	30	63	119	244	366	704	1,120	1,980	4,050
1600	29	61	115	236	353	680	1,080	1,920	3,910
1700	28	59	111	228	342	658	1,050	1,850	3,780
1800	27	57	108	221	331	638	1,020	1,800	3,670
1900	27	56	105	215	322	619	987	1,750	3,560
2000	26	54	102	209	313	602	960	1,700	3,460

Note: All table entries are rounded to 3 significant digits.

Table 6.2.1(d) Schedule 40 Metallic Pipe

					Gas:	Natural
					Inlet Pressure:	Less than 2 psi
					Pressure Drop:	6.0 in. w.c.
					Specific Gravity:	0.6

INTENDED USE: Initial supply pressure of 11.0 in. w.c. or greater

	Pipe Size (in.)								
Nominal:	½	¾	1	1¼	1½	2	2½	3	4
Actual ID:	0.622	0.824	1.049	1.38	1.61	2.067	2.469	3.068	4.026
Length (ft)	Capacity in Cubic Feet of Gas per Hour								
10	660	1,380	2,600	5,340	8,000	15,400	24,600	43,400	88,500
20	454	949	1,790	3,670	5,500	10,600	16,900	29,800	60,800
30	364	762	1,440	2,950	4,410	8,500	13,600	24,000	48,900
40	312	652	1,230	2,520	3,780	7,280	11,600	20,500	41,800
50	276	578	1,090	2,240	3,350	6,450	10,300	18,200	37,100
60	250	524	986	2,030	3,030	5,840	9,310	16,500	33,600
70	230	482	907	1,860	2,790	5,380	8,570	15,100	30,900
80	214	448	844	1,730	2,600	5,000	7,970	14,100	28,700
90	201	420	792	1,630	2,440	4,690	7,480	13,200	27,000
100	190	397	748	1,540	2,300	4,430	7,060	12,500	25,500
125	168	352	663	1,360	2,040	3,930	6,260	11,100	22,600
150	153	319	601	1,230	1,850	3,560	5,670	10,000	20,500
175	140	293	553	1,140	1,700	3,270	5,220	9,230	18,800
200	131	273	514	1,056	1,580	3,050	4,860	8,580	17,500
250	116	242	456	936	1,400	2,700	4,300	7,610	15,500
300	105	219	413	848	1,270	2,450	3,900	6,890	14,100
350	96	202	380	780	1,170	2,250	3,590	6,340	12,900
400	90	188	353	726	1,090	2,090	3,340	5,900	12,000
450	84	176	332	681	1,020	1,960	3,130	5,540	11,300
500	80	166	313	643	964	1,860	2,960	5,230	10,700
550	76	158	297	611	915	1,760	2,810	4,970	10,100
600	72	151	284	583	873	1,680	2,680	4,740	9,660
650	69	144	272	558	836	1,610	2,570	4,540	9,250
700	66	139	261	536	803	1,550	2,470	4,360	8,890
750	64	134	252	516	774	1,490	2,380	4,200	8,560
800	62	129	243	499	747	1,440	2,290	4,050	8,270
850	60	125	235	483	723	1,390	2,220	3,920	8,000
900	58	121	228	468	701	1,350	2,150	3,800	7,760
950	56	118	221	454	681	1,310	2,090	3,690	7,540
1,000	55	114	215	442	662	1,280	2,030	3,590	7,330
1,100	52	109	204	420	629	1,210	1,930	3,410	6,960
1,200	50	104	195	400	600	1,160	1,840	3,260	6,640
1,300	47	99	187	384	575	1,110	1,760	3,120	6,360
1,400	46	95	179	368	552	1,060	1,690	3,000	6,110
1,500	44	92	173	355	532	1,020	1,630	2,890	5,890
1,600	42	89	167	343	514	989	1,580	2,790	5,680
1,700	41	86	162	332	497	957	1,530	2,700	5,500
1,800	40	83	157	322	482	928	1,480	2,610	5,330
1,900	39	81	152	312	468	901	1,440	2,540	5,180
2,000	38	79	148	304	455	877	1,400	2,470	5,040

Note: All table entries are rounded to 3 significant digits.

Table 6.2.1(e) Schedule 40 Metallic Pipe

						Gas:	Natural		
						Inlet Pressure:	2.0 psi		
						Pressure Drop:	1.0 psi		
						Specific Gravity:	0.60		

	Pipe Size (in.)								
Nominal:	½	¾	1	1¼	1½	2	2½	3	4
Actual ID:	0.622	0.824	1.049	1.380	1.610	2.067	2.469	3.068	4.026
Length (ft)	Capacity in Cubic Feet of Gas per Hour								
10	1,510	3,040	5,560	11,400	17,100	32,900	52,500	92,800	189,000
20	1,070	2,150	3,930	8,070	12,100	23,300	37,100	65,600	134,000
30	869	1,760	3,210	6,590	9,880	19,000	30,300	53,600	109,000
40	753	1,520	2,780	5,710	8,550	16,500	26,300	46,400	94,700
50	673	1,360	2,490	5,110	7,650	14,700	23,500	41,500	84,700
60	615	1,240	2,270	4,660	6,980	13,500	21,400	37,900	77,300
70	569	1,150	2,100	4,320	6,470	12,500	19,900	35,100	71,600
80	532	1,080	1,970	4,040	6,050	11,700	18,600	32,800	67,000
90	502	1,010	1,850	3,810	5,700	11,000	17,500	30,900	63,100
100	462	934	1,710	3,510	5,260	10,100	16,100	28,500	58,200
125	414	836	1,530	3,140	4,700	9,060	14,400	25,500	52,100
150	372	751	1,370	2,820	4,220	8,130	13,000	22,900	46,700
175	344	695	1,270	2,601	3,910	7,530	12,000	21,200	43,300
200	318	642	1,170	2,410	3,610	6,960	11,100	19,600	40,000
250	279	583	1,040	2,140	3,210	6,180	9,850	17,400	35,500
300	253	528	945	1,940	2,910	5,600	8,920	15,800	32,200
350	232	486	869	1,790	2,670	5,150	8,210	14,500	29,600
400	216	452	809	1,660	2,490	4,790	7,640	13,500	27,500
450	203	424	759	1,560	2,330	4,500	7,170	12,700	25,800
500	192	401	717	1,470	2,210	4,250	6,770	12,000	24,400
550	182	381	681	1,400	2,090	4,030	6,430	11,400	23,200
600	174	363	650	1,330	2,000	3,850	6,130	10,800	22,100
650	166	348	622	1,280	1,910	3,680	5,870	10,400	21,200
700	160	334	598	1,230	1,840	3,540	5,640	9,970	20,300
750	154	322	576	1,180	1,770	3,410	5,440	9,610	19,600
800	149	311	556	1,140	1,710	3,290	5,250	9,280	18,900
850	144	301	538	1,100	1,650	3,190	5,080	8,980	18,300
900	139	292	522	1,070	1,600	3,090	4,930	8,710	17,800
950	135	283	507	1,040	1,560	3,000	4,780	8,460	17,200
1,000	132	275	493	1,010	1,520	2,920	4,650	8,220	16,800
1,100	125	262	468	960	1,440	2,770	4,420	7,810	15,900
1,200	119	250	446	917	1,370	2,640	4,220	7,450	15,200
1,300	114	239	427	878	1,320	2,530	4,040	7,140	14,600
1,400	110	230	411	843	1,260	2,430	3,880	6,860	14,000
1,500	106	221	396	812	1,220	2,340	3,740	6,600	13,500
1,600	102	214	382	784	1,180	2,260	3,610	6,380	13,000
1,700	99	207	370	759	1,140	2,190	3,490	6,170	12,600
1,800	96	200	358	736	1,100	2,120	3,390	5,980	12,200
1,900	93	195	348	715	1,070	2,060	3,290	5,810	11,900
2,000	91	189	339	695	1,040	2,010	3,200	5,650	11,500

Note: All table entries are rounded to 3 significant digits.

Table 6.2.1(f) Schedule 40 Metallic Pipe

							Gas:	Natural	
							Inlet Pressure:	3.0 psi	
							Pressure Drop:	2.0 psi	
							Specific Gravity:	0.60	

	Pipe Size (in.)								
Nominal:	½	¾	1	1¼	1½	2	2½	3	4
Actual ID:	0.622	0.824	1.049	1.380	1.610	2.067	2.469	3.068	4.026
Length (ft)	Capacity in Cubic Feet of Gas per Hour								
10	2,350	4,920	9,270	19,000	28,500	54,900	87,500	155,000	316,000
20	1,620	3,380	6,370	13,100	19,600	37,700	60,100	106,000	217,000
30	1,300	2,720	5,110	10,500	15,700	30,300	48,300	85,400	174,000
40	1,110	2,320	4,380	8,990	13,500	25,900	41,300	73,100	149,000
50	985	2,060	3,880	7,970	11,900	23,000	36,600	64,800	132,000
60	892	1,870	3,520	7,220	10,800	20,800	33,200	58,700	120,000
70	821	1,720	3,230	6,640	9,950	19,200	30,500	54,000	110,000
80	764	1,600	3,010	6,180	9,260	17,800	28,400	50,200	102,000
90	717	1,500	2,820	5,800	8,680	16,700	26,700	47,100	96,100
100	677	1,420	2,670	5,470	8,200	15,800	25,200	44,500	90,800
125	600	1,250	2,360	4,850	7,270	14,000	22,300	39,500	80,500
150	544	1,140	2,140	4,400	6,590	12,700	20,200	35,700	72,900
175	500	1,050	1,970	4,040	6,060	11,700	18,600	32,900	67,100
200	465	973	1,830	3,760	5,640	10,900	17,300	30,600	62,400
250	412	862	1,620	3,330	5,000	9,620	15,300	27,100	55,300
300	374	781	1,470	3,020	4,530	8,720	13,900	24,600	50,100
350	344	719	1,350	2,780	4,170	8,020	12,800	22,600	46,100
400	320	669	1,260	2,590	3,870	7,460	11,900	21,000	42,900
450	300	627	1,180	2,430	3,640	7,000	11,200	19,700	40,200
500	283	593	1,120	2,290	3,430	6,610	10,500	18,600	38,000
550	269	563	1,060	2,180	3,260	6,280	10,000	17,700	36,100
600	257	537	1,010	2,080	3,110	5,990	9,550	16,900	34,400
650	246	514	969	1,990	2,980	5,740	9,150	16,200	33,000
700	236	494	931	1,910	2,860	5,510	8,790	15,500	31,700
750	228	476	897	1,840	2,760	5,310	8,470	15,000	30,500
800	220	460	866	1,780	2,660	5,130	8,180	14,500	29,500
850	213	445	838	1,720	2,580	4,960	7,910	14,000	28,500
900	206	431	812	1,670	2,500	4,810	7,670	13,600	27,700
950	200	419	789	1,620	2,430	4,670	7,450	13,200	26,900
1,000	195	407	767	1,580	2,360	4,550	7,240	12,800	26,100
1,100	185	387	729	1,500	2,240	4,320	6,890	12,200	24,800
1,200	177	369	695	1,430	2,140	4,120	6,570	11,600	23,700
1,300	169	353	666	1,370	2,050	3,940	6,290	11,100	22,700
1,400	162	340	640	1,310	1,970	3,790	6,040	10,700	21,800
1,500	156	327	616	1,270	1,900	3,650	5,820	10,300	21,000
1,600	151	316	595	1,220	1,830	3,530	5,620	10,000	20,300
1,700	146	306	576	1,180	1,770	3,410	5,440	9,610	19,600
1,800	142	296	558	1,150	1,720	3,310	5,270	9,320	19,000
1,900	138	288	542	1,110	1,670	3,210	5,120	9,050	18,400
2,000	134	280	527	1,080	1,620	3,120	4,980	8,800	18,000

Note: All table entries are rounded to 3 significant digits.

Table 6.2.1(g) Schedule 40 Metallic Pipe

						Gas:	Natural		
						Inlet Pressure:	5.0 psi		
						Pressure Drop:	3.5 psi		
						Specific Gravity:	0.60		

	Pipe Size (in.)								
Nominal:	½	¾	1	1¼	1½	2	2½	3	4
Actual ID:	0.622	0.824	1.049	1.380	1.610	2.067	2.469	3.068	4.026
Length (ft)	Capacity in Cubic Feet of Gas per Hour								
10	3,190	6,430	11,800	24,200	36,200	69,700	111,000	196,000	401,000
20	2,250	4,550	8,320	17,100	25,600	49,300	78,600	139,000	283,000
30	1,840	3,720	6,790	14,000	20,900	40,300	64,200	113,000	231,000
40	1,590	3,220	5,880	12,100	18,100	34,900	55,600	98,200	200,000
50	1,430	2,880	5,260	10,800	16,200	31,200	49,700	87,900	179,000
60	1,300	2,630	4,800	9,860	14,800	28,500	45,400	80,200	164,000
70	1,200	2,430	4,450	9,130	13,700	26,400	42,000	74,300	151,000
80	1,150	2,330	4,260	8,540	12,800	24,700	39,300	69,500	142,000
90	1,060	2,150	3,920	8,050	12,100	23,200	37,000	65,500	134,000
100	979	1,980	3,620	7,430	11,100	21,400	34,200	60,400	123,000
125	876	1,770	3,240	6,640	9,950	19,200	30,600	54,000	110,000
150	786	1,590	2,910	5,960	8,940	17,200	27,400	48,500	98,900
175	728	1,470	2,690	5,520	8,270	15,900	25,400	44,900	91,600
200	673	1,360	2,490	5,100	7,650	14,700	23,500	41,500	84,700
250	558	1,170	2,200	4,510	6,760	13,000	20,800	36,700	74,900
300	506	1,060	1,990	4,090	6,130	11,800	18,800	33,300	67,800
350	465	973	1,830	3,760	5,640	10,900	17,300	30,600	62,400
400	433	905	1,710	3,500	5,250	10,100	16,100	28,500	58,100
450	406	849	1,600	3,290	4,920	9,480	15,100	26,700	54,500
500	384	802	1,510	3,100	4,650	8,950	14,300	25,200	51,500
550	364	762	1,440	2,950	4,420	8,500	13,600	24,000	48,900
600	348	727	1,370	2,810	4,210	8,110	12,900	22,900	46,600
650	333	696	1,310	2,690	4,030	7,770	12,400	21,900	44,600
700	320	669	1,260	2,590	3,880	7,460	11,900	21,000	42,900
750	308	644	1,210	2,490	3,730	7,190	11,500	20,300	41,300
800	298	622	1,170	2,410	3,610	6,940	11,100	19,600	39,900
850	288	602	1,130	2,330	3,490	6,720	10,700	18,900	38,600
900	279	584	1,100	2,260	3,380	6,520	10,400	18,400	37,400
950	271	567	1,070	2,190	3,290	6,330	10,100	17,800	36,400
1,000	264	551	1,040	2,130	3,200	6,150	9,810	17,300	35,400
1,100	250	524	987	2,030	3,030	5,840	9,320	16,500	33,600
1,200	239	500	941	1,930	2,900	5,580	8,890	15,700	32,000
1,300	229	478	901	1,850	2,770	5,340	8,510	15,000	30,700
1,400	220	460	866	1,780	2,660	5,130	8,180	14,500	29,500
1,500	212	443	834	1,710	2,570	4,940	7,880	13,900	28,400
1,600	205	428	806	1,650	2,480	4,770	7,610	13,400	27,400
1,700	198	414	780	1,600	2,400	4,620	7,360	13,000	26,500
1,800	192	401	756	1,550	2,330	4,480	7,140	12,600	25,700
1,900	186	390	734	1,510	2,260	4,350	6,930	12,300	25,000
2,000	181	379	714	1,470	2,200	4,230	6,740	11,900	24,300

Note: All table entries are rounded to 3 significant digits.

Table 6.2.1(h) Semirigid Copper Tubing

		Gas:	Natural
		Inlet Pressure:	Less than 2 psi
		Pressure Drop:	0.3 in. w.c.
		Specific Gravity:	0.60

Nominal:	K & L:	1/4	3/8	1/2	5/8	3/4	1	1 1/4	1 1/2	2
	ACR:	3/8	1/2	5/8	3/4	7/8	1 1/8	1 3/8	—	—
	Outside:	0.375	0.500	0.625	0.750	0.875	1.125	1.375	1.625	2.125
	Inside:*	0.305	0.402	0.527	0.652	0.745	0.995	1.245	1.481	1.959
Length (ft)		Capacity in Cubic Feet of Gas per Hour								
10		20	42	85	148	210	448	806	1,270	2,650
20		14	29	58	102	144	308	554	873	1,820
30		11	23	47	82	116	247	445	701	1,460
40		10	20	40	70	99	211	381	600	1,250
50		NA	17	35	62	88	187	337	532	1,110
60		NA	16	32	56	79	170	306	482	1,000
70		NA	14	29	52	73	156	281	443	924
80		NA	13	27	48	68	145	262	413	859
90		NA	13	26	45	64	136	245	387	806
100		NA	12	24	43	60	129	232	366	761
125		NA	11	22	38	53	114	206	324	675
150		NA	10	20	34	48	103	186	294	612
175		NA	NA	18	31	45	95	171	270	563
200		NA	NA	17	29	41	89	159	251	523
250		NA	NA	15	26	37	78	141	223	464
300		NA	NA	13	23	33	71	128	202	420
350		NA	NA	12	22	31	65	118	186	387
400		NA	NA	11	20	28	61	110	173	360
450		NA	NA	11	19	27	57	103	162	338
500		NA	NA	10	18	25	54	97	153	319
550		NA	NA	NA	17	24	51	92	145	303
600		NA	NA	NA	16	23	49	88	139	289
650		NA	NA	NA	15	22	47	84	133	277
700		NA	NA	NA	15	21	45	81	128	266
750		NA	NA	NA	14	20	43	78	123	256
800		NA	NA	NA	14	20	42	75	119	247
850		NA	NA	NA	13	19	40	73	115	239
900		NA	NA	NA	13	18	39	71	111	232
950		NA	NA	NA	13	18	38	69	108	225
1,000		NA	NA	NA	12	17	37	67	105	219
1,100		NA	NA	NA	12	16	35	63	100	208
1,200		NA	NA	NA	11	16	34	60	95	199
1,300		NA	NA	NA	11	15	32	58	91	190
1,400		NA	NA	NA	10	14	31	56	88	183
1,500		NA	NA	NA	NA	14	30	54	84	176
1,600		NA	NA	NA	NA	13	29	52	82	170
1,700		NA	NA	NA	NA	13	28	50	79	164
1,800		NA	NA	NA	NA	13	27	49	77	159
1,900		NA	NA	NA	NA	12	26	47	74	155
2,000		NA	NA	NA	NA	12	25	46	72	151

NA: A flow of less than 10 cfh.
Note: All table entries are rounded to 3 significant digits.
*Table capacities are based on Type K copper tubing inside diameter (shown), which has the smallest inside diameter of the copper tubing products.

Table 6.2.1(i) Semirigid Copper Tubing

		Tube Size (in.)								
							Gas:	Natural		
							Inlet Pressure:	Less than 2 psi		
							Pressure Drop:	0.5 in. w.c.		
							Specific Gravity:	0.60		
Nominal:	K & L:	¼	⅜	½	⅝	¾	1	1¼	1½	2
	ACR:	⅜	½	⅝	¾	⅞	1⅛	1⅜	—	—
	Outside:	0.375	0.500	0.625	0.750	0.875	1.125	1.375	1.625	2.125
	Inside:*	0.305	0.402	0.527	0.652	0.745	0.995	1.245	1.481	1.959
Length (ft)		Capacity in Cubic Feet of Gas per Hour								
10		27	55	111	195	276	590	1,060	1,680	3,490
20		18	38	77	134	190	406	730	1,150	2,400
30		15	30	61	107	152	326	586	925	1,930
40		13	26	53	92	131	279	502	791	1,650
50		11	23	47	82	116	247	445	701	1,460
60		10	21	42	74	105	224	403	635	1,320
70		NA	19	39	68	96	206	371	585	1,220
80		NA	18	36	63	90	192	345	544	1,130
90		NA	17	34	59	84	180	324	510	1,060
100		NA	16	32	56	79	170	306	482	1,000
125		NA	14	28	50	70	151	271	427	890
150		NA	13	26	45	64	136	245	387	806
175		NA	12	24	41	59	125	226	356	742
200		NA	11	22	39	55	117	210	331	690
250		NA	NA	20	34	48	103	186	294	612
300		NA	NA	18	31	44	94	169	266	554
350		NA	NA	16	28	40	86	155	245	510
400		NA	NA	15	26	38	80	144	228	474
450		NA	NA	14	25	35	75	135	214	445
500		NA	NA	13	23	33	71	128	202	420
550		NA	NA	13	22	32	68	122	192	399
600		NA	NA	12	21	30	64	116	183	381
650		NA	NA	12	20	29	62	111	175	365
700		NA	NA	11	20	28	59	107	168	350
750		NA	NA	11	19	27	57	103	162	338
800		NA	NA	10	18	26	55	99	156	326
850		NA	NA	10	18	25	53	96	151	315
900		NA	NA	NA	17	24	52	93	147	306
950		NA	NA	NA	17	24	50	90	143	297
1,000		NA	NA	NA	16	23	49	88	139	289
1,100		NA	NA	NA	15	22	46	84	132	274
1,200		NA	NA	NA	15	21	44	80	126	262
1,300		NA	NA	NA	14	20	42	76	120	251
1,400		NA	NA	NA	13	19	41	73	116	241
1,500		NA	NA	NA	13	18	39	71	111	232
1,600		NA	NA	NA	13	18	38	68	108	224
1,700		NA	NA	NA	12	17	37	66	104	217
1,800		NA	NA	NA	12	17	36	64	101	210
1,900		NA	NA	NA	11	16	35	62	98	204
2,000		NA	NA	NA	11	16	34	60	95	199

NA: A flow of less than 10 cfh.
Note: All table entries are rounded to 3 significant digits.
*Table capacities are based on Type K copper tubing inside diameter (shown), which has the smallest inside diameter of the copper tubing products.

Table 6.2.1(j) Semirigid Copper Tubing

		Gas:	Natural
		Inlet Pressure:	Less than 2 psi
		Pressure Drop:	1.0 in. w.c.
		Specific Gravity:	0.60

INTENDED USE: Tube Sizing Between House Line Regulator and the Appliance.

Nominal:		Tube Size (in.)								
	K & L:	1/4	3/8	1/2	5/8	3/4	1	1 1/4	1 1/2	2
	ACR:	3/8	1/2	5/8	3/4	7/8	1 1/8	1 3/8	—	—
	Outside:	0.375	0.500	0.625	0.750	0.875	1.125	1.375	1.625	2.125
	Inside:*	0.305	0.402	0.527	0.652	0.745	0.995	1.245	1.481	1.959
Length (ft)		Capacity in Cubic Feet of Gas per Hour								
10		39	80	162	283	402	859	1,550	2,440	5,080
20		27	55	111	195	276	590	1,060	1,680	3,490
30		21	44	89	156	222	474	853	1,350	2,800
40		18	38	77	134	190	406	730	1,150	2,400
50		16	33	68	119	168	359	647	1,020	2,130
60		15	30	61	107	152	326	586	925	1,930
70		13	28	57	99	140	300	539	851	1,770
80		13	26	53	92	131	279	502	791	1,650
90		12	24	49	86	122	262	471	742	1,550
100		11	23	47	82	116	247	445	701	1,460
125		NA	20	41	72	103	219	394	622	1,290
150		NA	18	37	65	93	198	357	563	1,170
175		NA	17	34	60	85	183	329	518	1,080
200		NA	16	32	56	79	170	306	482	1,000
250		NA	14	28	50	70	151	271	427	890
300		NA	13	26	45	64	136	245	387	806
350		NA	12	24	41	59	125	226	356	742
400		NA	11	22	39	55	117	210	331	690
450		NA	10	21	36	51	110	197	311	647
500		NA	NA	20	34	48	103	186	294	612
550		NA	NA	19	32	46	98	177	279	581
600		NA	NA	18	31	44	94	169	266	554
650		NA	NA	17	30	42	90	162	255	531
700		NA	NA	16	28	40	86	155	245	510
750		NA	NA	16	27	39	83	150	236	491
800		NA	NA	15	26	38	80	144	228	474
850		NA	NA	15	26	36	78	140	220	459
900		NA	NA	14	25	35	75	135	214	445
950		NA	NA	14	24	34	73	132	207	432
1,000		NA	NA	13	23	33	71	128	202	420
1,100		NA	NA	13	22	32	68	122	192	399
1,200		NA	NA	12	21	30	64	116	183	381
1,300		NA	NA	12	20	29	62	111	175	365
1,400		NA	NA	11	20	28	59	107	168	350
1,500		NA	NA	11	19	27	57	103	162	338
1,600		NA	NA	10	18	26	55	99	156	326
1,700		NA	NA	10	18	25	53	96	151	315
1,800		NA	NA	NA	17	24	52	93	147	306
1,900		NA	NA	NA	17	24	50	90	143	297
2,000		NA	NA	NA	16	23	49	88	139	289

NA: A flow of less than 10 cfh.

Note: All table entries are rounded to 3 significant digits.

*Table capacities are based on Type K copper tubing inside diameter (shown), which has the smallest inside diameter of the copper tubing products.

Table 6.2.1(k) Semirigid Copper Tubing

		Gas:	Natural
		Inlet Pressure:	Less than 2.0 psi
		Pressure Drop:	17.0 in. w.c.
		Specific Gravity:	0.60

Nominal:	K & L:	¼	⅜	½	⅝	¾	1	1¼	1½	2
	ACR:	⅜	½	⅝	¾	⅞	1⅛	1⅜	—	—
	Outside:	0.375	0.500	0.625	0.750	0.875	1.125	1.375	1.625	2.125
	Inside:*	0.305	0.402	0.527	0.652	0.745	0.995	1.245	1.481	1.959
Length (ft)		Capacity in Cubic Feet of Gas per Hour								
10		190	391	796	1,390	1,970	4,220	7,590	12,000	24,900
20		130	269	547	956	1,360	2,900	5,220	8,230	17,100
30		105	216	439	768	1,090	2,330	4,190	6,610	13,800
40		90	185	376	657	932	1,990	3,590	5,650	11,800
50		79	164	333	582	826	1,770	3,180	5,010	10,400
60		72	148	302	528	749	1,600	2,880	4,540	9,460
70		66	137	278	486	689	1,470	2,650	4,180	8,700
80		62	127	258	452	641	1,370	2,460	3,890	8,090
90		58	119	243	424	601	1,280	2,310	3,650	7,590
100		55	113	229	400	568	1,210	2,180	3,440	7,170
125		48	100	203	355	503	1,080	1,940	3,050	6,360
150		44	90	184	321	456	974	1,750	2,770	5,760
175		40	83	169	296	420	896	1,610	2,540	5,300
200		38	77	157	275	390	834	1,500	2,370	4,930
250		33	69	140	244	346	739	1,330	2,100	4,370
300		30	62	126	221	313	670	1,210	1,900	3,960
350		28	57	116	203	288	616	1,110	1,750	3,640
400		26	53	108	189	268	573	1,030	1,630	3,390
450		24	50	102	177	252	538	968	1,530	3,180
500		23	47	96	168	238	508	914	1,440	3,000
550		22	45	91	159	226	482	868	1,370	2,850
600		21	43	87	152	215	460	829	1,310	2,720
650		20	41	83	145	206	441	793	1,250	2,610
700		19	39	80	140	198	423	762	1,200	2,500
750		18	38	77	135	191	408	734	1,160	2,410
800		18	37	74	130	184	394	709	1,120	2,330
850		17	35	72	126	178	381	686	1,080	2,250
900		17	34	70	122	173	370	665	1,050	2,180
950		16	33	68	118	168	359	646	1,020	2,120
1,000		16	32	66	115	163	349	628	991	2,060
1,100		15	31	63	109	155	332	597	941	1,960
1,200		14	29	60	104	148	316	569	898	1,870
1,300		14	28	57	100	142	303	545	860	1,790
1,400		13	27	55	96	136	291	524	826	1,720
1,500		13	26	53	93	131	280	505	796	1,660
1,600		12	25	51	89	127	271	487	768	1,600
1,700		12	24	49	86	123	262	472	744	1,550
1,800		11	24	48	84	119	254	457	721	1,500
1,900		11	23	47	81	115	247	444	700	1,460
2,000		11	22	45	79	112	240	432	681	1,420

Note: All table entries are rounded to 3 significant digits.
*Table capacities are based on Type K copper tubing inside diameter (shown), which has the smallest inside diameter of the copper tubing products.

Table 6.2.1(l) Semirigid Copper Tubing

								Gas:	Natural	
								Inlet Pressure:	2.0 psi	
								Pressure Drop:	1.0 psi	
								Specific Gravity:	0.60	

Nominal:		Tube Size (in.)								
	K & L:	¼	⅜	½	⅝	¾	1	1¼	1½	2
	ACR:	⅜	½	⅝	¾	⅞	1⅛	1⅜	—	—
	Outside:	0.375	0.500	0.625	0.750	0.875	1.125	1.375	1.625	2.125
	Inside:*	0.305	0.402	0.527	0.652	0.745	0.995	1.245	1.481	1.959
Length (ft)		Capacity in Cubic Feet of Gas per Hour								
10		245	506	1,030	1,800	2,550	5,450	9,820	15,500	32,200
20		169	348	708	1,240	1,760	3,750	6,750	10,600	22,200
30		135	279	568	993	1,410	3,010	5,420	8,550	17,800
40		116	239	486	850	1,210	2,580	4,640	7,310	15,200
50		103	212	431	754	1,070	2,280	4,110	6,480	13,500
60		93	192	391	683	969	2,070	3,730	5,870	12,200
70		86	177	359	628	891	1,900	3,430	5,400	11,300
80		80	164	334	584	829	1,770	3,190	5,030	10,500
90		75	154	314	548	778	1,660	2,990	4,720	9,820
100		71	146	296	518	735	1,570	2,830	4,450	9,280
125		63	129	263	459	651	1,390	2,500	3,950	8,220
150		57	117	238	416	590	1,260	2,270	3,580	7,450
175		52	108	219	383	543	1,160	2,090	3,290	6,850
200		49	100	204	356	505	1,080	1,940	3,060	6,380
250		43	89	181	315	448	956	1,720	2,710	5,650
300		39	80	164	286	406	866	1,560	2,460	5,120
350		36	74	150	263	373	797	1,430	2,260	4,710
400		33	69	140	245	347	741	1,330	2,100	4,380
450		31	65	131	230	326	696	1,250	1,970	4,110
500		30	61	124	217	308	657	1,180	1,870	3,880
550		28	58	118	206	292	624	1,120	1,770	3,690
600		27	55	112	196	279	595	1,070	1,690	3,520
650		26	53	108	188	267	570	1,030	1,620	3,370
700		25	51	103	181	256	548	986	1,550	3,240
750		24	49	100	174	247	528	950	1,500	3,120
800		23	47	96	168	239	510	917	1,450	3,010
850		22	46	93	163	231	493	888	1,400	2,920
900		22	44	90	158	224	478	861	1,360	2,830
950		21	43	88	153	217	464	836	1,320	2,740
1,000		20	42	85	149	211	452	813	1,280	2,670
1,100		19	40	81	142	201	429	772	1,220	2,540
1,200		18	38	77	135	192	409	737	1,160	2,420
1,300		18	36	74	129	183	392	705	1,110	2,320
1,400		17	35	71	124	176	376	678	1,070	2,230
1,500		16	34	68	120	170	363	653	1,030	2,140
1,600		16	33	66	116	164	350	630	994	2,070
1,700		15	31	64	112	159	339	610	962	2,000
1,800		15	30	62	108	154	329	592	933	1,940
1,900		14	30	60	105	149	319	575	906	1,890
2,000		14	29	59	102	145	310	559	881	1,830

Note: All table entries are rounded to 3 significant digits.
*Table capacities are based on Type K copper tubing inside diameter (shown), which has the smallest inside diameter of the copper tubing products.

Table 6.2.1(m) Semirigid Copper Tubing

	Gas:	Natural
	Inlet Pressure:	2.0 psi
	Pressure Drop:	1.5 psi
	Specific Gravity:	0.60

INTENDED USE: Pipe Sizing Between Point of Delivery and the House Line Regulator. Total Load Supplied by a Single House Line Regulator Not Exceeding 150 Cubic Feet per Hour.*

Nominal:	K & L:	1/4	3/8	1/2	5/8	3/4	1	1 1/4	1 1/2	2
	ACR:	3/8	1/2	5/8	3/4	7/8	1 1/8	1 3/8	—	—
Outside:		0.375	0.500	0.625	0.750	0.875	1.125	1.375	1.625	2.125
Inside:†		0.305	0.402	0.527	0.652	0.745	0.995	1.245	1.481	1.959
Length (ft)		**Capacity in Cubic Feet of Gas per Hour**								
10		303	625	1,270	2,220	3,150	6,740	12,100	19,100	39,800
20		208	430	874	1,530	2,170	4,630	8,330	13,100	27,400
30		167	345	702	1,230	1,740	3,720	6,690	10,600	22,000
40		143	295	601	1,050	1,490	3,180	5,730	9,030	18,800
50		127	262	532	931	1,320	2,820	5,080	8,000	16,700
60		115	237	482	843	1,200	2,560	4,600	7,250	15,100
70		106	218	444	776	1,100	2,350	4,230	6,670	13,900
80		98	203	413	722	1,020	2,190	3,940	6,210	12,900
90		92	190	387	677	961	2,050	3,690	5,820	12,100
100		87	180	366	640	907	1,940	3,490	5,500	11,500
125		77	159	324	567	804	1,720	3,090	4,880	10,200
150		70	144	294	514	729	1,560	2,800	4,420	9,200
175		64	133	270	472	670	1,430	2,580	4,060	8,460
200		60	124	252	440	624	1,330	2,400	3,780	7,870
250		53	110	223	390	553	1,180	2,130	3,350	6,980
300		48	99	202	353	501	1,070	1,930	3,040	6,320
350		44	91	186	325	461	984	1,770	2,790	5,820
400		41	85	173	302	429	916	1,650	2,600	5,410
450		39	80	162	283	402	859	1,550	2,440	5,080
500		36	75	153	268	380	811	1,460	2,300	4,800
550		35	72	146	254	361	771	1,390	2,190	4,560
600		33	68	139	243	344	735	1,320	2,090	4,350
650		32	65	133	232	330	704	1,270	2,000	4,160
700		30	63	128	223	317	676	1,220	1,920	4,000
750		29	60	123	215	305	652	1,170	1,850	3,850
800		28	58	119	208	295	629	1,130	1,790	3,720
850		27	57	115	201	285	609	1,100	1,730	3,600
900		27	55	111	195	276	590	1,060	1,680	3,490
950		26	53	108	189	268	573	1,030	1,630	3,390
1,000		25	52	105	184	261	558	1,000	1,580	3,300
1,100		24	49	100	175	248	530	954	1,500	3,130
1,200		23	47	95	167	237	505	910	1,430	2,990
1,300		22	45	91	160	227	484	871	1,370	2,860
1,400		21	43	88	153	218	465	837	1,320	2,750
1,500		20	42	85	148	210	448	806	1,270	2,650
1,600		19	40	82	143	202	432	779	1,230	2,560
1,700		19	39	79	138	196	419	753	1,190	2,470
1,800		18	38	77	134	190	406	731	1,150	2,400
1,900		18	37	74	130	184	394	709	1,120	2,330
2,000		17	36	72	126	179	383	690	1,090	2,270

Note: All table entries are rounded to 3 significant digits.
*When this table is used to size the tubing upstream of a line pressure regulator, the pipe or tubing downstream of the line pressure regulator shall be sized using a pressure drop no greater than 1 in. w.c.
†Table capacities are based on Type K copper tubing inside diameter (shown), which has the smallest inside diameter of the copper tubing products.

Table 6.2.1(n) Semirigid Copper Tubing

							Gas:	Natural		
							Inlet Pressure:	5.0 psi		
							Pressure Drop:	3.5 psi		
							Specific Gravity:	0.60		

Nominal:		Tube Size (in.)								
	K & L:	1/4	3/8	1/2	5/8	3/4	1	1 1/4	1 1/2	2
	ACR:	3/8	1/2	5/8	3/4	7/8	1 1/8	1 3/8	—	—
	Outside:	0.375	0.500	0.625	0.750	0.875	1.125	1.375	1.625	2.125
	Inside:*	0.305	0.402	0.527	0.652	0.745	0.995	1.245	1.481	1.959
Length (ft)		Capacity in Cubic Feet of Gas per Hour								
10		511	1,050	2,140	3,750	5,320	11,400	20,400	32,200	67,100
20		351	724	1,470	2,580	3,650	7,800	14,000	22,200	46,100
30		282	582	1,180	2,070	2,930	6,270	11,300	17,800	37,000
40		241	498	1,010	1,770	2,510	5,360	9,660	15,200	31,700
50		214	441	898	1,570	2,230	4,750	8,560	13,500	28,100
60		194	400	813	1,420	2,020	4,310	7,750	12,200	25,500
70		178	368	748	1,310	1,860	3,960	7,130	11,200	23,400
80		166	342	696	1,220	1,730	3,690	6,640	10,500	21,800
90		156	321	653	1,140	1,620	3,460	6,230	9,820	20,400
100		147	303	617	1,080	1,530	3,270	5,880	9,270	19,300
125		130	269	547	955	1,360	2,900	5,210	8,220	17,100
150		118	243	495	866	1,230	2,620	4,720	7,450	15,500
175		109	224	456	796	1,130	2,410	4,350	6,850	14,300
200		101	208	424	741	1,050	2,250	4,040	6,370	13,300
250		90	185	376	657	932	1,990	3,580	5,650	11,800
300		81	167	340	595	844	1,800	3,250	5,120	10,700
350		75	154	313	547	777	1,660	2,990	4,710	9,810
400		69	143	291	509	722	1,540	2,780	4,380	9,120
450		65	134	273	478	678	1,450	2,610	4,110	8,560
500		62	127	258	451	640	1,370	2,460	3,880	8,090
550		58	121	245	429	608	1,300	2,340	3,690	7,680
600		56	115	234	409	580	1,240	2,230	3,520	7,330
650		53	110	224	392	556	1,190	2,140	3,370	7,020
700		51	106	215	376	534	1,140	2,050	3,240	6,740
750		49	102	207	362	514	1,100	1,980	3,120	6,490
800		48	98	200	350	497	1,060	1,910	3,010	6,270
850		46	95	194	339	481	1,030	1,850	2,910	6,070
900		45	92	188	328	466	1,000	1,790	2,820	5,880
950		43	90	182	319	452	967	1,740	2,740	5,710
1,000		42	87	177	310	440	940	1,690	2,670	5,560
1,100		40	83	169	295	418	893	1,610	2,530	5,280
1,200		38	79	161	281	399	852	1,530	2,420	5,040
1,300		37	76	154	269	382	816	1,470	2,320	4,820
1,400		35	73	148	259	367	784	1,410	2,220	4,630
1,500		34	70	143	249	353	755	1,360	2,140	4,460
1,600		33	68	138	241	341	729	1,310	2,070	4,310
1,700		32	65	133	233	330	705	1,270	2,000	4,170
1,800		31	63	129	226	320	684	1,230	1,940	4,040
1,900		30	62	125	219	311	664	1,200	1,890	3,930
2,000		29	60	122	213	302	646	1,160	1,830	3,820

Note: All table entries are rounded to 3 significant digits.
*Table capacities are based on Type K copper tubing inside diameter (shown), which has the smallest inside diameter of the copper tubing products.

Table 6.2.1(o) Corrugated Stainless Steel Tubing (CSST)

													Gas:	Natural
													Inlet Pressure:	Less than 2 psi
													Pressure Drop:	0.5 in. w.c.
													Specific Gravity:	0.60

	Tube Size (EHD)													
Flow Designation:	13	15	18	19	23	25	30	31	37	39	46	48	60	62
Length (ft)	Capacity in Cubic Feet of Gas per Hour													
5	46	63	115	134	225	270	471	546	895	1,037	1,790	2,070	3,660	4,140
10	32	44	82	95	161	192	330	383	639	746	1,260	1,470	2,600	2,930
15	25	35	66	77	132	157	267	310	524	615	1,030	1,200	2,140	2,400
20	22	31	58	67	116	137	231	269	456	536	888	1,050	1,850	2,080
25	19	27	52	60	104	122	206	240	409	482	793	936	1,660	1,860
30	18	25	47	55	96	112	188	218	374	442	723	856	1,520	1,700
40	15	21	41	47	83	97	162	188	325	386	625	742	1,320	1,470
50	13	19	37	42	75	87	144	168	292	347	559	665	1,180	1,320
60	12	17	34	38	68	80	131	153	267	318	509	608	1,080	1,200
70	11	16	31	36	63	74	121	141	248	295	471	563	1,000	1,110
80	10	15	29	33	60	69	113	132	232	277	440	527	940	1,040
90	10	14	28	32	57	65	107	125	219	262	415	498	887	983
100	9	13	26	30	54	62	101	118	208	249	393	472	843	933
150	7	10	20	23	42	48	78	91	171	205	320	387	691	762
200	6	9	18	21	38	44	71	82	148	179	277	336	600	661
250	5	8	16	19	34	39	63	74	133	161	247	301	538	591
300	5	7	15	17	32	36	57	67	95	148	226	275	492	540

EHD: Equivalent hydraulic diameter. A measure of the relative hydraulic efficiency between different tubing sizes. The greater the value of EHD, the greater the gas capacity of the tubing.

Notes:
(1) Table includes losses for four 90 degree bends and two end fittings. Tubing runs with larger numbers of bends and/or fittings shall be increased by an equivalent length of tubing to the following equation: $L = 1.3n$, where L is additional length (ft) of tubing and n is the number of additional fittings and/or bends.
(2) All table entries are rounded to 3 significant digits.

Table 6.2.1(p) Corrugated Stainless Steel Tubing (CSST)

											Gas:	Natural
											Inlet Pressure:	Less than 2 psi
											Pressure Drop:	3.0 in. w.c.
											Specific Gravity:	0.60

INTENDED USE: Initial Supply Pressure of 8.0 in. w.c. or Greater.

Flow Designation:	\multicolumn{14}{c}{Tube Size (EHD)}
	13	15	18	19	23	25	30	31	37	39	46	48	60	62
Length (ft)	\multicolumn{14}{c}{Capacity in Cubic Feet of Gas per Hour}
5	120	160	277	327	529	649	1,180	1,370	2,140	2423	4,430	5,010	8,800	10,100
10	83	112	197	231	380	462	828	958	1,530	1740	3,200	3,560	6,270	7,160
15	67	90	161	189	313	379	673	778	1,250	1433	2,540	2,910	5,140	5,850
20	57	78	140	164	273	329	580	672	1,090	1249	2,200	2,530	4,460	5,070
25	51	69	125	147	245	295	518	599	978	1123	1,960	2,270	4,000	4,540
30	46	63	115	134	225	270	471	546	895	1029	1,790	2,070	3,660	4,140
40	39	54	100	116	196	234	407	471	778	897	1,550	1,800	3,180	3,590
50	35	48	89	104	176	210	363	421	698	806	1,380	1,610	2,850	3,210
60	32	44	82	95	161	192	330	383	639	739	1,260	1,470	2,600	2,930
70	29	41	76	88	150	178	306	355	593	686	1,170	1,360	2,420	2,720
80	27	38	71	82	141	167	285	331	555	644	1,090	1,280	2,260	2,540
90	26	36	67	77	133	157	268	311	524	609	1,030	1,200	2,140	2,400
100	24	34	63	73	126	149	254	295	498	579	974	1,140	2,030	2,280
150	19	27	52	60	104	122	206	240	409	477	793	936	1,660	1,860
200	17	23	45	52	91	106	178	207	355	415	686	812	1,440	1,610
250	15	21	40	46	82	95	159	184	319	373	613	728	1,290	1,440
300	13	19	37	42	75	87	144	168	284	342	559	665	1,180	1,320

EHD: Equivalent hydraulic diameter. A measure of the relative hydraulic efficiency between different tubing sizes. The greater the value of EHD, the greater the gas capacity of the tubing.

Notes:
(1) Table includes losses for four 90 degree bends and two end fittings. Tubing runs with larger numbers of bends and/or fittings shall be increased by an equivalent length of tubing to the following equation: $L = 1.3n$, where L is additional length (ft) of tubing and n is the number of additional fittings and/or bends.
(2) All table entries are rounded to 3 significant digits.

Table 6.2.1(q) Corrugated Stainless Steel Tubing (CSST)

							Gas:	Natural
							Inlet Pressure:	Less than 2 psi
							Pressure Drop:	6.0 in. w.c.
							Specific Gravity:	0.60

INTENDED USE: Initial Supply Pressure of 11.0 in. w.c. or Greater.

Flow Designation:	\multicolumn{14}{c}{Tube Size (EHD)}
	13	15	18	19	23	25	30	31	37	39	46	48	60	62
Length (ft)	\multicolumn{14}{c}{Capacity in Cubic Feet of Gas per Hour}
5	173	229	389	461	737	911	1,690	1,950	3,000	3375	6,280	7,050	12,400	14,260
10	120	160	277	327	529	649	1,180	1,370	2,140	2423	4,430	5,010	8,800	10,100
15	96	130	227	267	436	532	960	1,110	1,760	1996	3,610	4,100	7,210	8,260
20	83	112	197	231	380	462	828	958	1,530	1740	3,120	3,560	6,270	7,160
25	74	99	176	207	342	414	739	855	1,370	1564	2,790	3,190	5,620	6,400
30	67	90	161	189	313	379	673	778	1,250	1433	2,540	2,910	5,140	5,850
40	57	78	140	164	273	329	580	672	1,090	1249	2,200	2,530	4,460	5,070
50	51	69	125	147	245	295	518	599	978	1123	1,960	2,270	4,000	4,540
60	46	63	115	134	225	270	471	546	895	1029	1,790	2,070	3,660	4,140
70	42	58	106	124	209	250	435	505	830	956	1,660	1,920	3,390	3,840
80	39	54	100	116	196	234	407	471	778	897	1,550	1,800	3,180	3,590
90	37	51	94	109	185	221	383	444	735	848	1,460	1,700	3,000	3,390
100	35	48	89	104	176	210	363	421	698	806	1,380	1,610	2,850	3,210
150	28	39	73	85	145	172	294	342	573	664	1,130	1,320	2,340	2,630
200	24	34	63	73	126	149	254	295	498	579	974	1,140	2,030	2,280
250	21	30	57	66	114	134	226	263	447	520	870	1,020	1,820	2,040
300	19	27	52	60	104	122	206	240	409	477	793	936	1,660	1,860

EHD: Equivalent hydraulic diameter. A measure of the relative hydraulic efficiency between different tubing sizes. The greater the value of EHD, the greater the gas capacity of the tubing.

Notes:
(1) Table includes losses for four 90 degree bends and two end fittings. Tubing runs with larger numbers of bends and/or fittings shall be increased by an equivalent length of tubing to the following equation: $L = 1.3n$, where L is additional length (ft) of tubing and n is the number of additional fittings and/or bends.
(2) All table entries are rounded to 3 significant digits.

Table 6.2.1(r) Corrugated Stainless Steel Tubing (CSST)

														Gas:	Natural
														Inlet Pressure:	2.0 psi
														Pressure Drop:	1.0 psi
														Specific Gravity:	0.60

	Tube Size (EHD)													
Flow Designation:	13	15	18	19	23	25	30	31	37	39	46	48	60	62
Length (ft)	Capacity in Cubic Feet of Gas per Hour													
10	270	353	587	700	1,100	1,370	2,590	2,990	4,510	5,037	9,600	10,700	18,600	21,600
25	166	220	374	444	709	876	1,620	1,870	2,890	3,258	6,040	6,780	11,900	13,700
30	151	200	342	405	650	801	1,480	1,700	2,640	2,987	5,510	6,200	10,900	12,500
40	129	172	297	351	567	696	1,270	1,470	2,300	2,605	4,760	5,380	9,440	10,900
50	115	154	266	314	510	624	1,140	1,310	2,060	2,343	4,260	4,820	8,470	9,720
75	93	124	218	257	420	512	922	1,070	1,690	1,932	3,470	3,950	6,940	7,940
80	89	120	211	249	407	496	892	1,030	1,640	1,874	3,360	3,820	6,730	7,690
100	79	107	189	222	366	445	795	920	1,470	1,685	3,000	3,420	6,030	6,880
150	64	87	155	182	302	364	646	748	1,210	1,389	2,440	2,800	4,940	5,620
200	55	75	135	157	263	317	557	645	1,050	1,212	2,110	2,430	4,290	4,870
250	49	67	121	141	236	284	497	576	941	1,090	1,890	2,180	3,850	4,360
300	44	61	110	129	217	260	453	525	862	999	1,720	1,990	3,520	3,980
400	38	52	96	111	189	225	390	453	749	871	1,490	1,730	3,060	3,450
500	34	46	86	100	170	202	348	404	552	783	1,330	1,550	2,740	3,090

EHD: Equivalent hydraulic diameter. A measure of the relative hydraulic efficiency between different tubing sizes. The greater the value of EHD, the greater the gas capacity of the tubing.

Notes:

(1) Table does not include effect of pressure drop across the line regulator. Where regulator loss exceeds ¾ psi, do not use this table. Consult with regulator manufacturer for pressure drops and capacity factors. Pressure drops across a regulator may vary with flow rate.

(2) CAUTION: Capacities shown in table may exceed maximum capacity for a selected regulator. Consult with regulator or tubing manufacturer for guidance.

(3) Table includes losses for four 90 degree bends and two end fittings. Tubing runs with larger number of bends and/or fittings shall be increased by an equivalent length of tubing according to the following equation: $L = 1.3n$, where L is additional length (ft) of tubing and n is the number of additional fittings and/or bends.

(4) All table entries are rounded to 3 significant digits.

Table 6.2.1(s) Corrugated Stainless Steel Tubing (CSST)

												Gas:	Natural
												Inlet Pressure:	5.0 psi
												Pressure Drop:	3.5 psi
												Specific Gravity:	0.60

	Tube Size (EHD)													
Flow Designation:	13	15	18	19	23	25	30	31	37	39	46	48	60	62
Length (ft)	Capacity in Cubic Feet of Gas per Hour													
10	523	674	1,080	1,300	2,000	2,530	4,920	5,660	8,300	9,140	18,100	19,800	34,400	40,400
25	322	420	691	827	1,290	1,620	3,080	3,540	5,310	5,911	11,400	12,600	22,000	25,600
30	292	382	632	755	1,180	1,480	2,800	3,230	4,860	5,420	10,400	11,500	20,100	23,400
40	251	329	549	654	1,030	1,280	2,420	2,790	4,230	4,727	8,970	10,000	17,400	20,200
50	223	293	492	586	926	1,150	2,160	2,490	3,790	4,251	8,020	8,930	15,600	18,100
75	180	238	403	479	763	944	1,750	2,020	3,110	3,506	6,530	7,320	12,800	14,800
80	174	230	391	463	740	915	1,690	1,960	3,020	3,400	6,320	7,090	12,400	14,300
100	154	205	350	415	665	820	1,510	1,740	2,710	3,057	5,650	6,350	11,100	12,800
150	124	166	287	339	548	672	1,230	1,420	2,220	2,521	4,600	5,200	9,130	10,500
200	107	143	249	294	478	584	1,060	1,220	1,930	2,199	3,980	4,510	7,930	9,090
250	95	128	223	263	430	524	945	1,090	1,730	1,977	3,550	4,040	7,110	8,140
300	86	116	204	240	394	479	860	995	1,590	1,813	3,240	3,690	6,500	7,430
400	74	100	177	208	343	416	742	858	1,380	1,581	2,800	3,210	5,650	6,440
500	66	89	159	186	309	373	662	766	1,040	1,422	2,500	2,870	5,060	5,760

EHD: Equivalent hydraulic diameter. A measure of the relative hydraulic efficiency between different tubing sizes. The greater the value of EHD, the greater the gas capacity of the tubing.

Notes:
(1) Table does not include effect of pressure drop across line regulator. Where regulator loss exceeds 1 psi, do not use this table. Consult with regulator manufacturer for pressure drops and capacity factors. Pressure drop across regulator may vary with the flow rate.
(2) CAUTION: Capacities shown in table may exceed maximum capacity of selected regulator. Consult with tubing manufacturer for guidance.
(3) Table includes losses for four 90 degree bends and two end fittings. Tubing runs with larger numbers of bends and/or fittings shall be increased by an equivalent length of tubing to the following equation: $L = 1.3n$, where L is additional length (ft) of tubing and n is the number of additional fittings and/or bends.
(4) All table entries are rounded to 3 significant digits.

Table 6.2.1(t) Polyethylene Plastic Pipe

	Pipe Size (in.)							
	\: Natural							
	Inlet Pressure: Less than 2 psi							
	Pressure Drop: 0.3 in. w.c.							
	Specific Gravity: 0.60							
Nominal OD:	½	¾	1	1¼	1½	2	3	4
Designation:	SDR 9.3	SDR 11	SDR 11	SDR 10	SDR 11	SDR 11	SDR 11	SDR 11
Actual ID:	0.660	0.860	1.077	1.328	1.554	1.943	2.864	3.682
Length (ft)	Capacity in Cubic Feet of Gas per Hour							
10	153	305	551	955	1,440	2,590	7,170	13,900
20	105	210	379	656	991	1,780	4,920	9,520
30	84	169	304	527	796	1,430	3,950	7,640
40	72	144	260	451	681	1,220	3,380	6,540
50	64	128	231	400	604	1,080	3,000	5,800
60	58	116	209	362	547	983	2,720	5,250
70	53	107	192	333	503	904	2,500	4,830
80	50	99	179	310	468	841	2,330	4,500
90	46	93	168	291	439	789	2,180	4,220
100	44	88	159	275	415	745	2,060	3,990
125	39	78	141	243	368	661	1,830	3,530
150	35	71	127	221	333	598	1,660	3,200
175	32	65	117	203	306	551	1,520	2,940
200	30	60	109	189	285	512	1,420	2,740
250	27	54	97	167	253	454	1,260	2,430
300	24	48	88	152	229	411	1,140	2,200
350	22	45	81	139	211	378	1,050	2,020
400	21	42	75	130	196	352	974	1,880
450	19	39	70	122	184	330	914	1,770
500	18	37	66	115	174	312	863	1,670

Note: All table entries are rounded to 3 significant digits.

Table 6.2.1(u) Polyethylene Plastic Pipe

					Gas:	Natural
					Inlet Pressure:	Less than 2 psi
					Pressure Drop:	0.5 in. w.c.
					Specific Gravity:	0.60

	Pipe Size (in.)							
Nominal OD:	½	¾	1	1¼	1½	2	3	4
Designation:	SDR 9.3	SDR 11	SDR 11	SDR 10	SDR 11	SDR 11	SDR 11	SDR 11
Actual ID:	0.660	0.860	1.077	1.328	1.554	1.943	2.864	3.682
Length (ft)	Capacity in Cubic Feet of Gas per Hour							
10	201	403	726	1,260	1,900	3,410	9,450	18,260
20	138	277	499	865	1,310	2,350	6,490	12,550
30	111	222	401	695	1,050	1,880	5,210	10,080
40	95	190	343	594	898	1,610	4,460	8,630
50	84	169	304	527	796	1,430	3,950	7,640
60	76	153	276	477	721	1,300	3,580	6,930
70	70	140	254	439	663	1,190	3,300	6,370
80	65	131	236	409	617	1,110	3,070	5,930
90	61	123	221	383	579	1,040	2,880	5,560
100	58	116	209	362	547	983	2,720	5,250
125	51	103	185	321	485	871	2,410	4,660
150	46	93	168	291	439	789	2,180	4,220
175	43	86	154	268	404	726	2,010	3,880
200	40	80	144	249	376	675	1,870	3,610
250	35	71	127	221	333	598	1,660	3,200
300	32	64	115	200	302	542	1,500	2,900
350	29	59	106	184	278	499	1,380	2,670
400	27	55	99	171	258	464	1,280	2,480
450	26	51	93	160	242	435	1,200	2,330
500	24	48	88	152	229	411	1,140	2,200

Note: All table entries are rounded to 3 significant digits.

Table 6.2.1(v) Polyethylene Plastic Pipe

					Gas:	Natural		
					Inlet Pressure:	2.0 psi		
					Pressure Drop:	1.0 psi		
					Specific Gravity:	0.60		
	Pipe Size (in.)							
Nominal OD:	½	¾	1	1¼	1½	2	3	3
Designation:	SDR 9.3	SDR 11	SDR 11	SDR 10	SDR 11	SDR 11	SDR 11	SDR 11
Actual ID:	0.660	0.860	1.077	1.328	1.554	1.943	2.864	3.682
Length (ft)	Capacity in Cubic Feet of Gas per Hour							
10	1,860	3,720	6,710	11,600	17,600	31,600	87,300	169,000
20	1,280	2,560	4,610	7,990	12,100	21,700	60,000	116,000
30	1,030	2,050	3,710	6,420	9,690	17,400	48,200	93,200
40	878	1,760	3,170	5,490	8,300	14,900	41,200	79,700
50	778	1,560	2,810	4,870	7,350	13,200	36,600	70,700
60	705	1,410	2,550	4,410	6,660	12,000	33,100	64,000
70	649	1,300	2,340	4,060	6,130	11,000	30,500	58,900
80	603	1,210	2,180	3,780	5,700	10,200	28,300	54,800
90	566	1,130	2,050	3,540	5,350	9,610	26,600	51,400
100	535	1,070	1,930	3,350	5,050	9,080	25,100	48,600
125	474	949	1,710	2,970	4,480	8,050	22,300	43,000
150	429	860	1,550	2,690	4,060	7,290	20,200	39,000
175	395	791	1,430	2,470	3,730	6,710	18,600	35,900
200	368	736	1,330	2,300	3,470	6,240	17,300	33,400
250	326	652	1,180	2,040	3,080	5,530	15,300	29,600
300	295	591	1,070	1,850	2,790	5,010	13,900	26,800
350	272	544	981	1,700	2,570	4,610	12,800	24,700
400	253	506	913	1,580	2,390	4,290	11,900	22,900
450	237	475	856	1,480	2,240	4,020	11,100	21,500
500	224	448	809	1,400	2,120	3,800	10,500	20,300
550	213	426	768	1,330	2,010	3,610	9,990	19,300
600	203	406	733	1,270	1,920	3,440	9,530	18,400
650	194	389	702	1,220	1,840	3,300	9,130	17,600
700	187	374	674	1,170	1,760	3,170	8,770	16,900
750	180	360	649	1,130	1,700	3,050	8,450	16,300
800	174	348	627	1,090	1,640	2,950	8,160	15,800
850	168	336	607	1,050	1,590	2,850	7,890	15,300
900	163	326	588	1,020	1,540	2,770	7,650	14,800
950	158	317	572	990	1,500	2,690	7,430	14,400
1,000	154	308	556	963	1,450	2,610	7,230	14,000
1,100	146	293	528	915	1,380	2,480	6,870	13,300
1,200	139	279	504	873	1,320	2,370	6,550	12,700
1,300	134	267	482	836	1,260	2,270	6,270	12,100
1,400	128	257	463	803	1,210	2,180	6,030	11,600
1,500	124	247	446	773	1,170	2,100	5,810	11,200
1,600	119	239	431	747	1,130	2,030	5,610	10,800
1,700	115	231	417	723	1,090	1,960	5,430	10,500
1,800	112	224	404	701	1,060	1,900	5,260	10,200
1,900	109	218	393	680	1,030	1,850	5,110	9,900
2,000	106	212	382	662	1,000	1,800	4,970	9,600

Note: All table entries are rounded to 3 significant digits.

Table 6.2.1(w) Polyethylene Plastic Tubing

	Gas:	Natural
	Inlet Pressure:	Less than 2.0 psi
	Pressure Drop:	0.3 in. w.c.
	Specific Gravity:	0.60
	Plastic Tubing Size (CTS) (in.)	
Nominal OD:	½	1
Designation:	SDR 7	SDR 11
Actual ID:	0.445	0.927
Length (ft)	Capacity in Cubic Feet of Gas per Hour	
10	54	372
20	37	256
30	30	205
40	26	176
50	23	156
60	21	141
70	19	130
80	18	121
90	17	113
100	16	107
125	14	95
150	13	86
175	12	79
200	11	74
225	10	69
250	NA	65
275	NA	62
300	NA	59
350	NA	54
400	NA	51
450	NA	47
500	NA	45

CTS: Copper tube size.
NA: A flow of less than 10 cfh.
Note: All table entries are rounded to 3 significant digits.

Table 6.2.1(x) Polyethylene Plastic Tubing

	Gas:	Natural
	Inlet Pressure:	Less than 2.0 psi
	Pressure Drop:	0.5 in. w.c.
	Specific Gravity:	0.60
	Plastic Tubing Size (CTS) (in.)	
Nominal OD:	½	1
Designation:	SDR 7	SDR 11
Actual ID:	0.445	0.927
Length (ft)	Capacity in Cubic Feet of Gas per Hour	
10	72	490
20	49	337
30	39	271
40	34	232
50	30	205
60	27	186
70	25	171
80	23	159
90	22	149
100	21	141
125	18	125
150	17	113
175	15	104
200	14	97
225	13	91
250	12	86
275	11	82
300	11	78
350	10	72
400	NA	67
450	NA	63
500	NA	59

CTS: Copper tube size.
NA: A flow of less than 10 cfh.
Note: All table entries are rounded to 3 significant digits.

Table 6.3.1(a) Schedule 40 Metallic Pipe

				Gas:	Undiluted Propane
				Inlet Pressure:	10.0 psi
				Pressure Drop:	1.0 psi
				Specific Gravity:	1.50

INTENDED USE: Pipe Sizing Between First-Stage (High-Pressure) Regulator and Second-Stage (Low-Pressure) Regulator.

	Pipe Size (in.)								
Nominal Inside:	½	¾	1	1¼	1½	2	2½	3	4
Actual:	0.622	0.824	1.049	1.380	1.610	2.067	2.469	3.068	4.026
Length (ft)	Capacity in Thousands of Btu per Hour								
10	3,320	6,950	13,100	26,900	40,300	77,600	124,000	219,000	446,000
20	2,280	4,780	9,000	18,500	27,700	53,300	85,000	150,000	306,000
30	1,830	3,840	7,220	14,800	22,200	42,800	68,200	121,000	246,000
40	1,570	3,280	6,180	12,700	19,000	36,600	58,400	103,000	211,000
50	1,390	2,910	5,480	11,300	16,900	32,500	51,700	91,500	187,000
60	1,260	2,640	4,970	10,200	15,300	29,400	46,900	82,900	169,000
70	1,160	2,430	4,570	9,380	14,100	27,100	43,100	76,300	156,000
80	1,080	2,260	4,250	8,730	13,100	25,200	40,100	70,900	145,000
90	1,010	2,120	3,990	8,190	12,300	23,600	37,700	66,600	136,000
100	956	2,000	3,770	7,730	11,600	22,300	35,600	62,900	128,000
125	848	1,770	3,340	6,850	10,300	19,800	31,500	55,700	114,000
150	768	1,610	3,020	6,210	9,300	17,900	28,600	50,500	103,000
175	706	1,480	2,780	5,710	8,560	16,500	26,300	46,500	94,700
200	657	1,370	2,590	5,320	7,960	15,300	24,400	43,200	88,100
250	582	1,220	2,290	4,710	7,060	13,600	21,700	38,300	78,100
300	528	1,100	2,080	4,270	6,400	12,300	19,600	34,700	70,800
350	486	1,020	1,910	3,930	5,880	11,300	18,100	31,900	65,100
400	452	945	1,780	3,650	5,470	10,500	16,800	29,700	60,600
450	424	886	1,670	3,430	5,140	9,890	15,800	27,900	56,800
500	400	837	1,580	3,240	4,850	9,340	14,900	26,300	53,700
550	380	795	1,500	3,070	4,610	8,870	14,100	25,000	51,000
600	363	759	1,430	2,930	4,400	8,460	13,500	23,900	48,600
650	347	726	1,370	2,810	4,210	8,110	12,900	22,800	46,600
700	334	698	1,310	2,700	4,040	7,790	12,400	21,900	44,800
750	321	672	1,270	2,600	3,900	7,500	12,000	21,100	43,100
800	310	649	1,220	2,510	3,760	7,240	11,500	20,400	41,600
850	300	628	1,180	2,430	3,640	7,010	11,200	19,800	40,300
900	291	609	1,150	2,360	3,530	6,800	10,800	19,200	39,100
950	283	592	1,110	2,290	3,430	6,600	10,500	18,600	37,900
1,000	275	575	1,080	2,230	3,330	6,420	10,200	18,100	36,900
1,100	261	546	1,030	2,110	3,170	6,100	9,720	17,200	35,000
1,200	249	521	982	2,020	3,020	5,820	9,270	16,400	33,400
1,300	239	499	940	1,930	2,890	5,570	8,880	15,700	32,000
1,400	229	480	903	1,850	2,780	5,350	8,530	15,100	30,800
1,500	221	462	870	1,790	2,680	5,160	8,220	14,500	29,600
1,600	213	446	840	1,730	2,590	4,980	7,940	14,000	28,600
1,700	206	432	813	1,670	2,500	4,820	7,680	13,600	27,700
1,800	200	419	789	1,620	2,430	4,670	7,450	13,200	26,900
1,900	194	407	766	1,570	2,360	4,540	7,230	12,800	26,100
2,000	189	395	745	1,530	2,290	4,410	7,030	12,400	25,400

Note: All table entries are rounded to 3 significant digits.

Table 6.3.1(b) Schedule 40 Metallic Pipe

				Gas:	Undiluted Propane
				Inlet Pressure:	10.0 psi
				Pressure Drop:	3.0 psi
				Specific Gravity:	1.50

INTENDED USE: Pipe Sizing Between First-Stage (High-Pressure) Regulator and Second-Stage (Low-Pressure) Regulator.

	Pipe Size (in.)								
Nominal Inside:	½	¾	1	1¼	1½	2	2½	3	4
Actual:	0.622	0.824	1.049	1.380	1.610	2.067	2.469	3.068	4.026
Length (ft)	Capacity in Thousands of Btu per Hour								
10	5,890	12,300	23,200	47,600	71,300	137,000	219,000	387,000	789,000
20	4,050	8,460	15,900	32,700	49,000	94,400	150,000	266,000	543,000
30	3,250	6,790	12,800	26,300	39,400	75,800	121,000	214,000	436,000
40	2,780	5,810	11,000	22,500	33,700	64,900	103,000	183,000	373,000
50	2,460	5,150	9,710	19,900	29,900	57,500	91,600	162,000	330,000
60	2,230	4,670	8,790	18,100	27,100	52,100	83,000	147,000	299,000
70	2,050	4,300	8,090	16,600	24,900	47,900	76,400	135,000	275,000
80	1,910	4,000	7,530	15,500	23,200	44,600	71,100	126,000	256,000
90	1,790	3,750	7,060	14,500	21,700	41,800	66,700	118,000	240,000
100	1,690	3,540	6,670	13,700	20,500	39,500	63,000	111,000	227,000
125	1,500	3,140	5,910	12,100	18,200	35,000	55,800	98,700	201,000
150	1,360	2,840	5,360	11,000	16,500	31,700	50,600	89,400	182,000
175	1,250	2,620	4,930	10,100	15,200	29,200	46,500	82,300	167,800
200	1,160	2,430	4,580	9,410	14,100	27,200	43,300	76,500	156,100
250	1,030	2,160	4,060	8,340	12,500	24,100	38,400	67,800	138,400
300	935	1,950	3,680	7,560	11,300	21,800	34,800	61,500	125,400
350	860	1,800	3,390	6,950	10,400	20,100	32,000	56,500	115,300
400	800	1,670	3,150	6,470	9,690	18,700	29,800	52,600	107,300
450	751	1,570	2,960	6,070	9,090	17,500	27,900	49,400	100,700
500	709	1,480	2,790	5,730	8,590	16,500	26,400	46,600	95,100
550	673	1,410	2,650	5,450	8,160	15,700	25,000	44,300	90,300
600	642	1,340	2,530	5,200	7,780	15,000	23,900	42,200	86,200
650	615	1,290	2,420	4,980	7,450	14,400	22,900	40,500	82,500
700	591	1,240	2,330	4,780	7,160	13,800	22,000	38,900	79,300
750	569	1,190	2,240	4,600	6,900	13,300	21,200	37,400	76,400
800	550	1,150	2,170	4,450	6,660	12,800	20,500	36,200	73,700
850	532	1,110	2,100	4,300	6,450	12,400	19,800	35,000	71,400
900	516	1,080	2,030	4,170	6,250	12,000	19,200	33,900	69,200
950	501	1,050	1,970	4,050	6,070	11,700	18,600	32,900	67,200
1,000	487	1,020	1,920	3,940	5,900	11,400	18,100	32,000	65,400
1,100	463	968	1,820	3,740	5,610	10,800	17,200	30,400	62,100
1,200	442	923	1,740	3,570	5,350	10,300	16,400	29,000	59,200
1,300	423	884	1,670	3,420	5,120	9,870	15,700	27,800	56,700
1,400	406	849	1,600	3,280	4,920	9,480	15,100	26,700	54,500
1,500	391	818	1,540	3,160	4,740	9,130	14,600	25,700	52,500
1,600	378	790	1,490	3,060	4,580	8,820	14,100	24,800	50,700
1,700	366	765	1,440	2,960	4,430	8,530	13,600	24,000	49,000
1,800	355	741	1,400	2,870	4,300	8,270	13,200	23,300	47,600
1,900	344	720	1,360	2,780	4,170	8,040	12,800	22,600	46,200
2,000	335	700	1,320	2,710	4,060	7,820	12,500	22,000	44,900

Note: All table entries are rounded to 3 significant digits.

Table 6.3.1(c) Schedule 40 Metallic Pipe

	Gas:	Undiluted Propane
	Inlet Pressure:	2.0 psi
	Pressure Drop:	1.0 psi
	Specific Gravity:	1.50

INTENDED USE: Pipe Sizing Between 2 psig Service and Line Pressure Regulator.

	Pipe Size (in.)								
Nominal:	½	¾	1	1¼	1½	2	2½	3	4
Actual ID:	0.622	0.824	1.049	1.380	1.610	2.067	2.469	3.068	4.026
Length (ft)	Capacity in Thousands of Btu per Hour								
10	2,680	5,590	10,500	21,600	32,400	62,400	99,500	176,000	359,000
20	1,840	3,850	7,240	14,900	22,300	42,900	68,400	121,000	247,000
30	1,480	3,090	5,820	11,900	17,900	34,500	54,900	97,100	198,000
40	1,260	2,640	4,980	10,200	15,300	29,500	47,000	83,100	170,000
50	1,120	2,340	4,410	9,060	13,600	26,100	41,700	73,700	150,000
60	1,010	2,120	4,000	8,210	12,300	23,700	37,700	66,700	136,000
70	934	1,950	3,680	7,550	11,300	21,800	34,700	61,400	125,000
80	869	1,820	3,420	7,020	10,500	20,300	32,300	57,100	116,000
90	815	1,700	3,210	6,590	9,880	19,000	30,300	53,600	109,000
100	770	1,610	3,030	6,230	9,330	18,000	28,600	50,600	103,000
125	682	1,430	2,690	5,520	8,270	15,900	25,400	44,900	91,500
150	618	1,290	2,440	5,000	7,490	14,400	23,000	40,700	82,900
175	569	1,190	2,240	4,600	6,890	13,300	21,200	37,400	76,300
200	529	1,110	2,080	4,280	6,410	12,300	19,700	34,800	71,000
250	469	981	1,850	3,790	5,680	10,900	17,400	30,800	62,900
300	425	889	1,670	3,440	5,150	9,920	15,800	27,900	57,000
350	391	817	1,540	3,160	4,740	9,120	14,500	25,700	52,400
400	364	760	1,430	2,940	4,410	8,490	13,500	23,900	48,800
450	341	714	1,340	2,760	4,130	7,960	12,700	22,400	45,800
500	322	674	1,270	2,610	3,910	7,520	12,000	21,200	43,200
550	306	640	1,210	2,480	3,710	7,140	11,400	20,100	41,100
600	292	611	1,150	2,360	3,540	6,820	10,900	19,200	39,200
650	280	585	1,100	2,260	3,390	6,530	10,400	18,400	37,500
700	269	562	1,060	2,170	3,260	6,270	9,990	17,700	36,000
750	259	541	1,020	2,090	3,140	6,040	9,630	17,000	34,700
800	250	523	985	2,020	3,030	5,830	9,300	16,400	33,500
850	242	506	953	1,960	2,930	5,640	9,000	15,900	32,400
900	235	490	924	1,900	2,840	5,470	8,720	15,400	31,500
950	228	476	897	1,840	2,760	5,310	8,470	15,000	30,500
1,000	222	463	873	1,790	2,680	5,170	8,240	14,600	29,700
1,100	210	440	829	1,700	2,550	4,910	7,830	13,800	28,200
1,200	201	420	791	1,620	2,430	4,680	7,470	13,200	26,900
1,300	192	402	757	1,550	2,330	4,490	7,150	12,600	25,800
1,400	185	386	727	1,490	2,240	4,310	6,870	12,100	24,800
1,500	178	372	701	1,440	2,160	4,150	6,620	11,700	23,900
1,600	172	359	677	1,390	2,080	4,010	6,390	11,300	23,000
1,700	166	348	655	1,340	2,010	3,880	6,180	10,900	22,300
1,800	161	337	635	1,300	1,950	3,760	6,000	10,600	21,600
1,900	157	327	617	1,270	1,900	3,650	5,820	10,300	21,000
2,000	152	318	600	1,230	1,840	3,550	5,660	10,000	20,400

Note: All table entries are rounded to 3 significant digits.

Table 6.3.1(d) Schedule 40 Metallic Pipe

						Gas:	Undiluted Propane
						Inlet Pressure:	11.0 in. w.c.
						Pressure Drop:	0.5 in. w.c.
						Specific Gravity:	1.50

INTENDED USE: Pipe Sizing Between Single- or Second-Stage (Low-Pressure) Regulator and Appliance.

	Pipe Size (in.)								
Nominal Inside:	½	¾	1	1¼	1½	2	2½	3	4
Actual:	0.622	0.824	1.049	1.380	1.610	2.067	2.469	3.068	4.026
Length (ft)	Capacity in Thousands of Btu per Hour								
10	291	608	1,150	2,350	3,520	6,790	10,800	19,100	39,000
20	200	418	787	1,620	2,420	4,660	7,430	13,100	26,800
30	160	336	632	1,300	1,940	3,750	5,970	10,600	21,500
40	137	287	541	1,110	1,660	3,210	5,110	9,030	18,400
50	122	255	480	985	1,480	2,840	4,530	8,000	16,300
60	110	231	434	892	1,340	2,570	4,100	7,250	14,800
70	101	212	400	821	1,230	2,370	3,770	6,670	13,600
80	94	197	372	763	1,140	2,200	3,510	6,210	12,700
90	89	185	349	716	1,070	2,070	3,290	5,820	11,900
100	84	175	330	677	1,010	1,950	3,110	5,500	11,200
125	74	155	292	600	899	1,730	2,760	4,880	9,950
150	67	140	265	543	814	1,570	2,500	4,420	9,010
175	62	129	243	500	749	1,440	2,300	4,060	8,290
200	58	120	227	465	697	1,340	2,140	3,780	7,710
250	51	107	201	412	618	1,190	1,900	3,350	6,840
300	46	97	182	373	560	1,080	1,720	3,040	6,190
350	42	89	167	344	515	991	1,580	2,790	5,700
400	40	83	156	320	479	922	1,470	2,600	5,300
450	37	78	146	300	449	865	1,380	2,440	4,970
500	35	73	138	283	424	817	1,300	2,300	4,700
550	33	70	131	269	403	776	1,240	2,190	4,460
600	32	66	125	257	385	741	1,180	2,090	4,260
650	30	64	120	246	368	709	1,130	2,000	4,080
700	29	61	115	236	354	681	1,090	1,920	3,920
750	28	59	111	227	341	656	1,050	1,850	3,770
800	27	57	107	220	329	634	1,010	1,790	3,640
850	26	55	104	213	319	613	978	1,730	3,530
900	25	53	100	206	309	595	948	1,680	3,420
950	25	52	97	200	300	578	921	1,630	3,320
1,000	24	50	95	195	292	562	895	1,580	3,230
1,100	23	48	90	185	277	534	850	1,500	3,070
1,200	22	46	86	176	264	509	811	1,430	2,930
1,300	21	44	82	169	253	487	777	1,370	2,800
1,400	20	42	79	162	243	468	746	1,320	2,690
1,500	19	40	76	156	234	451	719	1,270	2,590
1,600	19	39	74	151	226	436	694	1,230	2,500
1,700	18	38	71	146	219	422	672	1,190	2,420
1,800	18	37	69	142	212	409	652	1,150	2,350
1,900	17	36	67	138	206	397	633	1120	2280
2,000	17	35	65	134	200	386	615	1090	2220

Note: All table entries are rounded to 3 significant digits.

Table 6.3.1(e) Semirigid Copper Tubing

		Gas:	Undiluted Propane
		Inlet Pressure:	10.0 psi
		Pressure Drop:	1.0 psi
		Specific Gravity:	1.50

INTENDED USE: Tube Sizing Between First-Stage (High-Pressure) Regulator and Second-Stage (Low-Pressure) Regulator.

Nominal:	K & L:	¼	⅜	½	⅝	¾	1	1¼	1½	2
	ACR:	⅜	½	⅝	¾	⅞	1⅛	1⅜	—	—
	Outside:	0.375	0.500	0.625	0.750	0.875	1.125	1.375	1.625	2.125
	Inside:*	0.305	0.402	0.527	0.652	0.745	0.995	1.245	1.481	1.959
Length (ft)		Capacity in Thousands of Btu per Hour								
10		513	1,060	2,150	3,760	5,330	11,400	20,500	32,300	67,400
20		352	727	1,480	2,580	3,670	7,830	14,100	22,200	46,300
30		283	584	1,190	2,080	2,940	6,290	11,300	17,900	37,200
40		242	500	1,020	1,780	2,520	5,380	9,690	15,300	31,800
50		215	443	901	1,570	2,230	4,770	8,590	13,500	28,200
60		194	401	816	1,430	2,020	4,320	7,780	12,300	25,600
70		179	369	751	1,310	1,860	3,980	7,160	11,300	23,500
80		166	343	699	1,220	1,730	3,700	6,660	10,500	21,900
90		156	322	655	1,150	1,630	3,470	6,250	9,850	20,500
100		147	304	619	1,080	1,540	3,280	5,900	9,310	19,400
125		131	270	549	959	1,360	2,910	5,230	8,250	17,200
150		118	244	497	869	1,230	2,630	4,740	7,470	15,600
175		109	225	457	799	1,130	2,420	4,360	6,880	14,300
200		101	209	426	744	1,060	2,250	4,060	6,400	13,300
250		90	185	377	659	935	2,000	3,600	5,670	11,800
300		81	168	342	597	847	1,810	3,260	5,140	10,700
350		75	155	314	549	779	1,660	3,000	4,730	9,840
400		70	144	292	511	725	1,550	2,790	4,400	9,160
450		65	135	274	480	680	1,450	2,620	4,130	8,590
500		62	127	259	453	643	1,370	2,470	3,900	8,120
550		59	121	246	430	610	1,300	2,350	3,700	7,710
600		56	115	235	410	582	1,240	2,240	3,530	7,350
650		54	111	225	393	558	1,190	2,140	3,380	7,040
700		51	106	216	378	536	1,140	2,060	3,250	6,770
750		50	102	208	364	516	1,100	1,980	3,130	6,520
800		48	99	201	351	498	1,060	1,920	3,020	6,290
850		46	96	195	340	482	1,030	1,850	2,920	6,090
900		45	93	189	330	468	1,000	1,800	2,840	5,910
950		44	90	183	320	454	970	1,750	2,750	5,730
1,000		42	88	178	311	442	944	1,700	2,680	5,580
1,100		40	83	169	296	420	896	1,610	2,540	5,300
1,200		38	79	161	282	400	855	1,540	2,430	5,050
1,300		37	76	155	270	383	819	1,470	2,320	4,840
1,400		35	73	148	260	368	787	1,420	2,230	4,650
1,500		34	70	143	250	355	758	1,360	2,150	4,480
1,600		33	68	138	241	343	732	1,320	2,080	4,330
1,700		32	66	134	234	331	708	1,270	2,010	4,190
1,800		31	64	130	227	321	687	1,240	1,950	4,060
1,900		30	62	126	220	312	667	1,200	1,890	3,940
2,000		29	60	122	214	304	648	1,170	1,840	3,830

Note: All table entries are rounded to 3 significant digits.
*Table capacities are based on Type K copper tubing inside diameter (shown), which has the smallest inside diameter of the copper tubing products.

Table 6.3.1(f) Semirigid Copper Tubing

							Gas:	Undiluted Propane		
							Inlet Pressure:	11.0 in. w.c.		
							Pressure Drop:	0.5 in. w.c.		
							Specific Gravity:	1.50		

INTENDED USE: Tube Sizing Between Single- or Second-Stage (Low-Pressure) Regulator and Appliance.

Nominal:	K & L:	¼	⅜	½	⅝	¾	1	1¼	1½	2
	ACR:	⅜	½	⅝	¾	⅞	1⅛	1⅜	—	—
	Outside:	0.375	0.500	0.625	0.750	0.875	1.125	1.375	1.625	2.125
	Inside:*	0.305	0.402	0.527	0.652	0.745	0.995	1.245	1.481	1.959
Length (ft)		Capacity in Thousands of Btu per Hour								
10		45	93	188	329	467	997	1,800	2,830	5,890
20		31	64	129	226	321	685	1,230	1,950	4,050
30		25	51	104	182	258	550	991	1,560	3,250
40		21	44	89	155	220	471	848	1,340	2,780
50		19	39	79	138	195	417	752	1,180	2,470
60		17	35	71	125	177	378	681	1,070	2,240
70		16	32	66	115	163	348	626	988	2,060
80		15	30	61	107	152	324	583	919	1,910
90		14	28	57	100	142	304	547	862	1,800
100		13	27	54	95	134	287	517	814	1,700
125		11	24	48	84	119	254	458	722	1,500
150		10	21	44	76	108	230	415	654	1,360
175		NA	20	40	70	99	212	382	602	1,250
200		NA	18	37	65	92	197	355	560	1,170
250		NA	16	33	58	82	175	315	496	1,030
300		NA	15	30	52	74	158	285	449	936
350		NA	14	28	48	68	146	262	414	861
400		NA	13	26	45	63	136	244	385	801
450		NA	12	24	42	60	127	229	361	752
500		NA	11	23	40	56	120	216	341	710
550		NA	11	22	38	53	114	205	324	674
600		NA	10	21	36	51	109	196	309	643
650		NA	NA	20	34	49	104	188	296	616
700		NA	NA	19	33	47	100	180	284	592
750		NA	NA	18	32	45	96	174	274	570
800		NA	NA	18	31	44	93	168	264	551
850		NA	NA	17	30	42	90	162	256	533
900		NA	NA	17	29	41	87	157	248	517
950		NA	NA	16	28	40	85	153	241	502
1,000		NA	NA	16	27	39	83	149	234	488
1,100		NA	NA	15	26	37	78	141	223	464
1,200		NA	NA	14	25	35	75	135	212	442
1,300		NA	NA	14	24	34	72	129	203	423
1,400		NA	NA	13	23	32	69	124	195	407
1,500		NA	NA	13	22	31	66	119	188	392
1,600		NA	NA	12	21	30	64	115	182	378
1,700		NA	NA	12	20	29	62	112	176	366
1,800		NA	NA	11	20	28	60	108	170	355
1,900		NA	NA	11	19	27	58	105	166	345
2,000		NA	NA	11	19	27	57	102	161	335

NA: A flow of less than 10,000 Btu/hr.
Note: All table entries are rounded to 3 significant digits.
*Table capacities are based on Type K copper tubing inside diameter (shown), which has the smallest inside diameter of the copper tubing products.

Table 6.3.1(g) Semirigid Copper Tubing

		Gas:	Undiluted Propane
		Inlet Pressure:	2.0 psi
		Pressure Drop:	1.0 psi
		Specific Gravity:	1.50

INTENDED USE: Tube Sizing Between 2 psig Service and Line Pressure Regulator.

Nominal:	K & L:	¼	⅜	½	⅝	¾	1	1¼	1½	2
	ACR:	⅜	½	⅝	¾	⅞	1⅛	1⅜	—	—
	Outside:	0.375	0.500	0.625	0.750	0.875	1.125	1.375	1.625	2.125
	Inside:*	0.305	0.402	0.527	0.652	0.745	0.995	1.245	1.481	1.959
Length (ft)		Capacity in Thousands of Btu per Hour								
10		413	852	1,730	3,030	4,300	9,170	16,500	26,000	54,200
20		284	585	1,190	2,080	2,950	6,310	11,400	17,900	37,300
30		228	470	956	1,670	2,370	5,060	9,120	14,400	29,900
40		195	402	818	1,430	2,030	4,330	7,800	12,300	25,600
50		173	356	725	1,270	1,800	3,840	6,920	10,900	22,700
60		157	323	657	1,150	1,630	3,480	6,270	9,880	20,600
70		144	297	605	1,060	1,500	3,200	5,760	9,090	18,900
80		134	276	562	983	1,390	2,980	5,360	8,450	17,600
90		126	259	528	922	1,310	2,790	5,030	7,930	16,500
100		119	245	498	871	1,240	2,640	4,750	7,490	15,600
125		105	217	442	772	1,100	2,340	4,210	6,640	13,800
150		95	197	400	700	992	2,120	3,820	6,020	12,500
175		88	181	368	644	913	1,950	3,510	5,540	11,500
200		82	168	343	599	849	1,810	3,270	5,150	10,700
250		72	149	304	531	753	1,610	2,900	4,560	9,510
300		66	135	275	481	682	1,460	2,620	4,140	8,610
350		60	124	253	442	628	1,340	2,410	3,800	7,920
400		56	116	235	411	584	1,250	2,250	3,540	7,370
450		53	109	221	386	548	1,170	2,110	3,320	6,920
500		50	103	209	365	517	1,110	1,990	3,140	6,530
550		47	97	198	346	491	1,050	1,890	2,980	6,210
600		45	93	189	330	469	1,000	1,800	2,840	5,920
650		43	89	181	316	449	959	1,730	2,720	5,670
700		41	86	174	304	431	921	1,660	2,620	5,450
750		40	82	168	293	415	888	1,600	2,520	5,250
800		39	80	162	283	401	857	1,540	2,430	5,070
850		37	77	157	274	388	829	1,490	2,350	4,900
900		36	75	152	265	376	804	1,450	2,280	4,750
950		35	72	147	258	366	781	1,410	2,220	4,620
1,000		34	71	143	251	356	760	1,370	2,160	4,490
1,100		32	67	136	238	338	721	1,300	2,050	4,270
1,200		31	64	130	227	322	688	1,240	1,950	4,070
1,300		30	61	124	217	309	659	1,190	1,870	3,900
1,400		28	59	120	209	296	633	1,140	1,800	3,740
1,500		27	57	115	201	286	610	1,100	1,730	3,610
1,600		26	55	111	194	276	589	1,060	1,670	3,480
1,700		26	53	108	188	267	570	1,030	1,620	3,370
1,800		25	51	104	182	259	553	1,000	1,570	3,270
1,900		24	50	101	177	251	537	966	1,520	3,170
2,000		23	48	99	172	244	522	940	1,480	3,090

Note: All table entries are rounded to 3 significant digits.
*Table capacities are based on Type K copper tubing inside diameter (shown), which has the smallest inside diameter of the copper tubing products.

Table 6.3.1(h) Corrugated Stainless Steel Tubing (CSST)

													Gas:	Undiluted Propane
													Inlet Pressure:	11.0 in. w.c.
													Pressure Drop:	0.5 in. w.c.
													Specific Gravity:	1.50

INTENDED USE: CSST Sizing Between Single- or Second-Stage (Low-Pressure) Regulator and Appliance Shutoff Valve.

Flow Designation:	Tube Size (EHD)													
	13	15	18	19	23	25	30	31	37	39	46	48	60	62
Length (ft)	Capacity in Thousands of Btu per Hour													
5	72	99	181	211	355	426	744	863	1,420	1,638	2,830	3,270	5,780	6,550
10	50	69	129	150	254	303	521	605	971	1,179	1,990	2,320	4,110	4,640
15	39	55	104	121	208	248	422	490	775	972	1,620	1,900	3,370	3,790
20	34	49	91	106	183	216	365	425	661	847	1,400	1,650	2,930	3,290
25	30	42	82	94	164	192	325	379	583	762	1,250	1,480	2,630	2,940
30	28	39	74	87	151	177	297	344	528	698	1,140	1,350	2,400	2,680
40	23	33	64	74	131	153	256	297	449	610	988	1,170	2,090	2,330
50	20	30	58	66	118	137	227	265	397	548	884	1,050	1,870	2,080
60	19	26	53	60	107	126	207	241	359	502	805	961	1,710	1,900
70	17	25	49	57	99	117	191	222	330	466	745	890	1,590	1,760
80	15	23	45	52	94	109	178	208	307	438	696	833	1,490	1,650
90	15	22	44	50	90	102	169	197	286	414	656	787	1,400	1,550
100	14	20	41	47	85	98	159	186	270	393	621	746	1,330	1,480
150	11	15	31	36	66	75	123	143	217	324	506	611	1,090	1,210
200	9	14	28	33	60	69	112	129	183	283	438	531	948	1,050
250	8	12	25	30	53	61	99	117	163	254	390	476	850	934
300	8	11	23	26	50	57	90	107	147	234	357	434	777	854

EHD: Equivalent hydraulic diameter. A measure of the relative hydraulic efficiency between different tubing sizes. The greater the value of EHD, the greater the gas capacity of the tubing.

Notes:
(1) Table includes losses for four 90 degree bends and two end fittings. Tubing runs with larger numbers of bends and/or fittings shall be increased by an equivalent length of tubing to the following equation: $L = 1.3n$, where L is additional length (ft) of tubing and n is the number of additional fittings and/or bends.
(2) All table entries are rounded to 3 significant digits.

Table 6.3.1(i) Corrugated Stainless Steel Tubing (CSST)

	Gas:	Undiluted Propane
	Inlet Pressure:	2.0 psi
	Pressure Drop:	1.0 psi
	Specific Gravity:	1.50

INTENDED USE: CSST Sizing Between 2 psig Service and Line Pressure Regulator.

Flow Designation:	Tube Size (EHD)													
	13	15	18	19	23	25	30	31	37	39	46	48	60	62
Length (ft)	Capacity in Thousands of Btu per Hour													
10	426	558	927	1,110	1,740	2,170	4,100	4,720	7,130	7,958	15,200	16,800	29,400	34,200
25	262	347	591	701	1,120	1,380	2,560	2,950	4,560	5,147	9,550	10,700	18,800	21,700
30	238	316	540	640	1,030	1,270	2,330	2,690	4,180	4,719	8,710	9,790	17,200	19,800
40	203	271	469	554	896	1,100	2,010	2,320	3,630	4,116	7,530	8,500	14,900	17,200
50	181	243	420	496	806	986	1,790	2,070	3,260	3,702	6,730	7,610	13,400	15,400
75	147	196	344	406	663	809	1,460	1,690	2,680	3,053	5,480	6,230	11,000	12,600
80	140	189	333	393	643	768	1,410	1,630	2,590	2,961	5,300	6,040	10,600	12,200
100	124	169	298	350	578	703	1,260	1,450	2,330	2,662	4,740	5,410	9,530	10,900
150	101	137	245	287	477	575	1,020	1,180	1,910	2,195	3,860	4,430	7,810	8,890
200	86	118	213	248	415	501	880	1,020	1,660	1,915	3,340	3,840	6,780	7,710
250	77	105	191	222	373	448	785	910	1,490	1,722	2,980	3,440	6,080	6,900
300	69	96	173	203	343	411	716	829	1,360	1,578	2,720	3,150	5,560	6,300
400	60	82	151	175	298	355	616	716	1,160	1,376	2,350	2,730	4,830	5,460
500	53	72	135	158	268	319	550	638	1,030	1,237	2,100	2,450	4,330	4,880

EHD: Equivalent hydraulic diameter. A measure of the relative hydraulic efficiency between different tubing sizes. The greater the value of EHD, the greater the gas capacity of the tubing.

Notes:
(1) Table does not include effect of pressure drop across the line regulator. Where regulator loss exceeds ½ psi (based on 13 in. w.c. outlet pressure), do not use this table. Consult with regulator manufacturer for pressure drops and capacity factors. Pressure drops across a regulator may vary with flow rate.
(2) CAUTION: Capacities shown in table may exceed maximum capacity for a selected regulator. Consult with regulator or tubing manufacturer for guidance.
(3) Table includes losses for four 90 degree bends and two end fittings. Tubing runs with larger number of bends and/or fittings shall be increased by an equivalent length of tubing according to the following equation: $L = 1.3n$, where L is additional length (ft) of tubing and n is the number of additional fittings and/or bends.
(4) All table entries are rounded to 3 significant digits.

Table 6.3.1(j) Corrugated Stainless Steel Tubing (CSST)

										Gas:	Undiluted Propane
										Inlet Pressure:	5.0 psi
										Pressure Drop:	3.5 psi
										Specific Gravity:	1.50

Flow Designation:	Tube Size (EHD)													
	13	15	18	19	23	25	30	31	37	39	46	48	60	62
Length (ft)	Capacity in Thousands of Btu per Hour													
10	826	1,070	1,710	2,060	3,150	4,000	7,830	8,950	13,100	14,441	28,600	31,200	54,400	63,800
25	509	664	1,090	1,310	2,040	2,550	4,860	5,600	8,400	9,339	18,000	19,900	34,700	40,400
30	461	603	999	1,190	1,870	2,340	4,430	5,100	7,680	8,564	16,400	18,200	31,700	36,900
40	396	520	867	1,030	1,630	2,030	3,820	4,400	6,680	7,469	14,200	15,800	27,600	32,000
50	352	463	777	926	1,460	1,820	3,410	3,930	5,990	6,717	12,700	14,100	24,700	28,600
75	284	376	637	757	1,210	1,490	2,770	3,190	4,920	5,539	10,300	11,600	20,300	23,400
80	275	363	618	731	1,170	1,450	2,680	3,090	4,770	5,372	9,990	11,200	19,600	22,700
100	243	324	553	656	1,050	1,300	2,390	2,760	4,280	4,830	8,930	10,000	17,600	20,300
150	196	262	453	535	866	1,060	1,940	2,240	3,510	3,983	7,270	8,210	14,400	16,600
200	169	226	393	464	755	923	1,680	1,930	3,050	3,474	6,290	7,130	12,500	14,400
250	150	202	352	415	679	828	1,490	1,730	2,740	3,124	5,620	6,390	11,200	12,900
300	136	183	322	379	622	757	1,360	1,570	2,510	2,865	5,120	5,840	10,300	11,700
400	117	158	279	328	542	657	1,170	1,360	2,180	2,498	4,430	5,070	8,920	10,200
500	104	140	251	294	488	589	1,050	1,210	1,950	2,247	3,960	4,540	8,000	9,110

EHD: Equivalent hydraulic diameter. A measure of the relative hydraulic efficiency between different tubing sizes. The greater the value of EHD, the greater the gas capacity of the tubing.

Notes:
(1) Table does not include effect of pressure drop across the line regulator. Where regulator loss exceeds ½ psi (based on 13 in. w.c. outlet pressure), do not use this table. Consult with regulator manufacturer for pressure drops and capacity factors. Pressure drops across a regulator may vary with flow rate.
(2) CAUTION: Capacities shown in table may exceed maximum capacity for a selected regulator. Consult with regulator or tubing manufacturer for guidance.
(3) Table includes losses for four 90 degree bends and two end fittings. Tubing runs with larger number of bends and/or fittings shall be increased by an equivalent length of tubing according to the following equation: $L = 1.3n$, where L is additional length (ft) of tubing and n is the number of additional fittings and/or bends.
(4) All table entries are rounded to 3 significant digits.

Table 6.3.1(k) Polyethylene Plastic Pipe

	Gas:	Undiluted Propane
	Inlet Pressure:	11.0 in. w.c.
	Pressure Drop:	0.5 in. w.c.
	Specific Gravity:	1.50

INTENDED USE: PE Pipe Sizing Between Integral Second-Stage Regulator at Tank or Second-Stage (Low-Pressure) Regulator and Building.

Nominal OD:	Pipe Size (in.)							
	½	¾	1	1¼	1½	2	3	4
Designation:	SDR 9.3	SDR 11	SDR 11	SDR 10	SDR 11	SDR 11	SDR 11	SDR 11
Actual ID:	0.660	0.860	1.077	1.328	1.554	1.943	2.864	3.682
Length (ft)	Capacity in Thousands of Btu per Hour							
10	340	680	1,230	2,130	3,210	5,770	16,000	30,900
20	233	468	844	1,460	2,210	3,970	11,000	21,200
30	187	375	677	1,170	1,770	3,180	8,810	17,000
40	160	321	580	1,000	1,520	2,730	7,540	14,600
50	142	285	514	890	1,340	2,420	6,680	12,900
60	129	258	466	807	1,220	2,190	6,050	11,700
70	119	237	428	742	1,120	2,010	5,570	10,800
80	110	221	398	690	1,040	1,870	5,180	10,000
90	103	207	374	648	978	1,760	4,860	9,400
100	98	196	353	612	924	1,660	4,590	8,900
125	87	173	313	542	819	1,470	4,070	7,900
150	78	157	284	491	742	1,330	3,690	7,130
175	72	145	261	452	683	1,230	3,390	6,560
200	67	135	243	420	635	1,140	3,160	6,100
250	60	119	215	373	563	1,010	2,800	5,410
300	54	108	195	338	510	916	2,530	4,900
350	50	99	179	311	469	843	2,330	4,510
400	46	92	167	289	436	784	2,170	4,190
450	43	87	157	271	409	736	2,040	3,930
500	41	82	148	256	387	695	1,920	3,720

Note: All table entries are rounded to 3 significant digits.

Table 6.3.1(l) Polyethylene Plastic Pipe

					Gas:	Undiluted Propane
					Inlet Pressure:	2.0 psi
					Pressure Drop:	1.0 psi
					Specific Gravity:	1.50

INTENDED USE: PE Pipe Sizing Between 2 psi Service Regulator and Line Pressure Regulator.

	Pipe Size (in.)							
Nominal OD:	½	¾	1	1¼	1½	2	3	4
Designation:	SDR 9.3	SDR 11	SDR 11	SDR 10	SDR 11	SDR 11	SDR 11	SDR 11
Actual ID:	0.660	0.860	1.077	1.328	1.554	1.943	2.864	3.682
Length (ft)	Capacity in Thousands of Btu per Hour							
10	3,130	6,260	11,300	19,600	29,500	53,100	147,000	284,000
20	2,150	4,300	7,760	13,400	20,300	36,500	101,000	195,000
30	1,730	3,450	6,230	10,800	16,300	29,300	81,100	157,000
40	1,480	2,960	5,330	9,240	14,000	25,100	69,400	134,100
50	1,310	2,620	4,730	8,190	12,400	22,200	61,500	119,000
60	1,190	2,370	4,280	7,420	11,200	20,100	55,700	108,000
70	1,090	2,180	3,940	6,830	10,300	18,500	51,300	99,100
80	1,010	2,030	3,670	6,350	9,590	17,200	47,700	92,200
90	952	1,910	3,440	5,960	9,000	16,200	44,700	86,500
100	899	1,800	3,250	5,630	8,500	15,300	42,300	81,700
125	797	1,600	2,880	4,990	7,530	13,500	37,500	72,400
150	722	1,450	2,610	4,520	6,830	12,300	33,900	65,600
175	664	1,330	2,400	4,160	6,280	11,300	31,200	60,300
200	618	1,240	2,230	3,870	5,840	10,500	29,000	56,100
250	548	1,100	1,980	3,430	5,180	9,300	25,700	49,800
300	496	994	1,790	3,110	4,690	8,430	23,300	45,100
350	457	914	1,650	2,860	4,320	7,760	21,500	41,500
400	425	851	1,530	2,660	4,020	7,220	12,000	38,600
450	399	798	1,440	2,500	3,770	6,770	18,700	36,200
500	377	754	1,360	2,360	3,560	6,390	17,700	34,200
550	358	716	1,290	2,240	3,380	6,070	16,800	32,500
600	341	683	1,230	2,140	3,220	5,790	16,000	31,000
650	327	654	1,180	2,040	3,090	5,550	15,400	29,700
700	314	628	1,130	1,960	2,970	5,330	14,700	28,500
750	302	605	1,090	1,890	2,860	5,140	14,200	27,500
800	292	585	1,050	1,830	2,760	4,960	13,700	26,500
850	283	566	1,020	1,770	2,670	4,800	13,300	25,700
900	274	549	990	1,710	2,590	4,650	12,900	24,900
950	266	533	961	1,670	2,520	4,520	12,500	24,200
1,000	259	518	935	1,620	2,450	4,400	12,200	23,500
1,100	246	492	888	1,540	2,320	4,170	11,500	22,300
1,200	234	470	847	1,470	2,220	3,980	11,000	21,300
1,300	225	450	811	1,410	2,120	3,810	10,600	20,400
1,400	216	432	779	1,350	2,040	3,660	10,100	19,600
1,500	208	416	751	1,300	1,960	3,530	9,760	18,900
1,600	201	402	725	1,260	1,900	3,410	9,430	18,200
1,700	194	389	702	1,220	1,840	3,300	9,130	17,600
1,800	188	377	680	1,180	1,780	3,200	8,850	17,100
1,900	183	366	661	1,140	1,730	3,110	8,590	16,600
2,000	178	356	643	1,110	1,680	3,020	8,360	16,200

Note: All table entries are rounded to 3 significant digits.

Table 6.3.1(m) Polyethylene Plastic Tubing

Gas:	Undiluted Propane
Inlet Pressure:	11.0 in. w.c.
Pressure Drop:	0.5 in. w.c.
Specific Gravity:	1.50

INTENDED USE: Sizing Between Integral 2-Stage Regulator at Tank or Second-Stage (Low-Pressure Regulator) and the Building.

Plastic Tubing Size (CTS) (in.)		
Nominal OD:	½	1
Designation:	SDR 7	SDR 11
Actual ID:	0.445	0.927
Length (ft)	Capacity in Thousands of Btu per Hour	
10	121	828
20	83	569
30	67	457
40	57	391
50	51	347
60	46	314
70	42	289
80	39	269
90	37	252
100	35	238
125	31	211
150	28	191
175	26	176
200	24	164
225	22	154
250	21	145
275	20	138
300	19	132
350	18	121
400	16	113
450	15	106
500	15	100

CTS: Copper tube size.
Note: All table entries are rounded to 3 significant digits.

Table 6.4.2 C_r and Y for Natural Gas and Undiluted Propane at Standard Conditions

	Formula Factors	
Gas	C_r	Y
Natural gas	0.6094	0.9992
Undiluted propane	1.2462	0.9910

Chapter 7 Gas Piping Installation

7.1 Installation of Underground Piping.

7.1.1 Clearances.

7.1.1.1 Underground gas piping shall be installed with sufficient clearance from any other underground structure to avoid contact therewith, to allow maintenance, and to protect against damage from proximity to other structures.

7.1.1.2 Underground plastic piping shall be installed with sufficient clearance or shall be insulated from any source of heat so as to prevent the heat from impairing the serviceability of the pipe.

7.1.2 Protection Against Damage. Means shall be provided to prevent excessive stressing of the piping where vehicular traffic is heavy or soil conditions are unstable and settling of piping or foundation walls could occur. Piping shall be buried or covered in a manner so as to protect the piping from physical damage. Piping shall be protected from physical damage where it passes through flower beds, shrub beds, and other such cultivated areas where such damage is reasonably expected.

7.1.2.1 Cover Requirements. Underground piping systems shall be installed with a minimum of 12 in. (300 mm) of cover.

(A) The minimum cover shall be increased to 18 in. (460 mm) if external damage to the pipe or tubing from external forces is likely to result.

(B)* Where a minimum of 12 in. (300 mm) of cover cannot be provided, the piping shall be installed in conduit.

7.1.2.2 Trenches. The trench shall be graded so that the pipe has a firm, substantially continuous bearing on the bottom of the trench.

7.1.2.3 Backfilling. Where flooding of the trench is done to consolidate the backfill, care shall be exercised to see that the pipe is not floated from its firm bearing on the trench bottom.

7.1.3* Corrosion Protection of Piping. Steel pipe and steel tubing installed underground shall be installed in accordance with the 7.1.3.1 through 7.1.3.9.

7.1.3.1 Zinc coating (galvanizing) shall not be deemed adequate protection for underground gas piping.

7.1.3.2 Underground piping shall comply with one or more of the following unless approved technical justification is provided to demonstrate that protection is unnecessary:

(1) The piping shall be made of corrosion-resistant material that is suitable for the environment in which it will be installed.
(2) Pipe shall have a factory-applied, electrically insulating coating. Fittings and joints between sections of coated pipe shall be coated in accordance with the coating manufacturer's instructions.
(3) The piping shall have a cathodic protection system installed, and the system shall be maintained in accordance with 7.1.3.3 or 7.1.3.6.

7.1.3.3 Cathodic protection systems shall be monitored by testing and the results shall be documented. The test results shall demonstrate one of the following:

(1) A pipe-to-soil voltage of –0.85 volts or more negative is produced, with reference to a saturated copper-copper sulfate half cell
(2) A pipe-to-soil voltage of –0.78 volts or more negative is produced, with reference to a saturated KCl calomel half cell
(3) A pipe-to-soil voltage of –0.80 volts or more negative is produced, with reference to a silver-silver chloride half cell
(4) Compliance with a method described in Appendix D of Title 49 of the Code of Federal Regulations, Part 192

7.1.3.4 Sacrificial anodes shall be tested in accordance with the following:

(1) Upon installation of the cathodic protection system, except where prohibited by climatic conditions, in which case the testing shall be performed not later than 180 days after the installation of the system
(2) 12 to 18 months after the initial test
(3) Upon successful verification testing in accordance with (1) and (2), periodic follow-up testing shall be performed at intervals not to exceed 36 months

7.1.3.5 Systems failing a test shall be repaired not more than 180 days after the date of the failed testing. The testing schedule shall be restarted as required in 7.1.3.4(1) and 7.1.3.4(2), and the results shall comply with 7.1.3.3.

7.1.3.6 Impressed current cathodic protection systems shall be inspected and tested in accordance with the following schedule:

(1) The impressed current rectifier voltage output shall be checked at intervals not exceeding two months.
(2) The pipe-to-soil voltage shall be tested at least annually.

7.1.3.7 Documentation of the results of the two most recent tests shall be retained.

7.1.3.8 Where dissimilar metals are joined underground, an insulating coupling or fitting shall be used.

7.1.3.9 Steel risers, other than anodeless risers, connected to plastic piping shall be cathodically protected by means of a welded anode.

7.1.4* Protection Against Freezing. Where the formation of hydrates or ice is known to occur, piping shall be protected against freezing.

7.1.5 Piping Through Foundation Wall. Piping through a foundation wall shall comply with all of the following:

(1) Underground piping, where installed through the outer foundation or basement wall of a building, shall be encased in a protective sleeve or protected by an approved device or method.
(2) The spaces between the gas piping and the sleeve and between the sleeve and the wall shall be sealed to prevent entry of gas and water.
(3) Sealing materials shall be compatible with the piping and sleeve.

7.1.6 Piping Underground Beneath Buildings. Where gas piping is installed underground beneath buildings, the piping shall be either of the following:

(1) Encased in an approved conduit designed to withstand the imposed loads and installed in accordance with 7.1.6.1 or 7.1.6.2

(2) A piping/encasement system listed for installation beneath buildings.

7.1.6.1 Conduit with One End Terminating Outdoors. The conduit shall extend into an accessible portion of the building and, at the point where the conduit terminates in the building, the space between the conduit and the gas piping shall be sealed to prevent the possible entrance of any gas leakage. Where the end sealing is of a type that retains the full pressure of the pipe, the conduit shall be designed for the same pressure as the pipe. The conduit shall extend at least 4 in. (100 mm) outside the building, be vented outdoors above finished ground level, and be installed so as to prevent the entrance of water and insects.

7.1.6.2 Conduit with Both Ends Terminating Indoors. Where the conduit originates and terminates within the same building, the conduit shall originate and terminate in an accessible portion of the building and shall not be sealed.

7.1.7 Plastic Piping.

7.1.7.1 Connection of Plastic Piping. Plastic piping shall be installed outdoors, underground only.

Exception No. 1: Plastic piping shall be permitted to terminate aboveground where an anodeless riser is used.

Exception No. 2: Plastic piping shall be permitted to terminate with a wall head adapter aboveground in buildings, including basements, where the plastic piping is inserted in a piping material permitted for use in buildings.

7.1.7.2 Connections Between Metallic and Plastic Piping. Connections made between metallic and plastic piping shall be made with fittings conforming to one of the following:

(1) ASTM D2513, *Standard Specification for Polyethylene (PE) Gas Pressure Pipe, Tubing, and Fittings*, Category 1 transition fittings
(2) ASTM F1973, *Standard Specification for Factory Assembled Anodeless Risers and Transition Fittings in Polyethylene (PE) and Polyamide 11 (PA11) and Polyamide 12 (PA 12) Fuel Gas Distribution Systems*
(3) ASTM F2509, *Standard Specification for Field-Assembled Anodeless Riser Kits for Use on Outside Diameter Controlled Polyethylene Gas Distribution Pipe and Tubing*

7.1.7.3 Tracer Wire. An electrically continuous corrosion-resistant tracer shall be buried with the plastic pipe to facilitate locating.

7.1.7.3.1 The tracer shall be one of the following:

(1) A product specifically designed for that purpose
(2) Insulated copper conductor not less than 14 AWG

7.1.7.3.2 Where tracer wire is used, access shall be provided from aboveground or one end of the tracer wire or tape shall be brought aboveground at a building wall or riser.

7.1.8 CSST piping systems shall be installed in accordance with this code and the manufacturer's installation instructions.

7.2 Installation of Aboveground Piping.

7.2.1 Piping installed aboveground shall comply with all of the following:

(1) Piping shall be securely supported and located where it will be protected from physical damage.
(2) Where passing through an exterior wall, the piping shall also be protected from corrosion by coating or wrapping with an inert material approved for such applications.
(3) The piping shall be sealed around its circumference at the point of the exterior penetration to prevent the entry of water, insects, and rodents.
(4) Where piping is encased in a protective pipe sleeve, the annular spaces between the gas piping and the sleeve and between the sleeve and the wall opening shall be sealed.
(5) Piping installed outdoors shall be elevated not less than 3½ in. (89 mm) above the ground.
(6) Sealing materials shall be compatible with the piping and sleeve.

7.2.2* Protective Coating. Where piping is in contact with a material or an atmosphere corrosive to the piping system, the piping and fittings shall be coated with a corrosion-resistant material. Any such coating used on piping or components shall not be considered as adding strength to the system.

7.2.3 Building Structure.

7.2.3.1 The installation of gas piping shall not cause structural stresses within building components to exceed allowable design limits.

7.2.3.2 Approval shall be obtained before any beams or joists are cut or notched.

7.2.4 Gas Piping to Be Sloped. Piping for other than dry gas conditions shall be sloped not less than ¼ in. in 15 ft (7 mm in 4.6 m) to prevent traps.

7.2.5* Prohibited Locations. Gas piping inside any building shall not be installed in or through a clothes chute, chimney or gas vent, dumbwaiter, elevator shaft, or air duct, other than combustion air ducts.

7.2.6 Hangers, Supports, and Anchors.

7.2.6.1 Piping shall be supported with metal pipe hooks, metal pipe straps, metal bands, metal brackets, metal hangers, or building structural components, suitable for the size of piping, of adequate strength and quality, and located at intervals so as to prevent or damp out excessive vibration. Piping shall be anchored to prevent undue strains on connected appliances and equipment and shall not be supported by other piping. Pipe hangers and supports shall conform to the requirements of ANSI/MSS SP-58, *Pipe Hangers and Supports — Materials, Design Manufacture, Selection, Application, and Installation*.

7.2.6.2 Spacings of supports in gas piping installations shall not be greater than shown in Table 7.2.6.2. Spacing of supports of CSST shall be in accordance with the CSST manufacturer's instructions.

7.2.6.3 Supports, hangers, and anchors shall be installed so as not to interfere with the free expansion and contraction of the piping between anchors. All parts of the supporting system shall be designed and installed so they are not disengaged by movement of the supported piping.

7.2.6.4 Piping on Roofs.

7.2.6.4.1 Gas piping installed on the roof surfaces shall be supported in accordance with Table 7.2.6.2.

7.2.6.4.2 Gas piping shall be elevated not less than 3½ in. (89 mm) above the roof surface.

Table 7.2.6.2 Support of Piping

Steel Pipe, Nominal Size of Pipe (in.)	Spacing of Supports (ft)	Nominal Size of Tubing Smooth Wall (in. O.D.)	Spacing of Supports (ft)
½	6	½	4
¾ or 1	8	⅝ or ¾	6
1¼ or larger (horizontal)	10	⅞ or 1 (horizontal)	8
1¼ or larger (vertical)	Every floor level	1 or larger (vertical)	Every floor level

For SI units, 1 ft = 0.305 m.

7.2.7 CSST. CSST piping systems shall be installed in accordance with this code and the manufacturer's installation instructions.

7.3 Concealed Piping in Buildings.

7.3.1 General. Gas piping in concealed locations shall be installed in accordance with this section.

7.3.2 Fittings in Concealed Locations. Fittings installed in concealed locations shall be limited to the following types:

(1) Threaded elbows, tees, couplings, caps, and plugs
(2) Brazed fittings
(3) Welded fittings
(4) Fittings listed to ANSI LC 1/CSA 6.26, *Fuel Gas Piping Systems Using Corrugated Stainless Steel Tubing (CSST)*, or ANSI LC 4/CSA 6.32, *Press-Connect Metallic Fittings for Use in Fuel Gas Distribution Systems*

7.3.3 Piping in Partitions. Concealed gas piping shall not be located in solid partitions.

7.3.4 Tubing in Partitions. This provision shall not apply to tubing that pierces walls, floors, or partitions. Tubing installed vertically and horizontally inside hollow walls or partitions without protection along its entire concealed length shall meet the following requirements:

(1) A steel striker barrier not less than 0.0508 in. (1.3 mm) thick, or equivalent, is installed between the tubing and the finished wall and extends at least 4 in. (100 mm) beyond concealed penetrations of plates, firestops, wall studs, and so on.
(2) The tubing is installed in single runs and is not rigidly secured.

7.3.5 Piping in Floors.

7.3.5.1 Industrial Occupancies. In industrial occupancies, gas piping in solid floors such as concrete shall be laid in channels in the floor and covered to permit access to the piping with a minimum of damage to the building. Where piping in floor channels could be exposed to excessive moisture or corrosive substances, the piping shall be protected in an approved manner.

7.3.5.2 Other Occupancies. In other than industrial occupancies and where approved by the authority having jurisdiction, gas piping embedded in concrete floor slabs constructed with Portland cement shall be surrounded with a minimum of 1½ in. (38 mm) of concrete and shall not be in physical contact with other metallic structures such as reinforcing rods or electrically neutral conductors. All piping, fittings, and risers shall be protected against corrosion in accordance with 7.2.2. Piping shall not be embedded in concrete slabs containing quickset additives or cinder aggregate.

7.3.6 Shutoff Valves in Tubing Systems. Shutoff valves in tubing systems in concealed locations shall be rigidly and securely supported independently of the tubing.

7.4 Piping in Vertical Chases. Where gas piping exceeding 5 psi (34 kPa) is located within vertical chases in accordance with 5.4.1, the requirements of 7.4.1 through 7.4.3 shall apply.

7.4.1 Pressure Reduction. Where pressure reduction is required in branch connections for compliance with 5.4.1, such reduction shall take place either inside the chase or immediately adjacent to the outside wall of the chase. Regulator venting and downstream overpressure protection shall comply with 5.7.5 and Section 5.8. The regulator shall be accessible for service and repair and vented in accordance with one of the following:

(1) Where the fuel gas is lighter than air, regulators equipped with a vent limiting means shall be permitted to be vented into the chase. Regulators not equipped with a vent limiting means shall be permitted to be vented either directly to the outdoors or to a point within the top 1 ft (0.3 m) of the chase.
(2) Where the fuel gas is heavier than air, the regulator vent shall be vented only directly to the outdoors.

7.4.2 Chase Construction. Chase construction shall comply with local building codes with respect to fire resistance and protection of horizontal and vertical openings.

7.4.3* Ventilation. A chase shall be ventilated to the outdoors and only at the top. The opening(s) shall have a minimum free area [in square inches (square meters)] equal to the product of one-half of the maximum pressure in the piping [in pounds per square inch (kilopascals)] times the largest nominal diameter of that piping [in inches (millimeters)], or the cross-sectional area of the chase, whichever is smaller. Where more than one fuel gas piping system is present, the free area for each system shall be calculated and the largest area used.

7.5 Gas Pipe Turns. Changes in direction of gas pipe shall be made by the use of fittings, factory bends, or field bends.

7.5.1 Metallic Pipe. Metallic pipe bends shall comply with the following:

(1) Bends shall be made only with bending tools and procedures intended for that purpose.
(2) All bends shall be smooth and free from buckling, cracks, or other evidence of mechanical damage.
(3) The longitudinal weld of the pipe shall be near the neutral axis of the bend.
(4) Pipe shall not be bent through an arc of more than 90 degrees.
(5) The inside radius of a bend shall be not less than 6 times the outside diameter of the pipe.

7.5.2 Plastic Pipe. Plastic pipe bends shall comply with the following:

(1) The pipe shall not be damaged, and the internal diameter of the pipe shall not be effectively reduced.
(2) Joints shall not be located in pipe bends.
(3) The radius of the inner curve of such bends shall not be less than 25 times the inside diameter of the pipe.

(4) Where the piping manufacturer specifies the use of special bending tools or procedures, such tools or procedures shall be used.

7.5.3 Elbows. Factory-made welding elbows or transverse segments cut therefrom shall have an arc length measured along the crotch of at least 1 in. (25 mm) for pipe sizes 2 in. (50 mm) and larger.

7.6 Drips and Sediment Traps.

7.6.1 Provide Drips Where Necessary. For other than dry gas conditions, a drip shall be provided at any point in the line of pipe where condensate could collect. Where required by the authority having jurisdiction or the serving gas supplier, a drip shall also be provided at the outlet of the meter. This drip shall be installed so as to constitute a trap wherein an accumulation of condensate shuts off the flow of gas before it runs back into the meter.

7.6.2 Location of Drips. All drips shall be installed only in such locations that they are readily accessible to permit cleaning or emptying. A drip shall not be located where the condensate is likely to freeze.

7.6.3 Sediment Traps. The installation of sediment traps shall be in accordance with 9.6.8.

7.7 Outlets.

7.7.1 Location and Installation.

7.7.1.1 The outlet fittings or piping shall be securely fastened in place.

7.7.1.2 Outlets shall not be located behind doors.

7.7.1.3 Outlets shall be located far enough from floors, walls, patios, slabs, and ceilings to permit the use of wrenches without straining, bending, or damaging the piping.

7.7.1.4 The unthreaded portion of gas piping outlets shall extend not less than 1 in. (25 mm) through finished ceilings or indoor or outdoor walls.

7.7.1.5 The unthreaded portion of gas piping outlets shall extend not less than 2 in. (50 mm) above the surface of floors or outdoor patios or slabs.

7.7.1.6 The provisions of 7.7.1.4 and 7.7.1.5 shall not apply to listed quick-disconnect devices of the flush-mounted type or listed gas convenience outlets. Such devices shall be installed in accordance with the manufacturers' installation instructions.

7.7.2 Cap All Outlets.

7.7.2.1 Each outlet, including a valve, shall be closed gastight with a threaded plug or cap immediately after installation and shall be left closed until the appliance or equipment is connected thereto. When an appliance or equipment is disconnected from an outlet and the outlet is not to be used again immediately, it shall be capped or plugged gastight.

Exception No. 1: Laboratory appliances installed in accordance with 9.6.2(1) shall be permitted.

Exception No. 2: The use of a listed quick-disconnect device with integral shutoff or listed gas convenience outlet shall be permitted.

7.7.2.2 Appliance shutoff valves installed in fireplaces shall be removed and the piping capped gastight where the fireplace is used for solid fuel burning.

7.8 Manual Gas Shutoff Valves.

7.8.1 Accessibility of Gas Valves.

7.8.1.1 System shutoff valves shall be readily accessible for operation and installed so as to be protected from physical damage.

7.8.1.2 System shutoff valves shall be marked with a metal tag or other permanent means attached by the installing agency so that the gas piping systems supplied through them can be readily identified.

7.8.2 Valves at Regulators. An accessible gas shutoff valve shall be provided upstream of each gas pressure regulator. Where two gas pressure regulators are installed in series in a single gas line, a manual valve shall not be required at the second regulator.

7.8.3 Valves Controlling Multiple Systems.

7.8.3.1 Shutoff Valves for Multiple House Lines. In multiple-tenant buildings supplied through a master meter, through one service regulator where a meter is not provided, or where meters or service regulators are not readily accessible from the appliance or equipment location, an individual shutoff valve for each apartment or tenant line shall be provided at a convenient point of general accessibility. In a common system serving a number of individual buildings, shutoff valves shall be installed at each building.

7.8.3.2 Emergency Shutoff Valves. An exterior shutoff valve to permit turning off the gas supply to each building in an emergency shall be provided. The emergency shutoff valves shall be plainly marked as such and their locations posted as required by the authority having jurisdiction.

7.8.3.3 Shutoff Valve for Laboratories. Each laboratory space containing two or more gas outlets installed on tables, benches, or in hoods in educational, research, commercial, and industrial occupancies shall have a single shutoff valve through which all such gas outlets are supplied. The shutoff valve shall be accessible, located within the laboratory or adjacent to the laboratory's egress door, and identified.

7.8.4* System Shutoff Valves. Where a system shutoff valve is installed, the valve shall comply with Section 5.11.

7.9 Prohibited Devices.
Devices shall not be placed within the interior of gas piping or fittings where such devices reduce the cross-sectional area or otherwise obstruct the free flow of gas, except where allowance in the piping system design has been made for such devices.

7.10 Systems Containing Gas–Air Mixtures Outside the Flammable Range.
Where gas–air mixing machines are employed to produce mixtures above or below the flammable range, they shall be provided with stops to prevent adjustment of the mixture to within or approaching the flammable range.

7.11 Systems Containing Flammable Gas–Air Mixtures.

7.11.1 Required Components. A central premix system with a flammable mixture in the blower or compressor shall consist of the following components:

(1) Gas-mixing machine in the form of an automatic gas–air proportioning device combined with a downstream blower or compressor
(2) Flammable mixture piping, minimum Schedule 40

(3) Automatic firecheck(s)
(4) Safety blowout(s) or backfire preventers for systems utilizing flammable mixture lines above 2½ in. (64 mm) nominal pipe size or the equivalent

7.11.2 Optional Components. The following components shall also be permitted to be utilized in any type of central premix system:

(1) Flowmeter(s)
(2) Flame arrester(s)

7.11.3 Additional Requirements. Gas-mixing machines shall have nonsparking blowers and shall be constructed so that a flashback does not rupture machine casings.

7.11.4* Special Requirements for Mixing Blowers. A mixing blower system shall be limited to applications with minimum practical lengths of mixture piping, limited to a maximum mixture pressure of 10 in. w.c. (2.5 kPa) and limited to gases containing no more than 10 percent hydrogen. The blower shall be equipped with a gas control valve at its air entrance arranged so that gas is admitted to the airstream, entering the blower in proper proportions for correct combustion by the type of burners employed, the said gas control valve being of either the zero governor or mechanical ratio valve type that controls the gas and air adjustment simultaneously. No valves or other obstructions shall be installed between the blower discharge and the burner or burners.

7.11.5 Installation of Gas-Mixing Machines.

7.11.5.1* Location. The gas-mixing machine shall be located in a well-ventilated area or in a detached building or cutoff room provided with room construction and explosion vents in accordance with engineering methods. Such rooms or below-grade installations shall have adequate positive ventilation.

7.11.5.2 Electrical Requirements. Where gas-mixing machines are installed in well-ventilated areas, the type of electrical equipment shall be in accordance with *NFPA 70* for general service conditions unless other hazards in the area prevail. Where gas-mixing machines are installed in small detached buildings or cutoff rooms, the electrical equipment and wiring shall be installed in accordance with *NFPA 70* for hazardous locations (Articles 500 and 501, Class I, Division 2).

7.11.5.3 Air Intakes. Air intakes for gas-mixing machines using compressors or blowers shall be taken from outdoors whenever practical.

7.11.5.4* Controls. Controls for gas-mixing machines shall include interlocks and a safety shutoff valve of the manual reset type in the gas supply connection to each machine arranged to automatically shut off the gas supply in the event of high or low gas pressure. Except for open burner installations only, the controls shall be interlocked so that the blower or compressor stops operating following a gas supply failure. Where a system employs pressurized air, means shall be provided to shut off the gas supply in the event of air failure.

7.11.5.5 Installation in Parallel. Centrifugal gas-mixing machines in parallel shall be reviewed by the user and equipment manufacturer before installation, and means or plans for minimizing the effects of downstream pulsation and equipment overload shall be prepared and utilized as needed.

7.11.6 Use of Automatic Firechecks, Safety Blowouts, or Backfire Preventers. Automatic firechecks and safety blowouts or backfire preventers shall be provided in piping systems distributing flammable air–gas mixtures from gas-mixing machines to protect the piping and the machines in the event of flashback, in accordance with the following:

(1)* Approved automatic firechecks shall be installed upstream as close as practical to the burner inlets following the firecheck manufacturers' instructions.
(2) A separate manually operated gas valve shall be provided at each automatic firecheck for shutting off the flow of the gas–air mixture through the firecheck after a flashback has occurred. The valve shall be located upstream as close as practical to the inlet of the automatic firecheck. Caution: these valves shall not be reopened after a flashback has occurred until the firecheck has cooled sufficiently to prevent re-ignition of the flammable mixture and has been reset properly.
(3) A safety blowout or backfiring preventer shall be provided in the mixture line near the outlet of each gas-mixing machine where the size of the piping is larger than 2½ in. (64 mm) NPS, or equivalent, to protect the mixing equipment in the event of an explosion passing through an automatic firecheck. The manufacturers' instructions shall be followed when installing these devices, particularly after a disc has burst. The discharge from the safety blowout or backfire preventer shall be located or shielded so that particles from the ruptured disc cannot be directed toward personnel. Wherever there are interconnected installations of gas-mixing machines with safety blowouts or backfire preventers, provision shall be made to keep the mixture from other machines from reaching any ruptured disc opening. Check valves shall not be used for this purpose.
(4) Large-capacity premix systems provided with explosion heads (rupture discs) to relieve excessive pressure in pipelines shall be located at and vented to a safe outdoor location. Provisions shall be provided for automatically shutting off the supply of the gas–air mixture in the event of rupture.

7.12 Electrical Bonding and Grounding.

7.12.1 Pipe and Tubing Other than CSST. Each aboveground portion of a gas piping system, other than CSST, that is likely to become energized shall be electrically continuous and bonded to an effective ground-fault current path. Gas piping, other than CSST, shall be considered to be bonded when it is connected to appliances that are connected to the appliance grounding conductor of the circuit supplying that appliance.

7.12.2* CSST. CSST gas piping systems, and gas piping systems containing one or more segments of CSST, shall be electrically continuous and bonded to the electrical service grounding electrode system or, where provided, lightning protection grounding electrode system.

7.12.2.1 The bonding jumper shall connect to a metallic pipe, pipe fitting, or CSST fitting.

7.12.2.2 The bonding jumper shall not be smaller than 6 AWG copper wire or equivalent.

7.12.2.3* The length of the jumper between the connection to the gas piping system and the grounding electrode system shall not exceed 75 ft (22 m). Any additional grounding electrodes installed to meet this requirement shall be bonded to the electrical service grounding electrode system or, where provided, lightning protection grounding electrode system.

7.12.2.4 Bonding connections shall be in accordance with *NFPA 70*.

7.12.2.5 Devices used for the bonding connection shall be listed for the application in accordance with UL 467, *Grounding and Bonding Equipment*.

7.12.3 Arc-Resistant Jacketed CSST. CSST listed with an arc-resistant jacket or coating system in accordance with ANSI LC 1/CSA 6.26, *Fuel Gas Piping Systems Using Corrugated Stainless Steel Tubing*, shall be electrically continuous and bonded to an effective ground fault current path. Where any CSST component of a piping system does not have an arc-resistant jacket or coating system, the bonding requirements of 7.12.2 shall apply. Arc-resistant jacketed CSST shall be considered to be bonded when it is connected to appliances that are connected to the appliance grounding conductor of the circuit supplying that appliance.

7.12.4 Electrical Isolation.

7.12.4.1* Gas piping shall not be used as a grounding conductor or electrode.

7.12.4.2 Underground metallic piping shall be provided with a dielectric fitting installed at building penetrations.

7.12.4.2.1 Dielectric fittings shall not be installed underground.

7.12.5* Lightning Protection Systems. Where a lightning protection system is installed, the bonding of the gas piping shall be in accordance with NFPA 780.

7.13 Electrical Circuits. Electrical circuits shall not utilize gas piping or components as conductors.

Exception: Low-voltage (50 V or less) control circuits, ignition circuits, and electronic flame detection device circuits shall be permitted to make use of piping or components as a part of an electric circuit.

7.14 Electrical Connections.

7.14.1 All electrical connections between wiring and electrically operated control devices in a piping system shall conform to the requirements of *NFPA 70*.

7.14.2 Any essential safety control depending on electric current as the operating medium shall be of a type that shuts off (fail safe) the flow of gas in the event of current failure.

Chapter 8 Inspection, Testing, and Purging

8.1 Pressure Testing and Inspection.

8.1.1* General.

8.1.1.1 Prior to acceptance and initial operation, all piping installations shall be visually inspected and pressure tested to determine that the materials, design, fabrication, and installation practices comply with the requirements of this code.

8.1.1.2 Inspection shall consist of visual examination, during or after manufacture, fabrication, assembly, or pressure tests.

8.1.1.3 Where repairs or additions are made following the pressure test, the affected piping shall be tested. Minor repairs and additions are not required to be pressure tested, provided that the work is inspected and connections are tested with a noncorrosive leak-detecting fluid or other leak-detecting methods approved by the authority having jurisdiction.

8.1.1.4 Where new branches are installed to new appliance(s), only the newly installed branch(es) shall be required to be pressure tested. Connections between the new piping and the existing piping shall be tested with a noncorrosive leak-detecting fluid or approved leak-detecting methods.

8.1.1.5 A piping system shall be tested as a complete unit or in sections. Under no circumstances shall a valve in a line be used as a bulkhead between gas in one section of the piping system and test medium in an adjacent section, unless a double block and bleed valve system is installed. A valve shall not be subjected to the test pressure unless it can be determined that the valve, including the valve closing mechanism, is designed to safely withstand the pressure.

8.1.1.6 Regulator and valve assemblies fabricated independently of the piping system in which they are to be installed shall be permitted to be tested with inert gas or air at the time of fabrication.

8.1.1.7* Prior to testing, the interior of the pipe shall be cleared of all foreign material.

8.1.2 Test Medium. The test medium shall be air, nitrogen, carbon dioxide, or an inert gas. Oxygen shall not be used as a test medium.

8.1.3 Test Preparation.

8.1.3.1 Pipe joints, including welds, shall be left exposed for examination during the test.

Exception: Covered or concealed pipe end joints that have been previously tested in accordance with this code.

8.1.3.2 Expansion joints shall be provided with temporary restraints, if required, for the additional thrust load under test.

8.1.3.3 Appliances and equipment that are not to be included in the test shall be either disconnected from the piping or isolated by blanks, blind flanges, or caps. Flanged joints at which blinds are inserted to blank off other equipment during the test shall not be required to be tested.

8.1.3.4 Where the piping system is connected to appliances or equipment designed for operating pressures of less than the test pressure, such appliances or equipment shall be isolated from the piping system by disconnecting them and capping the outlet(s).

8.1.3.5 Where the piping system is connected to appliances or equipment designed for operating pressures equal to or greater than the test pressure, such appliances or equipment shall be isolated from the piping system by closing the individual appliance or equipment shutoff valve(s).

8.1.3.6 All testing of piping systems shall be performed in a manner that protects the safety of employees and the public during the test.

8.1.4 Test Pressure.

8.1.4.1 Test pressure shall be measured with a manometer or with a pressure measuring device designed and calibrated to read, record, or indicate a pressure loss due to leakage during the pressure test period. The source of pressure shall be isolated before the pressure tests are made. Mechanical gauges used to measure test pressures shall have a range such that the highest end of the scale is not greater than 5 times the test pressure.

8.1.4.2 The test pressure to be used shall be no less than 1½ times the proposed maximum working pressure, but not less than 3 psi (20 kPa), irrespective of design pressure. Where the test pressure exceeds 125 psi (862 kPa), the test pressure shall not exceed a value that produces a hoop stress in the piping greater than 50 percent of the specified minimum yield strength of the pipe.

8.1.4.3* Test duration shall be not less than ½ hour for each 500 ft^3 (14 m^3) of pipe volume or fraction thereof. When testing a system having a volume less than 10 ft^3 (0.28 m^3) or a system in a single-family dwelling, the test duration shall be a minimum of 10 minutes. The duration of the test shall not be required to exceed 24 hours.

8.1.5 Detection of Leaks and Defects.

8.1.5.1 The piping system shall withstand the test pressure specified without showing any evidence of leakage or other defects. Any reduction of test pressures as indicated by pressure gauges shall be deemed to indicate the presence of a leak unless such reduction can be readily attributed to some other cause.

8.1.5.2 The leakage shall be located by means of an approved gas detector, a noncorrosive leak detection fluid, or other approved leak detection methods.

8.1.5.3 Where leakage or other defects are located, the affected portion of the piping system shall be repaired or replaced and retested.

8.2 Piping System Leak Check.

8.2.1 Test Gases. Leak checks using fuel gas shall be permitted in piping systems that have been pressure tested in accordance with Section 8.1.

8.2.2 Turning Gas On. During the process of turning gas on into a system of new gas piping, the entire system shall be inspected to determine that there are no open fittings or ends and that all valves at unused outlets are closed and plugged or capped.

8.2.3* Leak Check. Immediately after the gas is turned on into a new system or into a system that has been initially restored after an interruption of service, the piping system shall be checked for leakage. Where leakage is indicated, the gas supply shall be shut off until the necessary repairs have been made.

8.2.4 Placing Appliances and Equipment in Operation. Appliances and equipment shall not be placed in operation until after the piping system has been checked for leakage in accordance with 8.2.3, the piping system is purged in accordance with Section 8.3, and connections to the appliance are checked for leakage.

8.3* Purging Requirements. The purging of piping shall be in accordance with 8.3.1 through 8.3.3.

8.3.1* Piping Systems Required to Be Purged Outdoors. The purging of piping systems shall be in accordance with 8.3.1.1 through 8.3.1.4 where the piping system meets either of the following:

(1) The design operating gas pressure is greater than 2 psig (14 kPag).
(2) The piping being purged contains one or more sections of pipe or tubing meeting the size and length criteria of Table 8.3.1.

Table 8.3.1 Size and Length of Piping*

Nominal Piping Size (in.)	Length of Piping (ft)
≥2½ <3	> 50
≥3 <4	> 30
≥4 <6	> 15
≥6 <8	> 10
≥8	Any length

For SI units, 1 in. = 25.4 mm; 1 ft = 0.305 m.
* CSST EHD size of 62 is equivalent to 2 in. nominal size pipe or tubing.

8.3.1.1 Removal from Service. Where existing gas piping is opened, the section that is opened shall be isolated from the gas supply and the line pressure vented in accordance with 8.3.1.3. Where gas piping meeting the criteria of Table 8.3.1 is removed from service, the residual fuel gas in the piping shall be displaced with an inert gas.

8.3.1.2* Placing in Operation. Where gas piping containing air and meeting the criteria of Table 8.3.1 is placed in operation, the air in the piping shall first be displaced with an inert gas. The inert gas shall then be displaced with fuel gas in accordance with 8.3.1.3.

8.3.1.3 Outdoor Discharge of Purged Gases. The open end of a piping system being pressure vented or purged shall discharge directly to an outdoor location. Purging operations shall comply with all of the following requirements:

(1) The point of discharge shall be controlled with a shutoff valve.
(2) The point of discharge shall be located at least 10 ft (3.0 m) from sources of ignition, at least 10 ft (3.0 m) from building openings and at least 25 ft (7.6 m) from mechanical air intake openings.
(3) During discharge, the open point of discharge shall be continuously attended and monitored with a combustible gas indicator that complies with 8.3.1.4.
(4) Purging operations introducing fuel gas shall be stopped when 90 percent fuel gas by volume is detected within the pipe.
(5) Persons not involved in the purging operations shall be evacuated from all areas within 10 ft (3.0 m) of the point of discharge.

8.3.1.4* Combustible Gas Indicator. Combustible gas indicators shall be listed and calibrated in accordance with the manufacturer's instructions. Combustible gas indicators shall numerically display a volume scale from 0 percent to 100 percent in 1 percent or smaller increments.

8.3.2* Piping Systems Allowed to Be Purged Indoors or Outdoors. The purging of piping systems shall be in accordance with the provisions of 8.3.2.1 where the piping system meets both of the following:

(1) The design operating pressure is 2 psig (14 kPag) or less.

(2) The piping being purged is constructed entirely from pipe or tubing not meeting the size and length criteria of Table 8.3.1.

8.3.2.1* Purging Procedure. The piping system shall be purged in accordance with one or more of the following:

(1) The piping shall be purged with fuel gas and shall discharge to the outdoors.
(2) The piping shall be purged with fuel gas and shall discharge to the indoors or outdoors through an appliance burner not located in a combustion chamber. Such burner shall be provided with a continuous source of ignition.
(3) The piping shall be purged with fuel gas and shall discharge to the indoors or outdoors through a burner that has a continuous source of ignition and that is designed for such purpose.
(4) The piping shall be purged with fuel gas that is discharged to the indoors or outdoors, and the point of discharge shall be monitored with a listed combustible gas detector in accordance with 8.3.2.2. Purging shall be stopped when fuel gas is detected.
(5) The piping shall be purged by the gas supplier in accordance with written procedures.

8.3.2.2 Combustible Gas Detector. Combustible gas detectors shall be listed and calibrated or tested in accordance with the manufacturer's instructions. Combustible gas detectors shall be capable of indicating the presence of fuel gas.

8.3.3 Purging Appliances and Equipment. After the piping system has been placed in operation, appliances and equipment shall be purged before being placed into operation.

Chapter 9 Appliance, Equipment, and Accessory Installation

9.1 General.

9.1.1* Appliances, Equipment, and Accessories to Be Approved. Appliances, equipment, and accessories shall be approved.

9.1.1.1 Listed appliances, equipment, and accessories shall be installed in accordance with Chapter 9 and the manufacturers' installation instructions.

9.1.1.2 Acceptance of unlisted appliances, equipment, and accessories shall be on the basis of engineering methods.

9.1.1.3 The unlisted appliance, equipment, or accessory shall be safe and suitable for the proposed service and shall be recommended for the service by the manufacturer.

9.1.2 Added or Converted Appliances. When additional or replacement appliances or equipment is installed or an appliance is converted to gas from another fuel, the location in which the appliances or equipment is to be operated shall be checked to verify the following:

(1) Air for combustion and ventilation is provided where required, in accordance with the provisions of Section 9.3. Where existing facilities are not adequate, they shall be upgraded to meet Section 9.3 specifications.
(2) The installation components and appliances meet the clearances to combustible material provisions of 9.2.2. It shall be determined that the installation and operation of the additional or replacement appliances do not render the remaining appliances unsafe for continued operation.
(3) The venting system is constructed and sized in accordance with the provisions of Chapter 12. Where the existing venting system is not adequate, it shall be upgraded to comply with Chapter 12.

9.1.3 Type of Gas(es). The appliance shall be connected to the fuel gas for which it was designed. No attempt shall be made to convert the appliance from the gas specified on the rating plate for use with a different gas without consulting the installation instructions, the serving gas supplier, or the appliance manufacturer for complete instructions. Listed appliances shall not be converted unless permitted by and in accordance with the manufacturer's installation instructions.

9.1.4 Safety Shutoff Devices for Unlisted LP-Gas Appliances Used Indoors. Unlisted appliances for use with undiluted LP-Gases and installed indoors, except attended laboratory equipment, shall be equipped with safety shutoff devices of the complete shutoff type.

9.1.5 Use of Air or Oxygen Under Pressure. Where air or oxygen under pressure is used in connection with the gas supply, effective means such as a back pressure regulator and relief valve shall be provided to prevent air or oxygen from passing back into the gas piping. Where oxygen is used, installation shall be in accordance with NFPA 51.

9.1.6* Protection of Appliances from Fumes or Gases Other than Products of Combustion.

9.1.6.1 Where corrosive or flammable process fumes or gases, such as carbon monoxide, hydrogen sulfide, ammonia, chlorine, and halogenated hydrocarbons, as are present, means for their safe disposal shall be provided.

9.1.6.2 Non-direct-vent appliances installed in beauty shops, barber shops, or other facilities where chemicals that generate corrosive or flammable products such as aerosol sprays are routinely used shall be located in a mechanical room separate or partitioned off from other areas with provisions for combustion and dilution air from outdoors. Direct vent appliances in such facilities shall be in accordance with the appliance manufacturer's installation instructions.

9.1.7 Process Air. In addition to air needed for combustion in commercial or industrial processes, process air shall be provided as required for cooling of appliances, equipment, or material; for controlling dew point, heating, drying, oxidation, dilution, safety exhaust, odor control, and air for compressors; and for comfort and proper working conditions for personnel.

9.1.8 Appliance Support.

9.1.8.1 Appliances and equipment shall be furnished either with load distributing bases or with a sufficient number of supports to prevent damage to either the building structure or the appliance and the equipment.

9.1.8.2 At the locations selected for installation of appliances and equipment, the dynamic and static load carrying capacities of the building structure shall be checked to determine whether they are adequate to carry the additional loads. The appliances and equipment shall be supported and shall be connected to the piping so as not to exert undue stress on the connections.

9.1.9 Flammable Vapors. Appliances shall not be installed in areas where the open use, handling, or dispensing of flammable liquids occurs, unless the design, operation, or installation reduces the potential of ignition of the flammable vapors. Appliances installed in compliance with 9.1.10 through 9.1.12 shall be considered to comply with the intent of this provision.

9.1.10 Installation in Residential Garages.

9.1.10.1 Appliances in residential garages and in adjacent spaces that open to the garage and are not part of the living space of a dwelling unit shall be installed so that all burners and burner ignition devices are located not less than 18 in. (460 mm) above the floor unless listed as flammable vapor ignition resistant.

9.1.10.2 Such appliances shall be located or protected so they are not subject to physical damage by a moving vehicle.

9.1.10.3 Where appliances are installed in a separate, enclosed space having access only from outside of the garage, such appliances shall be permitted to be installed at floor level, providing the required combustion air is taken from the exterior of the garage.

9.1.11 Installation in Commercial Garages.

9.1.11.1 Parking Structures. Appliances installed in enclosed, basement, and underground parking structures shall be installed in accordance with NFPA 88A.

9.1.11.2 Repair Garages. Appliances installed in repair garages shall be installed in accordance with NFPA 30A.

9.1.12 Installation in Aircraft Hangars. Heaters in aircraft hangars shall be installed in accordance with NFPA 409.

9.1.13 Appliance Physical Protection. Where locating appliances close to a passageway traveled by vehicles or machinery is necessary, guardrails or bumper plates shall be installed to protect the equipment from damage.

9.1.14 Venting of Flue Gases. Appliances shall be vented in accordance with the provisions of Chapter 12.

9.1.15 Extra Device or Attachment. No device or attachment shall be installed on any appliance that could in any way impair the combustion of gas.

9.1.16 Avoiding Strain on Gas Piping. Appliances shall be supported and connected to the piping so as not to exert undue strain on the connections.

9.1.17 Gas Appliance Pressure Regulators. Where the gas supply pressure is higher than that at which the appliance is designed to operate or varies beyond the design pressure limits of the appliance, a gas appliance pressure regulator listed in accordance with ANSI Z21.18/CSA 6.3, *Gas Appliance Pressure Regulators*, shall be installed.

9.1.18 Bleed Lines for Diaphragm-Type Valves. Bleed lines shall comply with the following requirements:

(1) Diaphragm-type valves shall be equipped to convey bleed gas to the outdoors or into the combustion chamber adjacent to a continuous pilot.
(2) In the case of bleed lines leading outdoors, means shall be employed to prevent water from entering this piping and also to prevent blockage of vents by insects and foreign matter.
(3) Bleed lines shall not terminate in the appliance flue or exhaust system.
(4) In the case of bleed lines entering the combustion chamber, the bleed line shall be located so the bleed gas is readily ignited by the pilot and the heat liberated thereby does not adversely affect the normal operation of the safety shutoff system. The terminus of the bleed line shall be securely held in a fixed position relative to the pilot. For manufactured gas, the need for a flame arrester in the bleed line piping shall be determined.
(5) A bleed line(s) from a diaphragm-type valve and a vent line(s) from an appliance pressure regulator shall not be connected to a common manifold terminating in a combustion chamber. Bleed lines shall not terminate in positive-pressure-type combustion chambers.

9.1.19 Combination of Appliances and Equipment. Any combination of appliances, equipment, attachments, or devices used together in any manner shall comply with the standards that apply to the individual appliance and equipment.

9.1.20* Installation Instructions. The installer shall conform to the appliance and equipment manufacturers' recommendations in completing an installation. The installer shall leave the manufacturers' installation, operating, and maintenance instructions on the premises.

9.1.21 Protection of Outdoor Appliances. Appliances not listed for outdoor installation but installed outdoors shall be provided with protection to the degree that the environment requires. Appliances listed for outdoor installation shall be permitted to be installed without protection in accordance with the manufacturer's installation instructions.

9.1.22* Existing Appliances. Existing appliance installations shall be inspected to verify compliance with the provisions of Section 9.3 and Chapter 12 where a component of the building envelope is modified as described by one or more of 9.1.22(1) through 9.1.22(6). Where the appliance installation does not comply with Section 9.3 and Chapter 12, the installation shall be altered as necessary to be in compliance with Section 9.3 and Chapter 12.

(1) The building is modified under a weatherization program.
(2) A building permit is issued for a building addition or exterior building modification.
(3) Three or more window assemblies are replaced.
(4) Three or more storm windows are installed over existing windows.
(5) One or more exterior door and frame assemblies are replaced.
(6) A building air barrier is installed or replaced.

9.2 Accessibility and Clearance.

9.2.1 Accessibility for Service. All appliances shall be located with respect to building construction and other equipment so as to permit access to the appliance. Sufficient clearance shall be maintained to permit cleaning of heating surfaces; the replacement of filters, blowers, motors, burners, controls, and vent connections; the lubrication of moving parts where necessary; the adjustment and cleaning of burners and pilots; and the proper functioning of explosion vents, if provided. For attic installation, the passageway and servicing area adjacent to the appliance shall be floored.

9.2.2 Clearance to Combustible Materials. Appliances and their vent connectors shall be installed with clearances from combustible material so their operation does not create a hazard to persons or property. Minimum clearances between combustible walls and the back and sides of various conventional types of appliances and their vent connectors are specified in Chapters 10 and 12. *(Reference can also be made to NFPA 211.)*

9.2.3 Installation on Carpeting. Appliances shall not be installed on carpeting, unless the appliances are listed for such installation.

9.3* Air for Combustion and Ventilation.

9.3.1 General.

9.3.1.1 Air for combustion, ventilation, and dilution of flue gases for appliances installed in buildings shall be obtained by application of one of the methods covered in 9.3.2 through 9.3.6. Where the requirements of 9.3.2 are not met, outdoor air shall be introduced in accordance with methods covered in 9.3.3 through 9.3.6.

Exception No. 1: This provision shall not apply to direct vent appliances.

Exception No. 2: Type 1 clothes dryers that are provided with make-up air in accordance with 10.4.4.

9.3.1.2 Appliances of other than natural draft design, appliances not designated as Category I vented appliances, and appliances equipped with power burners shall be provided with combustion, ventilation, and dilution air in accordance with the appliance manufacturer's instructions.

9.3.1.3 Appliances shall be located so as not to interfere with proper circulation of combustion, ventilation, and dilution air.

9.3.1.4 Where used, a draft hood or a barometric draft regulator shall be installed in the same room or enclosure as the appliance served so as to prevent any difference in pressure between the hood or regulator and the combustion air supply.

9.3.1.5 Where exhaust fans, clothes dryers, and kitchen ventilation systems interfere with the operation of appliances, make-up air shall be provided.

9.3.2 Indoor Combustion Air. The required volume of indoor air shall be determined in accordance with the method in 9.3.2.1 or 9.3.2.2 except that where the air infiltration rate is known to be less than 0.40 *ACH* (air change per hour), the method in 9.3.2.2 shall be used. The total required volume shall be the sum of the required volume calculated for all appliances located within the space. Rooms communicating directly with the space in which the appliances are installed through openings not furnished with doors, and through combustion air openings sized and located in accordance with 9.3.2.3, are considered a part of the required volume.

9.3.2.1* Standard Method. The minimum required volume shall be 50 ft^3/1000 Btu/hr (4.8 m^3/kW).

9.3.2.2* Known Air Infiltration Rate Method. Where the air infiltration rate of a structure is known, the minimum required volume shall be determined as follows:

(1) For appliances other than fan assisted, calculate using the following equation:

$$\text{Required Volume}_{other} \geq \frac{21 \text{ ft}^3}{ACH} \left(\frac{I_{other}}{1000 \text{ Btu/hr}} \right) \quad [9.3.2.2a]$$

(2) For fan-assisted appliances, calculate using the following equation:

$$\text{Required Volume}_{fan} \geq \frac{15 \text{ ft}^3}{ACH} \left(\frac{I_{fan}}{1000 \text{ Btu/hr}} \right) \quad [9.3.2.2b]$$

where:
I_{other} = all appliances other than fan-assisted input (Btu/hr)
I_{fan} = fan-assisted appliance input (Btu/hr)
ACH = air change per hour (percent of volume of space exchanged per hour, expressed as a decimal)

(3) For purposes of these calculations, an infiltration rate greater than 0.60 *ACH* shall not be used in Equations 9.3.2.2a and 9.3.2.2b.

9.3.2.3 Indoor Opening Size and Location. Openings used to connect indoor spaces shall be sized and located in accordance with the following:

(1)* *Combining spaces on the same story.* Each opening shall have a minimum free area of 1 in.^{2}/1000 Btu/hr (2200 mm^2/kW) of the total input rating of all appliances in the space but not less than 100 in.^{2} (0.06 m^2). One permanent opening shall commence within 12 in. (300 mm) of the top of the enclosure and one permanent opening shall commence within 12 in. (300 mm) of the bottom of the enclosure. The minimum dimension of air openings shall not be less than 3 in. (80 mm).

(2) *Combining spaces in different stories.* The volumes of spaces in different stories shall be considered as communicating spaces where such spaces are connected by one or more permanent openings in doors or floors having a total minimum free area of 2 in.^{2}/1000 Btu/hr (4400 mm^2/kW) of total input rating of all appliances.

9.3.3 Outdoor Combustion Air. Outdoor combustion air shall be provided through opening(s) to the outdoors in accordance with the methods in 9.3.3.1 or 9.3.3.2. The minimum dimension of air openings shall not be less than 3 in. (80 mm).

9.3.3.1 Two Permanent Openings Method. Two permanent openings, one commencing within 12 in. (300 mm) of the top of the enclosure and one commencing within 12 in. (300 mm) of the bottom of the enclosure, shall be provided. The openings shall communicate directly, or by ducts, with the outdoors or spaces that freely communicate with the outdoors, as follows:

(1)* Where directly communicating with the outdoors or where communicating to the outdoors through vertical ducts, each opening shall have a minimum free area of 1 in.^{2}/4000 Btu/hr (550 mm^2/kW) of total input rating of all appliances in the enclosure.

(2)* Where communicating with the outdoors through horizontal ducts, each opening shall have a minimum free area of 1 in.^{2}/2000 Btu/hr (1100 mm^2/kW) of total input rating of all appliances in the enclosure.

9.3.3.2* One Permanent Opening Method. One permanent opening, commencing within 12 in. (300 mm) of the top of the enclosure, shall be provided. The appliance shall have clearances of at least 1 in. (25 mm) from the sides and back and 6 in. (150 mm) from the front of the appliance. The opening shall directly communicate with the outdoors or shall communicate through a vertical or horizontal duct to the outdoors or spaces that freely communicate with the outdoors and shall have a minimum free area of the following:

(1) 1 in.^{2}/3000 Btu/hr (700 mm^2/kW) of the total input rating of all appliances located in the enclosure
(2) Not less than the sum of the areas of all vent connectors in the space

9.3.4 Combination Indoor and Outdoor Combustion Air. The use of a combination of indoor and outdoor combustion air shall be in accordance with the following:

(1) *Indoor openings.* Where used, openings connecting the interior spaces shall comply with 9.3.2.3.
(2) *Outdoor opening(s) location.* Outdoor opening(s) shall be located in accordance with 9.3.3.
(3) *Outdoor opening(s) size.* The outdoor opening(s) size shall be calculated in accordance with the following:
   (a) The ratio of the interior spaces shall be the available volume of all communicating spaces divided by the required volume.
   (b) The outdoor size reduction factor shall be 1 minus the ratio of interior spaces.
   (c) The minimum size of outdoor opening(s) shall be the full size of outdoor opening(s) calculated in accordance with 9.3.3, multiplied by the reduction factor. The minimum dimension of air openings shall not be less than 3 in. (80 mm).

9.3.5 Engineered Installations. Engineered combustion air installations shall provide an adequate supply of combustion, ventilation, and dilution air determined using engineering methods.

9.3.6 Mechanical Combustion Air Supply. Where all combustion air is provided by a mechanical air supply system, the combustion air shall be supplied from outdoors at the minimum rate of 0.35 ft^3/min/1000 Btu/hr (0.034 m^3/min/kW) for all appliances located within the space.

9.3.6.1 Where exhaust fans are installed, additional air shall be provided to replace the exhausted air.

9.3.6.2 Each of the appliances served shall be interlocked to the mechanical air supply system to prevent main burner operation where the mechanical air supply system is not in operation.

9.3.6.3 Where combustion air is provided by the building's mechanical ventilation system, the system shall provide the specified combustion air rate in addition to the required ventilation air.

9.3.7 Louvers, Grilles, and Screens.

9.3.7.1 Louvers and Grilles. The required size of openings for combustion, ventilation, and dilution air shall be based on the net free area of each opening. Where the free area through a design of louver, grille, or screen is known, it shall be used in calculating the size opening required to provide the free area specified. Where the louver and grille design and free area are not known, it shall be assumed that wood louvers have 25 percent free area, and metal louvers and grilles have 75 percent free area. Nonmotorized louvers and grilles shall be fixed in the open position.

9.3.7.2 Minimum Screen Mesh Size. Screens shall not be smaller than ¼ in. (7 mm) mesh.

9.3.7.3 Motorized Louvers. Motorized louvers shall be interlocked with the appliance so they are proven in the full open position prior to main burner ignition and during main burner operation. Means shall be provided to prevent the main burner from igniting should the louver fail to open during burner startup and to shut down the main burner if the louvers close during burner operation.

9.3.8 Combustion Air Ducts. Combustion air ducts shall comply with 9.3.8.1 through 9.3.8.8.

9.3.8.1 Ducts shall be constructed of galvanized steel or a material having equivalent corrosion resistance, strength, and rigidity.

Exception: Within dwellings units, unobstructed stud and joist spaces shall not be prohibited from conveying combustion air, provided that not more than one fireblock is removed.

9.3.8.2 Ducts shall terminate in an unobstructed space, allowing free movement of combustion air to the appliances.

9.3.8.3 Ducts shall serve a single space.

9.3.8.4 Ducts shall not serve both upper and lower combustion air openings where both such openings are used. The separation between ducts serving upper and lower combustion air openings shall be maintained to the source of combustion air.

9.3.8.5 Ducts shall not be screened where terminating in an attic space.

9.3.8.6 Horizontal upper combustion air ducts shall not slope downward toward the source of combustion air.

9.3.8.7 The remaining space surrounding a chimney liner, gas vent, special gas vent, or plastic piping installed within a masonry, metal, or factory built chimney shall not be used to supply combustion air.

Exception: Direct vent appliances designed for installation in a solid fuel–burning fireplace where installed in accordance with the manufacturer's installation instructions.

9.3.8.8 Combustion air intake openings located on the exterior of the building shall have the lowest side of the combustion air intake openings located at least 12 in. (300 mm) vertically from the adjoining finished ground level.

9.4 Appliances on Roofs.

9.4.1 General.

9.4.1.1 Appliances on roofs shall be designed or enclosed so as to withstand climatic conditions in the area in which they are installed. Where enclosures are provided, each enclosure shall permit easy entry and movement, shall be of reasonable height, and shall have at least a 30 in. (760 mm) clearance between the entire service access panel(s) of the appliance and the wall of the enclosure.

9.4.1.2 Roofs on which appliances are to be installed shall be capable of supporting the additional load or shall be reinforced to support the additional load.

9.4.1.3 All access locks, screws, and bolts shall be of corrosion-resistant material.

9.4.2 Installation of Appliances on Roofs.

9.4.2.1 Appliances shall be installed in accordance with the manufacturers' installation instructions.

9.4.2.2 Appliances shall be installed on a well-drained surface of the roof. At least 6 ft (1.8 m) of clearance shall be available between any part of the appliance and the edge of a roof or similar hazard, or rigidly fixed rails, guards, parapets, or other building structures at least 42 in. (1.1 m) in height shall be provided on the exposed side.

9.4.2.3 Appliances requiring an external source of electrical power shall be installed in accordance with *NFPA 70*.

9.4.2.4 Where water stands on the roof at the appliance or in the passageways to the appliance, or where the roof is of a design having a water seal, a suitable platform, walkway, or both shall be provided above the water line. Such platform(s) or walkway(s) shall be located adjacent to the appliance and control panels so that the appliance can be safely serviced where water stands on the roof.

9.4.3 Access to Appliances on Roofs.

9.4.3.1 Appliances located on roofs or other elevated locations shall be accessible.

9.4.3.2 Buildings of more than 15 ft (4.6 m) in height shall have an inside means of access to the roof, unless other means acceptable to the authority having jurisdiction are used.

9.4.3.3 The inside means of access shall be a permanent or foldaway inside stairway or ladder, terminating in an enclosure, scuttle, or trapdoor. Such scuttles or trapdoors shall be at least 22 in. × 24 in. (560 mm × 610 mm) in size, shall open easily and safely under all conditions, especially snow, and shall be constructed so as to permit access from the roof side unless deliberately locked on the inside. At least 6 ft (1.8 m) of clearance shall be available between the access opening and the edge of the roof or similar hazard, or rigidly fixed rails or guards a minimum of 42 in. (1.1 m) in height shall be provided on the exposed side. Where parapets or other building structures are utilized in lieu of guards or rails, they shall be a minimum of 42 in. (1.1 m) in height.

9.4.3.4 Permanent lighting shall be provided at the roof access. The switch for such lighting shall be located inside the building near the access means leading to the roof.

9.5 Appliances in Attics.

9.5.1 Attic Access. An attic in which an appliance is installed shall be accessible through an opening and passageway at least as large as the largest component of the appliance and not less than 22 in. × 30 in. (560 mm × 760 mm).

9.5.1.1 Where the height of the passageway is less than 6 ft (1.8 m), the distance from the passageway access to the appliance shall not exceed 20 ft (6.1 m) measured along the centerline of the passageway.

9.5.1.2 The passageway shall be unobstructed and shall have solid flooring not less than 24 in. (610 mm) wide from the entrance opening to the appliance.

9.5.2 Work Platform. A level working platform not less than 30 in. × 30 in. (760 mm × 760 mm) shall be provided in front of the service side of the appliance.

9.5.3 Lighting and Convenience Outlet. A permanent 120 V receptacle outlet and a luminaire shall be installed near the appliance. The switch controlling the luminaire shall be located at the entrance to the passageway.

9.6 Appliance and Equipment Connections to Building Piping.

9.6.1 Connecting Appliances and Equipment. Appliances and equipment shall be connected to the building piping in compliance with 9.6.5 through 9.6.7 by one of the following:

(1) Rigid metallic pipe and fittings.
(2) Semirigid metallic tubing and metallic fittings. Aluminum alloy tubing shall not be used in exterior locations.
(3) A connector for gas appliances listed in accordance with ANSI Z21.24/CSA 6.10, *Connectors for Gas Appliances*. The connector shall be used in accordance with the manufacturer's installation instructions and shall be in the same room as the appliance. Only one connector shall be used per appliance.
(4) A connector for outdoor gas appliances and manufactured homes listed in accordance with ANSI Z21.75/CSA 6.27, *Connectors for Outdoor Gas Appliances and Manufactured Homes*. Only one connector shall be used per appliance.
(5) CSST where installed in accordance with the manufacturer's installation instructions. CSST shall not be directly routed into a metallic appliance enclosure where the appliance is connected to a metallic vent that terminates above a roofline. CSST shall connect only to appliances that are fixed in place.
(6) Listed nonmetallic gas hose connectors in accordance with 9.6.2.
(7) Unlisted gas hose connectors for use in laboratories and educational facilities in accordance with 9.6.3.

9.6.1.1 Protection of Connectors. Connectors and tubing addressed in 9.6.1(2), 9.6.1(3), 9.6.1(4), 9.6.1(5), and 9.6.1(6) shall be installed to be protected against physical and thermal damage. Aluminum alloy tubing and connectors shall be coated to protect against external corrosion where they are in contact with masonry, plaster, or insulation or are subject to repeated wettings by such liquids as detergents, sewage, or water other than rainwater.

9.6.1.2 Materials addressed in 9.6.1(2), 9.6.1(3), 9.6.1(4), 9.6.1(5), and 9.6.1(6) shall not be installed through an opening in an appliance housing, cabinet, or casing, unless the tubing or connector is protected against damage.

9.6.1.3 Food Service Appliance Connectors. Connectors used with food service appliances that are moved for cleaning and sanitation purposes shall be installed in accordance with the connector manufacturer's installation instructions. Such connectors shall be listed in accordance with ANSI Z21.69/CSA 6.16, *Connectors for Movable Gas Appliances*.

9.6.1.4 Restraint. Movement of appliances with casters shall be limited by a restraining device installed in accordance with the connector and appliance manufacturer's installation instructions.

9.6.1.5* Suspended Low-Intensity Infrared Tube Heaters. Suspended low-intensity infrared tube heaters shall be connected to the building piping system with a connector listed for the application in accordance with ANSI Z21.24/CSA 6.10, *Connectors for Gas Appliances*.

(A) The connector shall be installed in accordance with the tube heater installation instructions and shall be in the same room as the appliance.

(B) Only one connector shall be used per appliance.

9.6.2 Use of Nonmetallic Gas Hose Connectors. Listed gas hose connectors shall be used in accordance with the manufacturer's installation instructions and as follows:

(1) *Indoor.* Indoor gas hose connectors shall be used only to connect laboratory, shop, and ironing appliances requiring mobility during operation and installed in accordance with the following:
   (a) An appliance shutoff valve shall be installed where the connector is attached to the building piping.
   (b) The connector shall be of minimum length and shall not exceed 6 ft (1.8 m).
   (c) The connector shall not be concealed and shall not extend from one room to another or pass through wall partitions, ceilings, or floors.

(2) *Outdoor.* Where outdoor gas hose connectors are used to connect portable outdoor appliances, the connector shall be listed in accordance with ANSI Z21.54/CSA 8.4, *Gas Hose Connectors for Portable Outdoor Gas-Fired Appliances*, and installed in accordance with the following:
   (a) An appliance shutoff valve, a listed quick-disconnect device, or a listed gas convenience outlet shall be installed where the connector is attached to the supply piping and in such a manner so as to prevent the accumulation of water or foreign matter.
   (b) This connection shall be made only in the outdoor area where the appliance is to be used.

9.6.3* Injection (Bunsen) burners used in laboratories and educational facilities shall be permitted to be connected to the gas supply by an unlisted hose.

9.6.4 Connection of Portable and Mobile Industrial Appliances.

9.6.4.1 Where portable industrial appliances or appliances requiring mobility or subject to vibration are connected to the building gas piping system by the use of a flexible hose, the hose shall be suitable and safe for the conditions under which it can be used.

9.6.4.2 Where industrial appliances requiring mobility are connected to the rigid piping by the use of swivel joints or couplings, the swivel joints or couplings shall be suitable for the service required and only the minimum number required shall be installed.

9.6.4.3 Where industrial appliances subject to vibration are connected to the building piping system by the use of all metal flexible connectors, the connectors shall be suitable for the service required.

9.6.4.4 Where flexible connections are used, they shall be of the minimum practical length and shall not extend from one room to another or pass through any walls, partitions, ceilings, or floors. Flexible connections shall not be used in any concealed location. They shall be protected against physical or thermal damage and shall be provided with gas shutoff valves in readily accessible locations in rigid piping upstream from the flexible connections.

9.6.5 Appliance Shutoff Valves and Connections. Each appliance connected to a piping system shall have an accessible, approved manual shutoff valve with a nondisplaceable valve member, or a listed gas convenience outlet. Appliance shutoff valves and convenience outlets shall serve a single appliance only and shall be installed in accordance with 9.6.5.1.

9.6.5.1 The shutoff valve shall be located within 6 ft (1.8 m) of the appliance it serves except as permitted in 9.6.5.2 or 9.6.5.3.

(A) Where a connector is used, the valve shall be installed upstream of the connector. A union or flanged connection shall be provided downstream from the valve to permit removal of appliance controls.

(B) Shutoff valves serving decorative appliances in a fireplace shall not be located within the fireplace firebox except where the valve is listed for such use.

9.6.5.2 Shutoff valves serving appliances installed in vented fireplaces and ventless firebox enclosures shall not be required to be located within 6 ft (1.8 m) of the appliance where such valves are readily accessible and permanently identified. The piping from the shutoff valve to within 6 ft (1.8 m) of the appliance shall be designed, sized, installed, and tested in accordance with Chapters 5, 6, 7, and 8.

9.6.5.3 Where installed at a manifold, the appliance shutoff valve shall be located within 50 ft (15 m) of the appliance served and shall be readily accessible and permanently identified. The piping from the manifold to within 6 ft (1.8 m) of the appliance shall be designed, sized, installed, and tested in accordance with Chapters 5, 6, 7, and 8.

9.6.6 Quick-Disconnect Devices.

9.6.6.1 Quick-disconnect devices used to connect appliances to the building piping shall be listed in accordance with ANSI Z21.41/CSA 6.9, *Quick-Disconnect Devices for Use with Gas Fuel Appliances*.

9.6.6.2 Where installed indoors, an approved manual shutoff valve with a nondisplaceable valve member shall be installed upstream of the quick-disconnect device.

9.6.7 Gas Convenience Outlets. Gas convenience outlets shall be listed in accordance with ANSI Z21.90/CSA 6.24, *Gas Convenience Outlets and Optional Enclosures*, and installed in accordance with the manufacturer's installation instructions.

9.6.8 Sediment Trap. Where a sediment trap is not incorporated as a part of the appliance, a sediment trap shall be installed downstream of the appliance shutoff valve as close to the inlet of the appliance as practical at the time of appliance installation. The sediment trap shall be either a tee fitting with a capped nipple in the bottom outlet, as illustrated in Figure 9.6.8, or another device recognized as an effective sediment trap. Illuminating appliances, gas ranges, clothes dryers, decorative appliances for installation in vented fireplaces, gas fireplaces, and outdoor cooking appliances shall not be required to be so equipped.

9.6.9 Installation of Piping. Piping shall be installed in a manner not to interfere with inspection, maintenance, or servicing of the appliances.

9.7 Electrical.

9.7.1 Electrical Connections. Electrical connections between appliances and the building wiring, including the grounding of the appliances, shall conform to *NFPA 70*.

9.7.2 Electrical Ignition and Control Devices. Electrical ignition, burner control, and electrical vent damper devices shall not permit unsafe operation of the appliance in the event of electrical power interruption or when the power is restored.

9.7.3 Electrical Circuit. The electrical circuit employed for operating the automatic main gas control valve, automatic pilot, room temperature thermostat, limit control, or other electrical devices used with the appliances shall be in accordance with the wiring diagrams certified or approved by the original appliance manufacturer.

9.8 Room Temperature Thermostats.

9.8.1 Locations. Room temperature thermostats shall be installed in accordance with the manufacturer's instructions.

9.8.2 Drafts. Any hole in the plaster or panel through which the wires pass from the thermostat to the appliance being controlled shall be sealed so as to prevent drafts from affecting the thermostat.

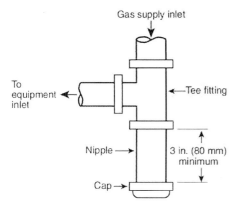

FIGURE 9.6.8 Method of Installing a Tee Fitting Sediment Trap.

Chapter 10 Installation of Specific Appliances

10.1 General.

10.1.1* Application. Appliances shall be installed in accordance with the manufacturers' installation instructions and, as elsewhere specified in this chapter, as applicable to the appliance. Unlisted appliances shall be installed as specified in this chapter as applicable to the appliances.

10.1.2* Installation in a Bedroom or Bathroom. Appliances shall not be installed so their combustion, ventilation, and dilution air are obtained only from a bedroom or bathroom unless the bedroom or bathroom has the required volume in accordance with 9.3.2.

10.1.3 Locations with Airhandlers. Where a draft hood–equipped appliance is installed in a space containing a furnace or other air handler, the ducts serving the furnace or air handler shall comply with 10.3.8.4.

10.2 Air-Conditioning Appliances.

10.2.1 Application. Gas-fired air conditioners and heat pumps shall be listed in accordance with ANSI Z21.40.1/CSA 2.91, *Gas-Fired Heat Activated Air Conditioning and Heat Pump Appliances*, or ANSI Z21.40.2/CSA 2.92, *Air Conditioning and Heat Pump Appliances (Internal Combustion)*.

10.2.2 Independent Gas Piping. Gas piping serving heating appliances shall be permitted to also serve cooling appliances where heating and cooling appliances cannot be operated simultaneously.

10.2.3 Connection of Gas Engine–Powered Air Conditioners. Gas engines shall not be rigidly connected to the gas supply piping.

10.2.4 Clearances for Indoor Installation. The installation of air-conditioning appliances shall comply with the following requirements:

(1) Air-conditioning appliances shall be installed with clearances in accordance with the manufacturer's instructions.
(2) Air-conditioning appliances shall be permitted to be installed with reduced clearances to combustible material, provided that the combustible material or appliance is protected as described in Table 10.2.4 and such reduction is allowed by the manufacturer's installation instructions.
(3) Where the furnace plenum is adjacent to plaster on metal lath or noncombustible material attached to combustible material, the clearance shall be measured to the surface of the plaster or other noncombustible finish where the clearance specified is 2 in. (50 mm) or less.
(4) Air-conditioning appliances shall have the clearance from supply ducts within 3 ft (0.9 m) of the furnace plenum be not less than that specified from the furnace plenum. No clearance is necessary beyond this distance.

10.2.5 Assembly and Installation. Unless the air-conditioning appliance is listed for installation on a combustible surface, or unless the surface is protected in an approved manner, it shall be installed on a surface of noncombustible construction with noncombustible material and surface finish and with no combustible material against the underside thereof.

Table 10.2.4 Reduction of Clearances with Specified Forms of Protection

Type of protection applied to and covering all surfaces of combustible material within the distance specified as the required clearance with no protection	Where the required clearance with no protection from appliance, vent connector, or single-wall metal pipe is:									
	36 in.		18 in.		12 in.		9 in.		6 in.	
	Allowable Clearances with Specified Protection (in.)									
	Use Col. 1 for clearances above appliance or horizontal connector. Use Col. 2 for clearances from appliance, vertical connector, and single-wall metal pipe.									
	Above (Col. 1)	Sides and Rear (Col. 2)	Above (Col. 1)	Sides and Rear (Col. 2)	Above (Col. 1)	Sides and Rear (Col. 2)	Above (Col. 1)	Sides and Rear (Col. 2)	Above (Col. 1)	Sides and Rear (Col. 2)
(1) 3½ in. thick masonry wall without ventilated air space	—	24	—	12	—	9	—	6	—	5
(2) ½ in. insulation board over 1 in. glass fiber or mineral wool batts	24	18	12	9	9	6	6	5	4	3
(3) 0.024 in. (nominal 24 gauge) sheet metal over 1 in. glass fiber or mineral wool batts reinforced with wire on rear face with ventilated air space	18	12	9	6	6	4	5	3	3	3
(4) 3½ in. thick masonry wall with ventilated air space	—	12	—	6	—	6	—	6	—	6
(5) 0.024 in. (nominal 24 gauge) sheet metal with ventilated air space	18	12	9	6	6	4	5	3	3	2
(6) ½ in. thick insulation board with ventilated air space	18	12	9	6	6	4	5	3	3	3
(7) 0.024 in. (nominal 24 gauge) sheet metal with ventilated air space over 0.024 in. (nominal 24 gauge) sheet metal with ventilated air space	18	12	9	6	6	4	5	3	3	3
(8) 1 in. glass fiber or mineral wool batts sandwiched between two sheets 0.024 in. (nominal 24 gauge) sheet metal with ventilated air space	18	12	9	6	6	4	5	3	3	3

For SI units, 1 in. = 25.4 mm.

Notes:
(1) Reduction of clearances from combustible materials shall not interfere with combustion air, draft hood clearance and relief, and accessibility of servicing.
(2) All clearances shall be measured from the outer surface of the combustible material to the nearest point on the surface of the appliance, disregarding any intervening protection applied to the combustible material.
(3) Spacers and ties shall be of noncombustible material. No spacer or tie shall be used directly opposite the appliance or connector.
(4) Where all clearance reduction systems use a ventilated air space, adequate provision for air circulation shall be provided as described.
(5) At least 1 in. (25 mm) shall be between clearance reduction systems and combustible walls and ceilings for reduction systems using a ventilated air space.
(6) Where a wall protector is installed on a single flat wall away from corners, it shall have a minimum 1 in. (25 mm) air gap. To provide adequate air circulation, the bottom and top edges, or only the side and top edges, or all edges shall be left open.
(7) Mineral wool batts (blanket or board) shall have a minimum density of 8 lb/ft^3 (128 kg/m^3) and a minimum melting point of 1500°F (816°C).
(8) Insulation material used as part of a clearance reduction system shall have a thermal conductivity of 1.0 Btu in./ft^2/hr-°F (0.144 W/m-K) or less.
(9) At least 1 in. (25 mm) shall be between the appliance and the protector. The clearance between the appliance and the combustible surface shall not be reduced below that allowed in Table 10.2.4.
(10) All clearances and thicknesses are minimum; larger clearances and thicknesses are acceptable.
(11) Listed single-wall connectors shall be installed in accordance with the manufacturers' installation instructions.

10.2.6 Furnace Plenums and Air Ducts. Where an air conditioner is installed within an enclosure, the installation shall comply with 10.3.8.4.

10.2.7* Refrigeration Coils. The installation of refrigeration coils shall be in accordance with 10.3.9 and 10.3.10.

10.2.8 Switches in Electrical Supply Line. Means for interrupting the electrical supply to the air-conditioning appliance and to its associated cooling tower shall be in accordance with *NFPA 70, National Electrical Code.*

10.3 Central Heating Boilers and Furnaces.

10.3.1 Application.

10.3.1.1 Central heating furnaces and boilers having input ratings up to and including 400,000 Btu/hr shall be listed in accordance with the following as applicable:

(1) Furnaces listed in accordance with ANSI Z21.47/CSA 2.3, *Gas-Fired Central Furnaces*
(2) Low-pressure boilers listed in accordance with ANSI Z21.13/CSA 4.9, *Gas-Fired Low-Pressure Steam and Hot Water Boilers*

10.3.1.2* Furnaces and boilers having input ratings greater than 400,000 Btu/hr shall be listed or in accordance with 9.1.1.2 and 9.1.1.3.

10.3.2 Location. Central heating furnace and low-pressure boiler installations in bedrooms or bathrooms shall comply with one of the following:

(1) Central heating furnaces and low-pressure boilers shall be installed in a closet equipped with a weather-stripped door with no openings, and with a self-closing device. All combustion air shall be obtained from the outdoors in accordance with 9.3.3.
(2) Central heating furnaces and low-pressure boilers shall be of the direct vent type.

10.3.3 Clearances.

10.3.3.1 Listed central heating furnaces and low-pressure boilers shall be installed with clearances in accordance with the manufacturer's instructions.

10.3.3.2 Unlisted central heating furnaces and low-pressure boilers shall be installed with clearances from combustible material not less than those specified in Table 10.3.3.2.

10.3.3.3 Central heating furnaces and low-pressure boilers shall be permitted to be installed with reduced clearances to combustible material, provided that the combustible material or appliance is protected as described in Table 10.2.4 and Figure 10.3.3.3(a) through Figure 10.3.3.3(c), and such reduction is allowed by the manufacturer's installation instructions.

10.3.3.4 Front clearance shall be sufficient for servicing the burner and the furnace or boiler.

10.3.3.5 Where the furnace plenum is adjacent to plaster on metal lath or noncombustible material attached to combustible material, the clearance shall be measured to the surface of the plaster or other noncombustible finish where the clearance specified is 2 in. (50 mm) or less.

10.3.3.6 The clearances to these appliances shall not interfere with combustion air, draft hood clearance and relief, and accessibility for servicing.

10.3.3.7 Supply air ducts connecting to listed central heating furnaces shall have the same minimum clearance to combustibles as required for the furnace supply plenum for a distance of not less than 3 ft (0.9 m) from the supply plenum. Clearance shall not be required beyond the 3 ft (0.9 m) distance.

10.3.3.8 Supply air ducts connecting to unlisted central heating furnaces equipped with temperature limit controls with a maximum setting of 250°F (121°C) shall have a minimum clearance to combustibles of 6 in. (150 mm) for a distance of not less than 6 ft (1.8 m) from the furnace supply plenum.

Table 10.3.3.2 Clearances to Combustible Material for Unlisted Furnaces and Boilers

	Minimum Clearance (in.)					
Appliance	Above and Sides of Furnace Plenum	Top of Boiler	Jacket Sides and Rear	Front	Draft Hood and Barometric Draft Regulator	Single-Wall Vent Connector
I Automatically fired, forced air or gravity system, equipped with temperature limit control that cannot be set higher than 250°F (121°C)	6	—	6	18	6	18
II Automatically fired heating boilers — steam boilers operating at not over 15 psi (103 kPa) and hot water boilers operating at 250°F (121°C) or less	6	6	6	18	18	18
III Central heating boilers and furnaces, other than in I or II	18	18	18	18	18	18

For SI units, 1 in. = 25.4 mm.
Note: See Section 10.3 for additional requirements for central heating boilers and furnaces.

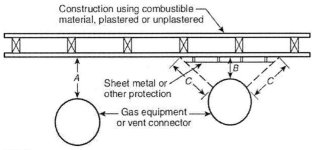

Notes:
(1) A equals the clearance with no protection specified in Tables 10.3.3.2 and 12.8.4.4 and in the sections applying to various types of equipment.
(2) B equals the reduced clearance permitted in accordance with Table 10.2.4.
(3) The protection applied to the construction using combustible material shall extend far enough in each direction to make C equal to A.

FIGURE 10.3.3.3(a) Extent of Protection Necessary to Reduce Clearances from Gas Appliance or Vent Connectors.

Clearance shall not be required beyond the 6 ft (1.8 m) distance.

10.3.3.9 Central heating furnaces other than those listed in 10.3.3.7 or 10.3.3.8 shall have clearances from the supply ducts of not less than 18 in. (460 mm) from the furnace plenum for the first 3 ft (0.9 m), then 6 in. (150 mm) for the next 3 ft (0.9 m), and 1 in. (25 mm) beyond 6 ft (1.8 m).

10.3.4 Assembly and Installation. A central heating boiler or furnace shall be installed in accordance with the manufacturer's instructions in one of the following manners:

(1) On a floor of noncombustible construction with noncombustible flooring and surface finish and with no combustible material against the underside thereof
(2) On fire-resistive slabs or arches having no combustible material against the underside thereof

Exception No. 1: Appliances listed for installation on a combustible floor.

Exception No. 2: Installation on a floor protected in an approved manner.

10.3.5 Temperature or Pressure Limiting Devices. Steam and hot water boilers, respectively, shall be provided with approved automatic limiting devices for shutting down the burner(s) to prevent boiler steam pressure or boiler water temperature from exceeding the maximum allowable working pressure or temperature. Safety limit controls shall not be used as operating controls.

10.3.6 Low-Water Cutoff. All water boilers and steam boilers shall be provided with an automatic means to shut off the fuel supply to the burner(s) if the boiler water level drops below the lowest safe water line. In lieu of the low-water cutoff, water tube or coil-type boilers that require forced circulation to prevent overheating and failure shall have an approved flow sensing device arranged to shut down the boiler when the flow rate is inadequate to protect the boiler against overheating.

10.3.7* Steam Safety and Pressure Relief Valves. Steam and hot water boilers shall be equipped, respectively, with listed or

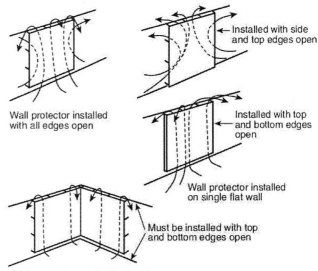

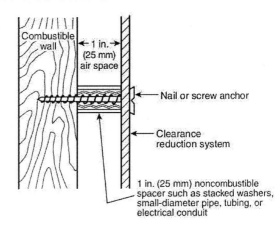

Notes:
(1) Masonry walls can be attached to combustible walls using wall ties.
(2) Spacers should not be used directly behind appliance or connector.

FIGURE 10.3.3.3(b) Wall Protector Clearance Reduction System.

approved steam safety or pressure relief valves of appropriate discharge capacity and conforming with ASME requirements. A shutoff valve shall not be placed between the relief valve and the boiler or on discharge pipes between such valves and the atmosphere.

10.3.7.1 Relief valves shall be piped to discharge near the floor.

10.3.7.2 The entire discharged piping shall be at least the same size as the relief valve discharge piping.

10.3.7.3 Discharge piping shall not contain threaded end connection at its termination point.

10.3.8 Furnace Plenums and Air Ducts.

10.3.8.1 Furnace plenums and air ducts shall be installed in accordance with NFPA 90A or NFPA 90B.

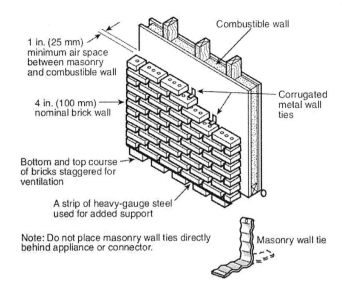

FIGURE 10.3.3.3(c) Masonry Clearance Reduction System.

10.3.8.2 A furnace plenum supplied as a part of a furnace shall be installed in accordance with the manufacturer's instructions.

10.3.8.3* Where a furnace plenum is not supplied with the furnace, any fabrication and installation instructions provided by the manufacturer shall be followed. The method of connecting supply and return ducts shall facilitate proper circulation of air.

10.3.8.4 Where a furnace is installed so supply ducts carry air circulated by the furnace to areas outside the space containing the furnace, the return air shall also be handled by a duct(s) sealed to the furnace casing and terminating outside the space containing the furnace. Return air shall not be taken from the mechanical room containing the furnace.

10.3.9 Refrigeration Coils. The installation of refrigeration coils shall comply with the following requirements:

(1) A refrigeration coil shall not be installed in conjunction with a forced air furnace where circulation of cooled air is provided by the furnace blower, unless the blower has sufficient capacity to overcome the external static pressure resistance imposed by the duct system and refrigeration coil at the air flow rate for heating or cooling, whichever is greater.
(2) Furnaces shall not be located upstream from refrigeration coils, unless the refrigeration coil is designed or equipped so as not to develop excessive temperature or pressure.
(3) Refrigeration coils shall be installed in parallel with or on the downstream side of central furnaces to avoid condensation in the heating element, unless the furnace has been specifically listed for downstream installation. With a parallel flow arrangement, the dampers or other means used to control flow of air shall be sufficiently tight to prevent any circulation of cooled air through the furnace.
(4) Means shall be provided for disposal of condensate and to prevent dripping of condensate on the heating element.

10.3.10 Cooling Units Used with Heating Boilers.

10.3.10.1 Boilers, where used in conjunction with refrigeration systems, shall be installed so that the chilled medium is piped in parallel with the heating boiler with appropriate valves to prevent the chilled medium from entering the heating boiler.

10.3.10.2 Where hot water heating boilers are connected to heating coils located in air-handling units where they can be exposed to refrigerated air circulation, such boiler piping systems shall be equipped with flow control valves or other automatic means to prevent gravity circulation of the boiler water during the cooling cycle.

10.4 Clothes Dryers.

10.4.1 Application. Clothes dryers shall be listed in accordance with ANSI Z21.5.1/CSA 7.1, *Gas Clothes Dryer, Volume I, Type 1 Clothes Dryers*, or ANSI Z21.5.2/CSA 7.2, *Gas Clothes Dryer, Volume II, Type 2 Clothes Dryers*.

10.4.2 Clearance. The installation of clothes dryers shall comply with the following requirements:

(1) Type 1 clothes dryers shall be installed with a minimum clearance of 6 in. (150 mm) from adjacent combustible material. Clothes dryers listed for installation at reduced clearances shall be installed in accordance with the manufacturer's installation instructions. Type 1 clothes dryers installed in closets shall be specifically listed for such installation.
(2) Type 2 clothes dryers shall be installed with clearances of not less than those shown on the marking plate and in the manufacturer's instructions. Type 2 clothes dryers designed and marked "For use only in noncombustible locations" shall not be installed elsewhere.

10.4.3 Exhausting to the Outdoors. Type 1 and Type 2 clothes dryers shall be exhausted to the outdoors.

10.4.4 Provisions for Make-Up Air.

10.4.4.1 Make-up air shall be provided for Type 1 clothes dryers in accordance with the manufacturers' installation instructions.

10.4.4.2 Provision for make-up air shall be provided for Type 2 clothes dryers, with a minimum free area of 1 in.^{2}/1000 Btu/hr (2200 mm^2/kW) total input rating of the dryer(s) installed.

10.4.5 Exhaust Ducts for Type 1 Clothes Dryers.

10.4.5.1 A clothes dryer exhaust duct shall not be connected into any vent connector, gas vent, chimney, crawl space, attic, or other similar concealed space.

10.4.5.2 Ducts for exhausting clothes dryers shall not be assembled with screws or other fastening means that extend into the duct and that would catch lint and reduce the efficiency of the exhaust system.

10.4.5.3 Exhaust ducts shall be constructed of rigid metallic material. Transition ducts used to connect the dryer to the exhaust duct shall be listed and labeled in accordance with UL 2158A, *Clothes Dryer Transition Ducts*, and installed in accordance with the clothes dryer manufacturer's installation instructions.

10.4.6 Exhaust Ducts for Type 2 Clothes Dryers.

10.4.6.1 Exhaust ducts for Type 2 clothes dryers shall comply with 10.4.5.

10.4.6.2 Exhaust ducts for Type 2 clothes dryers shall be constructed of sheet metal or other noncombustible material. Such ducts shall be equivalent in strength and corrosion resistance to ducts made of galvanized sheet steel not less than 0.0195 in. (0.5 mm) thick.

10.4.6.3 Type 2 clothes dryers shall be equipped or installed with lint-controlling means.

10.4.6.4 Where ducts pass through walls, floors, or partitions, the space around the duct shall be sealed with noncombustible material.

10.4.6.5 Multiple installations of Type 2 clothes dryers shall be made in a manner to prevent adverse operation due to back pressures that might be created in the exhaust systems.

10.4.7 Multiple-Family or Public Use.
All clothes dryers installed for multiple-family or public use shall be installed as specified for a Type 2 clothes dryer under 10.4.6.

10.5 Conversion Burners.
Installation of conversion burners shall conform to ANSI Z21.8, *Installation of Domestic Gas Conversion Burners*.

10.6 Decorative Appliances for Installation in Vented Fireplaces.

10.6.1 Application. Decorative appliances for installation in vented fireplaces shall be listed in accordance with ANSI Z21.60/CSA 2.26, *Decorative Gas Appliances for Installation in Solid-Fuel Burning Fireplaces*.

10.6.2* Prohibited Installations. Decorative appliances for installation in vented fireplaces shall not be installed in bathrooms or bedrooms unless the bedroom or bathroom has the required volume in accordance with 9.3.2.

10.6.3 Installation. A decorative appliance for installation in a vented fireplace shall be installed only in a vented fireplace having a working chimney flue and constructed of noncombustible materials. These appliances shall not be thermostatically controlled.

10.6.3.1 A decorative appliance for installation in a vented fireplace shall be installed in accordance with the manufacturer's installation instructions.

10.6.3.2 A decorative appliance for installation in a vented fireplace, where installed in a manufactured home, shall be listed for installation in manufactured homes.

10.6.4 Fireplace Screens. A fireplace screen shall be installed with a decorative appliance for installation in a vented fireplace.

10.7 Gas Fireplaces, Vented.

10.7.1 Application. Vented gas fireplaces shall be listed in accordance with ANSI Z21.50/CSA 2.22, *Vented Decorative Gas Appliances*.

10.7.2* Prohibited Installations. Vented gas fireplaces shall not be installed in bathrooms or bedrooms unless the bedroom or bathroom has the required volume in accordance with 9.3.2.

Exception: Direct vent gas fireplaces.

10.7.3 Installation. The installation of vented gas fireplaces shall comply with the following requirements:

(1) Vented gas fireplaces shall be installed in accordance with the manufacturer's installation instructions and where installed in or attached to combustible material shall be specifically listed for such installation.
(2) Panels, grilles, and access doors that are required to be removed for normal servicing operations shall not be attached to the building.
(3) Direct vent gas fireplaces shall be installed with the vent air intake terminal in the outdoors and in accordance with the manufacturer's instructions.

10.7.4 Combustion and Circulating Air. Combustion and circulating air shall be provided in accordance with Section 9.3.

10.8 Direct Gas-Fired Heating and Forced Ventilation Appliances.

10.8.1 Application. Direct gas-fired heating and forced ventilation appliances for commercial and industrial applications shall be listed in accordance with the following standards as applicable:

(1) ANSI Z83.4/CSA 3.7, *Non-Recirculating Direct Gas-Fired Heating and Forced Ventilation Appliances for Commercial and Industrial Application*.
(2) ANSI Z83.18, *Recirculating Direct Gas-Fired Heating and Forced Ventilation Appliances for Commercial and Industrial Application*.

10.8.2 Prohibited Installations.

10.8.2.1 Direct gas-fired heating and forced ventilation appliances shall not serve any area containing sleeping quarters.

10.8.2.2 Non-recirculating direct gas-fired heating and forced ventilation appliances shall not recirculate room air.

10.8.2.3* Recirculating direct gas-fired industrial air heaters shall not recirculate room air in buildings that contain flammable solids, liquids, or gases; explosive materials; or substances that can become toxic when exposed to flame or heat.

10.8.3 Installation. Installation of direct gas-fired heating and forced ventilation appliances shall comply with 10.8.3.1 through 10.8.3.3.

10.8.3.1 Direct gas-fired heating and forced ventilation appliances shall be installed in accordance with the manufacturer's instructions.

10.8.3.2 Direct gas-fired heating and forced ventilation appliances shall be permitted to provide fresh air ventilation.

10.8.3.3 Direct gas-fired heating and forced ventilation appliances shall be provided with access for removal of burners; for replacement of motors, controls, filters, and other working parts; and for adjustment and lubrication of parts requiring maintenance.

10.8.4 Clearance from Combustible Materials. Direct gas-fired heating and forced ventilation appliances shall be installed with a clearance from combustible materials of not less than that shown on the rating plate and the manufacturer's instructions.

10.8.5 Air Supply. The air supply to direct gas-fired heating and forced ventilation appliances shall be in accordance with 10.8.5.1 through 10.8.5.3.

10.8.5.1 All air to the non-recirculating direct gas-fired heating and forced ventilation appliance shall be ducted directly from outdoors.

10.8.5.2 Ventilation air to the recirculating direct gas-fired heating and forced ventilation appliance shall be ducted directly from outdoors. Air in excess of the minimum ventilation air specified on the heater's rating plate shall be taken from the building, ducted directly from outdoors, or a combination of both.

10.8.5.3 Where outdoor air dampers or closing louvers are used, they shall be verified to be in the open position prior to main burner operation.

10.8.6 Atmospheric Vents or Gas Reliefs or Bleeds. Direct gas-fired heating and forced ventilation appliances with valve train components equipped with atmospheric vents, gas reliefs, or bleeds shall have their vent lines, gas reliefs, or bleeds lead to a safe point outdoors. Means shall be employed on these lines to prevent water from entering and to prevent blockage from insects and foreign matter. An atmospheric vent line shall not be required to be provided on a valve train component equipped with a listed vent limiter.

10.8.7 Relief Openings. The design of the installation shall include adequate provisions to permit the direct gas-fired heating and forced ventilation appliances to operate at their rated airflow without overpressurizing the space served by the heater by taking into account the structure's designed infiltration rate, properly designed relief openings, or an interlocked powered exhaust system, or a combination of these methods.

10.8.7.1 The structure's designed infiltration rate and the size of relief opening(s) shall be determined by engineering methods.

10.8.7.2 Louver or counterbalanced gravity damper relief openings shall be permitted. Where motorized dampers or closable louvers are used, they shall be proved to be in their open position prior to main burner operation.

10.8.8 Purging. Inlet ducting, when used, shall be purged with at least four air changes prior to an ignition attempt.

10.9 Duct Furnaces.

10.9.1 Application. Duct furnaces with inputs of 10 MBtu/hr or less shall be listed in accordance with ANSI Z83.8/CSA 2.6, *Gas Unit Heaters, as Packaged Heaters, Gas Utility Heaters, and Gas-fired Duct Furnaces*.

10.9.2 Clearances. Duct furnaces shall be installed with clearances of at least 6 in. (150 mm) between adjacent walls, ceilings, and floors of combustible material, and the furnace draft hood and shall comply with the following:

(1) Duct furnaces listed for installation at lesser clearances shall be installed in accordance with the manufacturer's installation instructions.
(2) The clearance shall not interfere with combustion air and accessibility.

10.9.3 Installation of Duct Furnaces. Duct furnaces shall be installed in accordance with the manufacturers' instructions.

10.9.4 Access Panels. The ducts connected to duct furnaces shall have removable access panels on both the upstream and downstream sides of the furnace.

10.9.5 Location of Draft Hood and Controls. The controls, combustion air inlet, and draft hoods for duct furnaces shall be located outside the ducts. The draft hood shall be located in the same enclosure from which combustion air is taken.

10.9.6 Circulating Air. Where a duct furnace is installed so that supply ducts carry air circulated by the furnace to areas outside the space containing the furnace, the return air shall also be handled by a duct(s) sealed to the furnace casing and terminating outside the space containing the furnace. The duct furnace shall be installed on the positive-pressure side of the circulating air blower.

10.9.7 Duct Furnaces Used with Refrigeration Systems.

10.9.7.1 A duct furnace shall not be installed in conjunction with a refrigeration coil where circulation of cooled air is provided by the blower.

Exception: Where the blower has sufficient capacity to overcome the external static resistance imposed by the duct system, the furnace, and the cooling coil and the air throughput necessary for heating or cooling, whichever is greater.

10.9.7.2 Duct furnaces used in conjunction with cooling appliances shall be installed in parallel with or on the upstream side of cooling coils to avoid condensation within heating elements. With a parallel flow arrangement, the dampers or other means used to control the flow of air shall be sufficiently tight to prevent any circulation of cooled air through the unit.

Exception: Where the duct furnace has been specifically listed for downstream installation.

10.9.7.3* Where a duct furnace is installed downstream of an evaporative cooler or air washer, the heat exchanger shall be constructed of corrosion-resistant materials. Air washers operating with chilled water that deliver air below the dew point of the ambient air at the duct furnace shall be considered as refrigeration systems.

10.9.8 Installation in Commercial Garages and Aircraft Hangars. Duct furnaces installed in garages for more than three motor vehicles or in aircraft hangars shall be installed in accordance with 9.1.11 and 9.1.12.

10.10 Floor Furnaces.

10.10.1 Application. Floor furnaces shall be listed in accordance with ANSI Z21.86/CSA 2.32, *Vented Gas-Fired Space Heating Appliances*.

10.10.2 Installation. The installation of floor furnaces shall comply with the following requirements:

(1) Floor furnaces shall be installed in accordance with the manufacturers' installation instructions.
(2) Thermostats controlling floor furnaces shall not be located in a room or space that can be separated from the room or space in which the register of the floor furnace is located.

10.10.3 Temperature Limit Controls. Automatically operated floor furnaces shall be equipped with temperature limit controls.

10.10.4 Combustion and Circulating Air. Combustion and circulating air shall be provided in accordance with Section 9.3.

10.10.5 Placement. The following provisions apply to furnaces that serve one story:

(1) *Floors.* Floor furnaces shall not be installed in the floor of any doorway, stairway landing, aisle, or passageway of any enclosure, public or private, or in an exitway from any such room or space.
(2) *Walls and Corners.* The register of a floor furnace with a horizontal warm air outlet shall not be placed closer than 6 in. (150 mm) from the nearest wall. A distance of at least 18 in. (460 mm) from two adjoining sides of the floor furnace register to walls shall be provided to eliminate the necessity of occupants walking over the warm air discharge. The remaining sides shall be a minimum of 6 in. (150 mm) from a wall. Wall register models shall not be placed closer than 6 in. (150 mm) to a corner.
(3) *Draperies.* The furnace shall be placed so that a door, drapery, or similar object cannot be nearer than 12 in. (300 mm) to any portion of the register of the furnace.

10.10.6 Bracing. The space provided for the furnace shall be framed with doubled joists and with headers not lighter than the joists.

10.10.7 Support. Means shall be provided to support the furnace when the floor register is removed.

10.10.8 Clearance. The lowest portion of the floor furnace shall have at least a 6 in. (150 mm) clearance from the general ground level. A reduced clearance to a minimum of 2 in. (50 mm) shall be permitted, provided the lower 6 in. (150 mm) portion of the floor furnace is sealed by the manufacturer to prevent entrance of water. Where these clearances are not present, the ground below and to the sides shall be excavated to form a "basin-like" pit under the furnace so that the required clearance is provided beneath the lowest portion of the furnace. A 12 in. (300 mm) clearance shall be provided on all sides except the control side, which shall have an 18 in. (460 mm) clearance.

10.10.9 Access. The space in which any floor furnace is installed shall be accessible by an opening in the foundation not less than 24 in. × 18 in. (610 mm × 460 mm) or by a trapdoor not less than 24 in. × 24 in. (610 mm × 610 mm) in any cross-section thereof, and a passageway not less than 24 in. × 18 in. (610 mm × 460 mm) in any cross-section thereof.

10.10.10 Seepage Pan. Where the excavation exceeds 12 in. (300 mm) in depth or water seepage is likely to collect, a watertight copper pan, concrete pit, or other suitable material shall be used, unless adequate drainage is provided or the appliance is sealed by the manufacturer to meet this condition. A copper pan shall be made of not less than 16 oz/ft^2 (4.9 kg/m^2) sheet copper. The pan shall be anchored in place so as to prevent floating, and the walls shall extend at least 4 in. (100 mm) above the ground level with at least a 6 in. (150 mm) clearance on all sides, except on the control side, which shall have at least an 18 in. (460 mm) clearance.

10.10.11 Wind Protection. Floor furnaces shall be protected, where necessary, against severe wind conditions.

10.10.12 Upper Floor Installations. Floor furnaces shall be permitted to be installed in an upper floor, provided the furnace assembly projects below into a utility room, closet, garage, or similar nonhabitable space. In such installations, the floor furnace shall be enclosed completely (entirely separated from the nonhabitable space) with means for air intake to meet the provisions of Section 9.3, with access for servicing, minimum furnace clearances of 6 in. (150 mm) to all sides and bottom, and with the enclosure constructed of Portland cement plaster or metal lath or other noncombustible material.

10.10.13 First Floor Installation. Floor furnaces installed in the first or ground floors of buildings shall not be required to be enclosed unless the basements of these buildings have been converted to apartments or sleeping quarters, in which case the floor furnace shall be enclosed as specified for upper floor installations and shall project into a nonhabitable space.

10.11 Food Service Appliance, Floor-Mounted.

10.11.1 Application. Floor-mounted food service appliances shall be listed in accordance with ANSI Z83.11/CSA 1.8, *Gas Food Service Equipment*.

10.11.2 Clearance for Listed Appliances. Floor-mounted food service appliances, such as ranges for hotels and restaurants, deep fat fryers, unit broilers, kettles, steam cookers, steam generators, and baking and roasting ovens, shall be installed at least 6 in. (150 mm) from combustible material except that at least a 2 in. (50 mm) clearance shall be maintained between a draft hood and combustible material. Floor-mounted food service appliances listed for installation at lesser clearances shall be installed in accordance with the manufacturer's installation instructions. Appliances designed and marked "For use only in noncombustible locations" shall not be installed elsewhere.

10.11.3 Mounting on Combustible Floor.

10.11.3.1 Floor-mounted food service appliances that are listed specifically for installation on floors constructed of combustible material shall be permitted to be installed on combustible floors in accordance with the manufacturer's installation instructions.

10.11.3.2 Floor-mounted food service appliances that are not listed for installation on a combustible floor shall be installed in accordance with 10.11.4 or be installed in accordance with one of the following:

(1) Where the appliance is set on legs that provide not less than 18 in. (460 mm) open space under the base of the appliance or where it has no burners and no portion of any oven or broiler within 18 in. (460 mm) of the floor, it shall be permitted to be installed on a combustible floor without special floor protection, provided at least one sheet metal baffle is between the burner and the floor.
(2) Where the appliance is set on legs that provide not less than 8 in. (200 mm) open space under the base of the appliance, it shall be permitted to be installed on combustible floors, provided the floor under the appliance is protected with not less than 3/8 in. (9.5 mm) insulating millboard covered with sheet metal not less than 0.0195 in. (0.5 mm) thick. The preceding specified floor protection shall extend not less than 6 in. (150 mm) beyond the appliance on all sides.
(3) Where the appliance is set on legs that provide not less than 4 in. (100 mm) under the base of the appliance, it shall be permitted to be installed on combustible floors, provided the floor under the appliance is protected with hollow masonry not less than 4 in. (100 mm) in thickness covered with sheet metal not less than 0.0195 in. (0.5 mm) thick. Such masonry courses shall be laid with ends unsealed and joints matched in such a way as to provide for free circulation of air through the masonry.

(4) Where the appliance does not have legs at least 4 in. (100 mm) high, it shall be permitted to be installed on combustible floors, provided the floor under the appliance is protected by two courses of 4 in. (100 mm) hollow clay tile, or equivalent, with courses laid at right angles and with ends unsealed and joints matched in such a way as to provide for free circulation of air through such masonry courses, and covered with steel plate not less than $\frac{3}{16}$ in. (4.8 mm) in thickness.

10.11.4 Installation on Noncombustible Floor.

10.11.4.1 Floor-installed food service appliances that are designed and marked "For use only in noncombustible locations" shall be installed on floors of noncombustible construction with noncombustible flooring and surface finish and with no combustible material against the underside thereof, or on noncombustible slabs or arches having no combustible material against the underside thereof.

10.11.4.2 Such construction shall in all cases extend not less than 12 in. (300 mm) beyond the appliance on all sides.

10.11.5 Combustible Material Adjacent to Cooking Top. Food service ranges shall be installed to provide clearance to combustible material of not less than 18 in. (460 mm) horizontally for a distance up to 2 ft (0.6 m) above the surface of the cooking top where the combustible material is not completely shielded by high shelving, a warming closet, or other system. Reduced combustible material clearances are permitted where protected in accordance with Table 10.2.4.

10.11.6 Use with Casters. Floor-mounted appliances with casters shall be listed for such construction and shall be installed in accordance with the manufacturer's installation instructions for limiting the movement of the appliance to prevent strain on the connection.

10.11.7 Level Installation. Floor-mounted food service appliances shall be installed level on a firm foundation.

10.11.8* Ventilation. Means shall be provided to properly ventilate the space in which a food service appliance is installed to permit proper combustion of the gas.

10.12 Food Service Appliances, Counter Appliances.

10.12.1 Application. Food service counter appliances shall be listed in accordance with ANSI Z83.11/CSA 1.8, *Gas Food Service Equipment*.

10.12.2 Vertical Clearance. A vertical distance of not less than 48 in. (1.2 m) shall be provided between the top of all food service hot plates and griddles and combustible material.

10.12.3 Clearance for Appliances. Food service counter appliances, where installed on combustible surfaces, shall be installed with a minimum horizontal clearance of 6 in. (150 mm) from combustible material, except that at least a 2 in. (50 mm) clearance shall be maintained between a draft hood and combustible material. Food service counter appliances listed for installation at lesser clearances shall be installed in accordance with the manufacturer's installation instructions.

10.13 Household Cooking Appliances.

10.13.1 Application. Household cooking appliances shall be listed in accordance with ANSI Z21.1/CSA 1.1, *Household Cooking Gas Appliances*.

10.13.2 Installation. Floor-mounted and built-in household cooking appliances shall be installed in accordance with the manufacturer's installation instructions.

10.13.3 Clearances. Floor-mounted household cooking appliances, where installed on combustible floors, shall be set on their own bases or legs and shall not interfere with combustion air, accessibility for operation, and servicing.

10.13.3.1* Vertical Clearance Above Cooking Top. Household cooking appliances shall have a vertical clearance above the cooking top of not less than 30 in. (760 mm) to combustible material or metal cabinets. A minimum clearance of 24 in. (610 mm) shall be permitted when one of the following is installed:

(1) The underside of the combustible material or metal cabinet above the cooking top is protected with not less than $\frac{1}{4}$ in. (6 mm) insulating millboard covered with sheet metal not less than 0.0122 in. (0.3 mm) thick.
(2) A metal ventilating hood of sheet metal not less than 0.0122 in. (0.3 mm) thick is installed above the cooking top with a clearance of not less than $\frac{1}{4}$ in. (6 mm) between the hood and the underside of the combustible material or metal cabinet, and the hood is at least as wide as the appliance and is centered over the appliance.
(3) A cooking appliance or microwave oven is installed over a cooking appliance and conforms to the terms of the upper appliance's manufacturer's installation instructions.

10.14 Illuminating Appliances.

10.14.1 Clearances for Listed Appliances. Listed illuminating appliances shall be installed in accordance with the manufacturer's installation instructions.

10.14.2 Clearances for Unlisted Appliances.

10.14.2.1 Enclosed Type. Clearance shall comply with the following:

(1) Unlisted enclosed illuminating appliances installed outdoors shall be installed with clearances in any direction from combustible material of not less than 12 in. (300 mm).
(2) Unlisted enclosed illuminating appliances installed indoors shall be installed with clearances in any direction from combustible material of not less than 18 in. (460 mm).

10.14.2.2 Open-Flame Type. Clearance shall comply with the following:

(1) Unlisted open-flame illuminating appliances installed outdoors shall have clearances from combustible material not less than that specified in Table 10.14.2.2. The distance from ground level to the base of the burner shall be a minimum of 7 ft (2.1 m) where installed within 2 ft (0.6 m) of walkways. Lesser clearances shall be permitted to be used where acceptable to the authority having jurisdiction.
(2) Unlisted open-flame illuminating appliances installed outdoors shall be equipped with a limiting orifice or other limiting devices that maintain a flame height consistent with the clearance from combustible material, as given in Table 10.14.2.2.

(3) Appliances designed for flame heights in excess of 30 in. (760 mm) shall be approved. Such appliances shall be equipped with a safety shutoff device or automatic ignition.
(4) Clearances to combustible material from unlisted open-flame illuminating appliances shall be approved.

10.14.3 Installation on Buildings. Illuminating appliances designed for installation on a wall or ceiling shall be securely attached to substantial structures in such a manner that they are not dependent on the gas piping for support.

10.14.4 Installation on Posts. Illuminating appliances designed for installation on a post shall be securely and rigidly attached to a post. Posts shall be rigidly installed. The strength and rigidity of posts greater than 3 ft (0.9 m) in height shall be at least equivalent to that of a 2½ in. (64 mm) diameter post constructed of 0.064 in. (1.6 mm) thick steel or a 1 in. Schedule 40 steel pipe. Posts 3 ft (0.9 m) or less in height shall not be smaller than a ¾ in. Schedule 40 steel pipe. Drain openings shall be provided near the base of posts where water collecting inside the posts is possible.

10.14.5 Appliance Pressure Regulators. Where an appliance pressure regulator is not supplied with an illuminating appliance and the service line is not equipped with a service pressure regulator, an appliance pressure regulator shall be installed in the line serving one or more illuminating appliances.

10.15 Incinerators, Commercial-Industrial. Commercial-industrial-type incinerators shall be constructed and installed in accordance with NFPA 82.

10.16 Infrared Heaters.

10.16.1 Application. Infrared heaters having an input rating of 400,000 Btu/hr or less shall be listed in accordance with ANSI Z83.19/CSA 2.35, *Gas-Fired High Intensity Infrared Heaters*, or ANSI Z83.20/CSA 2.34, *Gas-Fired Tubular and Low-Intensity Infrared Heaters*.

10.16.2 Support. Suspended-type infrared heaters shall be fixed in position independent of gas and electric supply lines. Hangers and brackets shall be of noncombustible material. Heaters subject to vibration shall be provided with vibration-isolating hangers.

Table 10.14.2.2 Clearances for Unlisted Outdoor Open-Flame Illuminating Appliances

Flame Height Above Burner Head (in.)	Minimum Clearance from Combustible Material (ft)*	
	Horizontal	Vertical
12	2	6
18	3	8
24	3	10
30	4	12

For SI units, 1 in. = 25.4 mm, 1 ft = 0.305 m.
*Measured from the nearest portion of the burner head.

10.16.3 Clearance. The installation of infrared heaters shall meet the following clearance requirements:

(1) Listed heaters shall be installed with clearances from combustible material in accordance the manufacturer's installation instructions.
(2) Unlisted heaters shall be installed in accordance with clearances from combustible material acceptable to the authority having jurisdiction.
(3) In locations used for the storage of combustible materials, signs shall be posted to specify the maximum permissible stacking height to maintain required clearances from the heater to the combustibles.

10.16.4 Combustion and Ventilation Air.

10.16.4.1 Where unvented infrared heaters are used, natural or mechanical means shall be provided to supply and exhaust at least 4 ft^3/min/1000 Btu/hr (0.38 m^3/min/kW) input of installed heaters.

10.16.4.2 Exhaust openings for removing flue products shall be above the level of the heaters.

10.16.5 Installation in Commercial Garages and Aircraft Hangars. Overhead heaters installed in garages for more than three motor vehicles or in aircraft hangars shall be listed and shall be installed in accordance with 9.1.11 and 9.1.12.

10.17 Open-Top Broiler Units.

10.17.1 Application. Open-top broiler units shall be listed in accordance with ANSI Z83.11/CSA 1.8, *Gas Food Service Equipment*, or ANSI Z21.1/CSA 1.1, *Household Cooking Gas Appliances*, and installed in accordance with the manufacturer's installation instructions.

10.17.2 Protection Above Domestic Units. Domestic open-top broiler units shall be provided with a metal ventilating hood not less than 0.0122 in. (0.3 mm) thick with a clearance of not less than ¼ in. (6 mm) between the hood and the underside of combustible material or metal cabinets. A clearance of at least 24 in. (610 mm) shall be maintained between the cooking top and the combustible material or metal cabinet, and the hood shall be at least as wide as the open-top broiler unit and centered over the unit. Domestic open-top broiler units incorporating an integral exhaust system and listed for use without a ventilating hood shall not be required to be provided with a ventilating hood if installed in accordance with 10.13.3.1(1).

10.17.3 Commercial Units. Commercial open-top broiler units shall be provided with ventilation in accordance with NFPA 96.

10.18 Outdoor Cooking Appliances. Outdoor cooking appliances shall be listed in accordance with ANSI Z83.11/CSA 1.8, *Gas Food Service Equipment*, ANSI Z21.58/CSA 1.6, *Outdoor Cooking Gas Appliances*, or ANSI Z21.89/CSA 1.18, *Outdoor Cooking Specialty Gas Appliances*, and installed in accordance with the manufacturer's installation instructions.

10.19 Pool Heaters.

10.19.1 Application. Pool heaters shall be listed in accordance with ANSI Z21.56/CSA 4.7, *Gas-Fired Pool Heaters*.

10.19.2 Location. A pool heater shall be located or protected so as to minimize accidental contact of hot surfaces by persons.

10.19.3 Clearance. The installation of pool heaters shall meet the following requirements:

(1) The clearances shall not interfere with combustion air, draft hood or vent terminal clearance and relief, and accessibility for servicing.
(2) A pool heater shall be installed in accordance with the manufacturer's installation instructions.

10.19.4 Temperature or Pressure Limiting Devices. Where a pool heater is provided with overtemperature protection only and is installed with any device in the discharge line of the heater that can restrict the flow of water from the heater to the pool (such as a check valve, shutoff valve, therapeutic pool valving, or flow nozzles), a pressure relief valve shall be installed either in the heater or between the heater and the restrictive device.

10.19.5 Bypass Valves. Where an integral bypass system is not provided as a part of the pool heater, a bypass line and valve shall be installed between the inlet and outlet piping for use in adjusting the flow of water through the heater.

10.19.6 Venting. A pool heater listed for outdoor installation shall be installed with the venting means supplied by the manufacturer and in accordance with the manufacturer's instructions.

10.20 Refrigerators.

10.20.1 Application. Refrigerators shall be listed in accordance with ANSI Z21.19/CSA 1.4, *Refrigerators Using Gas Fuel*.

10.20.2 Clearance. Refrigerators shall be provided with clearances for ventilation at the top and back in accordance with the manufacturers' instructions. Where such instructions are not available, at least 2 in. (50 mm) shall be provided between the back of the refrigerator and the wall and at least 12 in. (300 mm) above the top.

10.20.3 Venting or Ventilating Kits Approved for Use with a Refrigerator. Where an accessory kit is used for conveying air for burner combustion or unit cooling to the refrigerator from areas outside the room in which it is located, or for conveying combustion products diluted with air containing waste heat from the refrigerator to areas outside the room in which it is located, the kit shall be installed in accordance with the refrigerator manufacturer's instructions.

10.21 Room Heaters.

10.21.1 Application. Room heaters shall be listed in accordance with 10.21.1.1 or 10.21.1.2.

10.21.1.1 Vented Room Heaters. Vented room heaters shall be listed in accordance with ANSI Z21.86/CSA 2.32, *Vented Gas-Fired Space Heating Appliances*, or ANSI Z21.88/CSA 2.33, *Vented Gas Fireplace Heaters*.

10.21.1.2 Unvented Room Heaters. Unvented room heaters shall be listed in accordance with ANSI Z21.11.2, *Gas-Fired Room Heaters—Volume II, Unvented Room Heaters*.

10.21.2* Prohibited Installations. Unvented room heaters shall not be installed in bathrooms or bedrooms.

Exception No. 1: Where approved, one listed wall-mounted, unvented room heater equipped with an oxygen depletion safety shutoff system shall be permitted to be installed in a bathroom, provided that the input rating does not exceed 6000 Btu/hr (1760 W/hr) and combustion and ventilation air is provided as specified in 10.1.2.

Exception No. 2: Where approved, one listed wall-mounted unvented room heater equipped with an oxygen depletion safety shutoff system shall be permitted to be installed in a bedroom, provided that the input rating does not exceed 10,000 Btu/hr (2930 W/hr) and combustion and ventilation air is provided as specified in 10.1.2.

10.21.3 Installations in Institutions. Room heaters shall not be installed in the following occupancies:

(1) Residential board and care
(2) Health care

10.21.4 Wall-Mounted Room Heaters. Wall-mounted room heaters shall not be installed in or attached to walls of combustible material unless listed for such installation.

10.22 Stationary Gas Engines. The installation of gas engines shall conform to NFPA 37.

10.22.1 Stationary gas engines shall not be rigidly connected to the gas supply piping.

10.23 Gas-Fired Toilets.

10.23.1 Clearance. A listed gas-fired toilet shall be installed in accordance with the manufacturer's installation instructions, provided that the clearance is in any case sufficient to afford ready accessibility for use, cleanout, and necessary servicing.

10.23.2 Installation on Combustible Floors. Listed gas-fired toilets installed on combustible floors shall be listed for such installation.

10.23.3 Installation. Vents or vent connectors that are capable of being contacted during casual use of the room in which the toilet is installed shall be protected or shielded to prevent such contact.

10.24 Unit Heaters.

10.24.1 Application. Unit heaters shall be listed in accordance with ANSI Z83.8/CSA 2.6, *Gas Unit Heaters, Gas Packaged Heaters, Gas Utility Heaters, and Gas-Fired Duct Furnaces*, and installed in accordance with the manufacturer's installation instructions.

10.24.2 Support. Suspended-type unit heaters shall be safely and adequately supported, with due consideration given to their weight and vibration characteristics. Hangers and brackets shall be of noncombustible material.

10.24.3 Clearance for Suspended-Type Unit Heaters. Suspended-type unit heaters shall meet the following requirements:

(1) Unit heaters shall be installed with clearances from combustible material of not less than 18 in. (460 mm) at the sides, 12 in. (300 mm) at the bottom, and 6 in. (150 mm) above the top where the unit heater has an internal draft hood, or 1 in. (25 mm) above the top of the sloping side of a vertical draft hood. A unit heater listed for reduced clearances shall be installed in accordance with the manufacturer's installation instructions.
(2) Clearances for servicing shall be in accordance with the manufacturers' installation instructions.

10.24.4 Combustion and Circulating Air. Combustion and circulating air shall be provided in accordance with Section 9.3.

10.24.5 Ductwork. A unit heater shall not be attached to a warm air duct system unless listed and marked for such installation.

10.24.6 Installation in Commercial Garages and Aircraft Hangars. Unit heaters installed in garages for more than three motor vehicles or in aircraft hangars shall be installed in accordance with 9.1.11 and 9.1.12.

10.25 Wall Furnaces.

10.25.1 Application. Wall furnaces shall be listed in accordance with ANSI Z21.86/CSA 2.32, *Vented Gas-Fired Space Heating Appliances.*

10.25.2 Installation.

10.25.2.1 Wall furnaces shall be installed in accordance with the manufacturer's installation instructions. Wall furnaces installed in or attached to combustible material shall be listed for such installation.

10.25.2.2 Vented wall furnaces connected to a Type B-W gas vent system listed only for a single story shall be installed only in single-story buildings or the top story of multistory buildings. Vented wall furnaces connected to a Type B-W gas vent system listed for installation in multistory buildings shall be permitted to be installed in single-story or multistory buildings. Type B-W gas vents shall be attached directly to a solid header plate that serves as a firestop at that point and that shall be permitted to be an integral part of the vented wall furnace, as illustrated in Figure 10.25.2.2. The stud space in which the vented wall furnace is installed shall be ventilated at the first ceiling level by installation of the ceiling plate spacers furnished with the gas vent. Firestop spacers shall be installed at each subsequent ceiling or floor level penetrated by the vent.

10.25.2.3 Direct vent wall furnaces shall be installed with the combustion air intake terminal outdoors.

10.25.2.4 Panels, grilles, and access doors that are required to be removed for normal servicing operations shall not be attached to the building. *(For additional information on the venting of wall furnaces, see Chapter 12.)*

10.25.3 Location. Wall furnaces shall be located so as not to cause a hazard to walls, floors, curtains, furniture, or doors. Wall furnaces installed between bathrooms and adjoining rooms shall not circulate air from bathrooms to other parts of the building.

10.25.4 Combustion and Circulating Air. Combustion and circulating air shall be provided in accordance with Section 9.3.

10.26 Water Heaters.

10.26.1 Application. Water heaters shall be listed in accordance with ANSI Z21.10.1/CSA 4.1, *Gas Water Heaters, Volume I, Storage Water Heaters with Input Ratings of 75,000 Btu per Hour or Less*, or ANSI Z21.10.3/CSA 4.3, *Gas Water Heaters, Volume III, Storage Water Heaters with Input Ratings Above 75,000 Btu per Hour, Circulating or Instantaneous*, and shall be installed in accordance with the manufacturer's installation instructions.

10.26.2 Location. Water heater installations in bedrooms and bathrooms shall comply with one of the following:

(1) Water heater shall be installed in a closet equipped with a weather-stripped door with no openings and with a self-

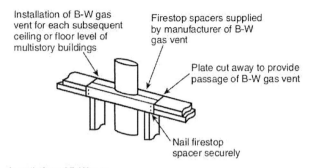

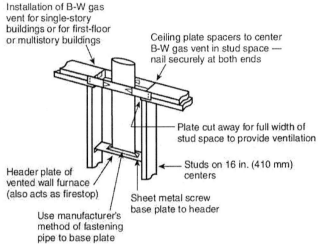

FIGURE 10.25.2.2 Installation of Type B-W Gas Vents for Vented Wall Furnaces.

closing device. All combustion air shall be obtained from the outdoors in accordance with 9.3.3.

(2) Water heater shall be of the direct vent type.

10.26.3 Clearance. The clearances shall not be such as to interfere with combustion air, draft hood clearance and relief, and accessibility for servicing. Listed water heaters shall be installed in accordance with the manufacturer's installation instructions.

10.26.4 Pressure Relief Devices. A water heater installation shall be provided with overpressure protection by means of a device listed in accordance with ANSI Z21.22/CSA 4.4, *Relief Valves for Hot Water Supply Systems*, and installed in accordance with the manufacturer's installation instructions. The pressure setting of the device shall exceed the water service pressure and shall not exceed the maximum pressure rating of the water heater.

10.26.5 Temperature Limiting Devices. A water heater installation or a hot water storage vessel installation shall be provided with overtemperature protection by means of an approved, listed device installed in accordance with the manufacturer's installation instructions.

10.26.6 Temperature, Pressure, and Vacuum Relief Devices. Temperature, pressure, and vacuum relief devices, or combinations thereof, and automatic gas shutoff devices shall be installed in accordance with the manufacturer's installation instructions. A shutoff valve shall not be placed between the relief valve and the water heater or on discharge pipes between such valves and the atmosphere. The hourly Btu discharge capacity or the rated steam relief capacity of the device shall not be less than the input rating of the water heater.

10.26.7 Automatic Instantaneous Type: Cold Water Supply. The water supply to an automatic instantaneous water heater that is equipped with a water flow-actuated control shall be such as to provide sufficient pressure to properly operate the control when water is drawn from the highest faucet served by the heater.

10.26.8* Antisiphon Devices. Means acceptable to the authority having jurisdiction shall be provided to prevent siphoning in any water heater or any tank to which a circulating water heater that incorporates a cold water inlet tube is attached.

10.27 Compressed Natural Gas (CNG) Vehicular Fuel Systems. The installation of compressed natural gas (CNG) fueling (dispensing) systems shall be in accordance with NFPA 52. Residential CNG fueling appliances shall be listed in accordance with ANSI/CSA NGV 5.1, *Residential Fueling Appliances*, and installed in accordance to the appliance manufacturer's installation instructions. Non-residential CNG fueling appliances shall be listed in accordance with ANSI/CSA NGV 5.2, *Vehicle Fueling Appliances (VFA)*, and installed in accordance with the appliance manufacturer's installation instructions.

10.28 Appliances for Installation in Manufactured Housing. Appliances installed in manufactured housing after the initial sale shall be listed for installation in manufactured housing, or approved, and shall be installed in accordance with the requirements of this code and the manufacturers' installation instructions. Appliances installed in the living space of manufactured housing shall be in accordance with the requirements of Section 9.3.

10.29 Fuel Cell Power Plants. Fuel cell power plants with a power output of less than 50 kW shall be listed in accordance with ANSI/CSA FC 1, *Fuel Cell Technologies — Part 3-100: Stationary Fuel Cell Power Systems — Safety*, and installed in accordance with the manufacturer's instructions. Fuel cell power plants with a power output of greater than 50 kW shall be installed in accordance with NFPA 853.

10.30 Outdoor Open Flame Decorative Appliances. Permanently fixed in place outdoor open flame decorative appliances shall be installed in accordance with 10.30.1 through 10.30.2.

10.30.1 Application. Outdoor open flame decorative appliances shall be listed in accordance with ANSI Z21.97/CSA 2.41, *Outdoor Decorative Gas Appliances*, and shall be installed in accordance with the manufacturer's installation instructions.

10.30.2 Connection to Piping System. The connection to the gas piping system shall be in accordance with 9.6.1(1), 9.6.1(2), 9.6.1(4), or 9.6.1(5).

10.31 Outdoor Infrared Heaters. Outdoor infrared heaters for residential and commercial applications shall be listed in accordance with ANSI Z83.26/CSA 2.27, *Gas-Fired Outdoor Infrared Patio Heaters*, and shall be installed in accordance with the manufacturer's installation instructions.

Chapter 11 Procedures to Be Followed to Place Appliance in Operation

11.1 Adjusting the Burner Input.

11.1.1* Adjusting Input. The input rate of the burner shall be adjusted to the proper value in accordance with the appliance manufacturer's instructions. Firing at a rate in excess of the nameplate rating shall be prohibited.

11.1.1.1 The input rate can be adjusted by either changing the size of a fixed orifice, changing the adjustment of an adjustable orifice, or readjusting the appliance's gas pressure regulator outlet pressure (where a regulator is provided in the appliance).

11.1.1.2 The input rate shall be determined by one of the following:

(1) Checking burner input by using a gas meter
(2) Checking burner input by using manifold pressure and orifice size

11.1.1.3 Overfiring shall be prohibited.

11.1.2 High Altitude. Gas input ratings of appliances shall be used for elevations up to 2000 ft (600 m). The input ratings of appliances operating at elevations above 2000 ft (600 m) shall be reduced in accordance with one of the following methods:

(1) At the rate of 4 percent for each 1000 ft (300 m) above sea level before selecting appropriately sized appliance
(2) As permitted by the authority having jurisdiction
(3) In accordance with the manufacturer's installation instructions

11.2* Primary Air Adjustment. The primary air for injection (Bunsen)-type burners shall be adjusted for proper flame characteristics in accordance with the appliance manufacturer's instructions. After setting the primary air, the adjustment means shall be secured in position.

11.3 Safety Shutoff Devices. Where a safety shutoff device is provided, it shall be checked for proper operation and adjustment in accordance with the appliance manufacturer's instructions. Where the device does not turn off the gas supply in the event of pilot outage or other ignition malfunction, the device shall be serviced or replaced with a new device.

11.4 Automatic Ignition. Appliances supplied with means for automatic ignition shall be checked for operation within the parameters provided by the manufacturer. Any adjustments made shall be in accordance with the manufacturer's installation instructions.

11.5 Protective Devices. Where required by the manufacturer's installation instructions, all protective devices furnished with the appliance, such as a limit control, fan control to blower, temperature and pressure relief valve, low-water cutoff device, or manual operating features, shall be checked for operation within the parameters provided by the manufacturer. Any adjustments made shall be in accordance with the manufacturer's installation instructions.

11.6* Checking the Draft. Draft hood–equipped appliances shall be checked to verify that there is no draft hood spillage after 5 minutes of main burner operation.

11.7 Operating Instructions. Operating instructions shall be furnished and shall be left in a prominent position near the appliance for use by the consumer.

Chapter 12 Venting of Appliances

12.1* Minimum Safe Performance. Venting systems shall be designed and constructed to convey all flue and vent gases to the outdoors.

12.2 General.

12.2.1 Installation. Listed chimneys and vents shall be installed in accordance with Chapter 12 and the manufacturers' installation instructions.

12.3 Specification for Venting.

12.3.1 Connection to Venting Systems. Except as permitted in 12.3.2 through 12.3.6, all appliances shall be connected to venting systems.

12.3.2 Appliances Not Required to Be Vented. The following appliances shall not be required to be vented:

(1) Listed ranges
(2) Built-in domestic cooking units listed and marked for optional venting
(3) Listed hot plates
(4) Listed Type 1 clothes dryers exhausted in accordance with Section 10.4
(5) A single listed booster-type (automatic instantaneous) water heater, when designed and used solely for the sanitizing rinse requirements of a dishwashing machine, provided that the appliance is installed with the draft hood in place and unaltered, if a draft hood is required, in a commercial kitchen having a mechanical exhaust system [Where installed in this manner, the draft hood outlet shall not be less than 36 in. (910 mm) vertically and 6 in. (150 mm) horizontally from any surface other than the appliance.]
(6) Listed refrigerators
(7) Counter appliances
(8) Room heaters listed for unvented use
(9) Direct gas–fired make-up air heaters
(10) Other appliances listed for unvented use and not provided with flue collars
(11) Specialized appliances of limited input such as laboratory burners or gas lights

12.3.2.1 Where any or all of the appliances in 12.3.2(5) through 12.3.2(11) are installed so the aggregate input rating exceeds 20 Btu/hr/ft^3 (207 W/m^3) of room or space in which it is installed, one or more shall be provided with venting systems or other approved means for conveying the vent gases to the outdoors so that the aggregate input rating of the remaining unvented appliances does not exceed 20 Btu/hr/ft^3 (207 W/m^3).

12.3.2.2 Where the calculation includes the volume of an adjacent room or space, the room or space in which the appliances are installed shall be directly connected to the adjacent room or space by a doorway, archway, or other opening of comparable size that cannot be closed.

12.3.3* Ventilating Hoods. The use of ventilating hoods and exhaust systems to vent appliances shall be limited to industrial appliances and appliances installed in commercial applications.

12.3.4 Well-Ventilated Spaces. The flue gases from industrial-type appliances shall not be required to be vented to the outdoors where such gases are discharged into a large and well-ventilated industrial space.

12.3.5 Direct Vent Appliances.

12.3.5.1 Listed direct vent appliances shall be installed in accordance with the manufacturer's installation instructions.

12.3.5.2 Through-the-wall vent terminations for listed direct vent appliances shall be in accordance with 12.9.1.

12.3.6 Appliances with Integral Vents. Appliances incorporating integral venting means shall be installed in accordance with 12.9.1.

12.3.7 Incinerators. Incinerators shall be vented in accordance with NFPA 82.

12.4 Design and Construction.

12.4.1 Appliance Draft Requirements. A venting system shall satisfy the draft requirements of the appliance in accordance with the manufacturer's instructions.

12.4.2 Design and Construction. Appliances required to be vented shall be connected to a venting system designed and installed in accordance with the provisions of Sections 12.5 through 12.16.

12.4.3 Mechanical Draft Systems.

12.4.3.1 Mechanical draft systems shall be listed in accordance with UL 378, *Draft Equipment*, and installed in accordance with both the appliance and the mechanical draft system manufacturer's installation instructions.

12.4.3.2 Appliances requiring venting shall be permitted to be vented by means of mechanical draft systems of either forced or induced draft design.

12.4.3.3 Forced draft systems and all portions of induced draft systems under positive pressure during operation shall be designed and installed so as to prevent leakage of flue or vent gases into a building.

12.4.3.4 Vent connectors serving appliances vented by natural draft shall not be connected into any portion of mechanical draft systems operating under positive pressure.

12.4.3.5 Where a mechanical draft system is employed, provision shall be made to prevent the flow of gas to the main burners when the draft system is not performing so as to satisfy the operating requirements of the appliance for safe performance.

12.4.4* Ventilating Hoods and Exhaust Systems.

12.4.4.1 Where automatically operated appliances, other than food service appliances, are vented through a ventilating hood or exhaust system equipped with a damper or with a power means of exhaust, provisions shall be made to allow the flow of gas to the main burners only when the damper is open to a position to properly vent the appliance and when the power means of exhaust is in operation.

12.4.5 Circulating Air Ducts, Above-Ceiling Air-Handling Spaces, and Furnace Plenums.

12.4.5.1 Venting systems shall not extend into or pass through any fabricated air duct or furnace plenum.

12.4.5.2 Where a venting system passes through an above-ceiling air space or other nonducted portion of an air-handling system, it shall conform to one of the following requirements:

(1) The venting system shall be a listed special gas vent, other system serving a Category III or Category IV appliance, or other positive pressure vent, with joints sealed in accordance with the appliance or vent manufacturer's instructions.
(2) The vent system shall be installed such that no fittings or joints between sections are installed in the above-ceiling space.
(3) The venting system shall be installed in a conduit or enclosure with joints between the interior of the enclosure and the ceiling space sealed.

12.5 Type of Venting System to Be Used.

12.5.1 The type of venting system to be used shall be in accordance with Table 12.5.1.

12.5.2 Plastic Piping. Where plastic piping is used to vent an appliance, the appliance shall be listed for use with such venting materials and the appliance manufacturer's installation instructions shall identify the specific plastic piping material. The plastic pipe venting materials shall be labeled in accordance with the product standards specified by the appliance manufacturer or shall be listed and labeled in accordance with UL 1738, *Venting Systems for Gas-Burning Appliances, Categories II, III, and IV.*

12.5.3 Plastic Vent Joints. Plastic pipe and fittings used to vent appliances shall be installed in accordance with the appliance manufacturer's installation instructions. Plastic pipe venting materials listed and labeled in accordance with UL 1738, *Venting Systems for Gas-Burning Appliances, Categories II, III, and IV,* shall be installed in accordance with the vent manufacturer's installation instructions. Where primer is required, it shall be of a contrasting color.

12.5.4 Special Gas Vents. Special gas vents shall be listed and labeled in accordance with UL 1738, *Venting Systems for Gas-Burning Appliances, Categories II, III, and IV,* and installed in accordance with the special gas vent manufacturer's installation instructions.

12.6 Masonry, Metal, and Factory-Built Chimneys.

12.6.1 Listing or Construction.

12.6.1.1 Factory-built chimneys shall be listed in accordance with UL 103, *Chimneys, Factory-Built, Residential Type and Building Heating Appliances;* UL 959, *Medium Heat Appliance Factory-Built Chimneys;* or UL 2561, *1400 Degree Fahrenheit Factory-Built Chimneys.* Factory-built chimneys used to vent appliances that operate at positive vent pressure shall be listed for such application.

12.6.1.2 Metal chimneys shall be built and installed in accordance with NFPA 211.

Table 12.5.1 Type of Venting System to Be Used

Appliances	Type of Venting System	Location of Requirements
Listed Category I appliances	Type B gas vent	12.7
Listed appliances equipped with draft hood	Chimney	12.6
Appliances listed for use with Type B gas vent	Single-wall metal pipe	12.8
	Listed chimney lining system for gas venting	12.6.1.3
	Special gas vent listed for these appliances	12.5.4
Listed vented wall furnaces	Type B-W gas vent	12.7, 10.25
Category II, Category III, and Category IV appliances	As specified or furnished by manufacturers of listed appliances	12.5.2, 12.5.4
Incinerators	In accordance with NFPA 82	
Appliances that can be converted to use solid fuel Unlisted combination gas- and oil-burning appliances Combination gas- and solid fuel–burning appliances Appliances listed for use with chimneys only Unlisted appliances	Chimney	12.6
Listed combination gas- and oil-burning appliances	Type L vent Chimney	12.7 12.6
Decorative appliance in vented fireplace	Chimney	10.6.3
Gas-fired toilets	Single-wall metal pipe	12.8, 10.23.3
Direct vent appliances		12.3.5
Appliances with integral vents		12.3.6

12.6.1.3* Masonry chimneys shall be built and installed in accordance with NFPA 211 and lined with one of the following:

(1) Approved clay flue lining
(2) A chimney lining system listed and labeled in accordance with UL 1777, *Chimney Liners*
(3) Other approved material that resists corrosion, erosion, softening, or cracking from vent gases at temperatures up to 1800°F (982°C)

Exception: Masonry chimney flues lined with a chimney lining system specifically listed for use with listed appliances with draft hoods, Category I appliances, and other appliances listed for use with Type B vents shall be permitted. The liner shall be installed in accordance with the liner manufacturer's installation instructions. A permanent identifying label shall be attached at the point where the connection is to be made to the liner. The label shall read "This chimney liner is for appliances that burn gas only. Do not connect to solid or liquid fuel–burning appliances or incinerators."

12.6.2 Termination.

12.6.2.1* A chimney for residential-type or low-heat appliances shall extend at least 3 ft (0.9 m) above the highest point where it passes through a roof of a building and at least 2 ft (0.6 m) higher than any portion of a building within a horizontal distance of 10 ft (3 m).

12.6.2.2 A chimney for medium-heat appliances shall extend at least 10 ft (3 m) higher than any portion of any building within 25 ft (7.6 m).

12.6.2.3 A chimney shall extend at least 5 ft (1.5 m) above the highest connected appliance draft hood outlet or flue collar.

12.6.2.4 Decorative shrouds shall not be installed at the termination of factory-built chimneys except where such shrouds are listed and labeled for use with the specific factory-built chimney system and are installed in accordance with the manufacturers' installation instructions.

12.6.3 Size of Chimneys.

12.6.3.1 The effective area of a chimney venting system serving listed appliances with draft hoods, Category I appliances, and other appliances listed for use with Type B vents shall be in accordance with one of the following methods:

(1) Those listed in Chapter 13.
(2) The effective areas of the vent connector and chimney flue of a venting system serving a single appliance with a draft hood shall be not less than the area of the appliance flue collar or draft hood outlet or greater than seven times the draft hood outlet area.
(3) The effective area of the chimney flue of a venting system serving two appliances with draft hoods shall be not less than the area of the larger draft hood outlet plus 50 percent of the area of the smaller draft hood outlet or greater than seven times the smaller draft hood outlet area.
(4) Chimney venting systems using mechanical draft shall be sized in accordance with engineering methods.
(5) Other engineering methods.

12.6.4 Inspection of Chimneys.

12.6.4.1 Before replacing an existing appliance or connecting a vent connector to a chimney, the chimney passageway shall be examined to ascertain that it is clear and free of obstructions and shall be cleaned if previously used for venting solid or liquid fuel–burning appliances or fireplaces.

12.6.4.2 Chimneys shall be lined in accordance with NFPA 211.

12.6.4.3 Cleanouts shall be examined and where they do not remain tightly closed when not in use, they shall be repaired or replaced.

12.6.4.4 When inspection reveals that an existing chimney is not safe for the intended application, it shall be repaired, rebuilt, lined, relined, or replaced with a vent or chimney to conform to NFPA 211 and shall be suitable for the appliances to be attached.

12.6.5 Chimney Serving Appliances Burning Other Fuels.

12.6.5.1 An appliance shall not be connected to a chimney flue serving a separate appliance designed to burn solid fuel.

12.6.5.2 Where one chimney serves gas appliances and liquid fuel–burning appliances, the appliances shall be connected through separate openings or connected through a single opening where joined by a suitable fitting located as close as practical to the chimney. Where two or more openings are provided into one chimney flue, they shall be at different levels. Where the gas appliance is automatically controlled, it shall be equipped with a safety shutoff device.

12.6.5.3* A listed combination gas- and solid fuel–burning appliance connected to a single chimney flue shall be equipped with a manual reset device to shut off gas to the main burner in the event of sustained backdraft or flue gas spillage. The chimney flue shall be sized to properly vent the appliance.

12.6.5.4 A single chimney flue serving a listed combination gas- and oil-burning appliance shall be sized in accordance with the appliance manufacturer's instructions.

12.6.6 Support of Chimneys. All portions of chimneys shall be supported for the design and weight of the materials employed. Listed factory-built chimneys shall be supported and spaced in accordance with the manufacturer's installation instructions.

12.6.7 Cleanouts. Where a chimney that formerly carried flue products from liquid or solid fuel–burning appliances is used with an appliance using fuel gas, an accessible cleanout shall be provided. The cleanout shall have a tight-fitting cover and be installed so its upper edge is at least 6 in. (150 mm) below the lower edge of the lowest chimney inlet opening.

12.6.8 Space Surrounding Lining or Vent.

12.6.8.1 The remaining space surrounding a chimney liner, gas vent, special gas vent, or plastic piping installed within a masonry chimney shall not be used to vent another appliance.

Exception: The insertion of another liner or vent within the chimney as provided in this code and the liner or vent manufacturer's instructions.

12.6.8.2 The remaining space surrounding a chimney liner, gas vent, special gas vent, or plastic piping installed within a masonry, metal, or factory-built chimney flue shall not be used to supply combustion air.

Exception: Direct vent appliances designed for installation in a solid fuel–burning fireplace where installed in accordance with the manufacturer's installation instructions.

12.6.9 Insulation Shield. Where a factory-built chimney passes through insulated assemblies, an insulation shield constructed of steel having a minimum thickness of 0.0187 in. (0.4712 mm) (nominal 26 gage) shall be installed to provide clearance between the chimney and the insulation material. The clearance shall not be less than the clearance to combustibles specified by the chimney manufacturer's installation instructions. Where chimneys pass through attic space, the shield shall terminate not less than 2 in. (51 mm) above the insulation materials and shall be secured in place to prevent displacement.

12.7 Gas Vents.

12.7.1 Materials. Type B and Type BW gas vents shall be listed in accordance with UL 441, *Gas Vents*. Vents for listed combination gas- and oil-burning appliances shall be listed in accordance with UL 641, *Type L Low-Temperature Venting Systems*.

12.7.2 Installation. The installation of gas vents shall meet the following requirements:

(1) Gas vents shall be installed in accordance with the manufacturer's installation instructions.
(2) A Type B-W gas vent shall have a listed capacity not less than that of the listed vented wall furnace to which it is connected.
(3) Gas vents installed within masonry chimneys shall be installed in accordance with the manufacturer's installation instructions. Gas vents installed within masonry chimneys shall be identified with a permanent label installed at the point where the vent enters the chimney. The label shall contain the following language: "This gas vent is for appliances that burn gas. Do not connect to solid or liquid fuel–burning appliances or incinerators."
(4) Screws, rivets, and other fasteners shall not penetrate the inner wall of double-wall gas vents, except at the transition from the appliance draft hood outlet, flue collar, or single-wall metal connector to a double-wall vent.

12.7.3 Gas Vent Termination. The termination of gas vents shall comply with the following requirements:

(1) A gas vent shall terminate in accordance with one of the following:
  (a) Gas vents that are 12 in. (300 mm) or less in size and located not less than 8 ft (2.4 m) from a vertical wall or similar obstruction shall terminate above the roof in accordance with Figure 12.7.3 and Table 12.7.3.
  (b) Gas vents that are over 12 in. (300 mm) in size or are located less than 8 ft (2.4 m) from a vertical wall or similar obstruction shall terminate not less than 2 ft (0.6 m) above the highest point where they pass through the roof and not less than 2 ft (0.6 m) above any portion of a building within 10 ft (3.0 m) horizontally.
  (c) Industrial appliances as provided in 12.3.4.
  (d) Direct vent systems as provided in 12.3.5.
  (e) Appliances with integral vents as provided in 12.3.6.
  (f) Mechanical draft systems as provided in 12.4.3.
  (g) Ventilating hoods and exhaust systems as provided in 12.4.4.
(2) A Type B or a Type L gas vent shall terminate at least 5 ft (1.5 m) in vertical height above the highest connected appliance draft hood or flue collar.
(3) A Type B-W gas vent shall terminate at least 12 ft (3.7 m) in vertical height above the bottom of the wall furnace.
(4) A gas vent extending through an exterior wall shall not terminate adjacent to the wall or below eaves or parapets, except as provided in 12.3.5 and 12.4.3.
(5) Decorative shrouds shall not be installed at the termination of gas vents except where such shrouds are listed for use with the specific gas venting system and are installed in accordance with the manufacturer's installation instructions.
(6) All gas vents shall extend through the roof flashing, roof jack, or roof thimble and terminate with a listed cap or listed roof assembly.
(7) A gas vent shall terminate at least 3 ft (0.9 m) above a forced air inlet located within 10 ft (3.0 m).

12.7.4 Size of Gas Vents. Venting systems shall be sized and constructed in accordance with 12.7.4.1 through 12.7.4.3 and the appliance manufacturer's instructions.

Table 12.7.3 Roof Slope Heights

Roof Slope	H (minimum)	
	ft	m
Flat to 6/12	1.0	0.30
Over 6/12 to 7/12	1.25	0.38
Over 7/12 to 8/12	1.5	0.46
Over 8/12 to 9/12	2.0	0.61
Over 9/12 to 10/12	2.5	0.76
Over 10/12 to 11/12	3.25	0.99
Over 11/12 to 12/12	4.0	1.22
Over 12/12 to 14/12	5.0	1.52
Over 14/12 to 16/12	6.0	1.83
Over 16/12 to 18/12	7.0	2.13
Over 18/12 to 20/12	7.5	2.27
Over 20/12 to 21/12	8.0	2.44

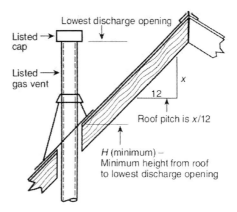

FIGURE 12.7.3 Termination Locations for Gas Vents with Listed Caps 12 in. (300 mm) or Less in Size at Least 8 ft (2.4 m) from a Vertical Wall.

12.7.4.1* Category I Appliances. The sizing of natural draft venting systems serving one or more listed appliances equipped with a draft hood or appliances listed for use with a Type B gas vent, installed in a single story of a building, shall be in accordance with one of the following:

(1) The provisions of Chapter 13.
(2) Vents serving fan-assisted combustion system appliances, or combinations of fan-assisted combustion system and draft hood–equipped appliances, shall be sized in accordance with Chapter 13 or other engineering methods.
(3) For sizing an individual gas vent for a single, draft hood–equipped appliance, the effective area of the vent connector and the gas vent shall be not less than the area of the appliance draft hood outlet or greater than seven times the draft hood outlet area.
(4) For sizing a gas vent connected to two appliances with draft hoods, the effective area of the vent shall be not less than the area of the larger draft hood outlet plus 50 percent of the area of the smaller draft hood outlet or greater than seven times the smaller draft hood outlet area.
(5) Engineering methods.

12.7.4.2 Vent Offsets. Type B and Type L vents sized in accordance with 12.7.4.1(3) or 12.7.4.1(4) shall extend in a generally vertical direction with offsets not exceeding 45 degrees, except that a vent system having not more than one 60 degree offset shall be permitted. Any angle greater than 45 degrees from the vertical is considered horizontal. The total horizontal distance of a vent plus the horizontal vent connector serving draft hood–equipped appliances shall not be greater than 75 percent of the vertical height of the vent.

12.7.4.3 Category II, Category III, and Category IV Appliances. The sizing of gas vents for Category II, Category III, and Category IV appliances shall be in accordance with the appliance manufacturers' instructions. The sizing of plastic pipe specified by the appliance manufacturer as a venting material for Category II, III, and IV appliances shall be in accordance with the appliance manufacturers' instructions.

12.7.4.4 Sizing. Chimney venting systems using mechanical draft shall be sized in accordance with engineering methods.

12.7.5 Gas Vents Serving Appliances on More than One Floor.

12.7.5.1 Where a common vent is installed in a multistory installation to vent Category I appliances located on more than one floor level, the venting system shall be designed and installed in accordance with engineering methods. Crawl spaces, basements, and attics shall be considered as floor levels.

12.7.5.2* All appliances connected to the common vent shall be located in rooms separated from occupiable space. Each of these rooms shall have provisions for an adequate supply of combustion, ventilation, and dilution air that is not supplied from occupiable space.

12.7.5.3 The size of the connectors and common segments of multistory venting systems for appliances listed for use with a Type B double-wall gas vent shall be in accordance with Table 13.2(a), provided all of the following apply:

(1) The available total height (H) for each segment of a multistory venting system is the vertical distance between the level of the highest draft hood outlet or flue collar on that floor and the centerline of the next highest interconnection tee.
(2) The size of the connector for a segment is determined from the appliance's gas input rate and available connector rise and shall not be smaller than the draft hood outlet or flue collar size.
(3) The size of the common vertical vent segment, and of the interconnection tee at the base of that segment, is based on the total appliance's gas input rate entering that segment and its available total height.

12.7.6 Support of Gas Vents. Gas vents shall be supported and spaced in accordance with the manufacturer's installation instructions.

12.7.7 Marking. In those localities where solid and liquid fuels are used extensively, gas vents shall be permanently identified by a label attached to the wall or ceiling at a point where the vent connector enters the gas vent. The label shall read: "This gas vent is for appliances that burn gas. Do not connect to solid or liquid fuel–burning appliances or incinerators." The authority having jurisdiction shall determine whether its area constitutes such a locality.

12.8 Single-Wall Metal Pipe.

12.8.1 Construction. Single-wall metal pipe shall be constructed of galvanized sheet steel not less than 0.0304 in. (0.7 mm) thick or of other approved, noncombustible, corrosion-resistant material.

12.8.2* Cold Climate. Uninsulated single-wall metal pipe shall not be used outdoors for venting appliances in regions where the 99 percent winter design temperature is below 32°F (0°C).

12.8.3 Termination. The termination of single-wall metal pipe shall meet the following requirements:

(1) Single-wall metal pipe shall terminate at least 5 ft (1.5 m) in vertical height above the highest connected appliance draft hood outlet or flue collar.
(2) Single-wall metal pipe shall extend at least 2 ft (0.6 m) above the highest point where it passes through a roof of a building and at least 2 ft (0.6 m) higher than any portion of a building within a horizontal distance of 10 ft (3 m).
(3) An approved cap or roof assembly shall be attached to the terminus of a single-wall metal pipe.

12.8.4 Installation with Appliances Permitted by 12.5.1.

12.8.4.1* Prohibited Use. Single-wall metal pipe shall not be used as a vent in dwellings and residential occupancies.

12.8.4.2 Single-wall metal pipe shall be used only for runs directly from the space in which the appliance is located through the roof or exterior wall to the outer air. A pipe passing through a roof shall extend without interruption through the roof flashing, roof jacket, or roof thimble.

12.8.4.3 Single-wall metal pipe shall not originate in any unoccupied attic or concealed space and shall not pass through any attic, inside wall, concealed space, or floor.

12.8.4.4 Minimum clearances from single-wall metal pipe to combustible material shall be in accordance with Table 12.8.4.4. Reduced clearances from single-wall metal pipe to combustible material shall be as specified for vent connectors in Table 10.2.4.

Table 12.8.4.4 Clearances for Connectors

Appliance	Minimum Distance from Combustible Material			
	Listed Type B Gas Vent Material	Listed Type L Vent Material	Single-Wall Metal Pipe	Factory-Built Chimney Sections
Listed appliance with draft hoods and appliance listed for use with Type B gas vents	As listed	As listed	6 in.	As listed
Residential boilers and furnaces with listed gas conversion burner and with draft hood	6 in.	6 in.	9 in.	As listed
Residential appliances listed for use with Type L vents	Not permitted	As listed	9 in.	As listed
Listed gas-fired toilets	Not permitted	As listed	As listed	As listed
Unlisted residential appliances with draft hood	Not permitted	6 in.	9 in.	As listed
Residential and low-heat appliances other than those above	Not permitted	9 in.	18 in.	As listed
Medium-heat appliance	Not permitted	Not permitted	36 in.	As listed

For SI units, 1 in. = 25.4 mm.
Note: These clearances shall apply unless the installation instructions of a listed appliance or connector specify different clearances, in which case the listed clearances shall apply.

12.8.4.5 Where a single-wall metal pipe passes through a roof constructed of combustible material, a noncombustible, nonventilating thimble shall be used at the point of passage. The thimble shall extend at least 18 in. (460 mm) above and 6 in. (150 mm) below the roof with the annular space open at the bottom and closed only at the top. The thimble shall be sized in accordance with 12.8.4.6.

12.8.4.6 Single-wall metal pipe shall not pass through a combustible exterior wall unless guarded at the point of passage by a ventilated metal thimble not smaller than the following:

(1) For listed appliances with draft hoods and appliances listed for use with Type B gas vents, the thimble shall be a minimum of 4 in. (100 mm) larger in diameter than the metal pipe. Where there is a run of not less than 6 ft (1.8 m) of metal pipe in the opening between the draft hood outlet and the thimble, the thimble shall be a minimum of 2 in. (50 mm) larger in diameter than the metal pipe.

(2) For unlisted appliances having draft hoods, the thimble shall be a minimum of 6 in. (150 mm) larger in diameter than the metal pipe.

(3) For residential and low-heat appliances, the thimble shall be a minimum of 12 in. (300 mm) larger in diameter than the metal pipe.

Exception: In lieu of thimble protection, all combustible material in the wall shall be removed a sufficient distance from the metal pipe to provide the specified clearance from such metal pipe to combustible material. Any material used to close up such opening shall be noncombustible.

12.8.5 Size of Single-Wall Metal Pipe. Single-wall metal piping shall comply with the following requirements:

(1)* A venting system of a single-wall metal pipe shall be sized in accordance with one of the following methods and the appliance manufacturer's instructions:

  (a) For a draft hood–equipped appliance, in accordance with Chapter 13.
  (b) For a venting system for a single appliance with a draft hood, the areas of the connector and the pipe each shall not be less than the area of the appliance flue collar or draft hood outlet, whichever is smaller. The vent area shall not be greater than seven times the draft hood outlet area.
  (c) Engineering methods.

(2) Where a single-wall metal pipe is used and has a shape other than round, it shall have an equivalent effective area equal to the effective area of the round pipe for which it is substituted and the minimum internal dimension of the pipe shall be 2 in. (50 mm).

(3) The vent cap or a roof assembly shall have a venting capacity not less than that of the pipe to which it is attached.

12.8.6 Support of Single-Wall Metal Pipe. All portions of single-wall metal pipe shall be supported for the design and weight of the material employed.

12.8.7 Marking. Single-wall metal pipe shall comply with the marking provisions of 12.7.7.

12.9 Through-the-Wall Vent Termination.

12.9.1 The clearance for through-the-wall direct vent and non-direct vent terminals shall be in accordance with Table 12.9.1 and Figure 12.9.1.

Exception: The clearances in Table 12.9.1 shall not apply to the combustion air intake of a direct vent appliance.

12.9.2 Where vents, including those for direct-vent appliances or combustion air intake pipes, penetrate outside walls of buildings, the annular spaces around such penetrations shall be permanently sealed using approved materials to prevent entry of combustion products into the building.

12.9.3 Vent systems for Category IV appliances that terminate through an outside wall of a building and discharge flue gases perpendicular to the adjacent wall shall be located not less than 10 ft (3 m) horizontally from an operable opening in an adjacent building.

Exception: This shall not apply to vent terminals that are 2 ft (0.6 m) or more above or 25 ft (7.6 m) or more below operable openings.

Table 12.9.1 Through the Wall Vent Terminal Clearances

Figure Clearance	Clearance Location	Minimum Clearances for Direct Vent Terminals	Minimum Clearances for Non-Direct Vent Terminals
A	Clearance above finished grade level, veranda, porch, deck, or balcony	12 in.	12 in.
B	Clearance to window or door that is openable	6 in. Appliances ≤ 10,000 Btu/hr 9 in. Appliances > 10,000 Btu/hr ≤ 50,000 Btu/hr 12 in. Appliances > 50,000 Btu/hr ≤ 150,000 Btu/hr Appliances > 150,000 Btu/hr, in accordance with the appliance manufacturer's instructions and not less than the clearances specified for non-direct vent terminals in row B	4 ft below or to side of opening or 1 ft above opening
C	Clearance to non-openable window	None unless otherwise specified by the appliance manufacturer	
D	Vertical clearance to ventilated soffit located above the terminal within a horizontal distance of 2 ft (610 mm) from the center line of the terminal	None unless otherwise specified by the appliance manufacturer	
E	Clearance to unventilated soffit	None unless otherwise specified by the appliance manufacturer	
F	Clearance to outside corner of building	None unless otherwise specified by the appliance manufacturer	
G	Clearance to inside corner of building	None unless otherwise specified by the appliance manufacturer	
H	Clearance to non-mechanical air supply inlet to building and the combustion air inlet to any other appliance	Same clearance as specified for row B	
I	Clearance to a mechanical air supply inlet	10 ft horizontally from inlet or 3 ft above inlet	
J	Clearance above paved sidewalk or paved driveway located on public property or other areas where condensate or vapor can cause a nuisance or hazard	7 ft and not located above public walkways or other areas where condensate or vapor can cause a nuisance or hazard	
K	Clearance to underside of veranda, porch, deck, or balcony	12 in. where the area beneath the veranda, porch, deck, or balcony is open on not less than two sides. The vent terminal is prohibited in this location where only one side is open.	

For SI units, 1 in. = 25.4 mm, 1 ft = 0.3 m, 1 Btu/hr = 0.293 W.

12.10 Condensation Drain.

12.10.1 Provision shall be made to collect and dispose of condensate from venting systems serving Category II and Category IV appliances and noncategorized condensing appliances.

12.10.2 Drains for condensate shall be installed in accordance with the appliance and vent manufacturers' installation instructions.

12.11 Vent Connectors for Category I Appliances.

12.11.1 Where Required. A vent connector shall be used to connect an appliance to a gas vent, chimney, or single-wall metal pipe, except where the gas vent, chimney, or single-wall metal pipe is directly connected to the appliance.

12.11.2 Materials.

12.11.2.1 A vent connector shall be made of noncombustible, corrosion-resistant material capable of withstanding the vent gas temperature produced by the appliance and of sufficient thickness to withstand physical damage.

12.11.2.2 Where the vent connector used for an appliance having a draft hood or a Category I appliance is located in or passes through an unconditioned area, attic, or crawl space, that portion of the vent connector shall be listed Type B, Type L, or listed vent material having equivalent insulation qualities.

Exception: Single-wall metal pipe located within the exterior walls of the building and located in an unconditioned area other than an attic or a crawl space having a local 99 percent winter design temperature of 5°F (−15°C) or higher.

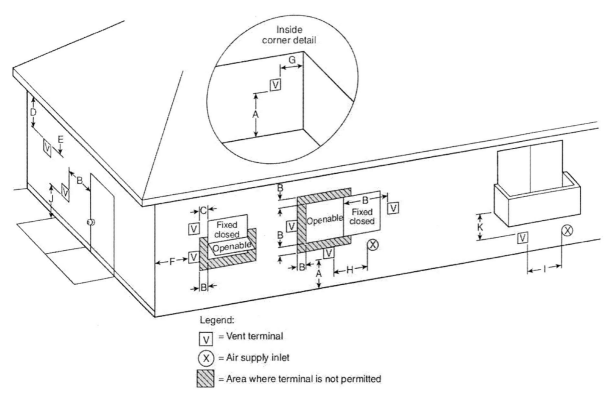

FIGURE 12.9.1 Through the Wall Vent Terminal Clearances.

12.11.2.3 Vent connectors for residential-type appliances shall comply with the following:

(1) Vent connectors for listed appliances having draft hoods, appliances having draft hoods and equipped with listed conversion burners, and Category I appliances that are not installed in attics, crawl spaces, or other unconditioned areas shall be one of the following:

 (a) Type B or Type L vent material
 (b) Galvanized sheet steel not less than 0.018 in. (0.46 mm) thick
 (c) Aluminum (1100 or 3003 alloy or equivalent) sheet not less than 0.027 in. (0.69 mm) thick
 (d) Stainless steel sheet not less than 0.012 in. (0.31 mm) thick
 (e) Smooth interior wall metal pipe having resistance to heat and corrosion equal to or greater than that of 12.11.2.3(1)(b), 12.11.2.3(1)(c), or 12.11.2.3(1)(d)
 (f) A listed vent connector

(2) Vent connectors shall not be covered with insulation.

Exception: Listed insulated vent connectors shall be installed in accordance with the manufacturer's installation instructions.

12.11.2.4 A vent connector for a nonresidential low-heat appliance shall be a factory-built chimney section or steel pipe having resistance to heat and corrosion equivalent to that for the appropriate galvanized pipe as specified in Table 12.11.2.4. Factory-built chimney sections shall be joined together in accordance with the chimney manufacturer's instructions.

12.11.2.5 Vent connectors for medium-heat appliances shall be constructed of factory-built, medium-heat chimney sections

Table 12.11.2.4 Minimum Thickness for Galvanized Steel Vent Connectors for Low-Heat Appliances

Diameter of Connector (in.)	Minimum Thickness (in.)
Less than 6	0.019
6 to less than 10	0.023
10 to 12 inclusive	0.029
14 to 16 inclusive	0.034
Over 16	0.056

For SI units, 1 in. = 25.4 mm, 1 in.^{2} = 645 mm^2.

or steel of a thickness not less than that specified in Table 12.11.2.5 and shall comply with the following:

(1) A steel vent connector for an appliance with a vent gas temperature in excess of 1000°F (538°C) measured at the entrance to the connector shall be lined with medium-duty fire brick or the equivalent.
(2) The lining shall be at least 2½ in. (64 mm) thick for a vent connector having a diameter or greatest cross-sectional dimension of 18 in. (460 mm) or less.
(3) The lining shall be at least 4½ in. (110 mm) thick laid on the 4½ in. (110 mm) bed for a vent connector having a diameter or greatest cross-sectional dimension greater than 18 in. (460 mm).
(4) Where factory-built chimney sections are installed, they shall be joined together in accordance with the chimney manufacturer's instructions.

Table 12.11.2.5 Minimum Thickness for Steel Vent Connectors for Medium-Heat Appliances

Vent Connector Size		Minimum Thickness (in.)
Diameter (in.)	Area (in.^{2})	
Up to 14	Up to 154	0.053
Over 14 to 16	154 to 201	0.067
Over 16 to 18	201 to 254	0.093
Over 18	Larger than 254	0.123

For SI units, 1 in. = 25.4 mm, 1 in.^{2} = 645 mm^2.

12.11.3* Size of Vent Connector.

12.11.3.1 A vent connector for an appliance with a single draft hood or for a Category I fan-assisted combustion system appliance shall be sized and installed in accordance with Chapter 13 or engineering methods.

12.11.3.2 Where a single appliance having more than one draft hood outlet or flue collar is installed, the manifold shall be constructed according to the instructions of the appliance manufacturer. Where there are no instructions, the manifold shall be designed and constructed in accordance with engineering methods. As an alternative method, the effective area of the manifold shall equal the combined area of the flue collars or draft hood outlets, and the vent connectors shall have a minimum 1 ft (0.3 m) rise.

12.11.3.3 Where two or more appliances are connected to a common vent or chimney, each vent connector shall be sized in accordance with Chapter 13 or engineering methods.

12.11.3.4 As an alternative method applicable only where all of the appliances are draft hood–equipped, each vent connector shall have an effective area not less than the area of the draft hood outlet of the appliance to which it is connected.

12.11.3.5 Where two or more appliances are vented through a common vent connector or vent manifold, the common vent connector or vent manifold shall be located at the highest level consistent with available headroom and clearance to combustible material and sized in accordance with Chapter 13 or engineering methods.

12.11.3.6 As an alternative method applicable only where there are two draft hood–equipped appliances, the effective area of the common vent connector or vent manifold and all junction fittings shall be not less than the area of the larger vent connector plus 50 percent of the area of the smaller flue collar outlet.

12.11.3.7 Where the size of a vent connector is increased to overcome installation limitations and obtain connector capacity equal to the appliance input, the size increase shall be made at the appliance draft hood outlet.

12.11.4 Two or More Appliances Connected to a Single Vent.

12.11.4.1 Where two or more openings are provided into one chimney flue or vent, either of the following shall apply:

(1) The openings shall be at different levels.
(2) The connectors shall be attached to the vertical portion of the chimney or vent at an angle of 45 degrees or less relative to the vertical.

12.11.4.2 Where two or more vent connectors enter a common vent, chimney flue, or single-wall metal pipe, the smaller connector shall enter at the highest level consistent with the available headroom or clearance to combustible material.

12.11.4.3 Vent connectors serving Category I appliances shall not be connected to any portion of a mechanical draft system operating under positive static pressure, such as those serving Category III or Category IV appliances.

12.11.5 Clearance. Minimum clearances from vent connectors to combustible material shall be in accordance with Table 12.8.4.4.

Exception: The clearance between a vent connector and combustible material shall be permitted to be reduced where the combustible material is protected as specified for vent connectors in Table 10.2.4.

12.11.6 Joints. Joints between sections of connector piping and connections to flue collars or draft hood outlets shall be fastened in accordance with one of the following methods:

(1) Sheet metal screws
(2) Vent connectors of listed vent material assembled and connected to flue collars or draft hood outlets in accordance with the manufacturers' instructions
(3) Other approved means

12.11.7 Connector Junctions. Where vent connectors are joined together, the connection shall be made with a manufactured tee or wye fitting.

12.11.8 Slope. A vent connector shall be installed without any dips or sags and shall slope upward toward the vent or chimney at least ¼ in./ft (20 mm/m).

Exception: Vent connectors attached to a mechanical draft system installed in accordance with appliance and the draft system manufacturers' instructions.

12.11.9* Length of Vent Connector.

12.11.9.1 The maximum horizontal length of a single-wall connector shall be 75 percent of the height of the chimney or vent, except for engineered systems.

12.11.9.2 The maximum horizontal length of a Type B double-wall connector shall be 100 percent of the height of the chimney or vent, except for engineered systems. The maximum length of an individual connector for a chimney or vent system serving multiple appliances, from the appliance outlet to the junction with the common vent or another connector, shall be 100 percent of the height of the chimney or vent.

12.11.10 Support. A vent connector shall be supported for the design and weight of the material employed to maintain clearances and prevent physical damage and separation of joints.

12.11.11 Chimney Connection.

12.11.11.1 Where entering a flue in a masonry or metal chimney, the vent connector shall be installed above the extreme bottom to avoid stoppage.

12.11.11.2 Where a thimble or slip joint is used to facilitate removal of the connector, the connector shall be firmly attached to or inserted into the thimble or slip joint to prevent the connector from falling out.

12.11.11.3 Means shall be employed to prevent the connector from entering so far as to restrict the space between its end and the opposite wall of the chimney flue.

12.11.12 Inspection. The entire length of a vent connector shall be readily accessible for inspection, cleaning, and replacement.

12.11.13 Fireplaces. A vent connector shall not be connected to a chimney flue serving a fireplace unless the fireplace flue opening is permanently sealed.

12.11.14 Passage Through Ceilings, Floors, or Walls.

12.11.14.1 Single-wall metal pipe connectors shall not pass through any wall, floor, or ceiling except as permitted by 12.8.4.2 and 12.8.4.6.

12.11.14.2 Vent connectors for medium-heat appliances shall not pass through walls or partitions constructed of combustible material.

12.12 Vent Connectors for Category II, Category III, and Category IV Appliances. The vent connectors for Category II, Category III, and Category IV appliances shall be in accordance with Section 12.5.

12.13 Draft Hoods and Draft Controls.

12.13.1 Appliances Requiring Draft Hoods. Vented appliances shall be installed with draft hoods.

Exception: Dual oven-type combination ranges; direct vent appliances; fan-assisted combustion system appliances; appliances requiring chimney draft for operation; single-firebox boilers equipped with conversion burners with inputs greater than 400,000 Btu/hr (117 kW); appliances equipped with blast, power, or pressure burners that are not listed for use with draft hoods; and appliances designed for forced venting.

12.13.2 Installation. A draft hood supplied with or forming a part of a listed vented appliance shall be installed without alteration, exactly as furnished and specified by the appliance manufacturer.

12.13.2.1 If a draft hood is not supplied by the appliance manufacturer where one is required, a draft hood shall be installed, be of a listed or approved type, and, in the absence of other instructions, be of the same size as the appliance flue collar. Where a draft hood is required with a conversion burner, it shall be of a listed or approved type.

12.13.3 Draft Control Devices. Where a draft control device is part of the appliance or is supplied by the appliance manufacturer, it shall be installed in accordance with the manufacturer's instructions. In the absence of manufacturer's instructions, the device shall be attached to the flue collar of the appliance or as near to the appliance as practical.

12.13.4* Additional Devices. Appliances requiring controlled chimney draft shall be permitted to be equipped with listed double-acting barometric draft regulators installed and adjusted in accordance with the manufacturer's instructions.

12.13.5 Location. Draft hoods and barometric draft regulators shall be installed in the same room or enclosure as the appliance in such a manner as to prevent any difference in pressure between the hood or regulator and the combustion air supply.

12.13.6 Positioning. Draft hoods and draft regulators shall be installed in the position for which they were designed with reference to the horizontal and vertical planes and shall be located so that the relief opening is not obstructed by any part of the appliance or adjacent construction. The appliance and its draft hood shall be located so that the relief opening is accessible for checking vent operation.

12.13.7 Clearance. A draft hood shall be located so that its relief opening is not less than 6 in. (150 mm) from any surface except that of the appliance it serves and the venting system to which the draft hood is connected. Where a greater or lesser clearance is indicated on the appliance label, the clearance shall not be less than that specified on the label. Such clearances shall not be reduced.

12.14 Manually Operated Dampers.

12.14.1 A manually operated damper shall not be placed in any appliance vent connector. Fixed baffles and balancing baffles shall not be classified as manually operated dampers.

12.14.2* Balancing baffles shall be mechanically locked in the desired position before placing the appliance in service.

12.14.3 Balancing baffles shall be listed in accordance with UL 378, *Draft Equipment*.

12.15 Automatically Operated Vent Dampers. An automatically operated vent damper shall be listed.

12.16 Obstructions. Devices that retard the flow of vent gases shall not be installed in a vent connector, chimney, or vent. The following shall not be considered as obstructions:

(1) Draft regulators and safety controls specifically listed for installation in venting systems and installed in accordance with the manufacturer's installation instructions
(2) Approved draft regulators and safety controls designed and installed in accordance with engineering methods
(3) Listed heat reclaimers and automatically operated vent dampers installed in accordance with the manufacturers' installation instructions
(4) Vent dampers serving listed appliances installed in accordance with 13.1.1 or 13.2.1 or engineering methods
(5) Approved economizers, heat reclaimers, and recuperators installed in venting systems of appliances not required to be equipped with draft hoods, provided the appliance manufacturer's instructions cover the installation of such a device in the venting system and performance in accordance with Section 12.1 and 12.4.1 is obtained

Chapter 13 Sizing of Category I Venting Systems

13.1 Additional Requirements to Single Appliance Vent. This section shall apply where Table 13.1(a) through Table 13.1(f) are used to size single appliance venting systems. Subsections 13.1.1 through 13.1.18 apply to Table 13.1(a) through Table 13.1(f).

Table 13.1(a) Type B Double-Wall Gas Vent

		Number of Appliances:	Single
		Appliance Type:	Category I
		Appliance Vent Connection:	Connected Directly to Vent

		Vent Diameter — D (in.)																		
		3			4			5			6			7			8			9		
		Appliance Input Rating in Thousands of Btu per Hour																				
Height H (ft)	Lateral L (ft)	FAN		NAT	FAN		NAT	FAN		NAT	FAN		NAT	FAN		NAT	FAN		NAT	FAN		NAT
		Min	Max	Max	Min	Max	Max	Min	Max	Max	Min	Max	Max	Min	Max	Max	Min	Max	Max	Min	Max	Max
6	0	0	78	46	0	152	86	0	251	141	0	375	205	0	524	285	0	698	370	0	897	470
	2	13	51	36	18	97	67	27	157	105	32	232	157	44	321	217	53	425	285	63	543	370
	4	21	49	34	30	94	64	39	153	103	50	227	153	66	316	211	79	419	279	93	536	362
	6	25	46	32	36	91	61	47	149	100	59	223	149	78	310	205	93	413	273	110	530	354
8	0	0	84	50	0	165	94	0	276	155	0	415	235	0	583	320	0	780	415	0	1006	537
	2	12	57	40	16	109	75	25	178	120	28	263	180	42	365	247	50	483	322	60	619	418
	5	23	53	38	32	103	71	42	171	115	53	255	173	70	356	237	83	473	313	99	607	407
	8	28	49	35	39	98	66	51	164	109	64	247	165	84	347	227	99	463	303	117	596	396
10	0	0	88	53	0	175	100	0	295	166	0	447	255	0	631	345	0	847	450	0	1096	585
	2	12	61	42	17	118	81	23	194	129	26	289	195	40	402	273	48	533	355	57	684	457
	5	23	57	40	32	113	77	41	187	124	52	280	188	68	392	263	81	522	346	95	671	446
	10	30	51	36	41	104	70	54	176	115	67	267	175	88	376	245	104	504	330	122	651	427
15	0	0	94	58	0	191	112	0	327	187	0	502	285	0	716	390	0	970	525	0	1263	682
	2	11	69	48	15	136	93	20	226	150	22	339	225	38	475	316	45	633	414	53	815	544
	5	22	65	45	30	130	87	39	219	142	49	330	217	64	463	300	76	620	403	90	800	529
	10	29	59	41	40	121	82	51	206	135	64	315	208	84	445	288	99	600	386	116	777	507
	15	35	53	37	48	112	76	61	195	128	76	301	198	98	429	275	115	580	373	134	755	491
20	0	0	97	61	0	202	119	0	349	202	0	540	307	0	776	430	0	1057	575	0	1384	752
	2	10	75	51	14	149	100	18	250	166	20	377	249	33	531	346	41	711	470	50	917	612
	5	21	71	48	29	143	96	38	242	160	47	367	241	62	519	337	73	697	460	86	902	599
	10	28	64	44	38	133	89	50	229	150	62	351	228	81	499	321	95	675	443	112	877	576
	15	34	58	40	46	124	84	59	217	142	73	337	217	94	481	308	111	654	427	129	853	557
	20	48	52	35	55	116	78	69	206	134	84	322	206	107	464	295	125	634	410	145	830	537
30	0	0	100	64	0	213	128	0	374	220	0	587	336	0	853	475	0	1173	650	0	1548	855
	2	9	81	56	13	166	112	14	283	185	18	432	280	27	613	394	33	826	535	42	1072	700
	5	21	77	54	28	160	108	36	275	176	45	421	273	58	600	385	69	811	524	82	1055	688
	10	27	70	50	37	150	102	48	262	171	59	405	261	77	580	371	91	788	507	107	1028	668
	15	33	64	NA	44	141	96	57	249	163	70	389	249	90	560	357	105	765	490	124	1002	648
	20	56	58	NA	53	132	90	66	237	154	80	374	237	102	542	343	119	743	473	139	977	628
	30	NA	NA	NA	73	113	NA	88	214	NA	104	346	219	131	507	321	149	702	444	171	929	594
50	0	0	101	67	0	216	134	0	397	232	0	633	363	0	932	518	0	1297	708	0	1730	952
	2	8	86	61	11	183	122	14	320	206	15	497	314	22	715	445	26	975	615	33	1276	813
	5	20	82	NA	27	177	119	35	312	200	43	487	308	55	702	438	65	960	605	77	1259	798
	10	26	76	NA	35	168	114	45	299	190	56	471	298	73	681	426	86	935	589	101	1230	773
	15	59	70	NA	42	158	NA	54	287	180	66	455	288	85	662	413	100	911	572	117	1203	747
	20	NA	NA	NA	50	149	NA	63	275	169	76	440	278	97	642	401	113	888	556	131	1176	722
	30	NA	NA	NA	69	131	NA	84	250	NA	99	410	259	123	605	376	141	844	522	161	1125	670
100	0	NA	NA	NA	0	218	NA	0	407	NA	0	665	400	0	997	560	0	1411	770	0	1908	1040
	2	NA	NA	NA	10	194	NA	12	354	NA	13	566	375	18	831	510	21	1155	700	25	1536	935
	5	NA	NA	NA	26	189	NA	33	347	NA	40	557	369	52	820	504	60	1141	692	71	1519	926
	10	NA	NA	NA	33	182	NA	43	335	NA	53	542	361	68	801	493	80	1118	679	94	1492	910
	15	NA	NA	NA	40	174	NA	50	321	NA	62	528	353	80	782	482	93	1095	666	109	1465	895
	20	NA	NA	NA	47	166	NA	59	311	NA	71	513	344	90	763	471	105	1073	653	122	1438	880
	30	NA	NA	NA	NA	NA	NA	78	290	NA	92	483	NA	115	726	449	131	1029	627	149	1387	849
	50	NA	NA	NA	NA	NA	NA	NA	NA	NA	147	428	NA	180	651	405	197	944	575	217	1288	787

Table 13.1(a) Continued

		Number of Appliances:	Single
		Appliance Type:	Category I
		Appliance Vent Connection:	Connected Directly to Vent

		Vent Diameter — D (in.)																					
		10			12			14			16			18			20			22			24		
		Appliance Input Rating in Thousands of Btu per Hour																					
Height H (ft)	Lateral L (ft)	FAN		NAT	FAN		NAT	FAN		NAT	FAN		NAT	FAN		NAT	FAN		NAT	FAN		NAT	FAN		NAT
		Min	Max	Max	Min	Max	Max	Min	Max	Max	Min	Max	Max	Min	Max	Max	Min	Max	Max	Min	Max	Max	Min	Max	Max
6	0	0	1121	570	0	1645	850	0	2267	1170	0	2983	1530	0	3802	1960	0	4721	2430	0	5737	2950	0	6853	3520
	2	75	675	455	103	982	650	138	1346	890	178	1769	1170	225	2250	1480	296	2782	1850	360	3377	2220	426	4030	2670
	4	110	668	445	147	975	640	191	1338	880	242	1761	1160	300	2242	1475	390	2774	1835	469	3370	2215	555	4023	2660
	6	128	661	435	171	967	630	219	1330	870	276	1753	1150	341	2235	1470	437	2767	1820	523	3363	2210	618	4017	2650
8	0	0	1261	660	0	1858	970	0	2571	1320	0	3399	1740	0	4333	2220	0	5387	2750	0	6555	3360	0	7838	4010
	2	71	770	515	98	1124	745	130	1543	1020	168	2030	1340	212	2584	1700	278	3196	2110	336	3882	2560	401	4634	3050
	5	115	758	503	154	1110	733	199	1528	1010	251	2013	1330	311	2563	1685	398	3180	2090	476	3863	2545	562	4612	3040
	8	137	746	490	180	1097	720	231	1514	1000	289	2000	1320	354	2552	1670	450	3163	2070	537	3850	2530	630	4602	3030
10	0	0	1377	720	0	2036	1060	0	2825	1450	0	3742	1925	0	4782	2450	0	5955	3050	0	7254	3710	0	8682	4450
	2	68	852	560	93	1244	850	124	1713	1130	161	2256	1480	202	2868	1890	264	3556	2340	319	4322	2840	378	5153	3390
	5	112	839	547	149	1229	829	192	1696	1105	243	2238	1461	300	2849	1871	382	3536	2318	458	4301	2818	540	5132	3371
	10	142	817	525	187	1204	795	238	1669	1080	298	2209	1430	364	2818	1840	459	3504	2280	546	4268	2780	641	5099	3340
15	0	0	1596	840	0	2380	1240	0	3323	1720	0	4423	2270	0	5678	2900	0	7099	3620	0	8665	4410	0	10,393	5300
	2	63	1019	675	86	1495	985	114	2062	1350	147	2719	1770	186	3467	2260	239	4364	2800	290	5232	3410	346	6251	4080
	5	105	1003	660	141	1476	967	182	2041	1327	229	2696	1748	283	3442	2235	355	4278	2777	426	5204	3385	501	6222	4057
	10	135	977	635	177	1446	936	227	2009	1289	283	2659	1712	346	3402	2193	432	4234	2739	510	5159	3343	599	6175	4019
	15	155	953	610	202	1418	905	257	1976	1250	318	2623	1675	385	3363	2150	479	4192	2700	564	5115	3300	665	6129	3980
20	0	0	1756	930	0	2637	1350	0	3701	1900	0	4948	2520	0	6376	3250	0	7988	4060	0	9785	4980	0	11,753	6000
	2	59	1150	755	81	1694	1100	107	2343	1520	139	3097	2000	175	3955	2570	220	4916	3200	269	5983	3910	321	7154	4700
	5	101	1133	738	135	1674	1079	174	2320	1498	219	3071	1978	270	3926	2544	337	4885	3174	403	5950	3880	475	7119	4662
	10	130	1105	710	172	1641	1045	220	2282	1460	273	3029	1940	334	3880	2500	413	4835	3130	489	5896	3830	573	7063	4600
	15	150	1078	688	195	1609	1018	248	2245	1425	306	2988	1910	372	3835	2465	459	4786	3090	541	5844	3795	631	7007	4575
	20	167	1052	665	217	1578	990	273	2210	1390	335	2948	1880	404	3791	2430	495	4737	3050	585	5792	3760	689	6953	4550
30	0	0	1977	1060	0	3004	1550	0	4252	2170	0	5725	2920	0	7420	3770	0	9341	4750	0	11,483	5850	0	13,848	7060
	2	54	1351	865	74	2004	1310	98	2786	1800	127	3696	2380	159	4734	3050	199	5900	3810	241	7194	4650	285	8617	5600
	5	96	1332	851	127	1981	1289	164	2759	1775	206	3666	2350	252	4701	3020	312	5863	3783	373	7155	4622	439	8574	5552
	10	125	1301	829	164	1944	1254	209	2716	1733	259	3617	2300	316	4647	2970	386	5803	3739	456	7090	4574	535	8505	5471
	15	143	1272	807	187	1908	1220	237	2674	1692	292	3570	2250	354	4594	2920	431	5744	3695	507	7026	4527	590	8437	5391
	20	160	1243	784	207	1873	1185	260	2633	1650	319	3523	2200	384	4542	2870	467	5686	3650	548	6964	4480	639	8370	5310
	30	195	1189	745	246	1807	1130	305	2555	1585	369	3433	2130	440	4442	2785	540	5574	3565	635	6842	4375	739	8239	5225
50	0	0	2231	1195	0	3441	1825	0	4934	2550	0	6711	3440	0	8774	4460	0	11,129	5635	0	13,767	6940	0	16,694	8430
	2	41	1620	1010	66	2431	1513	86	3409	2125	113	4554	2840	141	5864	3670	171	7339	4630	209	8980	5695	251	10,788	6860
	5	90	1600	996	118	2406	1495	151	3380	2102	191	4520	2813	234	5826	3639	283	7295	4597	336	8933	5654	394	10,737	6818
	10	118	1567	972	154	2366	1466	196	3332	2064	243	4464	2767	295	5763	3585	355	7224	4542	419	8855	5585	491	10,652	6749
	15	136	1536	948	177	2327	1437	222	3285	2026	274	4409	2721	330	5701	3534	396	7155	4511	465	8779	5546	542	10,570	6710
	20	151	1505	924	195	2288	1408	244	3239	1987	300	4356	2675	361	5641	3481	433	7086	4479	506	8704	5506	586	10,488	6670
	30	183	1446	876	232	2214	1349	287	3150	1910	347	4253	2631	412	5523	3431	494	6953	4421	577	8557	5444	672	10,328	6603
100	0	0	2491	1310	0	3925	2050	0	5729	2950	0	7914	4050	0	10,485	5300	0	13,454	6700	0	16,817	8600	0	20,578	10,300
	2	30	1975	1170	44	3027	1820	72	4313	2550	95	5834	3500	120	7591	4600	138	9577	5800	169	11,803	7200	204	14,264	8800
	5	82	1955	1159	107	3002	1803	136	4282	2531	172	5797	3475	208	7548	4566	245	9528	5769	293	11,748	7162	341	14,204	8756
	10	108	1923	1142	142	2961	1775	180	4231	2500	223	5737	3434	268	7478	4509	318	9447	5717	374	11,658	7100	436	14,105	8700
	15	126	1892	1124	163	2920	1747	206	4182	2469	252	5678	3392	304	7409	4451	358	9367	5665	418	11,569	7037	487	14,007	8610
	20	141	1861	1107	181	2880	1719	226	4133	2438	277	5619	3351	330	7341	4394	387	9289	5613	452	11,482	6975	523	13,910	8537
	30	170	1802	1071	215	2803	1663	265	4037	2375	319	5505	3267	378	7209	4279	446	9136	5509	514	11,310	6850	592	13,720	8391
	50	241	1688	1000	292	2657	1550	350	3856	2250	415	5289	3100	486	6956	4050	572	8841	5300	659	10,979	6600	752	13,354	8100

For SI units, 1 in. = 25.4 mm, 1 ft = 0.305 m, 1000 Btu/hr = 0.293 kW, 1 in.^{2} = 645 mm^2.

NA: Not applicable.

Table 13.1(b) Type B Double-Wall Vent

										Number of Appliances:			Single													
										Appliance Type:			Category I													
										Appliance Vent Connection:			Single-Wall Metal Connector													

		Vent Diameter — D (in.)																								
		3			4			5			6			7			8			9			10			12		
		Appliance Input Rating in Thousands of Btu per Hour																								
Height H (ft)	Lateral L (ft)	FAN		NAT	FAN		NAT	FAN		NAT	FAN		NAT	FAN		NAT	FAN		NAT	FAN		NAT	FAN		NAT	FAN	NAT
		Min	Max	Max	Min	Max	Max	Min	Max	Max	Min	Max	Max	Min	Max	Max	Min	Max	Max	Min	Max	Max	Min	Max	Max	Min Max	Max
6	0	38	77	45	59	151	85	85	249	140	126	373	204	165	522	284	211	695	369	267	894	469	371	1118	569	537 1639	849
	2	39	51	36	60	96	66	85	156	104	123	231	156	159	320	213	201	423	284	251	541	368	347	673	453	498 979	648
	4	NA	NA	33	74	92	63	102	152	102	146	225	152	187	313	208	237	416	277	295	533	360	409	664	443	584 971	638
	6	NA	NA	31	83	89	60	114	147	99	163	220	148	207	307	203	263	409	271	327	526	352	449	656	433	638 962	627
8	0	37	83	50	58	164	93	83	273	154	123	412	234	161	580	319	206	777	414	258	1002	536	360	1257	658	521 1852	967
	2	39	56	39	59	108	75	83	176	119	121	261	179	155	363	246	197	482	321	246	617	417	339	768	513	486 1120	743
	5	NA	NA	37	77	102	69	107	168	114	151	252	171	193	352	235	245	470	311	305	604	404	418	754	500	598 1104	730
	8	NA	NA	33	90	95	64	122	161	107	175	243	163	223	342	225	280	458	300	344	591	392	470	740	486	665 1089	715
10	0	37	87	53	57	174	99	82	293	165	120	444	254	158	628	344	202	844	449	253	1093	584	351	1373	718	507 2031	1057
	2	39	61	41	59	117	80	82	193	128	119	287	194	153	400	272	193	531	354	242	681	456	332	849	559	475 1242	848
	5	52	56	39	76	111	76	105	185	122	148	277	186	190	388	261	241	518	344	299	667	443	409	834	544	584 1224	825
	10	NA	NA	34	97	100	68	132	171	112	188	261	171	237	369	241	296	497	325	363	643	423	492	808	520	688 1194	788
15	0	36	93	57	56	190	111	80	325	186	116	499	283	153	713	388	195	966	523	244	1259	681	336	1591	838	488 2374	1237
	2	38	69	47	57	136	93	80	225	149	115	337	224	148	473	314	187	631	413	232	812	543	319	1015	673	457 1491	983
	5	51	63	44	75	128	86	102	216	140	144	326	217	182	459	298	231	616	400	287	795	526	392	997	657	562 1469	963
	10	NA	NA	39	95	116	79	128	201	131	182	308	203	228	438	284	284	592	381	349	768	501	470	966	628	664 1433	928
	15	NA	NA	NA	NA	NA	72	158	186	124	220	290	192	272	418	269	334	568	367	404	742	484	540	937	601	750 1399	894
20	0	35	96	60	54	200	118	78	346	201	114	537	306	149	772	428	190	1053	573	238	1379	750	326	1751	927	473 2631	1346
	2	37	74	50	56	148	99	78	248	165	113	375	248	144	528	344	182	708	468	227	914	611	309	1146	754	443 1689	1098
	5	50	68	47	73	140	94	100	239	158	141	363	239	178	514	334	224	692	457	279	896	596	381	1126	784	547 1665	1074
	10	NA	NA	41	93	129	86	125	223	146	177	344	224	222	491	316	277	666	437	339	866	570	457	1092	702	646 1626	1037
	15	NA	NA	NA	NA	NA	80	155	208	136	216	325	210	264	469	301	325	640	419	393	838	549	526	1060	677	730 1587	1005
	20	NA	NA	NA	NA	NA	NA	186	192	126	254	306	196	309	448	285	374	616	400	448	810	526	592	1028	651	808 1550	973
30	0	34	99	63	53	211	127	76	372	219	110	584	334	144	849	472	184	1168	647	229	1542	852	312	1971	1056	454 2996	1545
	2	37	80	56	55	164	111	76	281	183	109	429	279	139	610	392	175	823	533	219	1069	698	296	1346	863	424 1999	1308
	5	49	74	52	72	157	106	99	271	173	136	417	271	171	595	382	215	806	521	269	1049	684	366	1324	846	524 1971	1283
	10	NA	NA	NA	91	144	98	122	255	168	171	397	257	213	570	367	265	777	501	327	1017	662	440	1287	821	620 1927	1243
	15	NA	NA	NA	115	131	NA	151	239	157	208	377	242	255	547	349	312	750	481	379	985	638	507	1251	794	702 1884	1205
	20	NA	NA	NA	NA	NA	NA	181	223	NA	246	357	228	298	524	333	360	723	461	433	955	615	570	1216	768	780 1841	1166
	30	NA	NA	NA	NA	NA	NA	NA	NA	NA	389	NA	NA	389	477	305	461	670	426	541	895	574	704	1147	720	937 1759	1101
50	0	33	99	66	51	213	133	73	394	230	105	629	361	138	928	515	176	1292	704	220	1724	948	295	2223	1189	428 3432	1818
	2	36	84	61	53	181	121	73	318	205	104	495	312	133	712	443	168	971	613	209	1273	811	280	1615	1007	401 2426	1509
	5	48	80	NA	70	174	117	94	308	198	131	482	305	164	696	435	204	953	602	257	1252	795	347	1591	991	496 2396	1490
	10	NA	NA	NA	89	160	NA	118	292	186	162	461	292	203	671	420	253	923	583	313	1217	765	418	1551	963	589 2347	1455
	15	NA	NA	NA	112	148	NA	145	275	174	199	441	280	244	646	405	299	894	562	363	1183	736	481	1512	934	668 2299	1421
	20	NA	NA	NA	NA	NA	NA	176	257	NA	236	420	267	285	622	389	345	866	543	415	1150	708	544	1473	906	741 2251	1387
	30	NA	NA	NA	NA	NA	NA	NA	NA	NA	315	376	NA	373	573	NA	442	839	502	521	1086	649	674	1399	848	892 2159	1318
100	0	NA	NA	NA	49	214	NA	69	403	NA	100	659	395	131	991	555	166	1404	765	207	1900	1033	273	2479	1300	395 3912	2042
	2	NA	NA	NA	51	192	NA	70	351	NA	98	563	373	125	828	508	158	1152	698	196	1532	933	259	1970	1168	371 3021	1817
	5	NA	NA	NA	67	186	NA	90	342	NA	125	551	366	156	813	501	194	1134	688	240	1511	921	322	1945	1153	460 2990	1796
	10	NA	NA	NA	85	175	NA	113	324	NA	153	532	354	191	789	486	238	1104	672	293	1477	902	389	1905	1133	547 2938	1763
	15	NA	NA	NA	132	162	NA	138	310	NA	188	511	343	230	764	473	281	1075	656	342	1443	884	447	1865	1110	618 2888	1730
	20	NA	NA	NA	NA	NA	NA	168	295	NA	224	487	NA	270	739	458	325	1046	639	391	1410	864	507	1825	1087	690 2838	1696
	30	NA	NA	NA	NA	NA	NA	231	264	NA	301	448	NA	355	685	NA	418	988	NA	491	1343	824	631	1747	1041	834 2739	1627
	50	NA	NA	NA	NA	NA	NA	NA	NA	NA	NA	NA	NA	540	584	NA	617	866	NA	711	1205	NA	895	1591	NA	1138 2547	1489

For SI units, 1 in. = 25.4 mm, 1 ft = 0.305 m, 1000 Btu/hr = 0.293 kW, 1 in.^{2} = 645 mm^2.
NA: Not applicable.

Table 13.1(c) Masonry Chimney

		Number of Appliances:	Single
		Appliance Type:	Category I
		Appliance Vent Connection:	Type B Double-Wall Connector

Type B Double-Wall Connector Diameter — D (in.)
To be used with chimney areas within the size limits at bottom

Height H (ft)	Lateral L (ft)	3 FAN Min	3 FAN Max	3 NAT Max	4 FAN Min	4 FAN Max	4 NAT Max	5 FAN Min	5 FAN Max	5 NAT Max	6 FAN Min	6 FAN Max	6 NAT Max	7 FAN Min	7 FAN Max	7 NAT Max	8 FAN Min	8 FAN Max	8 NAT Max	9 FAN Min	9 FAN Max	9 NAT Max	10 FAN Min	10 FAN Max	10 NAT Max	12 FAN Min	12 FAN Max	12 NAT Max
6	2	NA	NA	28	NA	NA	52	NA	NA	86	NA	NA	130	NA	NA	180	NA	NA	247	NA	NA	320	NA	NA	401	NA	NA	581
	5	NA	NA	25	NA	NA	49	NA	NA	82	NA	NA	117	NA	NA	165	NA	NA	231	NA	NA	298	NA	NA	376	NA	NA	561
8	2	NA	NA	29	NA	NA	55	NA	NA	93	NA	NA	145	NA	NA	198	NA	NA	266	84	590	350	100	728	446	139	1024	651
	5	NA	NA	26	NA	NA	52	NA	NA	88	NA	NA	134	NA	NA	183	NA	NA	247	NA	NA	328	149	711	423	201	1007	640
	8	NA	NA	24	NA	NA	48	NA	NA	83	NA	NA	127	NA	NA	175	NA	NA	239	NA	NA	318	173	695	410	231	990	623
10	2	NA	NA	31	NA	NA	61	NA	NA	103	NA	NA	162	NA	NA	221	68	519	298	82	655	388	98	810	491	136	1144	724
	5	NA	NA	28	NA	NA	57	NA	NA	96	NA	NA	148	NA	NA	204	NA	NA	277	124	638	365	146	791	466	196	1124	712
	10	NA	NA	25	NA	NA	50	NA	NA	87	NA	NA	139	NA	NA	191	NA	NA	263	155	610	347	182	762	444	240	1093	668
15	2	NA	NA	35	NA	NA	67	NA	NA	114	NA	NA	179	53	475	250	64	613	336	77	779	441	92	968	562	127	1376	841
	5	NA	NA	35	NA	NA	62	NA	NA	107	NA	NA	164	NA	NA	231	99	594	313	118	759	416	139	946	533	186	1352	828
	10	NA	NA	28	NA	NA	55	NA	NA	97	NA	NA	153	NA	NA	216	126	565	296	148	727	394	173	912	567	229	1315	777
	15	NA	NA	NA	NA	NA	48	NA	NA	89	NA	NA	141	NA	NA	201	NA	NA	281	171	698	375	198	880	485	259	1280	742
20	2	NA	NA	38	NA	NA	74	NA	NA	124	NA	NA	201	51	522	274	61	678	375	73	867	491	87	1083	627	121	1548	953
	5	NA	NA	36	NA	NA	68	NA	NA	116	NA	NA	184	80	503	254	95	658	350	113	845	463	133	1059	597	179	1523	933
	10	NA	NA	NA	NA	NA	60	NA	NA	107	NA	NA	172	NA	NA	237	122	627	332	143	811	440	167	1022	566	221	1482	879
	15	NA	NA	NA	NA	NA	NA	NA	NA	97	NA	NA	159	NA	NA	220	NA	NA	314	165	780	418	191	987	541	251	1443	840
	20	NA	NA	NA	NA	NA	NA	NA	NA	83	NA	NA	148	NA	NA	206	NA	NA	296	186	750	397	214	955	513	277	1406	807
30	2	NA	NA	41	NA	NA	82	NA	NA	137	NA	NA	216	47	581	303	57	762	421	68	985	558	81	1240	717	111	1793	1112
	5	NA	NA	NA	NA	NA	76	NA	NA	128	NA	NA	198	75	561	281	90	741	393	106	962	526	125	1216	683	169	1766	1094
	10	NA	NA	NA	NA	NA	67	NA	NA	115	NA	NA	184	NA	NA	263	115	709	373	135	927	500	158	1176	648	210	1721	1025
	15	NA	NA	NA	NA	NA	NA	NA	NA	107	NA	NA	171	NA	NA	243	NA	NA	353	156	893	476	181	1139	621	239	1679	981
	20	NA	NA	NA	NA	NA	NA	NA	NA	91	NA	NA	159	NA	NA	227	NA	NA	332	176	860	450	203	1103	592	264	1638	940
	30	NA	NA	NA	NA	NA	NA	NA	NA	NA	NA	NA	NA	NA	NA	188	NA	NA	288	NA	NA	416	249	1035	555	318	1560	877
50	2	NA	NA	NA	NA	NA	92	NA	NA	161	NA	NA	251	NA	NA	351	51	840	477	61	1106	633	72	1413	812	99	2080	1243
	5	NA	NA	NA	NA	NA	NA	NA	NA	151	NA	NA	230	NA	NA	323	83	819	445	98	1083	596	116	1387	774	155	2052	1225
	10	NA	NA	NA	NA	NA	NA	NA	NA	138	NA	NA	215	NA	NA	304	NA	NA	424	126	1047	567	147	1347	733	195	2006	1147
	15	NA	NA	NA	NA	NA	NA	NA	NA	127	NA	NA	199	NA	NA	282	NA	NA	400	146	1010	539	170	1307	702	222	1961	1099
	20	NA	NA	NA	NA	NA	NA	NA	NA	NA	NA	NA	185	NA	NA	264	NA	NA	376	165	977	511	190	1269	669	246	1916	1050
	30	NA	NA	NA	NA	NA	NA	NA	NA	NA	NA	NA	NA	NA	NA	NA	NA	NA	327	NA	NA	468	233	1196	623	295	1832	984
Minimum internal area of chimney (in.^{2})			12			19			28			38			50			63			78			95			132	
Maximum internal area of chimney (in.^{2})		Seven times the listed appliance categorized vent area, flue collar area, or draft hood outlet areas.																										

For SI units, 1 in. = 25.4 mm, 1 ft = 0.305 m, 1000 Btu/hr = 0.293 kW, 1 in.^{2} = 645 mm^2.
NA: Not applicable.

Table 13.1(d) Masonry Chimney

		Number of Appliances:	Single
		Appliance Type:	Category I
		Appliance Vent Connection:	Single-Wall Metal Connector

Single-Wall Metal Connector Diameter — *D* (in.)
To be used with chimney areas within the size limits at bottom

Height H (ft)	Lateral L (ft)	3 FAN Min	3 FAN Max	3 NAT Max	4 FAN Min	4 FAN Max	4 NAT Max	5 FAN Min	5 FAN Max	5 NAT Max	6 FAN Min	6 FAN Max	6 NAT Max	7 FAN Min	7 FAN Max	7 NAT Max	8 FAN Min	8 FAN Max	8 NAT Max	9 FAN Min	9 FAN Max	9 NAT Max	10 FAN Min	10 FAN Max	10 NAT Max	12 FAN Min	12 FAN Max	12 NAT Max
6	2	NA	NA	28	NA	NA	52	NA	NA	86	NA	NA	130	NA	NA	180	NA	NA	247	NA	NA	319	NA	NA	400	NA	NA	580
	5	NA	NA	25	NA	NA	48	NA	NA	81	NA	NA	116	NA	NA	164	NA	NA	230	NA	NA	297	NA	NA	375	NA	NA	560
8	2	NA	NA	29	NA	NA	55	NA	NA	93	NA	NA	145	NA	NA	197	NA	NA	265	NA	NA	349	382	725	445	549	1021	650
	5	NA	NA	26	NA	NA	51	NA	NA	87	NA	NA	133	NA	NA	182	NA	NA	246	NA	NA	327	NA	NA	422	673	1003	638
	8	NA	NA	23	NA	NA	47	NA	NA	82	NA	NA	126	NA	NA	174	NA	NA	237	NA	NA	317	NA	NA	408	747	985	621
10	2	NA	NA	31	NA	NA	61	NA	NA	102	NA	NA	161	NA	NA	220	216	518	297	271	654	387	373	808	490	536	1142	722
	5	NA	NA	28	NA	NA	56	NA	NA	95	NA	NA	147	NA	NA	203	NA	NA	276	334	635	364	459	789	465	657	1121	710
	10	NA	NA	24	NA	NA	49	NA	NA	86	NA	NA	137	NA	NA	189	NA	NA	261	NA	NA	345	547	758	441	771	1088	665
15	2	NA	NA	35	NA	NA	67	NA	NA	113	NA	NA	178	166	473	249	211	611	335	264	776	440	362	965	560	520	1373	840
	5	NA	NA	32	NA	NA	61	NA	NA	106	NA	NA	163	NA	NA	230	261	591	312	325	755	414	444	942	531	637	1348	825
	10	NA	NA	27	NA	NA	54	NA	NA	96	NA	NA	151	NA	NA	214	NA	NA	294	392	722	392	531	907	504	749	1309	774
	15	NA	NA	NA	NA	NA	46	NA	NA	87	NA	NA	138	NA	NA	198	NA	NA	278	452	692	372	606	873	481	841	1272	738
20	2	NA	NA	38	NA	NA	73	NA	NA	123	NA	NA	200	163	520	273	206	675	374	258	864	490	252	1079	625	508	1544	950
	5	NA	NA	35	NA	NA	67	NA	NA	115	NA	NA	183	NA	NA	252	255	655	348	317	842	461	433	1055	594	623	1518	930
	10	NA	NA	NA	NA	NA	59	NA	NA	105	NA	NA	170	NA	NA	235	312	622	330	382	806	437	517	1016	562	733	1475	875
	15	NA	NA	NA	NA	NA	NA	NA	NA	95	NA	NA	156	NA	NA	217	NA	NA	311	442	773	414	591	979	539	823	1434	835
	20	NA	NA	NA	NA	NA	NA	NA	NA	80	NA	NA	144	NA	NA	202	NA	NA	292	NA	NA	392	663	944	510	911	1394	800
30	2	NA	NA	41	NA	NA	81	NA	NA	136	NA	NA	215	158	578	302	200	759	420	249	982	556	340	1237	715	489	1789	1110
	5	NA	NA	NA	NA	NA	75	NA	NA	127	NA	NA	196	NA	NA	279	245	737	391	306	958	524	417	1210	680	600	1760	1090
	10	NA	NA	NA	NA	NA	66	NA	NA	113	NA	NA	182	NA	NA	260	300	703	370	370	920	496	500	1168	644	708	1713	1020
	15	NA	NA	NA	NA	NA	NA	NA	NA	105	NA	NA	168	NA	NA	240	NA	NA	349	428	884	471	572	1128	615	798	1668	975
	20	NA	NA	NA	NA	NA	NA	NA	NA	88	NA	NA	155	NA	NA	223	NA	NA	327	NA	NA	445	643	1089	585	883	1624	932
	30	NA	NA	NA	NA	NA	NA	NA	NA	NA	NA	NA	NA	NA	NA	182	NA	NA	281	NA	NA	408	NA	NA	544	1055	1539	865
50	2	NA	NA	NA	NA	NA	91	NA	NA	160	NA	NA	250	NA	NA	350	191	837	475	238	1103	631	323	1408	810	463	2076	1240
	5	NA	NA	NA	NA	NA	NA	NA	NA	149	NA	NA	228	NA	NA	321	NA	NA	442	293	1078	593	398	1381	770	571	2044	1220
	10	NA	NA	NA	NA	NA	NA	NA	NA	136	NA	NA	212	NA	NA	301	NA	NA	420	355	1038	562	447	1337	728	674	1994	1140
	15	NA	NA	NA	NA	NA	NA	NA	NA	124	NA	NA	195	NA	NA	278	NA	NA	395	NA	NA	533	546	1294	695	761	1945	1090
	20	NA	NA	NA	NA	NA	NA	NA	NA	NA	NA	NA	180	NA	NA	258	NA	NA	370	NA	NA	504	616	1251	660	844	1898	1040
	30	NA	NA	NA	NA	NA	NA	NA	NA	NA	NA	NA	NA	NA	NA	NA	NA	NA	318	NA	NA	458	NA	NA	610	1009	1805	970
Minimum internal area of chimney (in.²)			12			19			28			38			50			63			78			95			132		
Maximum internal area of chimney (in.²)		Seven times the listed appliance categorized vent area, flue collar area, or draft hood outlet areas.																										

For SI units, 1 in. = 25.4 mm, 1 ft = 0.305 m, 1000 Btu/hr = 0.293 kW, 1 in.² = 645 mm².
NA: Not applicable.

Table 13.1(e) Single-Wall Metal Pipe or Type B Asbestos Cement Vent

		Number of Appliances:	Single
		Appliance Type:	Draft Hood–Equipped
		Appliance Vent Connection:	Connected Directly to Pipe or Vent

Height H (ft)	Lateral L (ft)	Diameter — D (in.) To be used with chimney areas within the size limits at bottom							
		3	4	5	6	7	8	10	12
		Appliance Input Rating in Thousands of Btu per Hour							
		Maximum Appliance Input Rating in Thousands of Btu per Hour							
6	0	39	70	116	170	232	312	500	750
	2	31	55	94	141	194	260	415	620
	5	28	51	88	128	177	242	390	600
8	0	42	76	126	185	252	340	542	815
	2	32	61	102	154	210	284	451	680
	5	29	56	95	141	194	264	430	648
	10	24	49	86	131	180	250	406	625
10	0	45	84	138	202	279	372	606	912
	2	35	67	111	168	233	311	505	760
	5	32	61	104	153	215	289	480	724
	10	27	54	94	143	200	274	455	700
	15	NA	46	84	130	186	258	432	666
15	0	49	91	151	223	312	420	684	1040
	2	39	72	122	186	260	350	570	865
	5	35	67	110	170	240	325	540	825
	10	30	58	103	158	223	308	514	795
	15	NA	50	93	144	207	291	488	760
	20	NA	NA	82	132	195	273	466	726
20	0	53	101	163	252	342	470	770	1190
	2	42	80	136	210	286	392	641	990
	5	38	74	123	192	264	364	610	945
	10	32	65	115	178	246	345	571	910
	15	NA	55	104	163	228	326	550	870
	20	NA	NA	91	149	214	306	525	832
30	0	56	108	183	276	384	529	878	1370
	2	44	84	148	230	320	441	730	1140
	5	NA	78	137	210	296	410	694	1080
	10	NA	68	125	196	274	388	656	1050
	15	NA	NA	113	177	258	366	625	1000
	20	NA	NA	99	163	240	344	596	960
	30	NA	NA	NA	NA	192	295	540	890
50	0	NA	120	210	310	443	590	980	1550
	2	NA	95	171	260	370	492	820	1290
	5	NA	NA	159	234	342	474	780	1230
	10	NA	NA	146	221	318	456	730	1190
	15	NA	NA	NA	200	292	407	705	1130
	20	NA	NA	NA	185	276	384	670	1080
	30	NA	NA	NA	NA	222	330	605	1010

For SI units, 1 in. = 25.4 mm, 1 ft = 0.305 m, 1000 Btu/hr = 0.293 kW, 1 in.^{2} = 645 mm^2.
NA: Not applicable.

Table 13.1(f) Exterior Masonry Chimney

			Number of Appliances:	Single
			Appliance Type:	NAT
			Appliance Vent Connection:	Type B Double-Wall Connector

Minimum Allowable Input Rating of Space-Heating Appliance in Thousands of Btu per Hour

Vent Height H (ft)	Internal Area of Chimney (in.^{2})							
	12	19	28	38	50	63	78	113
Local 99% winter design temperature: 37°F or greater								
6	0	0	0	0	0	0	0	0
8	0	0	0	0	0	0	0	0
10	0	0	0	0	0	0	0	0
15	NA	0	0	0	0	0	0	0
20	NA	NA	123	190	249	184	0	0
30	NA	NA	NA	NA	NA	393	334	0
50	NA	NA	NA	NA	NA	NA	NA	579
Local 99% winter design temperature: 27°F to 36°F								
6	0	0	68	116	156	180	212	266
8	0	0	82	127	167	187	214	263
10	0	51	97	141	183	201	225	265
15	NA	NA	NA	NA	233	253	274	305
20	NA	NA	NA	NA	NA	307	330	362
30	NA	NA	NA	NA	NA	419	445	485
50	NA	NA	NA	NA	NA	NA	NA	763
Local 99% winter design temperature: 17°F to 26°F								
6	NA	NA	NA	NA	NA	215	259	349
8	NA	NA	NA	NA	197	226	264	352
10	NA	NA	NA	NA	214	245	278	358
15	NA	NA	NA	NA	NA	296	331	398
20	NA	NA	NA	NA	NA	352	387	457
30	NA	NA	NA	NA	NA	NA	507	581
50	NA	NA	NA	NA	NA	NA	NA	NA
Local 99% winter design temperature: 5°F to 16°F								
6	NA	NA	NA	NA	NA	NA	NA	416
8	NA	NA	NA	NA	NA	NA	312	423
10	NA	NA	NA	NA	NA	289	331	430
15	NA	NA	NA	NA	NA	NA	393	485
20	NA	NA	NA	NA	NA	NA	450	547
30	NA	NA	NA	NA	NA	NA	NA	682
50	NA	NA	NA	NA	NA	NA	NA	972
Local 99% winter design temperature: −10°F to 4°F								
6	NA	NA	NA	NA	NA	NA	NA	484
8	NA	NA	NA	NA	NA	NA	NA	494
10	NA	NA	NA	NA	NA	NA	NA	513
15	NA	NA	NA	NA	NA	NA	NA	586
20	NA	NA	NA	NA	NA	NA	NA	650
30	NA	NA	NA	NA	NA	NA	NA	805
50	NA	NA	NA	NA	NA	NA	NA	1003
Local 99% winter design temperature: −11°F or lower *Not recommended for any vent configurations*								

For SI units, 1 in. = 25.4 mm, 1 in.^{2} = 645 mm^2, 1 ft = 0.305 m, 1000 Btu/hr = 0.293 kW, °C = (°F − 32)/1.8.

Note: See Figure F.2.4 for a map showing local 99 percent winter design temperatures in the United States.

NA: Not applicable.

13.1.1 Obstructions and Vent Dampers. Venting Table 13.1(a) through Table 13.1(f) shall not be used where obstructions are installed in the venting system. The installation of vents serving listed appliances with vent dampers shall be in accordance with the appliance manufacturer's instructions or in accordance with the following:

(1) The maximum capacity of the vent system shall be determined using the "NAT Max" column.
(2) The minimum capacity shall be determined as though the appliance were a fan-assisted appliance, using the "FAN Min" column to determine the minimum capacity of the vent system. Where the corresponding "Fan Min" is "NA," the vent configuration shall not be permitted and an alternative venting configuration shall be utilized.

13.1.2 Vent Downsizing. Where the vent size determined from the tables is smaller than the appliance draft hood outlet or flue collar, the use of the smaller size shall be permitted, provided that the installation complies with all of the following requirements:

(1) The total vent height (H) is at least 10 ft (3 m).
(2) Vents for appliance draft hood outlets or flue collars 12 in. (300 mm) in diameter or smaller are not reduced more than one table size.
(3) Vents for appliance draft hood outlets or flue collars larger than 12 in. (300 mm) in diameter are not reduced more than two table sizes.
(4) The maximum capacity listed in the tables for a fan-assisted appliance is reduced by 10 percent (0.90 × maximum table capacity).
(5) The draft hood outlet is greater than 4 in. (100 mm) in diameter. A 3 in. (80 mm) diameter vent shall not be connected to a 4 in. (100 mm) diameter draft hood outlet. This provision shall not apply to fan-assisted appliances.

13.1.3 Elbows. Single-appliance venting configurations with zero (0) lateral lengths in Table 13.1(a), Table 13.1(b), and Table 13.1(e) shall not have elbows in the venting system. Single-appliance venting with lateral lengths include two 90 degree elbows. For each additional elbow up to and including 45 degrees, the maximum capacity listed in the venting tables shall be reduced by 5 percent. For each additional elbow greater than 45 degrees up to and including 90 degrees, the maximum capacity listed in the venting tables shall be reduced by 10 percent. Where multiple offsets occur in a vent, the total lateral length of all offsets combined shall not exceed that specified in Table 13.1(a) through Table 13.1(e).

13.1.4 Zero Lateral. Zero (0) lateral (L) shall apply only to a straight vertical vent attached to a top outlet draft hood or flue collar.

13.1.5 High-Altitude Installations. Sea level input ratings shall be used when determining maximum capacity for high-altitude installation. Actual input (derated for altitude) shall be used for determining minimum capacity for high-altitude installation.

13.1.6 Two-Stage/Modulating Appliances. For appliances with more than one input rate, the minimum vent capacity (FAN Min) determined from the Chapter 13 tables shall be less than the lowest appliance input rating, and the maximum vent capacity (FAN Max/NAT Max) determined from the tables shall be greater than the highest appliance rating input.

13.1.7* Corrugated Chimney Liners. Listed corrugated metallic chimney liner systems in masonry chimneys shall be sized by using Table 13.1(a) or Table 13.1(b) for Type B vents, with the maximum capacity reduced by 20 percent (0.80 × maximum capacity) and the minimum capacity as shown in Table 13.1(a) or Table 13.1(b). Corrugated metallic liner systems installed with bends or offsets shall have their maximum capacity further reduced in accordance with 13.1.3. The 20 percent reduction for corrugated metallic chimney liner systems includes an allowance for one long radius 90-degree turn at the bottom of the liner.

13.1.8 Connection to Chimney Liners. Connections between chimney liners and listed double-wall connectors shall be made with listed adapters designed for such purpose.

13.1.9 Vertical Vent Upsizing/7 × Rule. Where the vertical vent has a larger diameter than the vent connector, the vertical vent diameter shall be used to determine the minimum vent capacity, and the connector diameter shall be used to determine the maximum vent capacity. The flow area of the vertical vent shall not exceed seven times the flow area of the listed appliance categorized vent area, flue collar area, or draft hood outlet area unless designed in accordance with engineering methods.

13.1.10 Draft Hood Conversion Accessories. Draft hood conversion accessories for use with masonry chimneys venting listed Category I fan-assisted appliances shall be listed and installed in accordance with the listed accessory manufacturers' installation instructions.

13.1.11 Chimneys and Vent Locations. Table 13.1(a) through Table 13.1(e) shall be used only for chimneys and vents not exposed to the outdoors below the roof line. A Type B vent or listed chimney lining system passing through an unused masonry chimney flue shall not be considered to be exposed to the outdoors. Where vents extend outdoors above the roof more than 5 ft (1.5 m) higher than required by Table 12.7.3, and where vents terminate in accordance with 12.7.3(1)(b), the outdoor portion of the vent shall be enclosed as required by this paragraph for vents not considered to be exposed to the outdoors, or such venting system shall be engineered. A Type B vent passing through an unventilated enclosure or chase insulated to a value of not less than R8 shall not be considered to be exposed to the outdoors. Table 13.1(c) in combination with Table 13.1(f) shall be used for clay tile–lined exterior masonry chimneys, provided all of the following requirements are met:

(1) The vent connector is Type B double wall.
(2) The vent connector length is limited to 18 in./in. (18 mm/mm) of vent connector diameter.
(3) The appliance is draft hood equipped.
(4) The input rating is less than the maximum capacity given in Table 13.1(c).
(5) For a water heater, the outdoor design temperature shall not be less than 5°F (−15°C).
(6) For a space-heating appliance, the input rating is greater than the minimum capacity given by Table 13.1(f).

13.1.12 Corrugated Vent Connector Size. Corrugated vent connectors shall not be smaller than the listed appliance categorized vent diameter, flue collar diameter, or draft hood outlet diameter.

13.1.13 Upsizing. Vent connectors shall not be upsized more than two sizes greater than the listed appliance categorized vent diameter, flue collar diameter, or draft hood outlet diameter.

13.1.14 Multiple Vertical Vent Sizes. In a single run of vent or vent connector, more than one diameter and type shall be permitted to be used, provided that all the sizes and types are permitted by the tables.

13.1.15 Interpolation. Interpolation shall be permitted in calculating capacities for vent dimensions that fall between table entries.

13.1.16 Extrapolation. Extrapolation beyond the table entries shall not be permitted.

13.1.17 Sizing Vents Not Covered by Tables. Where a vent height is lower than 6 ft (1.8 m) or higher than shown in the Chapter 13 tables, an engineering method shall be used to calculate the vent capacity.

13.1.18 Height Entries. Where the actual height of a vent falls between entries in the height column of the applicable table in Table 13.1(a) through Table 13.1(f) either of the following shall be used:

(1) Interpolation
(2) The lower appliance input rating shown in the table entries for FAN Max and NAT Max column values; and the higher appliance input rating for the FAN Min column values

13.2 Additional Requirements to Multiple-Appliance Vent. This section shall apply where Table 13.2(a) through Table 13.2(i) are used to size multiple appliance venting systems. Subsections 13.2.1 through 13.2.30 apply to Table 13.2(a) through Table 13.2(i).

13.2.1 Obstructions and Vent Dampers. Venting Table 13.2(a) through Table 13.2(i) shall not be used where obstructions are installed in the venting system. The installation of vents serving listed appliances with vent dampers shall be in accordance with the appliance manufacturer's instructions, or in accordance with the following:

(1) The maximum capacity of the vent connector shall be determined using the NAT Max column.
(2) The maximum capacity of the vertical vent or chimney shall be determined using the FAN+NAT column when the second appliance is a fan-assisted appliance, or the NAT+NAT column when the second appliance is equipped with a draft hood.
(3) The minimum capacity shall be determined as if the appliance were a fan-assisted appliance, as follows:
    (a) The minimum capacity of the vent connector shall be determined using the FAN Min column.
    (b) The FAN+FAN column shall be used when the second appliance is a fan-assisted appliance, and the FAN+NAT column shall be used when the second appliance is equipped with a draft hood, to determine whether the vertical vent or chimney configuration is not permitted (NA). Where the vent configuration is NA, the vent configuration shall not be permitted and an alternative venting configuration shall be utilized.

13.2.2 Vent Connector Maximum Length. The maximum vent connector horizontal length shall be 18 in./in. (18 mm/mm) of connector diameter as shown in Table 13.2.2, or as permitted by 13.2.3.

13.2.3 Vent Connector Exceeding Maximum Length. The vent connector shall be routed to the vent utilizing the shortest possible route. Connectors with longer horizontal lengths than those listed in Table 13.2.2 are permitted under the following conditions:

(1) The maximum capacity (FAN Max or NAT Max) of the vent connector shall be reduced 10 percent for each additional multiple of the length listed in Table 13.2.2. For example, the maximum length listed for a 4 in. (100 mm) connector is 6 ft (1.8 m). With a connector length greater than 6 ft (1.8 m) but not exceeding 12 ft (3.7 m), the maximum capacity must be reduced by 10 percent (0.90 × maximum vent connector capacity). With a connector length greater than 12 ft (3.7 m) but not exceeding 18 ft (5.5 m), the maximum capacity must be reduced by 20 percent (0.80 × maximum vent capacity).
(2) For a connector serving a fan-assisted appliance, the minimum capacity (FAN Min) of the connector shall be determined by referring to the corresponding single appliance table. For Type B double-wall connectors, Table 13.1(a) shall be used. For single-wall connectors, Table 13.1(b) shall be used. The height (H) and lateral (L) shall be measured according to the procedures for a single appliance vent, as if the other appliances were not present.

13.2.4 Vent Connector Manifolds. Where the vent connectors are combined prior to entering the vertical portion of the common vent to form a common vent manifold, the size of the common vent manifold and the common vent shall be determined by applying a 10 percent reduction (0.90 × maximum common vent capacity) to the common vent capacity part of the common vent tables. The length of the common vent manifold (LM) shall not exceed 18 in./in. (18 mm/mm) of common vent diameter (D).

13.2.5 Vent Offsets. Where the common vertical vent is offset, the maximum capacity of the common vent shall be reduced in accordance with 13.2.6 and the horizontal length of the common vent offset shall not exceed 18 in./in. (18 mm/mm) of common vent diameter (D). Where multiple offsets occur in a common vent, the total horizontal length of all offsets combined shall not exceed 18 in./in. (18 mm/mm) of the common vent diameter.

13.2.6 Elbows in Vents. For each elbow up to and including 45 degrees in the common vent, the maximum common vent capacity listed in the venting tables shall be reduced by 5 percent. For each elbow greater than 45 degrees up to and including 90 degrees, the maximum common vent capacity listed in the venting tables shall be reduced by 10 percent.

13.2.7 Elbows in Connectors. The vent connector capacities listed in the common vent sizing tables include allowance for two 90 degree elbows. For each additional elbow up to and including 45 degrees, the maximum vent connector capacity listed in the venting tables shall be reduced by 5 percent. For each elbow greater than 45 degrees up to and including 90 degrees, the maximum vent connector capacity listed in the venting tables shall be reduced by 10 percent.

13.2.8 Common Vent Minimum Size. The cross-sectional area of the common vent shall be equal to or greater than the cross-sectional area of the largest connector.

Table 13.2(a) Type B Double-Wall Vent

		Number of Appliances:	Two or More
		Appliance Type:	Category I
		Appliance Vent Connection:	Type B Double-Wall Connector

Vent Connector Capacity

Type B Double-Wall Vent and Connector Diameter — D (in.)

Appliance Input Rating Limits in Thousands of Btu per Hour

Vent Height H (ft)	Connector Rise R (ft)	3 FAN Min	3 FAN Max	3 NAT Max	4 FAN Min	4 FAN Max	4 NAT Max	5 FAN Min	5 FAN Max	5 NAT Max	6 FAN Min	6 FAN Max	6 NAT Max	7 FAN Min	7 FAN Max	7 NAT Max	8 FAN Min	8 FAN Max	8 NAT Max	9 FAN Min	9 FAN Max	9 NAT Max	10 FAN Min	10 FAN Max	10 NAT Max
6	1	22	37	26	35	66	46	46	106	72	58	164	104	77	225	142	92	296	185	109	376	237	128	466	289
	2	23	41	31	37	75	55	48	121	86	60	183	124	79	253	168	95	333	220	112	424	282	131	526	345
	3	24	44	35	38	81	62	49	132	96	62	199	139	82	275	189	97	363	248	114	463	317	134	575	386
8	1	22	40	27	35	72	48	49	114	76	64	176	109	84	243	148	100	320	194	118	408	248	138	507	303
	2	23	44	32	36	80	57	51	128	90	66	195	129	86	269	175	103	356	230	121	454	294	141	564	358
	3	24	47	36	37	87	64	53	139	101	67	210	145	88	290	198	105	384	258	123	492	330	143	612	402
10	1	22	43	28	34	78	50	49	123	78	65	189	113	89	257	154	106	341	200	125	436	257	146	542	314
	2	23	47	33	36	86	59	51	136	93	67	206	134	91	282	182	109	374	238	128	479	305	149	596	372
	3	24	50	37	37	92	67	52	146	104	69	220	150	94	303	205	111	402	268	131	515	342	152	642	417
15	1	21	50	30	33	89	53	47	142	83	64	220	120	88	298	163	110	389	214	134	493	273	162	609	333
	2	22	53	35	35	96	63	49	153	99	66	235	142	91	320	193	112	419	253	137	532	323	165	658	394
	3	24	55	40	36	102	71	51	163	111	68	248	160	93	339	218	115	445	286	140	565	365	167	700	444
20	1	21	54	31	33	99	56	46	157	87	62	246	125	86	334	171	107	436	224	131	552	285	158	681	347
	2	22	57	37	34	105	66	48	167	104	64	259	149	89	354	202	110	463	265	134	587	339	161	725	414
	3	23	60	42	35	110	74	50	176	116	66	271	168	91	371	228	113	486	300	137	618	383	164	764	466
30	1	20	62	33	31	113	59	45	181	93	60	288	134	83	391	182	103	512	238	125	649	305	151	802	372
	2	21	64	39	33	118	70	47	190	110	62	299	158	85	408	215	105	535	282	129	679	360	155	840	439
	3	22	66	44	34	123	79	48	198	124	64	309	178	88	423	242	108	555	317	132	706	405	158	874	494
50	1	19	71	36	30	133	64	43	216	101	57	349	145	78	477	197	97	627	257	120	797	330	144	984	403
	2	21	73	43	32	137	76	45	223	119	59	358	172	81	490	234	100	645	306	123	820	392	148	1014	478
	3	22	75	48	33	141	86	46	229	134	61	366	194	83	502	263	103	661	343	126	842	441	151	1043	538
100	1	18	82	37	28	158	66	40	262	104	53	442	150	73	611	204	91	810	266	112	1038	341	135	1285	417
	2	19	83	44	30	161	79	42	267	123	55	447	178	75	619	242	94	822	316	115	1054	405	139	1306	494
	3	20	84	50	31	163	89	44	272	138	57	452	200	78	627	272	97	834	355	118	1069	455	142	1327	555

Common Vent Capacity

Type B Double-Wall Common Vent Diameter — D (in.)

Combined Appliance Input Rating in Thousands of Btu per Hour

Vent Height H (ft)	4 FAN+FAN	4 FAN+NAT	4 NAT+NAT	5 FAN+FAN	5 FAN+NAT	5 NAT+NAT	6 FAN+FAN	6 FAN+NAT	6 NAT+NAT	7 FAN+FAN	7 FAN+NAT	7 NAT+NAT	8 FAN+FAN	8 FAN+NAT	8 NAT+NAT	9 FAN+FAN	9 FAN+NAT	9 NAT+NAT	10 FAN+FAN	10 FAN+NAT	10 NAT+NAT
6	92	81	65	140	116	103	204	161	147	309	248	200	404	314	260	547	434	335	672	520	410
8	101	90	73	155	129	114	224	178	163	339	275	223	444	348	290	602	480	378	740	577	465
10	110	97	79	169	141	124	243	194	178	367	299	242	477	377	315	649	522	405	800	627	495
15	125	112	91	195	164	144	283	228	206	427	352	280	556	444	365	753	612	465	924	733	565
20	136	123	102	215	183	160	314	255	229	475	394	310	621	499	405	842	688	523	1035	826	640
30	152	138	118	244	210	185	361	297	266	547	459	360	720	585	470	979	808	605	1209	975	740
50	167	153	134	279	244	214	421	353	310	641	547	423	854	706	550	1164	977	705	1451	1188	860
100	175	163	NA	311	277	NA	489	421	NA	751	658	479	1025	873	625	1408	1215	800	1784	1502	975

Table 13.2(a) Continued

		Number of Appliances:	Two or More
		Appliance Type:	Category I
		Appliance Vent Connection:	Type B Double-Wall Connector

Vent Connector Capacity

		Type B Double-Wall Vent and Connector Diameter — D (in.)																					
		12			14			16			18			20			22			24			
Vent Height H (ft)	Connector Rise R (ft)	\multicolumn{21}{c}{Appliance Input Rating Limits in Thousands of Btu per Hour}																				
		FAN		NAT	FAN		NAT	FAN		NAT	FAN		NAT	FAN		NAT	FAN		NAT	FAN		NAT
		Min	Max	Max	Min	Max	Max	Min	Max	Max	Min	Max	Max	Min	Max	Max	Min	Max	Max	Min	Max	Max
6	2	174	764	496	223	1046	653	281	1371	853	346	1772	1080	NA	NA	NA	NA	NA	NA	NA	NA	NA
	4	180	897	616	230	1231	827	287	1617	1081	352	2069	1370	NA	NA	NA	NA	NA	NA	NA	NA	NA
	6	NA	NA	NA	NA	NA	NA	NA	NA	NA	NA	NA	NA	NA	NA	NA	NA	NA	NA	NA	NA	NA
8	2	186	822	516	238	1126	696	298	1478	910	365	1920	1150	NA	NA	NA	NA	NA	NA	NA	NA	NA
	4	192	952	644	244	1307	884	305	1719	1150	372	2211	1460	471	2737	1800	560	3319	2180	662	3957	2590
	6	198	1050	772	252	1445	1072	313	1902	1390	380	2434	1770	478	3018	2180	568	3665	2640	669	4373	3130
10	2	196	870	536	249	1195	730	311	1570	955	379	2049	1205	NA	NA	NA	NA	NA	NA	NA	NA	NA
	4	201	997	664	256	1371	924	318	1804	1205	387	2332	1535	486	2887	1890	581	3502	2280	686	4175	2710
	6	207	1095	792	263	1509	1118	325	1989	1455	395	2556	1865	494	3169	2290	589	3849	2760	694	4593	3270
15	2	214	967	568	272	1334	790	336	1760	1030	408	2317	1305	NA	NA	NA	NA	NA	NA	NA	NA	NA
	4	221	1085	712	279	1499	1006	344	1978	1320	416	2579	1665	523	3197	2060	624	3881	2490	734	4631	2960
	6	228	1181	856	286	1632	1222	351	2157	1610	424	2796	2025	533	3470	2510	634	4216	3030	743	5085	3600
20	2	223	1051	596	291	1443	840	357	1911	1095	430	2533	1385	NA	NA	NA	NA	NA	NA	NA	NA	NA
	4	230	1162	748	298	1597	1064	365	2116	1395	438	2778	1765	554	3447	2180	661	4190	2630	772	5005	3130
	6	237	1253	900	307	1726	1288	373	2287	1695	450	2984	2145	567	3708	2650	671	4511	3190	785	5392	3790
30	2	216	1217	632	286	1664	910	367	2183	1190	461	2891	1540	NA	NA	NA	NA	NA	NA	NA	NA	NA
	4	223	1316	792	294	1802	1160	376	2366	1510	474	3110	1920	619	3840	2365	728	4861	2860	847	5606	3410
	6	231	1400	952	303	1920	1410	384	2524	1830	485	3299	2340	632	4080	2875	741	4976	3480	860	5961	4150
50	2	206	1479	689	273	2023	1007	350	2659	1315	435	3548	1665	NA	NA	NA	NA	NA	NA	NA	NA	NA
	4	213	1561	860	281	2139	1291	359	2814	1685	447	3730	2135	580	4601	2633	709	5569	3185	851	6633	3790
	6	221	1631	1031	290	2242	1575	369	2951	2055	461	3893	2605	594	4808	3208	724	5826	3885	867	6943	4620
100	2	192	1923	712	254	2644	1050	326	3490	1370	402	4707	1740	NA	NA	NA	NA	NA	NA	NA	NA	NA
	4	200	1984	888	263	2731	1346	336	3606	1760	414	4842	2220	523	5982	2750	639	7254	3330	769	8650	3950
	6	208	2035	1064	272	2811	1642	346	3714	2150	426	4968	2700	539	6143	3350	654	7453	4070	786	8892	4810

Common Vent Capacity

	Type B Double-Wall Common Vent Diameter — D (in.)																					
	12			14			16			18			20			22			24			
Vent Height H (ft)	\multicolumn{21}{c}{Combined Appliance Input Rating in Thousands of Btu per Hour}																				
	FAN +FAN	FAN +NAT	NAT +NAT	FAN +FAN	FAN +NAT	NAT +NAT	FAN +FAN	FAN +NAT	NAT +NAT	FAN +FAN	FAN +NAT	NAT +NAT	FAN +FAN	FAN +NAT	NAT +NAT	FAN +FAN	FAN +NAT	NAT +NAT	FAN +FAN	FAN +NAT	NAT +NAT
6	900	696	588	1284	990	815	1735	1336	1065	2253	1732	1345	2838	2180	1660	3488	2677	1970	4206	3226	2390
8	994	773	652	1423	1103	912	1927	1491	1190	2507	1936	1510	3162	2439	1860	3890	2998	2200	4695	3616	2680
10	1076	841	712	1542	1200	995	2093	1625	1300	2727	2113	1645	3444	2665	2030	4241	3278	2400	5123	3957	2920
15	1247	986	825	1794	1410	1158	2440	1910	1510	3184	2484	1910	4026	3133	2360	4971	3862	2790	6016	4670	3400
20	1405	1116	916	2006	1588	1290	2722	2147	1690	3561	2798	2140	4548	3552	2640	5573	4352	3120	6749	5261	3800
30	1658	1327	1025	2373	1892	1525	3220	2558	1990	4197	3326	2520	5303	4193	3110	6539	5157	3680	7940	6247	4480
50	2024	1640	1280	2911	2347	1863	3964	3183	2430	5184	4149	3075	6567	5240	3800	8116	6458	4500	9837	7813	5475
100	2569	2131	1670	3732	3076	2450	5125	4202	3200	6749	5509	4050	8597	6986	5000	10,681	8648	5920	13,004	10,499	7200

For SI units, 1 in. = 25.4 mm, 1 in.^{2} = 645 mm^2, 1 ft = 0.305 m, 1000 Btu/hr = 0.293 kW.

Table 13.2(b) Type B Double-Wall Vent

		Number of Appliances:	Two or More
		Appliance Type:	Category I
		Appliance Vent Connection:	Single-Wall Metal Connector

Vent Connector Capacity

		Single-Wall Metal Vent Connector Diameter — D (in.)																						
		3			4			5			6			7			8			9			10		
Vent Height H (ft)	Connector Rise R (ft)	Appliance Input Rating Limits in Thousands of Btu per Hour																							
		FAN		NAT	FAN		NAT	FAN		NAT	FAN		NAT	FAN		NAT	FAN		NAT	FAN		NAT	FAN		NAT
		Min	Max	Max	Min	Max	Max	Min	Max	Max	Min	Max	Max	Min	Max	Max	Min	Max	Max	Min	Max	Max	Min	Max	Max
6	1	NA	NA	26	NA	NA	46	NA	NA	71	NA	NA	102	207	223	140	262	293	183	325	373	234	447	463	286
	2	NA	NA	31	NA	NA	55	NA	NA	85	168	182	123	215	251	167	271	331	219	334	422	281	458	524	344
	3	NA	NA	34	NA	NA	62	121	131	95	175	198	138	222	273	188	279	361	247	344	462	316	468	574	385
8	1	NA	NA	27	NA	NA	48	NA	NA	75	NA	NA	106	226	240	145	285	316	191	352	403	244	481	502	299
	2	NA	NA	32	NA	NA	57	125	126	89	184	193	127	234	266	173	293	353	228	360	450	292	492	560	355
	3	NA	NA	35	NA	NA	64	130	138	100	191	208	144	241	287	197	302	381	256	370	489	328	501	609	400
10	1	NA	NA	28	NA	NA	50	119	121	77	182	186	110	240	253	150	302	335	196	372	429	252	506	534	308
	2	NA	NA	33	84	85	59	124	134	91	189	203	132	248	278	183	311	369	235	381	473	302	517	589	368
	3	NA	NA	36	89	91	67	129	144	102	197	217	148	257	299	203	320	398	265	391	511	339	528	637	413
15	1	NA	NA	29	79	87	52	116	138	81	177	214	116	238	291	158	312	380	208	397	482	266	556	596	324
	2	NA	NA	34	83	94	62	121	150	97	185	230	138	246	314	189	321	411	248	407	522	317	568	646	387
	3	NA	NA	39	87	100	70	127	160	109	193	243	157	255	333	215	331	438	281	418	557	360	579	690	437
20	1	49	56	30	78	97	54	115	152	84	175	238	120	233	325	165	306	425	217	390	538	276	546	664	336
	2	52	59	36	82	103	64	120	163	101	182	252	144	243	346	197	317	453	259	400	574	331	558	709	403
	3	55	62	40	87	107	72	125	172	113	190	264	164	252	363	223	326	476	294	412	607	375	570	750	457
30	1	47	60	31	77	110	57	112	175	89	169	278	129	226	380	175	296	497	230	378	630	294	528	779	358
	2	51	62	37	81	115	67	117	185	106	177	290	152	236	397	208	307	521	274	389	662	349	541	819	425
	3	54	64	42	85	119	76	122	193	120	185	300	172	244	412	235	316	542	309	400	690	394	555	855	482
50	1	46	69	34	75	128	60	109	207	96	162	336	137	217	460	188	284	604	245	364	768	314	507	951	384
	2	49	71	40	79	132	72	114	215	113	170	345	164	226	473	223	294	623	293	376	793	375	520	983	458
	3	52	72	45	83	136	82	119	221	123	178	353	186	235	486	252	304	640	331	387	816	423	535	1013	518
100	1	45	79	34	71	150	61	104	249	98	153	424	140	205	585	192	269	774	249	345	993	321	476	1236	393
	2	48	80	41	75	153	73	110	255	115	160	428	167	212	593	228	279	788	299	358	1011	383	490	1259	469
	3	51	81	46	79	157	85	114	260	129	168	433	190	222	603	256	289	801	339	368	1027	431	506	1280	527

Common Vent Capacity

	Type B Double-Wall Vent Diameter — D (in.)																			
	4			5			6			7			8			9			10		
Vent Height H (ft)	Combined Appliance Input Rating in Thousands of Btu per Hour																			
	FAN +FAN	FAN +NAT	NAT +NAT	FAN +FAN	FAN +NAT	NAT +NAT	FAN +FAN	FAN +NAT	NAT +NAT	FAN +FAN	FAN +NAT	NAT +NAT	FAN +FAN	FAN +NAT	NAT +NAT	FAN +FAN	FAN +NAT	NAT +NAT	FAN +FAN	FAN +NAT	NAT +NAT
6	NA	78	64	NA	113	99	200	158	144	304	244	196	398	310	257	541	429	332	665	515	407
8	NA	87	71	NA	126	111	213	173	159	331	269	218	436	342	285	592	473	373	730	569	460
10	NA	94	76	163	137	120	237	189	174	357	292	236	467	369	309	638	512	398	787	617	487
15	121	108	88	189	159	140	275	221	200	416	343	274	544	434	357	738	599	456	905	718	553
20	131	118	98	208	177	156	305	247	223	463	383	302	606	487	395	824	673	512	1013	808	626
30	145	132	113	236	202	180	350	286	257	533	446	349	703	570	459	958	790	593	1183	952	723
50	159	145	128	268	233	208	406	337	296	622	529	410	833	686	535	1139	954	689	1418	1157	838
100	166	153	NA	297	263	NA	469	398	NA	726	633	464	999	846	606	1378	1185	780	1741	1459	948

For SI units, 1 in. = 25.4 mm, 1 in.^{2} = 645 mm^2, 1 ft = 0.305 m, 1000 Btu/hr = 0.293 kW.

Table 13.2(c) Masonry Chimney

		Number of Appliances:	Two or More
		Appliance Type:	Category I
		Appliance Vent Connection:	Type B Double-Wall Connector

Vent Connector Capacity

		Type B Double-Wall Vent Connector Diameter — D (in.)																						
		3			4			5			6			7			8			9			10		
		Appliance Input Rating Limits in Thousands of Btu per Hour																						
Vent Height H (ft)	Connector Rise R (ft)	FAN		NAT	FAN		NAT	FAN		NAT	FAN		NAT	FAN		NAT	FAN		NAT	FAN		NAT	FAN		NAT
		Min	Max	Max	Min	Max	Max	Min	Max	Max	Min	Max	Max	Min	Max	Max	Min	Max	Max	Min	Max	Max	Min	Max	Max
6	1	24	33	21	39	62	40	52	106	67	65	194	101	87	274	141	104	370	201	124	479	253	145	599	319
	2	26	43	28	41	79	52	53	133	85	67	230	124	89	324	173	107	436	232	127	562	300	148	694	378
	3	27	49	34	42	92	61	55	155	97	69	262	143	91	369	203	109	491	270	129	633	349	151	795	439
8	1	24	39	22	39	72	41	55	117	69	71	213	105	94	304	148	113	414	210	134	539	267	156	682	335
	2	26	47	29	40	87	53	57	140	86	73	246	127	97	350	179	116	473	240	137	615	311	160	776	394
	3	27	52	34	42	97	62	59	159	98	75	269	145	99	383	206	119	517	276	139	672	358	163	848	452
10	1	24	42	22	38	80	42	55	130	71	74	232	108	101	324	153	120	444	216	142	582	277	165	739	348
	2	26	50	29	40	93	54	57	153	87	76	261	129	103	366	184	123	498	247	145	652	321	168	825	407
	3	27	55	35	41	105	63	58	170	100	78	284	148	106	397	209	126	540	281	147	705	366	171	893	463
15	1	24	48	23	38	93	44	54	154	74	72	277	114	100	384	164	125	511	229	153	658	297	184	824	375
	2	25	55	31	39	105	55	56	174	89	74	299	134	103	419	192	128	558	260	156	718	339	187	900	432
	3	26	59	35	41	115	64	57	189	102	76	319	153	105	448	215	131	597	292	159	760	382	190	960	486
20	1	24	52	24	37	102	46	53	172	77	71	313	119	98	437	173	123	584	239	150	752	312	180	943	397
	2	25	58	31	39	114	56	55	190	91	73	335	138	101	467	199	126	625	270	153	805	354	184	1011	452
	3	26	63	35	40	123	65	57	204	104	75	353	157	104	493	222	129	661	301	156	851	396	187	1067	505
30	1	24	54	25	37	111	48	52	192	82	69	357	127	96	504	187	119	680	255	145	883	337	175	1115	432
	2	25	60	32	38	122	58	54	208	95	72	376	145	99	531	209	122	715	287	149	928	378	179	1171	484
	3	26	64	36	40	131	66	56	221	107	74	392	163	101	554	233	125	746	317	152	968	418	182	1220	535
50	1	23	51	25	36	116	51	51	209	89	67	405	143	92	582	213	115	798	294	140	1049	392	168	1334	506
	2	24	59	32	37	127	61	53	225	102	70	421	161	95	604	235	118	827	326	143	1085	433	172	1379	558
	3	26	64	36	39	135	69	55	237	115	72	435	180	98	624	260	121	854	357	147	1118	474	176	1421	611
100	1	23	46	24	35	108	50	49	208	92	65	428	155	88	640	237	109	907	334	134	1222	454	161	1589	596
	2	24	53	31	37	120	60	51	224	105	67	444	174	92	660	260	113	933	368	138	1253	497	165	1626	651
	3	25	59	35	38	130	68	53	237	118	69	458	193	94	679	285	116	956	399	141	1282	540	169	1661	705

Common Vent Capacity

	Minimum Internal Area of Masonry Chimney Flue (in.^{2})																							
	12			19			28			38			50			63			78			113		
Vent Height H (ft)	Combined Appliance Input Rating in Thousands of Btu per Hour																							
	FAN +FAN	FAN +NAT	NAT +NAT	FAN +FAN	FAN +NAT	NAT +NAT	FAN +FAN	FAN +NAT	NAT +NAT	FAN +FAN	FAN +NAT	NAT +NAT	FAN +FAN	FAN +NAT	NAT +NAT	FAN +FAN	FAN +NAT	NAT +NAT	FAN +FAN	FAN +NAT	NAT +NAT	FAN +FAN	FAN +NAT	NAT +NAT
6	NA	74	25	NA	119	46	NA	178	71	NA	257	103	NA	351	143	NA	458	188	NA	582	246	1041	853	NA
8	NA	80	28	NA	130	53	NA	193	82	NA	279	119	NA	384	163	NA	501	218	724	636	278	1144	937	408
10	NA	84	31	NA	138	56	NA	207	90	NA	299	131	NA	409	177	606	538	236	776	686	302	1226	1010	454
15	NA	NA	36	NA	152	67	NA	233	106	NA	334	152	523	467	212	682	611	283	874	781	365	1374	1156	546
20	NA	NA	41	NA	NA	75	NA	250	122	NA	368	172	565	508	243	742	668	325	955	858	419	1513	1286	648
30	NA	NA	NA	NA	NA	NA	NA	270	137	NA	404	198	615	564	278	816	747	381	1062	969	496	1702	1473	749
50	NA	NA	NA	NA	NA	NA	NA	NA	NA	NA	NA	NA	NA	620	328	879	831	461	1165	1089	606	1905	1692	922
100	NA	NA	NA	NA	NA	NA	NA	NA	NA	NA	NA	NA	NA	NA	348	NA	NA	499	NA	NA	669	2053	1921	1058

For SI units, 1 in. = 25.4 mm, 1 in.^{2} = 645 mm^2, 1 ft = 0.305 m, 1000 Btu/hr = 0.293 kW.

Table 13.2(d) Masonry Chimney

		Number of Appliances:	Two or More
		Appliance Type:	Category I
		Appliance Vent Connection:	Single-Wall Metal Connector

Vent Connector Capacity

		Single-Wall Metal Vent Connector Diameter — D (in.)																						
		3			4			5			6			7			8			9			10		
Vent Height H (ft)	Connector Rise R (ft)	Appliance Input Rating Limits in Thousands of Btu per Hour																							
		FAN		NAT	FAN		NAT	FAN		NAT	FAN		NAT	FAN		NAT	FAN		NAT	FAN		NAT	FAN		NAT
		Min	Max	Max	Min	Max	Max	Min	Max	Max	Min	Max	Max	Min	Max	Max	Min	Max	Max	Min	Max	Max	Min	Max	Max
6	1	NA	NA	21	NA	NA	39	NA	NA	66	179	191	100	231	271	140	292	366	290	362	474	252	499	594	316
	2	NA	NA	28	NA	NA	52	NA	NA	84	186	227	123	239	321	172	301	432	231	373	557	299	509	696	376
	3	NA	NA	34	NA	NA	61	134	153	97	193	258	142	247	365	202	309	491	269	381	634	348	519	793	437
8	1	NA	NA	21	NA	NA	40	NA	NA	68	195	208	103	250	298	146	313	407	207	387	530	263	529	672	331
	2	NA	NA	28	NA	NA	52	137	139	85	202	240	125	258	343	177	323	465	238	397	607	309	540	766	391
	3	NA	NA	34	NA	NA	62	143	156	98	210	264	145	266	376	205	332	509	274	407	663	356	551	838	450
10	1	NA	NA	22	NA	NA	41	130	151	70	202	225	106	267	316	151	333	434	213	410	571	273	558	727	343
	2	NA	NA	29	NA	NA	53	136	150	86	210	255	128	276	358	181	343	489	244	420	640	317	569	813	403
	3	NA	NA	34	97	102	62	143	166	99	217	277	147	284	389	207	352	530	279	430	694	363	580	880	459
15	1	NA	NA	23	NA	NA	43	129	151	73	199	271	112	268	376	161	349	502	225	445	646	291	623	808	366
	2	NA	NA	30	92	103	54	135	170	88	207	295	132	277	411	189	359	548	256	456	706	334	634	884	424
	3	NA	NA	34	96	112	63	141	185	101	215	315	151	286	439	213	368	586	289	466	755	378	646	945	479
20	1	NA	NA	23	87	99	45	128	167	76	197	303	117	265	425	169	345	569	235	439	734	306	614	921	387
	2	NA	NA	30	91	111	55	134	185	90	205	325	136	274	455	195	355	610	266	450	787	348	627	986	443
	3	NA	NA	35	96	119	64	140	199	103	213	343	154	282	481	219	365	644	298	461	831	391	639	1042	496
30	1	NA	NA	24	86	108	47	126	187	80	193	347	124	259	492	183	338	665	250	430	864	330	600	1089	421
	2	NA	NA	31	91	119	57	132	203	93	201	366	142	269	518	205	348	699	282	442	908	372	613	1145	473
	3	NA	NA	35	95	127	65	138	216	105	209	381	160	277	540	229	358	729	312	452	946	412	626	1193	524
50	1	NA	NA	24	85	113	50	124	204	87	188	392	139	252	567	208	328	778	287	417	1022	383	582	1302	492
	2	NA	NA	31	89	123	60	130	218	100	196	408	158	262	588	230	339	806	320	429	1058	425	596	1346	545
	3	NA	NA	35	94	131	68	136	231	112	205	422	176	271	607	255	349	831	351	440	1090	466	610	1386	597
100	1	NA	NA	23	84	104	49	122	200	89	182	410	151	243	617	232	315	875	328	402	1181	444	560	1537	580
	2	NA	NA	30	88	115	59	127	215	102	190	425	169	253	636	254	326	899	361	415	1210	488	575	1570	634
	3	NA	NA	34	93	124	67	133	228	115	199	438	188	262	654	279	337	921	392	427	1238	529	589	1604	687

Common Vent Capacity

	Minimum Internal Area of Masonry Chimney Flue (in.²)																					
	12			19			28			38			50			63			78			113		
Vent Height H (ft)	Combined Appliance Input Rating in Thousands of Btu per Hour																					
	FAN +FAN	FAN +NAT	NAT +NAT	FAN +FAN	FAN +NAT	NAT +NAT	FAN +FAN	FAN +NAT	NAT +NAT	FAN +FAN	FAN +NAT	NAT +NAT	FAN +FAN	FAN +NAT	NAT +NAT	FAN +FAN	FAN +NAT	NAT +NAT	FAN +FAN	FAN +NAT	NAT +NAT	FAN +FAN	FAN +NAT	NAT +NAT
6	NA	NA	25	NA	118	45	NA	176	71	NA	255	102	NA	348	142	NA	455	187	NA	579	245	NA	846	NA
8	NA	NA	28	NA	128	52	NA	190	81	NA	276	118	NA	380	162	NA	497	217	NA	633	277	1136	928	405
10	NA	NA	31	NA	136	56	NA	205	89	NA	295	129	NA	405	175	NA	532	234	771	680	300	1216	1000	450
15	NA	NA	36	NA	NA	66	NA	230	105	NA	335	150	NA	400	210	677	602	280	866	772	360	1359	1139	540
20	NA	NA	NA	NA	NA	74	NA	247	120	NA	362	170	NA	503	240	765	661	321	947	849	415	1495	1264	640
30	NA	NA	NA	NA	NA	NA	NA	NA	135	NA	398	195	NA	558	275	808	739	377	1052	957	490	1682	1447	740
50	NA	NA	NA	NA	NA	NA	NA	NA	NA	NA	NA	NA	NA	612	325	NA	821	456	1152	1076	600	1879	1672	910
100	NA	NA	NA	NA	NA	NA	NA	NA	NA	NA	NA	NA	NA	NA	NA	NA	NA	494	NA	NA	663	2006	1885	1046

For SI units, 1 in. = 25.4 mm, 1 in.² = 645 mm², 1 ft = 0.305 m, 1000 Btu/hr = 0.293 kW.

Table 13.2(e) Single-Wall Metal Pipe or Type B Asbestos Cement Vent

		Number of Appliances:	Two or More
		Appliance Type:	Draft Hood–Equipped
		Appliance Vent Connection:	Direct to Pipe or Vent

Vent Connector Capacity

Total Vent Height H (ft)	Connector Rise R (ft)	Vent Connector Diameter — D (in.)					
		3	4	5	6	7	8
		Maximum Appliance Input Rating in Thousands of Btu per Hour					
6–8	1	21	40	68	102	146	205
	2	28	53	86	124	178	235
	3	34	61	98	147	204	275
15	1	23	44	77	117	179	240
	2	30	56	92	134	194	265
	3	35	64	102	155	216	298
30 and up	1	25	49	84	129	190	270
	2	31	58	97	145	211	295
	3	36	68	107	164	232	321

Common Vent Capacity

Total Vent Height H (ft)	Common Vent Diameter — D (in.)						
	4	5	6	7	8	10	12
	Combined Appliance Input Rating in Thousands of Btu per Hour						
6	48	78	111	155	205	320	NA
8	55	89	128	175	234	365	505
10	59	95	136	190	250	395	560
15	71	115	168	228	305	480	690
20	80	129	186	260	340	550	790
30	NA	147	215	300	400	650	940
50	NA	NA	NA	360	490	810	1190

For SI units, 1 in. = 25.4 mm, 1 in.^{2} = 645 mm^2, 1 ft = 0.305 m, 1000 Btu/hr = 0.293 kW.
Note: See Figure F.1(f) and Section 13.2.

Table 13.2(f) Exterior Masonry Chimney

					Number of Appliances:	Two or More
					Appliance Type:	NAT + NAT
					Appliance Vent Connection:	Type B Double-Wall Connector

Vent Height H (ft)	Combined Appliance Maximum Input Rating in Thousands of Btu per Hour							
	Internal Area of Chimney (in.^{2})							
	12	19	28	38	50	63	78	113
6	25	46	71	103	143	188	246	NA
8	28	53	82	119	163	218	278	408
10	31	56	90	131	177	236	302	454
15	NA	67	106	152	212	283	365	546
20	NA	NA	NA	NA	NA	325	419	648
30	NA	NA	NA	NA	NA	NA	496	749
50	NA	NA	NA	NA	NA	NA	NA	922
100	NA	NA	NA	NA	NA	NA	NA	NA

For SI units, 1 in. = 25.4 mm, 1 in.^{2} = 645 mm^2, 1 ft = 0.305 m, 1000 Btu/hr = 0.293 kW.

13.2.9 Tee and Wye Fittings. Tee and wye fittings connected to a common gas vent shall be considered as part of the common gas vent and constructed of materials consistent with that of the common gas vent.

13.2.10 Tee and Wye Sizing. At the point where tee or wye fittings connect to a common gas vent, the opening size of the fitting shall be equal to the size of the common vent. Such fittings shall not be prohibited from having reduced size openings at the point of connection of appliance gas vent connectors.

13.2.11 High-Altitude Installations. Sea level input ratings shall be used when determining maximum capacity for high-altitude installation. Actual input (derated for altitude) shall be used for determining minimum capacity for high-altitude installation.

13.2.12 Connector Rise. The connector rise (R) for each appliance connector shall be measured from the draft hood outlet or flue collar to the centerline where the vent gas streams come together.

13.2.13 Vent Height. The available total height (H) for multiple appliances on the same floor shall be measured from the highest draft hood outlet or flue collar up to the level of the outlet of the common vent.

13.2.14 Multistory Vent Height. Where appliances are located on more than one floor, the available total height (H) for each segment of the system shall be the vertical distance between the highest draft hood outlet or flue collar entering that segment and the centerline of the next higher interconnection tee.

13.2.15 Multistory Lowest Vent and Vent Connector Sizing. The size of the lowest connector and of the vertical vent leading to the lowest interconnection of a multistory system shall be in accordance with Table 13.1(a) or Table 13.1(b) for available total height (H) up to the lowest interconnection.

13.2.16 Multistory B Vents Required. Where used in multistory systems, vertical common vents shall be Type B double wall and shall be installed with a listed vent cap.

13.2.17 Multistory Vent Offsets and Capacity. Offsets in multistory common vent systems shall be limited to a single offset in each system, and systems with an offset shall comply with all of the following:

(1) The offset angle shall not exceed 45 degrees from vertical.
(2) The horizontal length of the offset shall not exceed 18 in./in. (18 mm/mm) of common vent diameter of the segment in which the offset is located.
(3) For the segment of the common vertical vent containing the offset, the common vent capacity listed in the common venting tables shall be reduced by 20 percent (0.80 × maximum common vent capacity).
(4) A multistory common vent shall not be reduced in size above the offset.

13.2.18 Vertical Vent Size Limitation. Where two or more appliances are connected to a vertical vent or chimney, the flow area of the largest section of vertical vent or chimney shall not exceed seven times the smallest listed appliance categorized vent areas, flue collar area, or draft hood outlet area unless designed in accordance with engineering methods.

13.2.19 Two-Stage/Modulating Appliances.

13.2.19.1 The minimum vent connector capacity (FAN Min) of appliances with more than one input rate shall be determined from the tables and shall be less than the lowest appliance input rating.

13.2.19.2 The maximum vent connector capacity (FAN Max or NAT Max) shall be determined from the tables and shall be greater than the highest appliance input rating.

13.2.20* Corrugated Chimney Liners. Listed corrugated metallic chimney liner systems in masonry chimneys shall be sized by using Table 13.2(a) or Table 13.2(b) for Type B vents, with the maximum capacity reduced by 20 percent (0.80 × maximum capacity) and the minimum capacity as shown in Table 13.2(a) or Table 13.2(b). Corrugated metallic liner systems installed with bends or offsets shall have their maximum capacity further reduced in accordance with 13.2.5 and 13.2.6. The 20 percent reduction for corrugated metallic chimney liner systems includes an allowance for one long radius 90-degree turn at the bottom of the liner.

Table 13.2(g) Exterior Masonry Chimney

	Number of Appliances:	Two or More
	Appliance Type:	NAT + NAT
	Appliance Vent Connection:	Type B Double-Wall Connector

Minimum Allowable Input Rating of Space-Heating Appliance in Thousands of Btu per Hour

Vent Height H (ft)	Internal Area of Chimney (in.^{2})							
	12	19	28	38	50	63	78	113
Local 99% winter design temperature: 37°F or greater								
6	0	0	0	0	0	0	0	NA
8	0	0	0	0	0	0	0	0
10	0	0	0	0	0	0	0	0
15	NA	0	0	0	0	0	0	0
20	NA	NA	NA	NA	NA	184	0	0
30	NA	NA	NA	NA	NA	393	334	0
50	NA	NA	NA	NA	NA	NA	NA	579
100	NA	NA	NA	NA	NA	NA	NA	NA
Local 99% winter design temperature: 27°F to 36°F								
6	0	0	68	NA	NA	180	212	NA
8	0	0	82	NA	NA	187	214	263
10	0	51	NA	NA	NA	201	225	265
15	NA	NA	NA	NA	NA	253	274	305
20	NA	NA	NA	NA	NA	307	330	362
30	NA	NA	NA	NA	NA	NA	445	485
50	NA	NA	NA	NA	NA	NA	NA	763
100	NA	NA	NA	NA	NA	NA	NA	NA
Local 99% winter design temperature: 17°F to 26°F								
6	NA	NA	NA	NA	NA	NA	NA	NA
8	NA	NA	NA	NA	NA	NA	264	352
10	NA	NA	NA	NA	NA	NA	278	358
15	NA	NA	NA	NA	NA	NA	331	398
20	NA	NA	NA	NA	NA	NA	387	457
30	NA	NA	NA	NA	NA	NA	NA	581
50	NA	NA	NA	NA	NA	NA	NA	862
100	NA	NA	NA	NA	NA	NA	NA	NA
Local 99% winter design temperature: 5°F to 16°F								
6	NA	NA	NA	NA	NA	NA	NA	NA
8	NA	NA	NA	NA	NA	NA	NA	NA
10	NA	NA	NA	NA	NA	NA	NA	430
15	NA	NA	NA	NA	NA	NA	NA	485
20	NA	NA	NA	NA	NA	NA	NA	547
30	NA	NA	NA	NA	NA	NA	NA	682
50	NA	NA	NA	NA	NA	NA	NA	NA
100	NA	NA	NA	NA	NA	NA	NA	NA
Local 99% winter design temperature: 4°F or lower *Not recommended for any vent configurations*								

For SI units, 1 in. = 25.4 mm, 1 in.^{2} = 645 mm^2, 1 ft = 0.305 m, 1000 Btu/hr = 0.293 kW, °C = (°F − 32)/1.8.

Note: See Figure F.2.4 for a map showing local 99 percent winter design temperatures in the United States.

Table 13.2(h) Exterior Masonry Chimney

	Number of Appliances:	Two or More
	Appliance Type:	FAN + NAT
	Appliance Vent Connection:	Type B Double-Wall Connector

Combined Appliance Maximum Input Rating in Thousands of Btu per Hour

Vent Height H (ft)	Internal Area of Chimney (in.²)							
	12	19	28	38	50	63	78	113
6	74	119	178	257	351	458	582	853
8	80	130	193	279	384	501	636	937
10	84	138	207	299	409	538	686	1010
15	NA	152	233	334	467	611	781	1156
20	NA	NA	250	368	508	668	858	1286
30	NA	NA	NA	404	564	747	969	1473
50	NA	NA	NA	NA	NA	831	1089	1692
100	NA	NA	NA	NA	NA	NA	NA	1921

For SI units, 1 in. = 25.4 mm, 1 in.² = 645 mm², 1 ft = 0.305 m, 1000 Btu/hr = 0.293 kW.

13.2.21 Connections to Chimney Liners. Where double-wall connectors are required, tee and wye fittings used to connect to the common vent chimney liner shall be listed double-wall fittings. Connections between chimney liners and listed double-wall fittings shall be made with listed adapter fittings designed for such purpose.

13.2.22 Chimneys and Vent Locations. Table 13.2(a) through Table 13.2(e) shall be used only for chimneys and vents not exposed to the outdoors below the roof line. A Type B vent or listed chimney lining system passing through an unused masonry chimney flue shall not be considered to be exposed to the outdoors. A Type B vent passing through an unventilated enclosure or chase insulated to a value of not less than R8 shall not be considered to be exposed to the outdoors. Where vents extend outdoors above the roof more than 5 ft (1.5 m) higher than required by Table 12.7.3, and where vents terminate in accordance with 12.7.3(1)(b), the outdoor portion of the vent shall be enclosed as required by this paragraph for vents not considered to be exposed to the outdoors, or such venting system shall be engineered. Table 13.2(f), Table 13.2(g), Table 13.2(h), and Table 13.2(i) shall be used for clay tile lined exterior masonry chimneys, provided all the following conditions are met:

(1) The vent connector is Type B double wall.
(2) At least one appliance is draft hood equipped.
(3) The combined appliance input rating is less than the maximum capacity given by Table 13.2(f) (for NAT+NAT) or Table 13.2(h) (for FAN+NAT).
(4) The input rating of each space-heating appliance is greater than the minimum input rating given by Table 13.2(g) (for NAT+NAT) or Table 13.2(i) (for FAN+NAT).
(5) The vent connector sizing is in accordance with Table 13.2(c).

13.2.23 Draft Hood Conversion Accessories. Draft hood conversion accessories for use with masonry chimney venting listed Category I fan-assisted appliances shall be listed and installed in accordance with the listed accessory manufacturer's installation instructions.

13.2.24 Vent Connector Sizing. Vent connectors shall not be increased more than two sizes greater than the listed appliance categorized vent diameter, flue collar diameter, or draft hood outlet diameter. Vent connectors for draft hood–equipped appliances shall not be smaller than the draft hood outlet diameter. Where a vent connector size(s) determined from the tables for a fan-assisted appliance(s) is smaller than the flue collar diameter, the use of the smaller size(s) shall be permitted, provided that the installation complies with all of the following conditions:

(1) Vent connectors for fan-assisted appliance flue collars 12 in. (300 mm) in diameter or smaller are not reduced by more than one table size [e.g., 12 in. to 10 in. (300 mm to 250 mm) is a one-size reduction], and those larger than 12 in. (300 mm) in diameter are not reduced more than two table sizes [e.g., 24 in. to 20 in. (610 mm to 510 mm) is a two-size reduction].
(2) The fan-assisted appliance(s) is common vented with a draft hood–equipped appliance(s).
(3) The vent connector has a smooth interior wall.

13.2.25 Multiple Vent and Connector Sizes. All combinations of pipe sizes, single-wall metal pipe, and double-wall metal pipe shall be allowed within any connector run(s) or within the common vent, provided ALL of the appropriate tables permit ALL of the desired sizes and types of pipe, as if they were used for the entire length of the subject connector or vent. Where single-wall and Type B double-wall metal pipes are used for vent connectors within the same venting system, the common vent shall be sized using Table 13.2(b) or Table 13.2(d) as appropriate.

13.2.26 Multiple Vent and Connector Sizes Permitted. Where a Chapter 13 table permits more than one diameter of pipe to be used for a connector or vent, all the permitted sizes shall be permitted to be used.

13.2.27 Interpolation. Interpolation shall be permitted in calculating capacities for vent dimensions that fall between table entries.

13.2.28 Extrapolation. Extrapolation beyond the table entries shall not be permitted.

Table 13.2(i) Exterior Masonry Chimney

	Number of Appliances:	Two or More
	Appliance Type:	FAN + NAT
	Appliance Vent Connection:	Type B Double-Wall Connector

Minimum Allowable Input Rating of Space-Heating Appliance in Thousands of Btu per Hour

Vent Height H (ft)	Internal Area of Chimney (in.²)							
	12	19	28	38	50	63	78	113
Local 99% winter design temperature: 37°F or greater								
6	0	0	0	0	0	0	0	0
8	0	0	0	0	0	0	0	0
10	0	0	0	0	0	0	0	0
15	NA	0	0	0	0	0	0	0
20	NA	NA	123	190	249	184	0	0
30	NA	NA	NA	334	398	393	334	0
50	NA	NA	NA	NA	NA	714	707	579
100	NA	NA	NA	NA	NA	NA	NA	1600
Local 99% winter design temperature: 27°F to 36°F								
6	0	0	68	116	156	180	212	266
8	0	0	82	127	167	187	214	263
10	0	51	97	141	183	201	225	265
15	NA	111	142	183	233	253	274	305
20	NA	NA	187	230	284	307	330	362
30	NA	NA	NA	330	419	419	445	485
50	NA	NA	NA	NA	NA	672	705	763
100	NA	NA	NA	NA	NA	NA	NA	1554
Local 99% winter design temperature: 17°F to 26°F								
6	0	55	99	141	182	215	259	349
8	52	74	111	154	197	226	264	352
10	NA	90	125	169	214	245	278	358
15	NA	NA	167	212	263	296	331	398
20	NA	NA	212	258	316	352	387	457
30	NA	NA	NA	362	429	470	507	581
50	NA	NA	NA	NA	NA	723	766	862
100	NA	NA	NA	NA	NA	NA	NA	1669
Local 99% winter design temperature: 5°F to 16°F								
6	NA	78	121	166	214	252	301	416
8	NA	94	135	182	230	269	312	423
10	NA	111	149	198	250	289	331	430
15	NA	NA	193	247	305	346	393	485
20	NA	NA	NA	293	360	408	450	547
30	NA	NA	NA	377	450	531	580	682
50	NA	NA	NA	NA	NA	797	853	972
100	NA	NA	NA	NA	NA	NA	NA	1833
Local 99% winter design temperature: −10°F to 4°F								
6	NA	NA	145	196	249	296	349	484
8	NA	NA	159	213	269	320	371	494
10	NA	NA	175	231	292	339	397	513
15	NA	NA	NA	283	351	404	457	586
20	NA	NA	NA	333	408	468	528	650
30	NA	NA	NA	NA	NA	603	667	805
50	NA	NA	NA	NA	NA	NA	955	1003
100	NA	NA	NA	NA	NA	NA	NA	NA
Local 99% winter design temperature: −11°F or lower *Not recommended for any vent configurations*								

For SI units, 1 in. = 25.4 mm, 1 in.² = 645 mm², 1 ft = 0.305 m, 1000 Btu/hr = 0.293 kW.

Note: See Figure F.2.4 for a map showing local 99 percent winter design temperatures in the United States.

Table 13.2.2 Vent Connector Maximum Length

Connector Diameter (in.)	Maximum Connector Horizontal Length (ft)
3	4½
4	6
5	7½
6	9
7	10½
8	12
9	13½
10	15
12	18
14	21
16	24
18	27
20	30
22	33
24	36

For SI units, 1 in. = 25.4 mm, 1 ft = 0.305 m.

13.2.29 Sizing Vents Not Covered by Tables. For vent heights lower than 6 ft (1.8 m) and higher than shown in the tables, engineering methods shall be used to calculate vent capacities.

13.2.30 Height Entries. Where the actual height of a vent falls between entries in the height column of the applicable table in Table 13.2(a) through Table 13.2(i), either of the following shall be used:

(1) Interpolation
(2) The lower appliance input rating shown in the table entries, for FAN Max and NAT Max column values; and the higher appliance input rating for the FAN Min column values

Annex A   Explanatory Material

Annex A is not a part of the requirements of this NFPA document but is included for informational purposes only. This annex contains explanatory material, numbered to correspond with the applicable text paragraphs.

A.1.1.1.1(A) The final pressure regulator in an undiluted liquefied petroleum gas (LP-Gas) system can include any one of the following:

(1) The second stage regulator or integral two-stage regulator
(2) A 2 psi (14 kPa) service regulator or integral 2 psi (14 kPa) service regulator
(3) A single-stage regulator, where single-stage systems are permitted by NFPA 58.

A.3.2.1 Approved. The American Gas Association, American National Standards Institute, and the National Fire Protection Association do not approve, inspect, or certify any installations, procedures, appliances, equipment, or materials; nor do they approve or evaluate testing laboratories. In determining the acceptability of installations, procedures, appliances, equipment, or materials, the authority having jurisdiction may base acceptance on compliance with NFPA or other appropriate standards. In the absence of such standards, said authority may require evidence of proper installation, procedure, or use. The authority having jurisdiction may also refer to the listings or labeling practices *(see 3.2.4)* of an organization that is concerned with product evaluations and is thus in a position to determine compliance with AGA, ANSI, CSA, NFPA, or appropriate standards for the current production of listed items.

A.3.2.2 Authority Having Jurisdiction (AHJ). The phrase "authority having jurisdiction," or its acronym AHJ, is used in NFPA documents in a broad manner, since jurisdictions and approval agencies vary, as do their responsibilities. Where public safety is primary, the authority having jurisdiction may be a federal, state, local, or other regional department or individual such as a fire chief; fire marshal; chief of a fire prevention bureau, labor department, or health department; building official; electrical inspector; or others having statutory authority. For insurance purposes, an insurance inspection department, rating bureau, or other insurance company representative may be the authority having jurisdiction. In many circumstances, the property owner or his or her designated agent assumes the role of the authority having jurisdiction; at government installations, the commanding officer or departmental official may be the authority having jurisdiction.

As used in the definition of Authority Having Jurisdiction, equipment includes appliances and materials.

A.3.2.3 Code. The decision to designate a standard as a "code" is based on such factors as the size and scope of the document, its intended use and form of adoption, and whether it contains substantial enforcement and administrative provisions.

A.3.2.5 Listed. The means for identifying listed appliances and equipment may vary for each organization concerned with product evaluation; some organizations do not recognize appliances and equipment as listed unless it is also labeled. The authority having jurisdiction should utilize the system employed by the listing organization to identify a listed product.

As used in the definition of Listed, equipment includes appliances and materials.

A.3.3.4.10.1 Category I Vented Appliance. For additional information on appliance categorization as shown in 3.3.4.10.1 through 3.3.4.10.4, see the appropriate Z21 and Z83 American National Standards.

A.3.3.53 Gas Vent. This definition does not apply to plastic plumbing piping that is specified as a venting material in the manufacturer's instructions for gas-fired appliances that are listed for venting with such piping.

A.3.3.64.1 Combustible (Material). Materials are considered to be combustible even if they have been fire-retardant treated.

A.3.3.84.4 Monitor Regulator. A monitor regulator is part of a two-regulator set in which one regulator is doing the work (i.e., the working regulator) and the second regulator (i.e., the monitor) is installed to back up the working regulator should it fail. The monitor regulator remains in a nearly full-open position until it senses a rise in the downstream pressure. Each regulator senses the same downstream pressure, which allows either regulator to limit that downstream pressure.

A.3.3.95.7 Venting System. A venting system is usually composed of a vent or a chimney and vent connector(s), if used, assembled to form the open passageway.

A.4.3.2.1 Gas suppliers intend to provide gas that is free of liquids. Where liquids or condensates are removed from a drip, the gas supplier can be notified if it is determined that the liquid accumulation impedes the appliance operation or if the liquid accumulation appears to be at an unusual rate. This could mean that the gas supplier's liquid removal equipment has failed or is in need of service.

Handling and disposal of liquids might need to be done with the consideration of an industrial hygienist to avoid possible contact with trace amounts of benzene. Contact the gas supplier for a safety data sheet (SDS) or consider laboratory sampling before handling or disposing of liquids.

A.4.4 The provisions of Section 4.4 do not require noncombustible materials to be tested in order to be classified as noncombustible materials. Materials such as steel, concrete, and cement blocks are generally accepted to be noncombustible.

A.4.5(3) The person performing the calculation or design can be one or more of the following:

(1) A registered/licensed professional engineer, with their stamp or registration/license number and state of registration/license
(2) A degreed engineer who is not registered/licensed
(3) Anyone who has experience in using the calculation method, along with a statement of their experience

A.5.3.1 The size of gas piping depends on the following factors:

(1) Allowable loss in pressure from point of delivery to appliance
(2) Maximum gas demand
(3) Length of piping and number of fittings
(4) Specific gravity of the gas
(5) Diversity factor
(6) Foreseeable future demand

A.5.3.2 To obtain the cubic feet per hour of gas required, divide the Btu per hour rating by the Btu per cubic foot heating value of the gas supplied. The heating value of the gas can be obtained from the local gas supplier.

Where the ratings of the appliances to be installed are not known, Table A.5.3.2.1 shows the approximate demand of typical appliances by types.

A.5.3.2.1 Some older appliances do not have a nameplate. In this case Table A.5.3.2.1 or an estimate of the appliance input should be used. The input can be based on the following:

(1) A rating provided by the manufacturer
(2) The rating of similar appliances
(3) Recommendations of the gas supplier
(4) Recommendations of a qualified agency
(5) A gas flow test
(6) Measurement of the orifice size of the appliance

The requirement of 5.3.1 that the piping system provide sufficient gas to each appliance inlet must be complied with.

Table A.5.3.2.1 Approximate Gas Input for Typical Appliances

Appliance	Input Btu/hr (Approx.)
Space Heating Units	
Warm air furnace	
Single family	100,000
Multifamily, per unit	60,000
Hydronic boiler	
Single family	100,000
Multifamily, per unit	60,000
Space and Water Heating Units	
Hydronic boiler	
Single family	120,000
Multifamily, per unit	75,000
Water Heating Appliances	
Water heater, automatic storage 30 gal to 40 gal tank	35,000
Water heater, automatic storage 50 gal tank	50,000
Water heater, automatic instantaneous	
Capacity at 2 gal/min	142,800
Capacity at 4 gal/min	285,000
Capacity at 6 gal/min	428,400
Water heater, domestic, circulating or side-arm	35,000
Cooking Appliances	
Range, freestanding, domestic	65,000
Built-in oven or broiler unit, domestic	25,000
Built-in top unit, domestic	40,000
Other Appliances	
Refrigerator	3,000
Clothes dryer, Type 1 (domestic)	35,000
Gas fireplace direct vent	40,000
Gas log	80,000
Barbecue	40,000
Gas light	2,500

A.5.3.3 The gas-carrying capacities for different sizes and lengths of iron pipe, or equivalent rigid pipe, and semirigid tubing are shown in the capacity tables in Chapter 6.

Table 6.2.1(a) through Table 6.2.1(x) indicate approximate capacities for single runs of piping. If the specific gravity of the gas is other than 0.60, correction factors should be applied. Correction factors for use with these tables are given in Table B.3.4.

For any gas piping system, for special appliances, or for conditions other than those covered by the capacity tables in Chapter 6, such as longer runs, greater gas demands, or greater pressure drops, the size of each gas piping system should be determined by the pipe sizing equations in Section 6.4 or by standard engineering methods acceptable to the authority having jurisdiction.

A suggested procedure for using the Chapter 6 tables to size a gas piping system is illustrated in Annex B.

A.5.4.4(1) For welding specifications and procedures that can be used, see the API STD 1104, *Welding of Pipelines and Related Facilities*; AWS B2.1/B2.1M, *Specification for Welding Procedure and*

Performance Qualification; or ASME *Boiler and Pressure Vessel Code*, Section IX.

A.5.5.2.3 An average of 0.3 grains of hydrogen sulfide per 100 scf of gas (0.7 mg/100 L) is equivalent to a trace as determined by ASTM D2385, *Test Method for Hydrogen Sulfide and Mercaptan Sulfur in Natural Gas (Cadmium Sulfate — Iodometric Titration Method)*, or ASTM D2420, *Test Method for Hydrogen Sulfide in Liquefied Petroleum (LP) Gases (Lead Acetate Method)*.

A.5.5.3.4 Copper and copper alloy tubing and fittings (except tin-lined copper tubing) should not be used if the gas contains more than an average of 0.3 grains of hydrogen sulfide per 100 scf of gas (0.7 mg/100 L).

A.5.5.4.2 The reference to UL 651, *Schedule 40 and 80 Rigid PVC Conduit and Fittings*, is to require that PVC be a minimum of Schedule 40 and that it be resistant to the effects of ultraviolet light because it is likely to be exposed to the outdoors when used for regulator vents.

A.5.5.6.4 Joint sealing compounds are used in tapered pipe thread joints to provide lubrication to the joint as it is tightened so that less tightening torque is "used up" to overcome friction and also to provide a seal of the small leak paths that would otherwise remain in a metal-to-metal threaded joint.

Commonly used joint sealing compounds include pipe dope and polytetrafluoroethylene tape, also known as PTFE tape. Some pipe dopes also contain PTFE. Joint sealing compounds should be applied so that no sealing compound finds its way into the interior of a completed joint.

Pipe dope application should be made only to the male pipe thread of the joint and should coat all of the threads commencing one thread back from the end of the threaded pipe.

PTFE tape application should be made by wrapping the tape tightly around the male thread in a clockwise direction when viewed from the end of the pipe to which the tape is being applied. Tape application should wrap all of the threads commencing one thread back from the end of the threaded pipe.

A.5.5.7.1 For welding and brazing specifications and procedures that can be used, see API STD 1104, *Welding Pipelines and Related Facilities*; AWS B2.1/B2.1M, *Specification for Welding Procedure and Performance Qualification*; AWS B2.2/B2.2M, *Specification for Brazing Procedure and Performance Qualification*; or ASME *Boiler and Pressure Vessel Code*, Section IX.

A.5.6 This section applies to premises-owned meters.

A.5.7 This section applies to premises-owned regulators.

A.5.10 Appliances that can produce a vacuum or dangerous reduction in pressure include, but are not limited to, gas compressors.

A.6.1 Table A.6.1 provides nominal metric pipe size equivalents.

A.6.1.1 The Longest Length Method is the traditional method used to determine the equivalent piping length L that is then used along with the pipe sizing tables to determine the appropriate pipe diameter size.

A.6.1.2 The Branch Length Method is an alternate sizing method that could permit slightly smaller pipe diameters in some segments of a piping system when compared with the Longest Length Method.

Table A.6.1 Nominal Pipe

Nominal Pipe Diameter	
in.	mm
1/8	6
3/16	7
1/4	8
3/8	10
1/2	15
5/8	18
3/4	20
1	25
1 1/4	32
1 1/2	40
2	50
2 1/2	65
3	80
3 1/2	90
4	100
4 1/2	115
5	125
6	150
8	200
10	250
12	300

For pipe sizes >12 in. diam., use 1 in. = 25 mm.

A.6.4.1 The Low-Pressure Formula is the standard flow formula located in Annex B but rearranged to solve for the pipe diameter.

A.6.4.2 The High-Pressure Formula is the standard flow formula located in Annex B but rearranged to solve for the pipe diameter.

A.7.1.2.1(B) Conduit as used here is intended to represent metallic or nonmetallic surround, which provides mechanical protection for the underground piping.

A.7.1.3 For information on corrosion protection of underground pipe, see NACE SP0169, *Control of External Corrosion on Underground or Submerged Metallic Piping Systems*. Information on installation, maintenance, and corrosion protection might be available from the gas supplier.

A.7.1.4 The gas supplier can be consulted for recommendations.

A.7.2.2 Painting can be an acceptable method of corrosion protection.

A.7.2.5 The intent is that gas piping, shutoff valves required by this code, and regulators be allowed to be installed in accessible portions of plenums, accessible ducts used to supply combustion and ventilation air in accordance with Section 9.3, and accessible spaces between a fixed ceiling and dropped ceiling.

A.7.4.3 Only vertical chases are recognized by the coverage. It is believed that welded joints for a horizontal gas line would be preferable to a horizontal chase.

A.7.8.4 System shutoff valves can serve as the emergency shutoff valve required by 7.8.3.2.

A.7.11.4 The mixing blower is acknowledged as a special case because of its inability to tolerate control valves or comparable restrictions between mixing blower(s) and burner(s). With these limitations, mixing blower installations are not required to utilize safety blowouts, backfire preventers, explosion heads, flame arresters, or automatic firechecks that introduce pressure losses.

A.7.11.5.1 For information on venting of deflagrations, see NFPA 68.

A.7.11.5.4 Additional interlocks might be necessary for safe operation of appliances supplied by the gas-mixing machine.

A.7.11.6(1) Two basic methods are generally used. One calls for a separate firecheck at each burner, the other a firecheck at each group of burners. The second method is generally more practical if a system consists of many closely spaced burners.

An approved automatic firecheck should be installed as near as practical upstream from a flame arrester used for local protection where test burners or lighting torches are employed.

A.7.12.2 The required bonding connection may be made from the piping to the electrical service equipment enclosure, to the grounded conductor at the electrical service, to the grounding electrode conductor (where of sufficient size), or directly to the grounding electrode. The bond may also be made to a lightning protection system grounding electrode (but not to down conductors) if the resulting length of the bonding conductor is shorter. Lightning protection grounding systems are bonded to the electrical service grounding electrodes, in accordance with NFPA 780, using a method to minimize impedance between the systems.

Listed clamps are manufactured to facilitate attachment of the bonding conductor to either a segment of rigid pipe or to a CSST-copper alloy fitting. Clamps should be installed to remain accessible when building construction is complete.

State and local laws can limit who can attach the bonding connection to the building grounding system.

The size of the bonding conductor, a 6 AWG copper wire, is a minimum size, and larger wire can be used. The requirement also permits conductors of different materials (of equivalent size) and both single wire and multi-strand.

A.7.12.2.3 The maximum length of the bonding connection was established based on studies conducted by the Gas Technology Institute in Project Number 21323, *Validation of Installation Methods for CSST Gas Piping to Mitigate Indirect Lightning Related Damage*. The shortest practical length should always be used.

If the bonding jumper required would be longer than 75 ft (22 m), an additional grounding electrode can be installed to allow a bonding jumper that is 75 ft (22 m) or less.

A.7.12.4.1 This requirement does not preclude the bonding of metallic piping to a grounding system.

A.7.12.5 Section 4.14 of NFPA 780 requires that all grounding media, including underground metallic piping systems, be interconnected to provide a common ground potential. These underground piping systems are not permitted to be substituted for grounding electrodes but must be bonded to the lightning protection grounding system. Where galvanic corrosion is of concern, the bond may be made via a spark gap or gas discharge tube.

A.8.1.1 Because it is sometimes necessary to divide a piping system into test sections and install test heads, connecting piping, and other necessary appurtenances for testing, it is not required that the tie-in sections of pipe be pressure-tested. Tie-in connections, however, should be tested with a noncorrosive leak detection fluid after gas has been introduced and the pressure has been increased sufficiently to give some indications whether leaks exist.

The test procedure used should be capable of disclosing all leaks in the section being tested and should be selected after giving due consideration to the volumetric content of the section and to its location.

Under no circumstances should a valve in a line be used as a bulkhead between gas in one section of the piping system and test medium in an adjacent section, unless two valves are installed in series with a valved "telltale" located between these valves. A valve should not be subjected to the test pressure unless it can be determined that the valve, including the valve closing mechanism, is designed to safely withstand the test pressure.

A.8.1.1.7 Fuel gas piping operating above 125 psi should be cleaned in accordance with NFPA 56.

A.8.1.4.3 During pressure tests conducted over long periods of time, such as overnight, the effects of temperature on pressure should be considered. Temperature drops can cause a drop in pressure great enough to be indicated by the test gauge. These temperature drops can cause test evaluators to think that a leak exists in the piping system when in fact the pressure drop was caused by a decrease in the ambient temperature. See Example 5 in B.7.5.

A.8.2.3 See Annex C for a suggested method.

A.8.3 The process of purging gas piping that contains fuel gas or charging gas piping that contains air must be performed in a manner that will minimize the potential for a flammable mixture to be developed within the piping.

Natural gas and propane suppliers add a distinctive odor to their gas. Persons conducting purging operations should not rely upon their sense of smell. When a gas piping system is brought into service and unodorized gas is detected, the company supplying the gas should be contacted to inform it of the situation and to determine what action should be taken. (More information on odorization of fuel gas is available in the *National Fuel Gas Code Handbook*, "Fuel Gas Odorization" supplement.)

A.8.3.1 Subsection 8.3.1 describes the characteristics of gas piping systems that are required to be purged only to the outdoors. The criteria were selected to distinguish between piping systems located in industrial, large commercial, and large multifamily buildings from those located in light commercial and smaller residential buildings. The gas piping systems installed in industrial, large commercial and large multifamily buildings are considered to be larger, more complex systems for the purposes of defining their purging requirements. Because of their larger pipe volumes or potential for higher flow rates, these systems require procedures to ensure that a large volume of fuel gas is not released to the indoors and that flammable mixtures do not occur within the piping itself. Installers of these complex systems deal with considerably more variables that can result in a higher potential for discharge of large gas volumes during purging operations.

Specific occupancy categories such as industrial, manufacturing, commercial and large multifamily were not included in the fuel gas code. United States building codes define these occupancies for the purpose of construction and safety requirements. There is no general relation between the occupancy types, as defined by the building codes, and the size of gas piping system to be installed in that occupancy. The gas piping size and operating pressure are based on the nature of the piping system and gas appliances to be installed and are not dependent upon a building's occupancy type or classification.

A.8.3.1.2 It is recommended that the oxygen levels in the piping be monitored during the purging process to determine when sufficient inert gas has been introduced. The manufacturer's instructions for monitoring instruments must be followed when performing purge operations.

A.8.3.1.4 Combustible gas indicators are available with different scales. For purging, it is necessary to use the percent gas in air scale and to follow the manufacturer's operating instructions. The percent lower explosible limit (% LEL) scale should not be used because it is not relevant to purging.

Users should verify that the indicator will detect fuel gas in the absence of oxygen. Many combustible gas indicators will not indicate fuel gas concentration accurately if no oxygen is present.

A.8.3.2 The criteria were selected to describe typical gas piping systems located in light commercial and the smaller residential family buildings. Gas piping systems installed in these buildings are considered to be smaller and less complex systems for the purposes of defining their purging requirements. Installers have familiarity with purging these systems and the potential for discharge of large gas volumes during purging operations is low. Also see A.8.3.1.

A.8.3.2.1 Where small piping systems contain air and are purged to either the indoors or outdoors with fuel gas, a rapid and uninterrupted flow of fuel gas must be introduced into one end of the piping system and vented out of the other end so as to prevent the development of a combustible fuel–air mixture. Purging these systems can be done either using a source of ignition to ignite the fuel gas or by using a listed combustible gas detector that can detect the presence of fuel gas.

A.9.1.1 The American Gas Association, American National Standards Institute, Inc., and the National Fire Protection Association do not approve, inspect, or certify any installations, procedures, appliances, equipment, or materials; nor do they approve or evaluate testing laboratories. In determining acceptability of installations, procedures, appliances, equipment, or materials, the authority having jurisdiction can base acceptance on compliance with AGA, ANSI, CSA, or NFPA, or other appropriate standards. In the absence of such standards, said authority can require evidence of proper installation, procedure, or use. The authority having jurisdiction can also refer to the listings or labeling practices of an organization concerned with product evaluations and is thus in a position to determine compliance with appropriate standards for the current production of listed items.

A.9.1.6 Halogenated hydrocarbons are particularly injurious and corrosive after contact with flames or hot surfaces.

A.9.1.20 The instructions are needed for reference and guidance for the authority having jurisdiction, service personnel, and the owner or operator.

A.9.1.22 Building envelope changes made under weatherization practices intended to reduce air infiltration and contractor activities, such as the replacement of whole windows and exterior doors and extensive exterior modifications, will reduce the amount of infiltration air and could impact the amount of combustion air that is available for existing appliance installations. Proper vent sizing and configuration is crucial to maintaining the required vent performance in structures that have reduced air infiltration.

A.9.3 Operation of exhaust fans, ventilation systems, clothes dryers, or fireplaces can create conditions requiring special attention to avoid unsatisfactory operation of installed appliances.

A.9.3.2.1 See Table A.9.3.2.1.

A.9.3.2.2 See Table A.9.3.2.2(a) and Table A.9.3.2.2(b).

A.9.3.2.3(1) See Figure A.9.3.2.3(1).

A.9.3.3.1(1) See Figure A.9.3.3.1(1)(a) and Figure A.9.3.3.1(1)(b).

A.9.3.3.1(2) See Figure A.9.3.3.1(2).

A.9.3.3.2 See Figure A.9.3.3.2.

A.9.6.1.5 The expansion and contraction of the heater and the vibration from the blower motor can lead to work hardening of the rigid pipe or semirigid metallic tubing, which can ultimately lead to fractures and leakage. Connectors for this type of heater should have adequate flexibility, temperature rating, and vibration resistance to accommodate the characteristics of the heater. Such flexible connectors for suspended heaters should meet the following criteria:

(1) Be determined to be appropriate for the application
(2) Be specified by the heater manufacturer
(3) Be installed in accordance with the manufacturer's installation instructions

A.9.6.3 Laboratory burners, commonly called Bunsen burners, are a type of burner used in laboratories. The original Bunsen burner was invented by Robert Bunsen in 1852. The use of the term in NFPA 54 is intended to include all types of portable laboratory burners used in laboratories and educational facilities.

A.10.1.1 This chapter is applicable primarily to nonindustrial-type appliances and installations and, unless specifically indicated, does not apply to industrial appliances and installations.

For additional information concerning particular gas appliances and accessories, including industrial types, reference can be made to the standards listed in Chapter 2 and Annex K.

A.10.1.2 Also see prohibited installations in 10.6.2, 10.7.2, 10.8.2, 10.9.2, and 10.21.2.

A.10.2.7 Reference can be made to NFPA 90A or to NFPA 90B.

Table A.9.3.2.1 Standard Method: Required Volume, All Appliances

Appliance Input (Btu/hr)	Required Volume (ft³)
5,000	250
10,000	500
15,000	750
20,000	1,000
25,000	1,250
30,000	1,500
35,000	1,750
40,000	2,000
45,000	2,250
50,000	2,500
55,000	2,750
60,000	3,000
65,000	3,250
70,000	3,500
75,000	3,750
80,000	4,000
85,000	4,250
90,000	4,500
95,000	4,750
100,000	5,000
105,000	5,250
110,000	5,500
115,000	5,750
120,000	6,000
125,000	6,250
130,000	6,500
135,000	6,750
140,000	7,000
145,000	7,250
150,000	7,500
160,000	8,000
170,000	8,500
180,000	9,000
190,000	9,500
200,000	10,000
210,000	10,500
220,000	11,000
230,000	11,500
240,000	12,000
250,000	12,500
260,000	13,000
270,000	13,500
280,000	14,000
290,000	14,500
300,000	15,000

For SI units, 1 ft³ = 0.028 m³, 1000 Btu/hr = 0.293 kW.

Table A.9.3.2.2(a) Known Air Infiltration Rate Method: Minimum Space Volume for Appliances Other than Fan-Assisted for Specified Infiltration Rates (ACH)

Appliance Input (Btu/hr)	Space Volume (ft³) 0.25 ACH	0.30 ACH	0.35 ACH
5,000	420	350	300
10,000	840	700	600
15,000	1,260	1,050	900
20,000	1,680	1,400	1,200
25,000	2,100	1,750	1,500
30,000	2,520	2,100	1,800
35,000	2,940	2,450	2,100
40,000	3,360	2,800	2,400
45,000	3,780	3,150	2,700
50,000	4,200	3,500	3,000
55,000	4,620	3,850	3,300
60,000	5,040	4,200	3,600
65,000	5,460	4,550	3,900
70,000	5,880	4,900	4,200
75,000	6,300	5,250	4,500
80,000	6,720	5,600	4,800
85,000	7,140	5,950	5,100
90,000	7,560	6,300	5,400
95,000	7,980	6,650	5,700
100,000	8,400	7,000	6,000
105,000	8,820	7,350	6,300
110,000	9,240	7,700	6,600
115,000	9,660	8,050	6,900
120,000	10,080	8,400	7,200
125,000	10,500	8,750	7,500
130,000	10,920	9,100	7,800
135,000	11,340	9,450	8,100
140,000	11,760	9,800	8,400
145,000	12,180	10,150	8,700
150,000	12,600	10,500	9,000
160,000	13,440	11,200	9,600
170,000	14,280	11,900	10,200
180,000	15,120	12,600	10,800
190,000	15,960	13,300	11,400
200,000	16,800	14,000	12,000
210,000	17,640	14,700	12,600
220,000	18,480	15,400	13,200
230,000	19,320	16,100	13,800
240,000	20,160	16,800	14,400
250,000	21,000	17,500	15,000
260,000	21,840	18,200	15,600
270,000	22,680	18,900	16,200
280,000	23,520	19,600	16,800
290,000	24,360	20,300	17,400
300,000	25,200	21,000	18,000

For SI units, 1 ft³ = 0.028 m³, 1000 Btu/hr = 0.293 kW.
ACH: Air change per hour.

Table A.9.3.2.2(b) Known Air Infiltration Rate Method: Minimum Space Volume for Fan-Assisted Appliance, for Specified Infiltration Rates (ACH)

Appliance Input (Btu/hr)	Required Volume (ft³)		
	0.25 ACH	0.30 ACH	0.35 ACH
5,000	300	250	214
10,000	600	500	429
15,000	900	750	643
20,000	1,200	1,000	857
25,000	1,500	1,250	1,071
30,000	1,800	1,500	1,286
35,000	2,100	1,750	1,500
40,000	2,400	2,000	1,714
45,000	2,700	2,250	1,929
50,000	3,000	2,500	2,143
55,000	3,300	2,750	2,357
60,000	3,600	3,000	2,571
65,000	3,900	3,250	2,786
70,000	4,200	3,500	3,000
75,000	4,500	3,750	3,214
80,000	4,800	4,000	3,429
85,000	5,100	4,250	3,643
90,000	5,400	4,500	3,857
95,000	5,700	4,750	4,071
100,000	6,000	5,000	4,286
105,000	6,300	5,250	4,500
110,000	6,600	5,500	4,714
115,000	6,900	5,750	4,929
120,000	7,200	6,000	5,143
125,000	7,500	6,250	5,357
130,000	7,800	6,500	5,571
135,000	8,100	6,750	5,786
140,000	8,400	7,000	6,000
145,000	8,700	7,250	6,214
150,000	9,000	7,500	6,429
160,000	9,600	8,000	6,857
170,000	10,200	8,500	7,286
180,000	10,800	9,000	7,714
190,000	11,400	9,500	8,143
200,000	12,000	10,000	8,571
210,000	12,600	10,500	9,000
220,000	13,200	11,000	9,429
230,000	13,800	11,500	9,857
240,000	14,400	12,000	10,286
250,000	15,000	12,500	10,714
260,000	15,600	13,000	11,143
270,000	16,200	13,500	11,571
280,000	16,800	14,000	12,000
290,000	17,400	14,500	12,429
300,000	18,000	15,000	12,857

For SI units, 1 ft³ = 0.028 m³, 1000 Btu/hr = 0.293 kW.
ACH: Air change per hour.

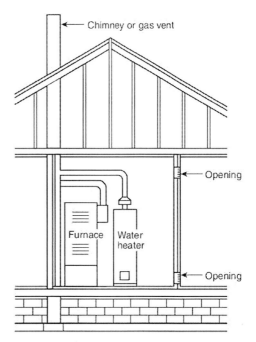

FIGURE A.9.3.2.3(1) All Combustion Air from Adjacent Indoor Spaces Through Indoor Combustion Air Openings.

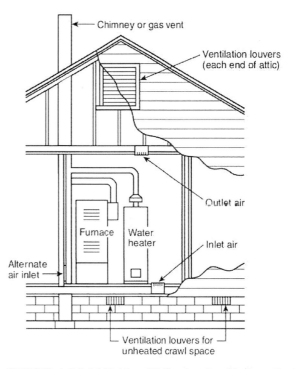

FIGURE A.9.3.3.1(1)(a) All Combustion Air from Outdoors — Inlet Air from Ventilated Crawl Space and Outlet Air to Ventilated Attic.

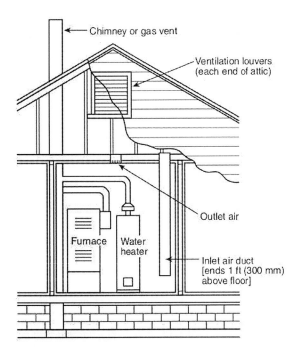

FIGURE A.9.3.3.1(1)(b) All Combustion Air from Outdoors Through Ventilated Attic.

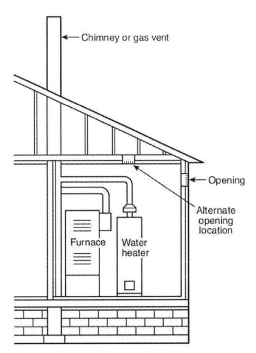

FIGURE A.9.3.3.2 All Combustion Air from Outdoors Through Single Combustion Air Opening.

A.10.3.1.2 Listing standards for furnaces or low-pressure boilers having input ratings greater than 400,000 Btu/hr include UL 795, *Commercial-Industrial Gas Heating Equipment*, or ANSI Z21.13/CSA 4.9, *Gas-Fired Low-Pressure Steam and Hot Water Boilers*.

A.10.3.7 For details of requirements on low-pressure heating boiler safety devices, refer to ASME *Boiler and Pressure Vessel Code*, Section IV, "Rules for Construction of Heating Boilers."

A.10.3.8.3 Reference can be made to NFPA 90A or to NFPA 90B.

A.10.6.2 For information on decorative appliances for installation in vented fireplaces, see ANSI Z21.60/CSA 2.26, *Decorative Gas Appliances for Installation in Solid-Fuel Burning Fireplaces*.

A.10.7.2 For information on vented gas fireplaces, see ANSI Z21.50/CSA 2.22, *Vented Decorative Gas Fireplaces*.

A.10.8.2.3 Recirculation of room air can be hazardous in the presence of flammable solids, liquids, gases, explosive materials (e.g., grain dust, coal dust, gun powder), and substances (e.g., refrigerants, aerosols) that can become toxic when exposed to flame or heat.

A.10.9.7.3 Stainless steel, ceramic-coated steel, and an aluminum-coated steel in which the bond between the steel and the aluminum is an iron-aluminum alloy are considered to be corrosion resistant.

A.10.11.8 Where exhaust fans are used for ventilation, precautions might be necessary to avoid interference with the operation of the appliance.

A.10.13.3.1 See Figure A.10.13.3.1

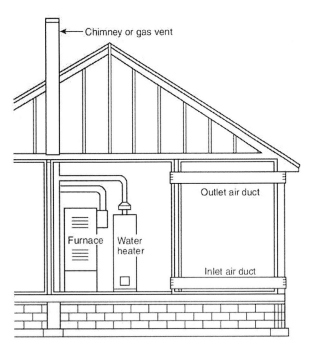

FIGURE A.9.3.3.1(2) All Combustion Air from Outdoors Through Horizontal Ducts.

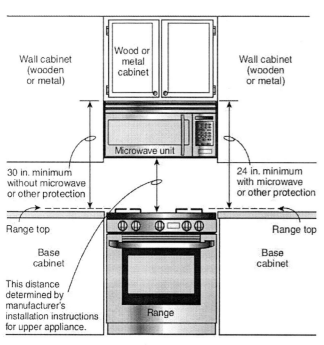

FIGURE A.10.13.3.1 Separation Requirements for Cooktops.

A.10.21.2 It is recommended that space heating appliances installed in all bedrooms or rooms generally kept closed be of the direct vent type.

A.10.26.8 A hole near the top of a cold water inlet tube that enters the top of the water heater or tank is commonly accepted for this purpose.

A.11.1.1 For most burners, the input rate can be changed only slightly by changing the input pressure. Burner input should be checked in accordance with the appliance manufacturer's installation instructions. If no appliance instructions are provided, burner input rate can be checked as follows:

(1) *Checking Burner Input Using a Meter (Clocking).* To check the Btu/hr input rate, the test hand on the gas meter should be timed for at least one revolution and the input determined from this timing. Test dials are generally marked ½, 1, 2, or 5 ft³/revolution depending on the size of the meter. Instructions for converting the test hand readings to cubic feet per hour are given in Table A.11.1.1. This table is provided for specific gas pressures within the meters and gives gas flow rate (corrected to standard conditions) in cubic feet of gas per hour. Standard temperature is 60°F (16°C), and standard pressure is 30.00 in. of mercury. Measure the time for at least one revolution of a dial. Look up the gas flow rate in Table A.11.1.1. Gas flow rates can be calculated for meter pressures other than in these tables in the following manner. A pressure correction factor **F** should be determined for use in the gas input calculation for the gas pressure difference ΔP between the meter inlet and the atmosphere. The gas supplier can provide the pressure at the meter inlet. The pressure correction factor **F** is calculated with the following formula. Table A.11.1.1 was calculated using this formula.

[A.11.1.1a]
$$F = \frac{\Delta P + (B \times 13.596)}{30.00 \times 13.596}$$

where:
F = pressure correction factor
ΔP = meter inlet pressure (in. w.c.)
B = barometric pressure, unadjusted to sea level (in. of mercury)

NOAA weather reports barometric pressure in inches of mercury, adjusted to sea level. The sea level adjustment must be subtracted from the barometric pressure reported by NOAA weather. The local sea level adjustment can be obtained from NOAA.

For example, NOAA reported barometric pressure to be 30.12 in. of mercury for a city at 250 ft elevation. The barometric pressure adjustment for 250 ft is 0.27 in. of mercury. Subtract the local sea level adjustment from the NOAA barometric pressure to get the unadjusted barometric pressure.

[A.11.1.1b]
$$30.12 - 0.27 = 29.85$$

The gas flow rate Q is calculated using the following formula:

[A.11.1.1c]
$$Q = F \times C$$

where:
Q = gas flow rate at standard conditions (ft³/hr)
F = pressure correction factor
C = timed gas flow rate (ft³/hr)

The gas input rate I is calculated with the following formula:

[A.11.1.1d]
$$I = Q \times HHV$$

where:
I = gas input rate (Btu/hr)
Q = gas flow rate at standard conditions (ft³/hr)
HHV = average higher heat value of the gas at standard temperature and pressure conditions (Btu/ft³), which can be obtained from the gas supplier

Appliances can be seriously overfired if the timed meter gas flow rate used to set input rate is not adjusted for meter pressure. At 2 psi (14 kPa) meter pressure, an appliance would be 13 percent overfired if the gas flow rate is not adjusted for meter pressure.

(2) *Checking Burner Input by Using Orifice Pressure Drop and Orifice Size.* The fixed orifice size for each burner can be determined in accordance with Table E.1.1(a) for utility gases and Table E.1.1(b) for undiluted LP-Gases.

Table A.11.1.1 Gas Flow Rate to Burner in Cubic Feet per Hour at Standard Temperature and Pressure

Meter Pressure:	7.0 in. w.c. or 0.25 psi				11.0 in. w.c. or 0.40 psi				55.4 in. w.c. or 2 psi			
Seconds for One Revolution	Size of Test Meter Dial											
	½ ft³	1 ft³	2 ft³	5 ft³	½ ft³	1 ft³	2 ft³	5 ft³	½ ft³	1 ft³	2 ft³	5 ft³
10	183	366	732	1831	185	370	739	1849	204	409	818	2044
11	166	333	666	1664	168	336	672	1680	186	372	743	1859
12	153	305	610	1526	154	308	616	1540	170	341	681	1704
13	141	282	563	1408	142	284	569	1422	157	315	629	1573
14	131	262	523	1308	132	264	528	1320	146	292	584	1460
15	122	244	488	1221	123	246	493	1232	136	273	545	1363
16	114	229	458	1144	116	231	462	1155	128	256	511	1278
17	108	215	431	1077	109	217	435	1087	120	241	481	1203
18	102	203	407	1017	103	205	411	1027	114	227	454	1136
19	96	193	385	964	97	195	389	973	108	215	430	1076
20	92	183	366	915	92	185	370	924	102	204	409	1022
21	87	174	349	872	88	176	352	880	97	195	389	974
22	83	166	333	832	84	168	336	840	93	186	372	929
23	80	159	318	796	80	161	321	804	89	178	356	889
24	76	153	305	763	77	154	308	770	85	170	341	852
25	73	146	293	732	74	148	296	739	82	164	327	818
26	70	141	282	704	71	142	284	711	79	157	315	786
27	68	136	271	678	68	137	274	685	76	151	303	757
28	65	131	262	654	66	132	264	660	73	146	292	730
29	63	126	253	631	64	127	255	637	70	141	282	705
30	61	122	244	610	62	123	246	616	68	136	273	681
31	59	118	236	591	60	119	239	596	66	132	264	660
32	57	114	229	572	58	116	231	578	64	128	256	639
33	55	111	222	555	56	112	224	560	62	124	248	620
34	54	108	215	538	54	109	217	544	60	120	241	601
35	52	105	209	523	53	106	211	528	58	117	234	584
36	51	102	203	509	51	103	205	513	57	114	227	568
37	49	99	198	495	50	100	200	500	55	111	221	553
38	48	96	193	482	49	97	195	486	54	108	215	538
39	47	94	188	469	47	95	190	474	52	105	210	524
40	46	92	183	458	46	92	185	462	51	102	204	511
41	45	89	179	447	45	90	180	451	50	100	199	499
42	44	87	174	436	44	88	176	440	49	97	195	487
43	43	85	170	426	43	86	172	430	48	95	190	475
44	42	83	166	416	42	84	168	420	46	93	186	465
45	41	81	163	407	41	82	164	411	45	91	182	454
46	40	80	159	398	40	80	161	402	44	89	178	444
47	39	78	156	390	39	79	157	393	43	87	174	435
48	38	76	153	381	39	77	154	385	43	85	170	426
49	37	75	149	374	38	75	151	377	42	83	167	417
50	37	73	146	366	37	74	148	370	41	82	164	409
51	36	72	144	359	36	72	145	362	40	80	160	401
52	35	70	141	352	36	71	142	355	39	79	157	393
53	35	69	138	345	35	70	140	349	39	77	154	386
54	34	68	136	339	34	68	137	342	38	76	151	379
55	33	67	133	333	34	67	134	336	37	74	149	372
56	33	65	131	327	33	66	132	330	37	73	146	365
57	32	64	128	321	32	65	130	324	36	72	143	359
58	32	63	126	316	32	64	127	319	35	70	141	352
59	31	62	124	310	31	63	125	313	35	69	139	347
60	31	61	122	305	31	62	123	308	34	68	136	341
62	30	59	118	295	30	60	119	298	33	66	132	330
64	29	57	114	286	29	58	116	289	32	64	128	319
66	28	55	111	277	28	56	112	280	31	62	124	310
68	27	54	108	269	27	54	109	272	30	60	120	301
70	26	52	105	262	26	53	106	264	29	58	117	292

(continues)

Table A.11.1.1 *Continued*

Meter Pressure:	7.0 in. w.c. or 0.25 psi				11.0 in. w.c. or 0.40 psi				55.4 in. w.c. or 2 psi			
Seconds for One Revolution	Size of Test Meter Dial											
	½ ft³	1 ft³	2 ft³	5 ft³	½ ft³	1 ft³	2 ft³	5 ft³	½ ft³	1 ft³	2 ft³	5 ft³
72	25	51	102	254	26	51	103	257	28	57	114	284
74	25	49	99	247	25	50	100	250	28	55	111	276
76	24	48	96	241	24	49	97	243	27	54	108	269
78	23	47	94	235	24	47	95	237	26	52	105	262
80	23	46	92	229	23	46	92	231	26	51	102	256
82	22	45	89	223	23	45	90	225	25	50	100	249
84	22	44	87	218	22	44	88	220	24	49	97	243
86	21	43	85	213	21	43	86	215	24	48	95	238
88	21	42	83	208	21	42	84	210	23	46	93	232
90	20	41	81	203	21	41	82	205	23	45	91	227
94	19	39	78	195	20	39	79	197	22	43	87	217
98	19	37	75	187	19	38	75	189	21	42	83	209
100	18	37	73	183	18	37	74	185	20	41	82	204
104	18	35	70	176	18	36	71	178	20	39	79	197
108	17	34	68	170	17	34	68	171	19	38	76	189
112	16	33	65	163	17	33	66	165	18	37	73	183
116	16	32	63	158	16	32	64	159	18	35	70	176
120	15	31	61	153	15	31	62	154	17	34	68	170
130	14	28	56	141	14	28	57	142	16	31	63	157
140	13	26	52	131	13	26	53	132	15	29	58	146
150	12	24	49	122	12	25	49	123	14	27	55	136
160	11	23	46	114	12	23	46	116	13	26	51	128
170	11	22	43	108	11	22	43	109	12	24	48	120
180	10	20	41	102	10	21	41	103	11	23	45	114
190	10	19	39	96	10	19	39	97	11	22	43	108
200	9	18	37	92	9	18	37	92	10	20	41	102

Note: To convert to Btu per hour, multiply the cubic feet per hour of gas by the Btu per cubic foot heating value of the gas used.

A.11.2 Normally, the primary air adjustment should first be set to give a soft blue flame having luminous tips and then increased to a point where the yellow tips just disappear. If the burner cannot be so adjusted, the manufacturer or serving gas supplier should be contacted.

A.11.6 A procedure for checking draft can be found in G.5.2.

A.12.1 This chapter recognizes that the choice of venting materials and the methods of installation of venting systems are dependent on the operating characteristics of any connected appliances. The operating characteristics of vented appliances can be categorized with respect to whether greater-than-atmospheric or sub-atmospheric pressure exists within the operating vent system and to whether an appliance generates flue or vent gases that can condense in the venting system.

Draft hood–equipped appliances require a vent design that provides a draft to draw vent products into and through the vent system. Vent design tables and the requirements within this code, both for vents and for provision of combustion air, should be used to ensure that vents will provide this draft.

Higher efficiency appliances that generate low-temperature vent gases that can condense require a venting system that can accommodate the condensate produced. Design of these venting systems is accomplished by the appliance manufacturer. Vent system installation requirements for these appliances are contained in the manufacturer's appliance installation instructions.

A.12.3.3 Information on the construction and installation of ventilating hoods can be obtained from NFPA 96.

A.12.4.4 See A.12.3.3.

A.12.6.1.3 For information on the installation of gas vents in existing masonry chimneys, see Section 12.7.

A.12.6.2.1 Chimney clearance requirements are illustrated in Figure A.12.6.2.1.

A.12.6.5.3 Reference can also be made to the chapter on chimney, gas vent, and fireplace systems of the *ASHRAE Handbook — HVAC Systems and Equipment*.

A.12.7.4.1 Additional information on sizing venting systems can be found in the following:

(1) Tables in Chapter 13
(2) The appliance manufacturer's instructions
(3) The vent system manufacturer's sizing instructions
(4) Drawings, calculations, and specifications provided by the vent system manufacturer
(5) Drawings, calculations, and specifications provided by a competent person
(6) The chapter on chimney, gas vent, and fireplace systems of the *ASHRAE Handbook — HVAC Systems and Equipment*

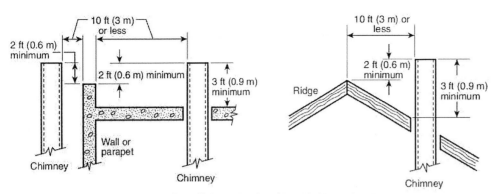

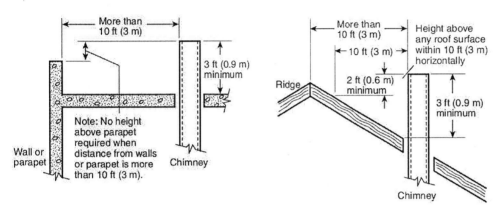

FIGURE A.12.6.2.1 Typical Termination Locations for Chimneys and Single-Wall Metal Pipes Serving Residential-Type and Low-Heat Appliances.

Category I appliances can be either draft hood–equipped or a fan-assisted combustion system in design. Different vent design methods are required for draft hood–equipped and fan-assisted combustion system appliances.

A.12.7.5.2 An example of practical separation of multistory gas venting is provided in Figure A.12.7.5.2.

A.12.8.2 Data on winter design temperature can be found in Figure F.2.4 and the *ASHRAE Handbook — Fundamentals*.

A.12.8.4.1 The prohibition only applies to a vent entirely constructed of single-wall metal pipe located in a residential occupancy. The prohibition does not apply to single-wall vent connectors used to connect an appliance to the vent as permitted in Section 12.11 and Chapter 13.

A.12.8.5(1) Reference can also be made to the chapter on chimney, gas vent, and fireplace systems of the *ASHRAE Handbook — HVAC Systems and Equipment*.

A.12.11.3 Reference can also be made to the chapter on chimney, gas vent, and fireplace systems of the *ASHRAE Handbook — HVAC Systems and Equipment*.

A.12.11.9 A vent connector should be installed so as to avoid turns or other construction features that create excessive resistance to flow of vent gases. A vent connector should be as short as practical, and the appliance located as close as practical, to the chimney or vent.

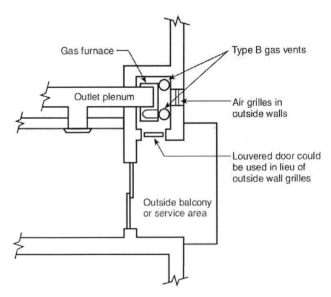

FIGURE A.12.7.5.2 Plan View of Practical Separation Method for Multistory Gas Venting.

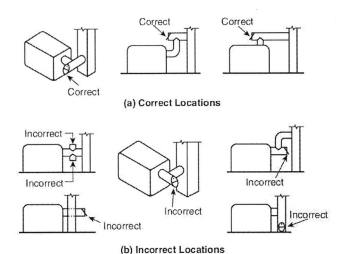

FIGURE A.12.13.4 Locations for Barometric Draft Regulators.

A.12.13.4 A device that automatically shuts off gas to the burner in the event of sustained backdraft is recommended if such backdraft might adversely affect burner operation or if flue gas spillage might introduce a hazard. Figure A.12.13.4 shows examples of correct and incorrect locations for barometric draft regulators.

A.12.14.2 Balancing baffles are typically used in engineered systems and are provided to allow draft adjustment during appliance and venting system commissioning. They are fixed in place and not adjusted after commissioning.

A.13.1.7 A long radius turn is a turn where the centerline radius is equal to or greater than 1.5 times the vent diameter.

A.13.2.20 A long radius turn is a turn where the centerline radius is equal to or greater than 1.5 times the vent diameter.

Annex B Sizing and Capacities of Gas Piping

This annex is not a part of the requirements of this NFPA document but is included for informational purposes only.

B.1 Sizing Factors. The first goal of determining the pipe sizing of a fuel gas piping system is to be assured that the gas pressure at the inlet to each appliance is sufficient. The majority of systems are residential, and the appliances all have the same, or nearly the same, requirement for minimum gas pressure at the appliance inlet. This pressure is about 5 in. (1.2 kPa) w.c., which is enough for proper operation of the appliance regulator to deliver about 3.5 in. (0.87 kPa) w.c. to the burner itself. The pressure drop in the piping is subtracted from the source delivery pressure to verify that the minimum is available at the appliance.

There are other systems, however, where the required inlet pressure to the different appliances could be quite varied. In such cases, the greatest inlet pressure required must be satisfied, as well as the farthest appliance, which is almost always the critical appliance in small systems.

There is an additional requirement to be observed besides the capacity of the system at 100 percent flow. That requirement is that at minimum flow, the pressure at the inlet to any appliance does not exceed the pressure rating of the appliance regulator. This factor would seldom be of concern in small systems if the source pressure is ½ psi (14 in. w.c.) (3.4 kPa) or less, but it should be verified for systems with greater gas pressure at the point of supply.

B.2 General Pipe Sizing Considerations. To determine the size of piping used in a gas piping system, the following factors must be considered:

(1) Allowable loss in pressure from point of delivery to appliance
(2) Maximum gas demand
(3) Length of piping and number of fittings
(4) Specific gravity of the gas
(5) Diversity factor

For any gas piping system, or special appliance, or for conditions other than those covered by the tables provided in this code, such as longer runs, greater gas demands, or greater pressure drops, the size of each gas piping system should be determined by standard engineering practices acceptable to the authority having jurisdiction.

B.3 Description of Tables.

B.3.1 General. The quantity of gas to be provided at each outlet should be determined, whenever possible, directly from the manufacturer's gas input Btu/hr rating of the appliance to be installed, adjusted for altitude where appropriate. In case the ratings of the appliances to be installed are not known, Table A.5.3.2.1 shows the approximate consumption (in Btu per hour) of certain types of typical household appliances.

To obtain the cubic feet per hour of gas required, divide the total Btu/hr input of all appliances by the average Btu heating value per cubic foot of the gas. The average Btu per cubic foot of the gas in the area of the installation can be obtained from the serving gas supplier.

B.3.2 Low-Pressure Natural Gas Tables. Capacities for gas at low pressure [2.0 psi (14 kPa gauge) or less] in cubic feet per hour of 0.60 specific gravity gas for different sizes and lengths are shown in Table 6.2.1(a) through Table 6.2.1(d) for iron pipe or equivalent rigid pipe, in Table 6.2.1(h) through Table 6.2.1(k) for smooth wall semirigid tubing, in Table 6.2.1(o) through Table 6.2.1(q) for corrugated stainless steel tubing, and in Table 6.2.1(t) and Table 6.2.1(u) for polyethylene plastic pipe. Table 6.2.1(a) and Table 6.2.1(h) are based on a pressure drop of 0.3 in. w.c. (75 Pa), whereas Table 6.2.1(b), Table 6.2.1(i), and Table 6.2.1(o) are based on a pressure drop of 0.5 in. w.c. (125 Pa). Table 6.2.1(j), Table 6.2.1(p), and Table 6.2.1(q) are special low-pressure applications based on pressure drops greater than 0.5 in. w.c. (125 Pa). In using Table 6.2.1(j), Table 6.2.1(p), or Table 6.2.1(q), an allowance (in equivalent length of pipe) should be considered for any piping run with four or more fittings *(see Table B.3.2)*.

Table B.3.2 Equivalent Lengths of Pipe Fittings and Valves

		Screwed Fittings[1]				90° Welding Elbows and Smooth Bends[2]					
		45°/Ell	90°/Ell	180° Close Return Bends	Tee	$R/d = 1$	$R/d = 1\frac{1}{3}$	$R/d = 2$	$R/d = 4$	$R/d = 6$	$R/d = 8$
k factor =		0.42	0.90	2.00	1.80	0.48	0.36	0.27	0.21	0.27	0.36
L/d' ratio[4] n =		14	30	67	60	16	12	9	7	9	12
Nominal Pipe Size (in.)	Inside Diam. d (in.), Sched. 40[6]										
		L = Equivalent Length in Feet of Schedule 40 (Standard Weight) Straight Pipe[6]									
½	0.622	0.73	1.55	3.47	3.10	0.83	0.62	0.47	0.36	0.47	0.62
¾	0.824	0.96	2.06	4.60	4.12	1.10	0.82	0.62	0.48	0.62	0.82
1	1.049	1.22	2.62	5.82	5.24	1.40	1.05	0.79	0.61	0.79	1.05
1¼	1.380	1.61	3.45	7.66	6.90	1.84	1.38	1.03	0.81	1.03	1.38
1½	1.610	1.88	4.02	8.95	8.04	2.14	1.61	1.21	0.94	1.21	1.61
2	2.067	2.41	5.17	11.5	10.3	2.76	2.07	1.55	1.21	1.55	2.07
2½	2.469	2.88	6.16	13.7	12.3	3.29	2.47	1.85	1.44	1.85	2.47
3	3.068	3.58	7.67	17.1	15.3	4.09	3.07	2.30	1.79	2.30	3.07
4	4.026	4.70	10.1	22.4	20.2	5.37	4.03	3.02	2.35	3.02	4.03
5	5.047	5.88	12.6	28.0	25.2	6.72	5.05	3.78	2.94	3.78	5.05
6	6.065	7.07	15.2	33.8	30.4	8.09	6.07	4.55	3.54	4.55	6.07
8	7.981	9.31	20.0	44.6	40.0	10.6	7.98	5.98	4.65	5.98	7.98
10	10.02	11.7	25.0	55.7	50.0	13.3	10.0	7.51	5.85	7.51	10.0
12	11.94	13.9	29.8	66.3	59.6	15.9	11.9	8.95	6.96	8.95	11.9
14	13.13	15.3	32.8	73.0	65.6	17.5	13.1	9.85	7.65	9.85	13.1
16	15.00	17.5	37.5	83.5	75.0	20.0	15.0	11.2	8.75	11.2	15.0
18	16.88	19.7	42.1	93.8	84.2	22.5	16.9	12.7	9.85	12.7	16.9
20	18.81	22.0	47.0	105	94.0	25.1	18.8	14.1	11.0	14.1	18.8
24	22.63	26.4	56.6	126	113	30.2	22.6	17.0	13.2	17.0	22.6

Miter Elbows[3] (No. of Miters)					Welding Tees		Valves (Screwed, Flanged, or Welded)			
1-45°	1-60°	1-90°	2-90°	3-90°	Forged	Miter[3]	Gate	Globe	Angle	Swing Check
0.45	0.90	1.80	0.60	0.45	1.35	1.80	0.21	10	5.0	2.5
15	30	60	20	15	45	60	7	333	167	83
L = Equivalent Length in Feet of Schedule 40 (Standard Weight) Straight Pipe[6]										
0.78	1.55	3.10	1.04	0.78	2.33	3.10	0.36	17.3	8.65	4.32
1.03	2.06	4.12	1.37	1.03	3.09	4.12	0.48	22.9	11.4	5.72
1.31	2.62	5.24	1.75	1.31	3.93	5.24	0.61	29.1	14.6	7.27
1.72	3.45	6.90	2.30	1.72	5.17	6.90	0.81	38.3	19.1	9.58
2.01	4.02	8.04	2.68	2.01	6.04	8.04	0.94	44.7	22.4	11.2
2.58	5.17	10.3	3.45	2.58	7.75	10.3	1.21	57.4	28.7	14.4
3.08	6.16	12.3	4.11	3.08	9.25	12.3	1.44	68.5	34.3	17.1
3.84	7.67	15.3	5.11	3.84	11.5	15.3	1.79	85.2	42.6	21.3
5.04	10.1	20.2	6.71	5.04	15.1	20.2	2.35	112	56.0	28.0
6.30	12.6	25.2	8.40	6.30	18.9	25.2	2.94	140	70.0	35.0

(continues)

Table B.3.2 *Continued*

Miter Elbows[3] (No. of Miters)					Welding Tees		Valves (Screwed, Flanged, or Welded)			
1-45°	1-60°	1-90°	2-90°	3-90°	Forged	Miter[3]	Gate	Globe	Angle	Swing Check
0.45	0.90	1.80	0.60	0.45	1.35	1.80	0.21	10	5.0	2.5
15	30	60	20	15	45	60	7	333	167	83
			5	5						
L = Equivalent Length in Feet of Schedule 40 (Standard Weight) Straight Pipe[6]										
7.58	15.2	30.4	10.1	7.58	22.8	30.4	3.54	168	84.1	42.1
9.97	20.0	40.0	13.3	9.97	29.9	40.0	4.65	222	111	55.5
12.5	25.0	50.0	16.7	12.5	37.6	50.0	5.85	278	139	69.5
14.9	29.8	59.6	19.9	14.9	44.8	59.6	6.96	332	166	83.0
16.4	32.8	65.6	21.9	16.4	49.2	65.6	7.65	364	182	91.0
18.8	37.5	75.0	25.0	18.8	56.2	75.0	8.75	417	208	104
21.1	42.1	84.2	28.1	21.1	63.2	84.2	9.85	469	234	117
23.5	47.0	94.0	31.4	23.5	70.6	94.0	11.0	522	261	131
28.3	56.6	113	37.8	28.3	85.0	113	13.2	629	314	157

For SI units, 1 ft = 0.305 m.

Note: Values for welded fittings are for conditions where bore is not obstructed by weld spatter or backing rings. If appreciably obstructed, use values for "Screwed Fittings."

[1] Flanged fittings have three-fourths the resistance of screwed elbows and tees.
[2] Tabular figures give the extra resistance due to curvature alone to which should be added the full length of travel.
[3] Small size socket-welding fittings are equivalent to miter elbows and miter tees.
[4] Equivalent resistance in number of diameters of straight pipe computed for a value of $f = 0.0075$ from the relation $n = k/4f$.
[5] For condition of minimum resistance where the centerline length of each miter is between d and $2\frac{1}{2}d$.
[6] For pipe having other inside diameters, the equivalent resistance may be computed from the above n values.
Source: From *Piping Handbook*, Table XIV, pp. 100–101. Used by permission of McGraw-Hill Book Company.

B.3.3 Undiluted LP-Gas Tables. Capacities in thousands of Btu per hour of undiluted LP-Gases based on a pressure drop of 0.5 in. w.c. (125 Pa) for different sizes and lengths are shown in Table 6.3.1(d) for iron pipe or equivalent rigid pipe, in Table 6.3.1(f) for smooth wall semirigid tubing, in Table 6.3.1(h) for corrugated stainless steel tubing, and in Table 6.3.1(k) and Table 6.3.1(m) for polyethylene plastic pipe and tubing. Table 6.3.1(i) and Table 6.3.1(j) for corrugated stainless steel tubing and Table 6.3.1(l) for polyethylene plastic pipe are based on operating pressures greater than 0.5 psi (3.5 kPa) and pressure drops greater than 0.5 in. w.c. (125 Pa). In using these tables, an allowance (in equivalent length of pipe) should be considered for any piping run with four or more fittings *(see Table B.3.2)*.

B.3.4 Natural Gas Specific Gravity. Gas piping systems that are to be supplied with gas of a specific gravity of 0.70 or less can be sized directly from the tables provided in this code, unless the authority having jurisdiction specifies that a gravity factor be applied. Where the specific gravity of the gas is greater than 0.70, the gravity factor should be applied.

Application of the gravity factor converts the figures given in the tables provided in this code to capacities for another gas of different specific gravity. Such application is accomplished by multiplying the capacities given in the tables by the multipliers shown in Table B.3.4. In case the exact specific gravity does not appear in the table, choose the next higher value specific gravity shown.

Table B.3.4 SPECIAL USE: Multipliers to Be Used with Tables 6.2.1(a) Through 6.2.1(x) When the Specific Gravity of the Gas Is Other than 0.60

Specific Gravity	Multiplier	Specific Gravity	Multiplier
0.35	1.31	1.00	0.78
0.40	1.23	1.10	0.74
0.45	1.16	1.20	0.71
0.50	1.10	1.30	0.68
0.55	1.04	1.40	0.66
0.60	1.00	1.50	0.63
0.65	0.96	1.60	0.61
0.70	0.93	1.70	0.59
0.75	0.90	1.80	0.58
0.80	0.87	1.90	0.56
0.85	0.84	2.00	0.55
0.90	0.82	2.10	0.54

B.3.5 Higher Pressure Natural Gas Tables. Capacities for gas at pressures of 2 psi (14 kPa) and greater in cubic feet per hour of 0.60 specific gravity gas for different sizes and lengths are shown in Table 6.2.1(e) and Table 6.2.1(f) for iron pipe or equivalent rigid pipe, Table 6.2.1(l) through Table 6.2.1(n) for semirigid tubing, Table 6.2.1(r) and Table 6.2.1(s) for corrugated stainless steel tubing, and Table 6.2.1(u) and Table 6.2.1(v) for polyethylene plastic pipe.

B.4 Use of Capacity Tables.

B.4.1 The Longest Length Method. This sizing method is conservative in its approach by applying the maximum operating conditions in the system as the norm for the system and by setting the length of pipe used to size any given part of the piping system to the maximum value.

To determine the size of each section of gas piping in a system within the range of the capacity tables, proceed as follows (*also see sample calculations included in this annex*):

(1) Divide the piping system into appropriate segments consistent with the presence of tees, branch lines, and main runs. For each segment, determine the gas load (assuming all appliances operate simultaneously) and its overall length. An allowance (in equivalent length of pipe) as determined from Table B.3.2 should be considered for piping segments that include four or more fittings.

(2) Determine the gas demand of each appliance to be attached to the piping system. Where Table 6.2.1(a) through Table 6.2.1(x) are to be used to select the piping size, calculate the gas demand in terms of cubic feet per hour for each piping system outlet. Where Table 6.3.1(a) through Table 6.3.1(m) are to be used to select the piping size, calculate the gas demand in terms of thousands of Btu per hour for each piping system outlet.

(3) Where the piping system is for use with other than undiluted LP-Gases, determine the design system pressure, the allowable loss in pressure (pressure drop), and specific gravity of the gas to be used in the piping system.

(4) Determine the length of piping from the point of delivery to the most remote outlet in the building/piping system.

(5) In the appropriate capacity table, select the row showing the measured length or the next longer length if the table does not give the exact length. This length is the only length used in determining the size of any section of gas piping. If the gravity factor is to be applied, the values in the selected row of the table are multiplied by the appropriate multiplier from Table B.3.4.

(6) Use this horizontal row to locate ALL gas demand figures for this particular system of piping.

(7) Starting at the most remote outlet, find the gas demand for that outlet in the horizontal row just selected. If the exact figure of demand is not shown, choose the next larger figure left in the row.

(8) Opposite this demand figure, in the first row at the top, the correct size of gas piping will be found.

(9) Proceed in a similar manner for each outlet and each section of gas piping. For each section of piping, determine the total gas demand supplied by that section.

When a large number of piping components (such as elbows, tees, and valves) are installed in a pipe run, additional pressure loss can be accounted for by the use of equivalent lengths. Pressure loss across any piping component can be equated to the pressure drop through a length of pipe. The equivalent length of a combination of only four elbows/tees can result in a jump to the next larger length row, resulting in a significant reduction in capacity. The equivalent lengths in feet shown in Table B.3.2 have been computed on a basis that the inside diameter corresponds to that of Schedule 40 (standard weight) steel pipe, which is close enough for most purposes involving other schedules of pipe. Where a more specific solution for equivalent length is desired, this can be made by multiplying the actual inside diameter of the pipe in inches by $n/12$, or the actual inside diameter in feet by n. N can be read from the table heading. The equivalent length values can be used with reasonable accuracy for copper or copper alloy fittings and bends, although the resistance per foot of copper or copper alloy pipe is less than that of steel. For copper or copper alloy valves, however, the equivalent length of pipe should be taken as 45 percent longer than the values in the table, which are for steel pipe.

B.4.2 The Branch Length Method. This sizing method reduces the amount of conservatism built into the traditional Longest Length Method. The longest length as measured from the meter to the farthest remote appliance is used only to size the initial parts of the overall piping system. The Branch Length Method is applied in the following manner:

(1) Determine the gas load for each of the connected appliances.

(2) Starting from the meter, divide the piping system into a number of connected segments, and determine the length and amount of gas that each segment would carry, assuming that all appliances were operated simultaneously. An allowance (in equivalent length of pipe) as determined from Table B.3.2 should be considered for piping segments that include four or more fittings.

(3) Determine the distance from the outlet of the gas meter to the appliance farthest removed from the meter.

(4) Using the longest distance (found in Step 3), size each piping segment from the meter to the most remote appliance outlet.

(5) For each of these piping segments, use the longest length and the calculated gas load for all of the connected appliances for the segment and begin the sizing process in Steps 6 through 8.

(6) Referring to the appropriate sizing table (based on operating conditions and piping material), find the longest length distance in the first column or the next larger distance if the exact distance is not listed. The use of alternative operating pressures and/or pressure drops requires the use of a different sizing table but does not alter the sizing methodology. In many cases, the use of alternative operating pressures and/or pressure drops requires the approval of both the authority having jurisdiction and the local gas serving utility.

(7) Trace across this row until the gas load is found or the closest larger capacity if the exact capacity is not listed.

(8) Read up the table column and select the appropriate pipe size in the top row. Repeat Steps 6, 7, and 8 for each pipe segment in the longest run.

(9) Size each remaining section of branch piping not previously sized by measuring the distance from the gas meter location to the most remote outlet in that branch, using the gas load of attached appliances, and follow the procedures of Steps 2 through 8.

B.4.3 Hybrid Pressure Method. The sizing of a 2 psi (14 kPa) gas piping system is performed using the traditional Longest Length Method but with modifications. The 2 psi (14 kPa) system consists of two independent pressure zones, and each zone is sized separately. The Hybrid Pressure Method is applied using the following steps.

The 2 psi (14 kPa) section (from the meter to the line regulator) is sized as follows:

(1) Calculate the gas load (by adding up the nameplate ratings) from all connected appliances. (In certain circumstances the installed gas load can be increased up to 50 percent to accommodate future addition of appliances.) Ensure that the line regulator capacity is adequate for the calculated gas load and that the required pressure drop (across the regulator) for that capacity does not exceed ¾ psi (5.2 kPa) for a 2 psi (14 kPa) system. If the pressure drop across the regulator is too high (for the connected gas load), select a larger regulator.
(2) Measure the distance from the meter to the line regulator located inside the building.
(3) If multiple line regulators are used, measure the distance from the meter to the regulator farthest removed from the meter.
(4) The maximum allowable pressure drop for the 2 psi (14 kPa) section is 1 psi (7 kPa).
(5) Referring to the appropriate sizing table (based on piping material) for 2 psi (14 kPa) systems with a 1 psi (7 kPa) pressure drop, find this distance in the first column, or the closest larger distance if the exact distance is not listed.
(6) Trace across this row until the gas load is found or the closest larger capacity if the exact capacity is not listed.
(7) Read up the table column to the top row and select the appropriate pipe size.
(8) If multiple regulators are used in this portion of the piping system, each line segment must be sized for its actual gas load, using the longest length previously determined.

The low-pressure section (all piping downstream of the line regulator) is sized as follows:

(1) Determine the gas load for each of the connected appliances.
(2) Starting from the line regulator, divide the piping system into a number of connected segments and/or independent parallel piping segments and determine the amount of gas that each segment would carry, assuming that all appliances were operated simultaneously. An allowance (in equivalent length of pipe) as determined from Table B.3.2 should be considered for piping segments that include four or more fittings.
(3) For each piping segment, use the actual length or longest length (if there are sub-branch lines) and the calculated gas load for that segment and begin the sizing process as follows:

   (a) Referring to the appropriate sizing table (based on operating pressure and piping material), find the longest length distance in the first column or the closest larger distance if the exact distance is not listed. The use of alternative operating pressures and/or pressure drops requires the use of a different sizing table but does not alter the sizing methodology. In many cases, the use of alternative operating pressures and/or pressure drops could require the approval of the authority having jurisdiction.
   (b) Trace across this row until the appliance gas load is found or the closest larger capacity if the exact capacity is not listed.
   (c) Read up the table column to the top row and select the appropriate pipe size.
   (d) Repeat this process for each segment of the piping system.

B.4.4 Pressure Drop per 100 ft Method. This sizing method is less conservative than the others, but it allows the designer to immediately see where the largest pressure drop occurs in the system. With this information, modifications can be made to bring the total drop to the critical appliance within the limitations that are presented to the designer.

Follow the procedures described in the Longest Length Method for steps (1) through (4) and step (9).

For each piping segment, calculate the pressure drop based on pipe size, length as a percentage of 100 ft, and gas flow. Table B.4.4 shows pressure drop per 100 ft for pipe sizes from ½ in. through 2 in. The sum of pressure drops to the critical appliance is subtracted from the supply pressure to verify that sufficient pressure is available. If not, the layout can be examined to find the high drop section(s), and sizing selections modified.

Table B.4.4 Thousands of Btu/hr of Natural Gas per 100 ft of Pipe at Various Pressure Drops and Pipe Diameters

| Press. Drop/ | Pipe Sizes (in.) | | | | | |
100 ft (in. w.c.)	½	¾	1	1¼	1½	2
0.2	31	64	121	248	372	716
0.3	38	79	148	304	455	877
0.5	50	104	195	400	600	1160
1.0	71	147	276	566	848	1640

Note: Other values can be obtained using the following equation:

[B.4.4a]
$$\text{Desired Value} = \text{thousands of Btu/hr} \times \sqrt{\frac{\text{Desired Drop}}{\text{Table Drop}}}$$

For example, if it is desired to get flow through ¾ in. pipe at 2 in. w.c./100 ft, multiply the capacity of ¾ in. pipe at 1 in./100 ft by the square root of the pressure ratio:

[B.4.4b]
$$147{,}000 \text{ Btu/hr} \times \sqrt{\frac{2 \text{ in. w.c.}}{1 \text{ in. w.c.}}} = 147{,}000 \times 1.414 = 208{,}000 \text{ Btu/hr}$$

B.5 Use of Sizing Equations. Capacities of smooth wall pipe or tubing can also be determined by using the following formulas:

(1) *High Pressure* [1.5 psi (10.3 kPa) and above]:

[B.5a]
$$Q = 181.6 \sqrt{\frac{D^5 \cdot (P_1^2 - P_2^2) \cdot Y}{Cr \cdot fba \cdot L}}$$
$$= 2237 D^{2.623} \left[\frac{(P_1^2 - P_2^2) \cdot Y}{Cr \cdot L}\right]^{0.541}$$

(2) *Low Pressure* [less than 1.5 psi (10.3 kPa)]:

[B.5b]
$$Q = 187.3 \sqrt{\frac{D^5 \cdot \Delta H}{Cr \cdot fba \cdot L}}$$
$$= 2313 D^{2.623} \left(\frac{\Delta H}{Cr \cdot L}\right)^{0.541}$$

where:
- Q = rate (cubic feet per hour at 60°F and 30 in. mercury column)
- D = inside diameter of pipe (in.)
- P_1 = upstream pressure (psia)
- P_2 = downstream pressure (psia)
- Y = superexpansibility factor = 1/supercompressibility factor
- Cr = factor for viscosity, density, and temperature
- fba = base friction factor for air at 60°F (CF = 1)
- L = length of pipe (ft)
- H = pressure drop [in. w.c. (27.7 in. H$_2$O = 1 psi) = $0.00354 ST(Z/S)^{0.152}$]

See Table 6.4.2 for values of Cr and Y for natural gas and propane.

B.6 Pipe and Tube Diameters. Where the internal diameter is determined by the formulas in Section 6.4, Table B.6(a) and Table B.6(b) can be used to select the nominal or standard pipe size based on the calculated internal diameter.

B.7 Examples of Piping System Design and Sizing.

B.7.1 Example 1 — Longest Length Method. Determine the required pipe size of each section and outlet of the piping system shown in Figure B.7.1, with a designated pressure drop of 0.50 in. w.c. (125 Pa), using the Longest Length Method.

Table B.6(a) Schedule 40 Steel Pipe Standard Sizes

Nominal Size (in.)	Internal Diameter (in.)	Nominal Size (in.)	Internal Diameter (in.)
1/4	0.364	1½	1.610
3/8	0.493	2	2.067
1/2	0.622	2½	2.469
3/4	0.824	3	3.068
1	1.049	3½	3.548
1¼	1.380	4	4.026

Table B.6(b) Copper Tube Standard Sizes

Tube Type	Nominal or Standard Size (in.)	Internal Diameter (in.)	Tube Type	Nominal or Standard Size (in.)	Internal Diameter (in.)
K	1/4	0.305	K	1	0.995
L	1/4	0.315	L	1	1.025
ACR (D)	3/8	0.315	ACR (D, A)	1⅛	1.025
ACR (A)	3/8	0.311	K	1¼	1.245
K	3/8	0.402	L	1¼	1.265
L	3/8	0.430	ACR (D, A)	1⅜	1.265
ACR (D)	1/2	0.430	K	1½	1.481
ACR (A)	1/2	0.436	L	1½	1.505
K	1/2	0.527	ACR (D, A)	1⅝	1.505
L	1/2	0.545	K	2	1.959
ACR (D)	5/8	0.545	L	2	1.985
ACR (A)	5/8	0.555	ACR (D, A)	2⅛	1.985
K	5/8	0.652	K	2½	2.435
L	5/8	0.666	L	2½	2.465
ACR (D)	3/4	0.666	ACR (D, A)	2⅝	2.465
ACR (A)	3/4	0.680	K	3	2.907
K	3/4	0.745	L	3	2.945
L	3/4	0.785	ACR (D, A)	3⅛	2.945
ACR (D, A)	7/8	0.785			

The gas to be used has 0.60 specific gravity and a heating value of 1000 Btu/ft^3 (37.5 MJ/m^3).

Solution

(1) Maximum gas demand for outlet A:

[B.7.1a]
$$\frac{\text{Consumption}\begin{pmatrix}\text{rating plate input, or}\\ \text{Table 5.4.2.1 if necessary}\end{pmatrix}}{\text{Btu of gas}}$$
$$= \frac{35{,}000 \text{ Btu/hr rating}}{1000 \text{ Btu/ft}^3} = 35 \text{ ft}^3/\text{hr} = 35 \text{ cfh}$$

Maximum gas demand for outlet B:

[B.7.1b]
$$\frac{\text{Consumption}}{\text{Btu of gas}} = \frac{75{,}000}{1000} = 75 \text{ cfh}$$

Maximum gas demand for outlet C:

[B.7.1c]
$$\frac{\text{Consumption}}{\text{Btu of gas}} = \frac{35{,}000}{1000} = 35 \text{ cfh}$$

Maximum gas demand for outlet D:

$$\frac{\text{Consumption}}{\text{Btu of gas}} = \frac{100{,}000}{1000} = 100 \text{ cfh} \qquad [\text{B.7.1d}]$$

(2) The length of pipe from the point of delivery to the most remote outlet (A) is 60 ft (18.3 m). This is the only distance used.

(3) Using the row marked 60 ft (18.3 m) in Table 6.2.1(b):

  (a) Outlet A, supplying 35 cfh (0.99 m³/hr), requires ½ in. pipe.

  (b) Outlet B, supplying 75 cfh (2.12 m³/hr), requires ¾ in. pipe.

  (c) Section 1, supplying outlets A and B, or 110 cfh (3.11 m³/hr), requires ¾ in. pipe.

  (d) Section 2, supplying outlets C and D, or 135 cfh (3.82 m³/hr), requires ¾ in. pipe.

  (e) Section 3, supplying outlets A, B, C, and D, or 245 cfh (6.94 m³/hr), requires 1 in. pipe.

(4) If a different gravity factor is applied to this example, the values in the row marked 60 ft (18.3 m) of Table 6.2.1(b) would be multiplied by the appropriate multiplier from Table B.3.4, and the resulting cubic feet per hour values would be used to size the piping.

B.7.2 Example 2 — Hybrid or Dual Pressure Systems. Determine the required CSST size of each section of the piping system shown in Figure B.7.2, with a designated pressure drop of 1 psi (7 kPa) for the 2 psi (14 kPa) section and 3 in. w.c. (0.75 kPa) pressure drop for the 10 in. w.c. (2.49 kPa) section. The gas to be used has 0.60 specific gravity and a heating value of 1000 Btu/ft³ (37.5 MJ/m³).

Solution

(1) Size 2 psi (14 kPa) line using Table 6.2.1(r).

(2) Size 10 in. w.c. (2.5 kPa) lines using Table 6.2.1(p).

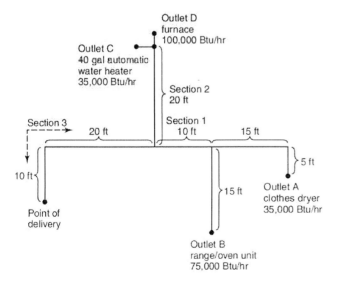

For SI units, 1 ft = 0.305 m, 1 gal = 3.785 L, 1000 Btu/hr = 0.293 kW.

FIGURE B.7.1 Piping Plan Showing a Steel Piping System.

(3) Using the following steps, determine if sizing tables can be used:

  (a) Total gas load shown in Figure B.7.2 equals 110 cfh (3.11 m³/hr).

  (b) Determine pressure drop across regulator [see notes in Table 6.2.1(r)].

  (c) If pressure drop across regulator exceeds ¾ psi (5.2 kPa), Table 6.2.1(r) cannot be used. Note that if pressure drop exceeds ¾ psi (5.2 kPa), a larger regulator must be selected or an alternative sizing method must be used.

  (d) Pressure drop across the line regulator [for 110 cfh/(3.11 m³/hr)] is 4 in. w.c. (0.99 kPa) based on manufacturer's performance data.

  (e) Assume the CSST manufacturer has tubing sizes or EHDs of 13, 18, 23, and 30.

(4) From Section A [2 psi (14 kPa) zone]:

  (a) Determine distance from meter to regulator = 100 ft (30.48 m).

  (b) Determine total load supplied by A = 110 cfh (3.11 m³/hr) (furnace + water heater + dryer).

  (c) Table 6.2.1(r) shows that EHD size 18 should be used. Note that it is not unusual to oversize the supply line by 25 to 50 percent of the as-installed load. EHD size 18 has a capacity of 189 cfh (5.35 m³/hr).

(5) From Section B (low-pressure zone):

  (a) Distance from regulator to furnace is 15 ft (4.57 m).

  (b) Load is 60 cfh (1.70 m³/hr).

  (c) Table 6.2.1(p) shows that EHD size 13 should be used.

(6) From Section C (low-pressure zone):

  (a) Distance from regulator to water heater is 10 ft (3 m).

  (b) Load is 30 cfh (0.85 m³/hr).

  (c) Table 6.2.1(p) shows that EHD size 13 should be used.

(7) From Section D (low-pressure zone):

  (a) Distance from regulator to dryer is 25 ft (7.62 m).

  (b) Load is 20 cfh (0.57 m³/hr).

  (c) Table 6.2.1(p) shows that EHD size 13 should be used.

B.7.3 Example 3 — Branch Length Method. Determine the required semirigid copper tubing size of each section of the piping system shown in Figure B.7.3, with a designated pressure drop of 1 in. w.c. (250 Pa) (using the Branch Length Method). The gas to be used has 0.60 specific gravity and a heating value of 1000 Btu/ft³ (37.5 MJ/m³).

Solution

(1) Section A:

  (a) The length of tubing from the point of delivery to the most remote appliance is 50 ft (15 m), A + C.

  (b) Use this longest length to size Sections A and C.

  (c) Using the row marked 50 ft (15 m) in Table 6.2.1(j), Section A supplying 220 cfh (6.23 m³/hr) for four appliances requires 1 in. (25 mm) tubing.

(2) Section B:

  (a) The length of tubing from the point of delivery to the range/oven at the end of Section B is 30 ft (9.14 m), A + B.

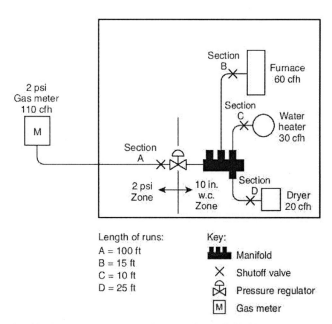

FIGURE B.7.2 Piping Plan Showing a CSST System.

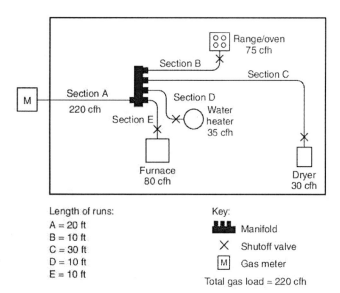

FIGURE B.7.3 Piping Plan Showing a Copper Tubing System.

(b) Use this branch length to size Section B only.
(c) Using the row marked 30 ft (9.14 m) in Table 6.2.1(j), Section B supplying 75 cfh (2.12 m³/hr) for the range/oven requires ½ in. (15 mm) tubing.

(3) Section C:
 (a) The length of tubing from the point of delivery to the dryer at the end of Section C is 50 ft (15 m), A + C.
 (b) Use this branch length (which is also the longest length) to size Section C.
 (c) Using the row marked 50 ft (15 m) in Table 6.2.1(j), Section C supplying 30 cfh (0.85 m³/hr) for the dryer requires ⅜ in. (10 mm) tubing.

(4) Section D:
 (a) The length of tubing from the point of delivery to the water heater at the end of Section D is 30 ft (9.14 m), A + D.
 (b) Use this branch length to size Section D only.
 (c) Using the row marked 30 ft (9.14 m) in Table 6.2.1(j), Section D supplying 35 cfh (0.99 m³/hr) for the water heater requires ⅜ in. (10 mm) tubing.

(5) Section E:
 (a) The length of tubing from the point of delivery to the furnace at the end of Section E is 30 ft (9.14 m), A + E.
 (b) Use this branch length to size Section E only.
 (c) Using the row marked 30 ft (9.14 m) in Table 6.2.1(j), Section E supplying 80 cfh (2.26 m³/hr) for the furnace requires ½ in. (15 mm) tubing.

B.7.4 Example 4 — Modification to Existing Piping System. Determine the required CSST size for Section G (retrofit application) of the piping system shown in Figure B.7.4, with a designated pressure drop of 0.50 in. w.c. (125 Pa) using the Branch Length Method. The gas to be used has 0.60 specific gravity and a heating value of 1000 Btu/ft³ (37.5 MJ/m³).

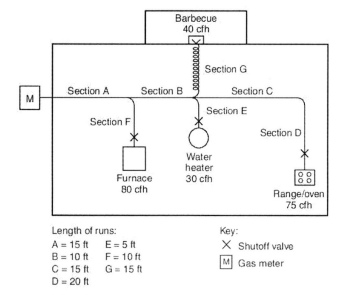

FIGURE B.7.4 Piping Plan Showing Modification to an Existing Piping System.

Solution

(1) The length of pipe and CSST from the point of delivery to the retrofit appliance (barbecue) at the end of Section G is 40 ft (12.19 m), A + B + G.
(2) Use this branch length to size Section G.
(3) Assume the CSST manufacturer has tubing sizes or EHDs of 13, 18, 23, and 30.
(4) Using the row marked 40 ft (12.19 m) in Table 6.2.1(o), Section G supplying 40 cfh (1.13 m³/hr) for the barbecue requires EHD 18 CSST.
(5) The sizing of Sections A, B, F, and E must be checked to ensure adequate gas carrying capacity since an appliance has been added to the piping system. See B.7.1 for details.

B.7.5 Example 5 — Calculating Pressure Drops Due to Temperature Changes. A test piping system is installed on a warm autumn afternoon when the temperature is 70°F (21°C). In accordance with local custom, the new piping system is subjected to an air pressure test at 20 psi (138 kPa). Overnight, the temperature drops, and when the inspector shows up first thing in the morning the temperature is 40°F (4°C).

If the volume of the piping system is unchanged, the formula based on Boyle's and Charles' law for determining the new pressure at a reduced temperature is as follows:

(1)
[B.7.5a]
$$\frac{T_1}{T_2} = \frac{P_1}{P_2}$$

where:
T_1 = initial temperature [absolute (T_1 + 459)]
T_2 = final temperature [absolute (T_2 + 459)]
P_1 = initial pressure [psia (P_1 + 14.7)]
P_2 = final pressure [psia (P_2 + 14.7)]

(2)
[B.7.5b]
$$\frac{(70+459)}{(40+459)} = \frac{(20+14.7)}{(P_2+14.7)}$$

(3)
[B.7.5c]
$$\frac{529}{499} = \frac{34.7}{(P_2+14.7)}$$

(4)
[B.7.5d]
$$(P_2+14.7) = \frac{34.7}{1.06}$$
$$P_2 = 32.7 - 14.7$$
$$P_2 = 18 \text{ psi}$$

Therefore, you could expect the gauge to register 18 psi (124 kPa) when the ambient temperature is 40°F (4°C).

B.7.6 Example 6 — Pressure Drop per 100 ft of Pipe Method. Using the layout shown in Figure B.7.1 and ΔH = pressure drop, in. w.c. (27.7 in. H₂O = 1 psi), proceed as follows:

(1) Length to A = 20 ft, with 35,000 Btu/hr:
For ½ in. pipe:

[B.7.6a]
$$\Delta H = \frac{20 \text{ ft}}{100 \text{ ft}} \times 0.3 \text{ in. w.c.} = 0.06 \text{ in. w.c.}$$

(2) Length to B = 15 ft, with 75,000 Btu/hr:
For ¾ in. pipe:

[B.7.6b]
$$\Delta H = \frac{15 \text{ ft}}{100 \text{ ft}} \times 0.3 \text{ in. w.c.} = 0.045 \text{ in. w.c.}$$

(3) Section 1 = 10 ft, with 110,000 Btu/hr. Here a choice is available:
For 1 in. pipe:

[B.7.6c]
$$\Delta H = \frac{10 \text{ ft}}{100 \text{ ft}} \times 0.2 \text{ in. w.c.} = 0.02 \text{ in. w.c.}$$

For ¾ in. pipe:

[B.7.6d]
$$\Delta H = \frac{10 \text{ ft}}{100 \text{ ft}} \times \left[0.5 \text{ in. w.c.} + \left(\frac{110{,}000 \text{ Btu/hr} - 104{,}000 \text{ Btu/hr}}{147{,}000 \text{ Btu/hr} - 104{,}000 \text{ Btu/hr}} \right) \times (1.0 \text{ in. w.c.} - 0.5 \text{ in. w.c.}) \right]$$
$$= 0.1 \times 0.57 \text{ in. w.c.} \approx 0.06 \text{ in. w.c.}$$

Notice that the pressure drop for 110,000 Btu/hr between 104,000 Btu/hr and 147,000 Btu/hr has been interpolated.

(4) Section 2 = 20 ft, with 135,000 Btu/hr. Here a choice is available:
For 1 in. pipe:

[B.7.6e]
$$\Delta H = \frac{20 \text{ ft}}{100 \text{ ft}} \times \left[0.2 \text{ in. w.c.} + \frac{14{,}000 \text{ Btu/hr}}{27{,}000 \text{ Btu/hr}} \times \Delta 0.1 \text{ in. w.c.} \right]$$
$$= 0.05 \text{ in. w.c.}$$

For ¾ in. pipe:

[B.7.6f]
$$\Delta H = \frac{20 \text{ ft}}{100 \text{ ft}} \times 1.0 \text{ in. w.c.} = 0.2 \text{ in. w.c.}$$

Notice that the pressure drop for 135,000 Btu/hr between 121,000 Btu/hr and 148,000 Btu/hr has been interpolated, but interpolation was not used for the ¾ in. pipe (trivial for 104,000 Btu/hr to 147,000 Btu/hr).

(5) Section 3 = 30 ft, with 245,000 Btu/hr. Here a choice is available:
For 1 in. pipe:

[B.7.6g]
$$\Delta H = \frac{30 \text{ ft}}{100 \text{ ft}} \times 1.0 \text{ in. w.c.} = 0.3 \text{ in. w.c.}$$

For 1¼ in. pipe:

[B.7.6h]
$$\Delta H = \frac{20 \text{ ft}}{100 \text{ ft}} \times 0.3 \text{ in. w.c.} = 0.06 \text{ in. w.c.}$$

Notice that interpolation was not used for these options, since the table values are close to the 245,000 Btu/hr carried by that section.

(6) The total pressure drop is the sum of the section approaching A, Section 1, and Section 3, or either of the following, depending on whether an absolute minimum is required or the larger drop can be accommodated:
Minimum Pressure Drop to farthest appliance:
ΔH = 0.06 in. w.c. + 0.02 in. w.c. + 0.06 in. w.c. = 0.14 in. w.c.
Larger Pressure Drop to the farthest appliance:
ΔH = 0.06 in. w.c. + 0.06 in. w.c. + 0.3 in. w.c. = 0.42 in. w.c.
Notice that Section 2 and the run to B do not enter into this calculation, provided that the appliances have similar input pressure requirements.
For SI units, 1 Btu/hr = 0.293 W, 1 ft^3 = 0.028 m^3, 1 ft = 0.305 m, 1 in. w.c. = 249 Pa.

Annex C Suggested Method of Checking for Leakage

This annex is not a part of the requirements of this NFPA document but is included for informational purposes only.

C.1 Use of Lights. Artificial illumination used in connection with a search for gas leakage should be restricted to battery-operated flashlights (preferably of the safety type) or approved safety lamps. In searching for leaks, electric switches should not be operated. If electric lights are already turned on, they should not be turned off.

C.2 Leak Check Using the Gas Meter. Immediately prior to the leak check, it should be determined that the meter is in operating condition and has not been bypassed.

The leak check can be done by carefully watching the test dial of the meter to determine whether gas is passing through the meter. To assist in observing any movement of the test hand, wet a small piece of paper and paste its edge directly over the centerline of the hand as soon as the gas is turned on. This observation should be made with the test hand on the upstroke. Table C.2 can be used for determining the length of observation time.

In case careful observation of the test hand for a sufficient length of time reveals no movement, the piping should be purged and a small gas burner turned on and lighted and the hand of the test dial again observed. If the dial hand moves (as it should), it shows that the meter is operating properly. If the test hand does not move or register flow of gas through the meter to the small burner, the meter is defective and the gas should be shut off and the serving gas supplier notified.

Table C.2 Observation Times for Various Meter Dials

Dial Styles (ft^3)	Test Time (min)
¼	5
½	5
1	7
2	10
5	20
10	30

For SI units, 1 ft^3 = 0.028 m^3.

C.3 Leak Check Not Using a Meter. This test can be done using one of the following methods:

(1) *For Any Gas System.*
  (a) Attach a manometer or pressure gauge between the inlet to the piping system and the first regulator in the piping system, momentarily turn on the gas supply, and observe the gauging device for pressure drop with the gas supply shut off. No discernible drop in pressure should occur during a period of 3 minutes.
  (b) Attach an in-line flow meter between the meter outlet and piping system inlet prior to the first regulator in the piping system. Slowly turn on the gas supply and observe the metering device. If flow does not drop to zero, leakage is indicated.

(2) *For Gas Systems Using Undiluted LP-Gas System Preparation for Propane.* A leak check performed on an LP-Gas system being placed back in service can be performed by using one of the following methods:
  (a) Insert a pressure gauge between the container gas shutoff valve and the first-stage regulator or integral two-stage regulator in the system, admitting full container pressure to the system and then closing the container shutoff valve. Enough gas should then be released from the system to lower the pressure gauge reading by 10 psi (69 kPa). The system should then be allowed to stand for 3 minutes without showing an increase or a decrease in the pressure gauge reading.
  (b) Insert a gauge/regulator test assembly between the container gas shutoff valve and first-stage regulator or integral two-stage regulator in the system. If a gauge/regulator test assembly with an inches water column gauge is inserted, follow the test requirements in C.3(2)(c); if a gauge/regulator test assembly with a 30 psi gauge is inserted, follow the test requirements in C.3(2)(d).
  (c) For systems with an integral two-stage, one or more second-stage, or one or more line pressure regulators serving appliances that receive gas at pressures of ½ psi (3.5 kPa) or less, insert a water manometer or inches water column gauge into the system downstream of the final stage regulator, pressurizing the system with either fuel gas or air to a test pressure of 9 in. w.c. ± ½ in. w.c. (2.2 kPa ± 0.1 kPa), and observing the device for a pressure change. If fuel gas is used as a pressure source, it is necessary to pressurize the system to full operating pressure, close the container service valve, and then release enough gas from the system through a range burner valve or other suitable means to drop the system pressure to 9 in. w.c. ± ½ in. w.c. (2.2 kPa ± 0.1 kPa). This ensures that all regulators in the system upstream of the test point are unlocked and that a leak anywhere in the system is communicated to the gauging device. The gauging device should indicate no loss or gain of pressure for a period of 3 minutes.

(d) When testing a system that has a first-stage regulator, or an integral two-stage regulator, insert a 30 psi (207 kPa) pressure gauge on the downstream side of the first-stage regulator or at the intermediate pressure tap of an integral two-stage regulator, admitting normal operating pressure to the system and then closing the container valve. Enough gas should be released from the system to lower the pressure gauge reading by a minimum of 2 psi (13.8 kPa) so that the first-stage regulator is unlocked. The system should be allowed to stand for 3 minutes without showing an increase or a decrease in pressure gauge reading.

(e) Insert a gauge/regulator test assembly on the downstream side of the first stage regulator or at the intermediate pressure tap of an integral two stage regulator. If a gauge/regulator test assembly with an inches water column gauge is inserted, follow the test requirements in C.3(2)(c); if a gauge/regulator test assembly with a 30 psi gauge is inserted, follow the test requirements in C.3(2)(d).

C.4 When Leakage Is Indicated. If leakage is indicated by a test device, all appliances and equipment or outlets supplied through the system should be examined to see whether they are shut off and do not leak. If they are found to be tight, the piping system has a leak.

Annex D Suggested Emergency Procedure for Gas Leaks

This annex is not a part of the requirements of this NFPA document but is included for informational purposes only.

D.1 Where an investigation discloses a concentration of gas inside of a building, it is suggested the following immediate actions be taken:

(1) Clear the room, building, or area of all occupants. Do not re-enter the room, building, or area until the space has been determined to be safe.
(2) Use every practical means to eliminate sources of ignition. Take precautions to prevent smoking, striking matches, operating electrical switches or devices, opening furnace doors, and so on. If possible, cut off all electric circuits at a remote source to eliminate operation of automatic switches in the dangerous area. Safety flashlights designed for use in hazardous atmospheres are recommended for use in such emergencies.
(3) Notify all personnel in the area and call 911 from an area remote from the leak.
(4) Ventilate the affected portion of the building by opening windows and doors.
(5) Shut off the supply of gas to the areas involved.
(6) Investigate other buildings in the immediate area to determine the presence of escaping gas therein.

Annex E Flow of Gas Through Fixed Orifices

This annex is not a part of the requirements of this NFPA document but is included for informational purposes only.

E.1 Use of Orifice Tables.

E.1.1 To Check Burner Input Not Using a Meter. Gauge the size of the burner orifice and determine flow rate at sea level from Table E.1.1(a), Utility Gases (cubic feet per hour), or from Table E.1.1(b), LP-Gases (Btu per hour). When the specific gravity of the utility gas is other than 0.60, select the multiplier from Table E.1.1(c) for the specific gravity of the utility gas served and apply to the flow rate as determined from Table E.1.1(a). When the altitude is above 2000 ft (600 m), first select the equivalent orifice size at sea level using Table E.1.1(d), then determine the flow rate from Table E.1.1(a) or Table E.1.1(b) as directed. Having determined the flow rate (as adjusted for specific gravity and/or altitude where necessary), check the burner input at sea level with the manufacturer's rated input.

E.1.2 To Select Correct Orifice Size for Rated Burner Input. The selection of a fixed orifice size for any rated burner input is affected by many variables, including orifice coefficient, and it is recommended that the appliance manufacturer be consulted for that purpose. When the correct orifice size cannot be readily determined, the orifice flow rates, as stated in the tables in this annex, can be used to select a fixed orifice size with a flow rate to approximately equal the required rated burner input.

For gases of the specific gravity and pressure conditions stipulated at elevations under 2000 ft (600 m), Table E.1.1(a) (in cubic feet per hour) or Table E.1.1(b) (in Btu per hour) can be used directly.

Where the specific gravity of the gas is other than 0.60, select the multiplier from Table E.1.1(c) for the utility gas served and divide the rated burner input by the selected factor to determine equivalent input at a specific gravity of 0.60, then select orifice size.

Where the appliance is located at an altitude of 2000 ft (600 m) or above, first use the manufacturer's rated input at sea level to select the orifice size as directed, then use Table E.1.1(d) to select the equivalent orifice size for use at the higher altitude.

Table E.1.1(a) Utility Gases (cubic feet per hour at sea level)

Orifice or Drill Size	Pressure at Orifice (in. w.c.)								
	3	3.5	4	5	6	7	8	9	10
80	0.48	0.52	0.55	0.63	0.69	0.73	0.79	0.83	0.88
79	0.55	0.59	0.64	0.72	0.80	0.84	0.90	0.97	1.01
78	0.70	0.76	0.78	0.88	0.97	1.04	1.10	1.17	1.24
77	0.88	0.95	0.99	1.11	1.23	1.31	1.38	1.47	1.55
76	1.05	1.13	1.21	1.37	1.52	1.61	1.72	1.83	1.92
75	1.16	1.25	1.34	1.52	1.64	1.79	1.91	2.04	2.14
74	1.33	1.44	1.55	1.74	1.91	2.05	2.18	2.32	2.44
73	1.51	1.63	1.76	1.99	2.17	2.32	2.48	2.64	2.78
72	1.64	1.77	1.90	2.15	2.40	2.52	2.69	2.86	3.00
71	1.82	1.97	2.06	2.33	2.54	2.73	2.91	3.11	3.26
70	2.06	2.22	2.39	2.70	2.97	3.16	3.38	3.59	3.78
69	2.25	2.43	2.61	2.96	3.23	3.47	3.68	3.94	4.14
68	2.52	2.72	2.93	3.26	3.58	3.88	4.14	4.41	4.64
67	2.69	2.91	3.12	3.52	3.87	4.13	4.41	4.69	4.94
66	2.86	3.09	3.32	3.75	4.11	4.39	4.68	4.98	5.24
65	3.14	3.39	3.72	4.28	4.62	4.84	5.16	5.50	5.78
64	3.41	3.68	4.14	4.48	4.91	5.23	5.59	5.95	6.26
63	3.63	3.92	4.19	4.75	5.19	5.55	5.92	6.30	6.63
62	3.78	4.08	4.39	4.96	5.42	5.81	6.20	6.59	6.94
61	4.02	4.34	4.66	5.27	5.77	6.15	6.57	7.00	7.37
60	4.21	4.55	4.89	5.52	5.95	6.47	6.91	7.35	7.74
59	4.41	4.76	5.11	5.78	6.35	6.78	7.25	7.71	8.11
58	4.66	5.03	5.39	6.10	6.68	7.13	7.62	8.11	8.53
57	4.84	5.23	5.63	6.36	6.96	7.44	7.94	8.46	8.90
56	5.68	6.13	6.58	7.35	8.03	8.73	9.32	9.92	10.44
55	7.11	7.68	8.22	9.30	10.18	10.85	11.59	12.34	12.98
54	7.95	8.59	9.23	10.45	11.39	12.25	13.08	13.93	14.65
53	9.30	10.04	10.80	12.20	13.32	14.29	15.27	16.25	17.09
52	10.61	11.46	12.31	13.86	15.26	16.34	17.44	18.57	19.53
51	11.82	12.77	13.69	15.47	16.97	18.16	19.40	20.64	21.71
50	12.89	13.92	14.94	16.86	18.48	19.77	21.12	22.48	23.65
49	14.07	15.20	16.28	18.37	20.20	21.60	23.06	24.56	25.83
48	15.15	16.36	17.62	19.88	21.81	23.31	24.90	26.51	27.89
47	16.22	17.52	18.80	21.27	23.21	24.93	26.62	28.34	29.81
46	17.19	18.57	19.98	22.57	24.72	26.43	28.23	30.05	31.61
45	17.73	19.15	20.52	23.10	25.36	27.18	29.03	30.90	32.51
44	19.45	21.01	22.57	25.57	27.93	29.87	31.89	33.96	35.72
43	20.73	22.39	24.18	27.29	29.87	32.02	34.19	36.41	38.30
42	23.10	24.95	26.50	29.50	32.50	35.24	37.63	40.07	42.14
41	24.06	25.98	28.15	31.69	34.81	37.17	39.70	42.27	44.46
40	25.03	27.03	29.23	33.09	36.20	38.79	41.42	44.10	46.38
39	26.11	28.20	30.20	34.05	37.38	39.97	42.68	45.44	47.80
38	27.08	29.25	31.38	35.46	38.89	41.58	44.40	47.27	49.73
37	28.36	30.63	32.99	37.07	40.83	43.62	46.59	49.60	52.17
36	29.76	32.14	34.59	39.11	42.76	45.77	48.88	52.04	54.74
35	32.36	34.95	36.86	41.68	45.66	48.78	52.10	55.46	58.34
34	32.45	35.05	37.50	42.44	46.52	49.75	53.12	56.55	59.49
33	33.41	36.08	38.79	43.83	48.03	51.46	54.96	58.62	61.55
32	35.46	38.30	40.94	46.52	50.82	54.26	57.95	61.70	64.89

(continues)

Table E.1.1(a) *Continued*

Orifice or Drill Size	Pressure at Orifice (in. w.c.)								
	3	3.5	4	5	6	7	8	9	10
31	37.82	40.85	43.83	49.64	54.36	58.01	61.96	65.97	69.39
30	43.40	46.87	50.39	57.05	62.09	66.72	71.22	75.86	79.80
29	48.45	52.33	56.19	63.61	69.62	74.45	79.52	84.66	89.04
28	51.78	55.92	59.50	67.00	73.50	79.50	84.92	90.39	95.09
27	54.47	58.83	63.17	71.55	78.32	83.59	89.27	95.04	99.97
26	56.73	61.27	65.86	74.57	81.65	87.24	93.17	99.19	104.57
25	58.87	63.58	68.22	77.14	84.67	90.36	96.50	102.74	108.07
24	60.81	65.67	70.58	79.83	87.56	93.47	99.83	106.28	111.79
23	62.10	67.07	72.20	81.65	89.39	94.55	100.98	107.49	113.07
22	64.89	70.08	75.21	85.10	93.25	99.60	106.39	113.24	119.12
21	66.51	71.83	77.14	87.35	95.63	102.29	109.24	116.29	122.33
20	68.22	73.68	79.08	89.49	97.99	104.75	111.87	119.10	125.28
19	72.20	77.98	83.69	94.76	103.89	110.67	118.55	125.82	132.36
18	75.53	81.57	87.56	97.50	108.52	116.03	123.92	131.93	138.78
17	78.54	84.82	91.10	103.14	112.81	120.33	128.52	136.82	143.91
16	82.19	88.77	95.40	107.98	118.18	126.78	135.39	144.15	151.63
15	85.20	92.02	98.84	111.74	122.48	131.07	139.98	149.03	156.77
14	87.10	94.40	100.78	114.21	124.44	133.22	142.28	151.47	159.33
13	89.92	97.11	104.32	118.18	128.93	138.60	148.02	157.58	165.76
12	93.90	101.41	108.52	123.56	135.37	143.97	153.75	163.69	172.13
11	95.94	103.62	111.31	126.02	137.52	147.20	157.20	167.36	176.03
10	98.30	106.16	114.21	129.25	141.82	151.50	161.81	172.26	181.13
9	100.99	109.07	117.11	132.58	145.05	154.71	165.23	175.91	185.03
8	103.89	112.20	120.65	136.44	149.33	160.08	170.96	182.00	191.44
7	105.93	114.40	123.01	139.23	152.56	163.31	174.38	185.68	195.30
6	109.15	117.88	126.78	142.88	156.83	167.51	178.88	190.46	200.36
5	111.08	119.97	128.93	145.79	160.08	170.82	182.48	194.22	204.30
4	114.75	123.93	133.22	150.41	164.36	176.18	188.16	200.25	210.71
3	119.25	128.79	137.52	156.26	170.78	182.64	195.08	207.66	218.44
2	128.48	138.76	148.61	168.64	184.79	197.66	211.05	224.74	235.58
1	136.35	147.26	158.25	179.33	194.63	209.48	223.65	238.16	250.54

For SI units, 1 Btu/hr = 0.293 W, 1 ft^3 = 0.028 m^3, 1 ft = 0.305 m, 1 in. w.c. = 249 Pa.

Notes:
(1) Specific gravity = 0.60; orifice coefficient = 0.90.
(2) For utility gases of another specific gravity, select multiplier from Table E.1.1(c). For altitudes above 2000 ft, first select the equivalent orifice size at sea level from Table E.1.1(d).

Table E.1.1(b) LP-Gases (Btu per hour at sea level)

Orifice or Drill Size	Propane	Butane
0.008	519	589
0.009	656	744
0.010	812	921
0.011	981	1,112
0.012	1,169	1,326
80	1,480	1,678
79	1,708	1,936
78	2,080	2,358
77	2,629	2,980
76	3,249	3,684
75	3,581	4,059
74	4,119	4,669
73	4,678	5,303
72	5,081	5,760
71	5,495	6,230
70	6,375	7,227
69	6,934	7,860
68	7,813	8,858
67	8,320	9,433
66	8,848	10,031
65	9,955	11,286
64	10,535	11,943
63	11,125	12,612
62	11,735	13,304
61	12,367	14,020
60	13,008	14,747
59	13,660	15,486
58	14,333	16,249
57	15,026	17,035
56	17,572	19,921
55	21,939	24,872
54	24,630	27,922
53	28,769	32,615
52	32,805	37,190
51	36,531	41,414
50	39,842	45,168
49	43,361	49,157
48	46,983	53,263
47	50,088	56,783
46	53,296	60,420
45	54,641	61,944
44	60,229	68,280
43	64,369	72,973
42	71,095	80,599
41	74,924	84,940
40	78,029	88,459
39	80,513	91,215
38	83,721	94,912
37	87,860	99,605
36	92,207	104,532

Table E.1.1(b) *Continued*

Orifice or Drill Size	Propane	Butane
35	98,312	111,454
34	100,175	113,566
33	103,797	117,672
32	109,385	124,007
31	117,043	132,689
30	134,119	152,046
29	150,366	170,466
28	160,301	181,728
27	168,580	191,114
26	175,617	199,092
25	181,619	205,896
24	187,828	212,935
23	192,796	218,567
22	200,350	227,131
21	205,525	232,997
20	210,699	238,863
19	223,945	253,880
18	233,466	264,673

Notes:

	Propane	Butane
(1) Btu per cubic foot	2516	3280
(2) Specific gravity	1.52	2.01
(3) Pressure at orifice (in. w.c.)	11	11
(4) Orifice coefficient	0.9	0.9

(5) For altitudes above 2000 ft (610 m), first select the equivalent orifice size at sea level from Table E.1.1(d).

Table E.1.1(c) Multipliers for Utility Gases of Another Specific Gravity

Specific Gravity	Multiplier	Specific Gravity	Multiplier
0.45	1.155	0.95	0.795
0.50	1.095	1.00	0.775
0.55	1.045	1.05	0.756
0.60	1.000	1.10	0.739
0.65	0.961	1.15	0.722
0.70	0.926	1.20	0.707
0.75	0.894	1.25	0.693
0.80	0.866	1.30	0.679
0.85	0.840	1.35	0.667
0.90	0.817	1.40	0.655

(continues)

Table E.1.1(d) Equivalent Orifice Sizes at High Altitudes (includes 4% input reduction for each 1000 ft above sea level)

Orifice Size at Sea Level	Orifice Size Required at Other Elevations (ft)								
	2000	3000	4000	5000	6000	7000	8000	9000	10,000
1	2	2	3	3	4	5	7	8	10
2	3	3	4	5	6	7	9	10	12
3	4	5	7	8	9	10	12	13	15
4	6	7	8	9	11	12	13	14	16
5	7	8	9	10	12	13	14	15	17
6	8	9	10	11	12	13	14	16	17
7	9	10	11	12	13	14	15	16	18
8	10	11	12	13	13	15	16	17	18
9	11	12	12	13	14	16	17	18	19
10	12	13	13	14	15	16	17	18	19
11	13	13	14	15	16	17	18	19	20
12	13	14	15	16	17	17	18	19	20
13	15	15	16	17	18	18	19	20	22
14	16	16	17	18	18	19	20	21	23
15	16	17	17	18	19	20	20	22	24
16	17	18	18	19	19	20	22	23	25
17	18	19	19	20	21	22	23	24	26
18	19	19	20	21	22	23	24	26	27
19	20	20	21	22	23	25	26	27	28
20	22	22	23	24	25	26	27	28	29
21	23	23	24	25	26	27	28	28	29
22	23	24	25	26	27	27	28	29	29
23	25	25	26	27	27	28	29	29	30
24	25	26	27	27	28	28	29	29	30
25	26	27	27	28	28	29	29	30	30
26	27	28	28	28	29	29	30	30	30
27	28	28	29	29	29	30	30	30	31
28	29	29	29	30	30	30	30	31	31
29	29	30	30	30	30	31	31	31	32
30	30	31	31	31	31	32	32	33	35
31	32	32	32	33	34	35	36	37	38
32	33	34	35	35	36	36	37	38	40
33	35	35	36	36	37	38	38	40	41
34	35	36	36	37	37	38	39	40	42
35	36	36	37	37	38	39	40	41	42
36	37	38	38	39	40	41	41	42	43
37	38	39	39	40	41	42	42	43	43
38	39	40	41	41	42	42	43	43	44
39	40	41	41	42	42	43	43	44	44
40	41	42	42	42	43	43	44	44	45
41	42	42	42	43	43	44	44	45	46
42	42	43	43	43	44	44	45	46	47
43	44	44	44	45	45	46	47	47	48
44	45	45	45	46	47	47	48	48	49
45	46	47	47	47	48	48	49	49	50
46	47	47	47	48	48	49	49	50	50
47	48	48	49	49	49	50	50	51	51
48	49	49	49	50	50	50	51	51	52

(continues)

Table E.1.1(d) Continued

Orifice Size at Sea Level	Orifice Size Required at Other Elevations (ft)								
	2000	3000	4000	5000	6000	7000	8000	9000	10,000
49	50	50	50	51	51	51	52	52	52
50	51	51	51	51	52	52	52	53	53
51	51	52	52	52	52	53	53	53	54
52	52	53	53	53	53	53	54	54	54
53	54	54	54	54	54	54	55	55	55
54	54	55	55	55	55	55	56	56	56
55	55	55	55	56	56	56	56	56	57
56	56	56	57	57	57	58	59	59	60
57	58	59	59	60	60	61	62	63	63
58	59	60	60	61	62	62	63	63	64
59	60	61	61	62	62	63	64	64	65
60	61	61	62	63	63	64	64	65	65
61	62	62	63	63	64	65	65	66	66
62	63	63	64	64	65	65	66	66	67
63	64	64	65	65	65	66	66	67	68
64	65	65	65	66	66	66	67	67	68
65	65	66	66	66	67	67	68	68	69
66	67	67	68	68	68	69	69	69	70
67	68	68	68	69	69	69	70	70	70
68	68	69	69	69	70	70	70	71	71
69	70	70	70	70	71	71	71	72	72
70	70	71	71	71	71	72	72	73	73
71	72	72	72	73	73	73	74	74	74
72	73	73	73	73	74	74	74	74	75
73	73	74	74	74	74	75	75	75	76
74	74	75	75	75	75	76	76	76	76
75	75	76	76	76	76	77	77	77	77
76	76	76	77	77	77	77	77	77	77
77	77	77	77	78	78	78	78	78	78
78	78	78	78	79	79	79	79	80	80
79	79	80	80	80	80	0.013	0.012	0.012	0.01
80	80	0.013	0.013	0.013	0.012	0.012	0.012	0.012	0.011

For SI units, 1 ft = 0.305 m.

Annex F Sizing of Venting Systems Serving Appliances Equipped with Draft Hoods, Category I Appliances, and Appliances Listed for Use with Type B Vents

This annex is not a part of the requirements of this NFPA document but is included for informational purposes only.

For SI units, 1 Btu/hr = 0.293 W, 1 ft^3 = 0.028 m^3, 1 ft = 0.305 m, 1 in. w.c. = 249 Pa.

F.1 Examples Using Single Appliance Venting Tables. See Figure F.1(a) through Figure F.1(n).

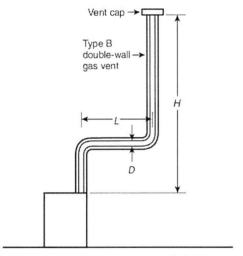

Table 13.1(a) is used when sizing Type B double-wall gas vent connected directly to the appliance.

Note: The appliance can be either Category I draft hood–equipped or fan-assisted type.

FIGURE F.1(a) Type B Double-Wall Vent System Serving a Single Appliance with a Type B Double-Wall Vent.

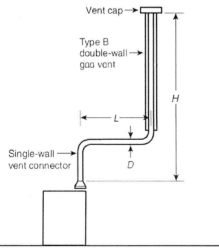

Table 13.1(b) is used when sizing a single-wall metal vent connector attached to a Type B double-wall gas vent.

Note: The appliance can be either Category I draft hood–equipped or fan-assisted type.

FIGURE F.1(b) Type B Double-Wall Vent System Serving a Single Appliance with a Single-Wall Metal Vent Connector.

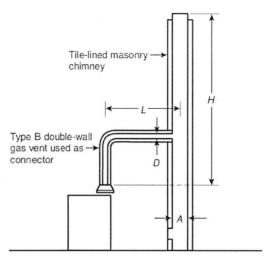

Table 13.1(c) is used when sizing a Type B double-wall gas vent connector attached to a tile-lined masonry chimney.

Notes:
(1) *A* is the equivalent cross-sectional area of the tile liner.
(2) The appliance can be either Category I draft hood–equipped or fan-assisted type.

FIGURE F.1(c) Vent System Serving a Single Appliance with a Masonry Chimney and a Type B Double-Wall Vent Connector.

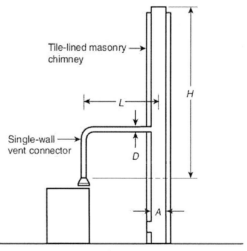

Table 13.1(d) is used when sizing a single-wall vent connector attached to a tile-lined masonry chimney.

Notes:
(1) *A* is the equivalent cross-sectional area of the tile liner.
(2) The appliance can be either Category I draft hood–equipped or fan-assisted type.

FIGURE F.1(d) Vent System Serving a Single Appliance Using a Masonry Chimney and a Single-Wall Metal Vent Connector.

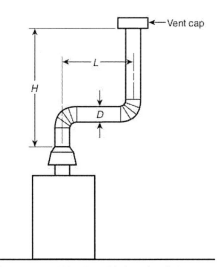

Asbestos cement Type B or single-wall metal vent serving a single draft hood–equipped appliance. *[See Table 13.1(e).]*

FIGURE F.1(e) Asbestos Cement Type B or Single-Wall Metal Vent System Serving a Single Draft Hood–Equipped Appliance.

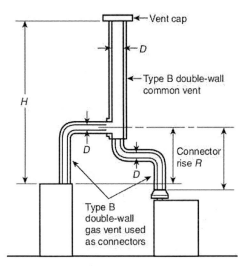

Table 13.2(a) is used when sizing Type B double-wall gas vent connectors attached to a Type B double-wall common vent.

Note: Each appliance can be either Category I draft hood–equipped or fan-assisted type.

FIGURE F.1(f) Vent System Serving Two or More Appliances with Type B Double-Wall Vent and Type B Double-Wall Vent Connectors.

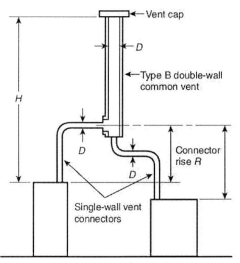

Table 13.2(b) is used when sizing single-wall vent connectors attached to a Type B double-wall common vent.

Note: Each appliance can be either Category I draft hood–equipped or fan-assisted type.

FIGURE F.1(g) Vent System Serving Two or More Appliances with Type B Double-Wall Vent and Single-Wall Metal Vent Connectors.

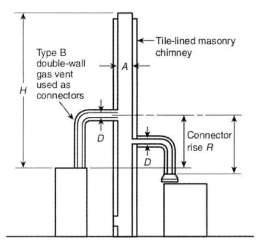

Table 13.2(c) is used when sizing Type B double-wall vent connectors attached to a tile-lined masonry chimney.

Notes:
(1) A is the equivalent cross-sectional area of the tile liner.
(2) Each appliance can be either Category I draft hood–equipped or fan-assisted type.

FIGURE F.1(h) Masonry Chimney Serving Two or More Appliances with Type B Double-Wall Vent Connectors.

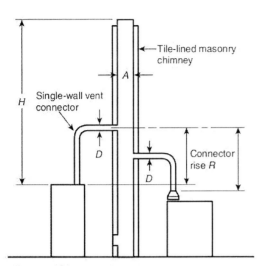

Table 13.2(d) is used when sizing single-wall metal vent connectors attached to a tile-lined masonry chimney.

Notes:
(1) A is the equivalent cross-sectional area of the tile liner.
(2) Each appliance can be either Category I draft hood–equipped or fan-assisted type.

FIGURE F.1(i) Masonry Chimney Serving Two or More Appliances with Single-Wall Metal Vent Connectors.

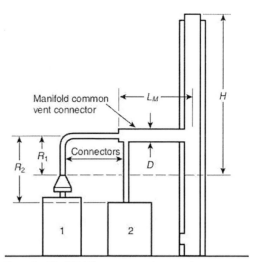

Example: Manifolded common vent connector L_M can be no greater than 18 times the common vent connector manifold inside diameter; that is, a 4 in. (100 mm) inside diameter common vent connector manifold should not exceed 72 in. (1800 mm) in length. (See 13.2.4.)

Note: This is an illustration of a typical manifolded vent connector. Different appliance, vent connector, or common vent types are possible. (See Section 13.2.)

FIGURE F.1(k) Use of Manifolded Common Vent Connector.

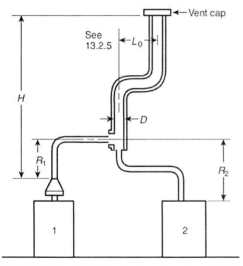

Asbestos cement Type B or single-wall metal pipe vent serving two or more draft hood–equipped appliances. [See Table 13.2(e).]

FIGURE F.1(j) Asbestos Cement Type B or Single-Wall Metal Vent System Serving Two or More Draft Hood–Equipped Appliances.

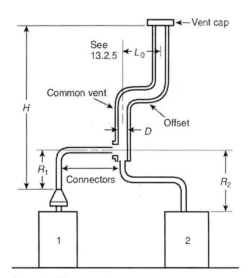

Example: Offset common vent.

Note: This is an illustration of a typical offset vent. Different appliance, vent connector, or vent types are possible. (See Sections 13.1 and 13.2.)

FIGURE F.1(l) Use of Offset Common Vent.

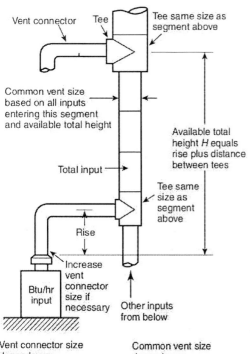

FIGURE F.1(m) Multistory Gas Vent Design Procedure for Each Segment of System.

F.1.1 Example 1: Single Draft Hood–Equipped Appliance.
An installer has a 120,000 Btu/hr input appliance with a 5 in. diameter draft hood outlet that needs to be vented into a 10 ft high Type B vent system. What size vent should be used assuming (1) a 5 ft lateral single-wall metal vent connector is used with two 90 degree elbows or (2) a 5 ft lateral single-wall metal vent connector is used with three 90-degree elbows in the vent system? See Figure F.1.1.

Solution

Table 13.1(b) should be used to solve this problem, because single-wall metal vent connectors are being used with a Type B vent, as follows:

(1) Read down the first column in Table 13.1(b) until the row associated with a 10 ft height and 5 ft lateral is found. Read across this row until a vent capacity greater than 120,000 Btu/hr is located in the shaded columns labeled NAT Max for draft hood–equipped appliances. In this case, a 5 in. diameter vent has a capacity of 122,000 Btu/hr and can be used for this application.

(2) If three 90 degree elbows are used in the vent system, the maximum vent capacity listed in the tables must be reduced by 10 percent. This implies that the 5 in. diameter vent has an adjusted capacity of only 110,000 Btu/hr. In this case, the vent system must be increased to 6 in. in diameter. See the following calculations:

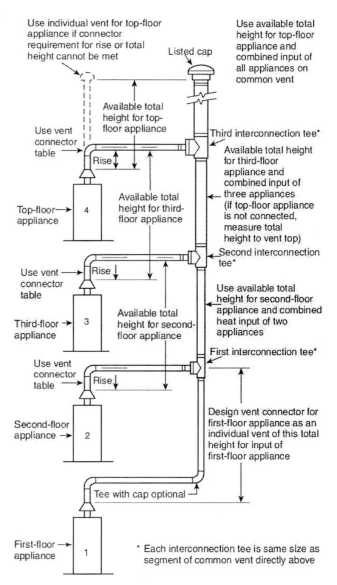

FIGURE F.1(n) Principles of Design of Multistory Vents Using Vent Connector and Common Vent Design Tables. *(See 13.2.14 through 13.2.17.)*

[F.1.1a]
$$122{,}000 \times 0.90 = 110{,}000 \text{ for 5 in. vent}$$

From Table 13.1(b), select 6 in. vent.

[F.1.1b]
$$186{,}000 \times 0.90 = 167{,}000$$

This figure is greater than the required 120,000. Therefore, use a 6 in. vent and connector where three elbows are used.

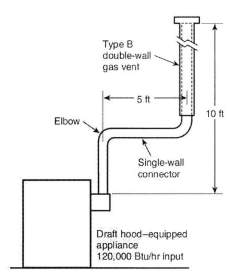

FIGURE F.1.1 Single Draft Hood–Equipped Appliance — Example 1.

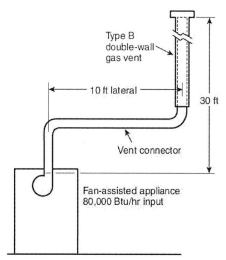

FIGURE F.1.2 Single Fan-Assisted Appliance — Example 2.

F.1.2 Example 2: Single Fan-Assisted Appliance. An installer has an 80,000 Btu/hr input fan-assisted appliance that must be installed using 10 ft of lateral connector attached to a 30 ft high Type B vent. Two 90-degree elbows are needed for the installation. Can a single-wall metal vent connector be used for this application? See Figure F.1.2.

Solution

Table 13.1(b) refers to the use of single-wall metal vent connectors with Type B vent. In the first column find the row associated with a 30 ft height and a 10 ft lateral. Read across this row, looking at the FAN Min and FAN Max columns, to find that a 3 in. diameter single-wall metal vent connector is not recommended. Moving to the next larger size single-wall connector (4 in.), we find that a 4 in. diameter single-wall metal connector has a recommended minimum vent capacity of 91,000 Btu/hr and a recommended maximum vent capacity of 144,000 Btu/hr. The 80,000 Btu/hr fan-assisted appliance is outside this range, so the conclusion is that a single-wall metal vent connector cannot be used to vent this appliance using 10 ft of lateral for the connector.

However, if the 80,000 Btu/hr input appliance could be moved to within 5 ft of the vertical vent, a 4 in. single-wall metal connector could be used to vent the appliance. Table 13.1(b) shows the acceptable range of vent capacities for a 4 in. vent with 5 ft of lateral to be between 72,000 Btu/hr and 157,000 Btu/hr.

If the appliance cannot be moved closer to the vertical vent, a Type B vent could be used as the connector material. In this case, Table 13.1(a) shows that, for a 30 ft high vent with 10 ft of lateral, the acceptable range of vent capacities for a 4 in. diameter vent attached to a fan-assisted appliance is between 37,000 Btu/hr and 150,000 Btu/hr.

F.1.3 Example 3: Interpolating Between Table Values. An installer has an 80,000 Btu/hr input appliance with a 4 in. diameter draft hood outlet that needs to be vented into a 12 ft high Type B vent. The vent connector has a 5 ft lateral length and is also Type B. Can this appliance be vented using a 4 in. diameter vent?

Solution

Table 13.1(a) is used in the case of an all Type B vent system. However, Table 13.1(a) does not have an entry for a height of 12 ft, and interpolation must be used. Read down the 4 in. diameter NAT Max column to the row associated with 10 ft height and 5 ft lateral to find the capacity value of 77,000 Btu/hr. Read further down to the 15 ft height, 5 ft lateral row to find the capacity value of 87,000 Btu/hr. The difference between the 15 ft height capacity value and the 10 ft height capacity value is 10,000 Btu/hr. The capacity for a vent system with a 12 ft height is equal to the capacity for a 10 ft height plus $2/5$ of the difference between the 10 ft and 15 ft height values, or $77,000 + 2/5 \times 10,000 = 81,000$ Btu/hr. Therefore, a 4 in. diameter vent can be used in the installation.

F.2 Examples Using Common Venting Tables.

F.2.1 Example 4: Common Venting Two Draft Hood–Equipped Appliances. A 35,000-Btu/hr water heater is to be common vented with a 150,000 Btu/hr furnace, using a common vent with a total height of 30 ft. The connector rise is 2 ft for the water heater with a horizontal length of 4 ft. The connector rise for the furnace is 3 ft with a horizontal length of 8 ft. Assume single-wall metal connectors will be used with Type B vent. What size connectors and combined vent should be used in this installation? See Figure F.2.1.

Solution

Table 13.2(b) should be used to size single-wall metal vent connectors attached to Type B vertical vents. In the vent connector capacity portion of Table 13.2(b), find the row associated with a 30 ft vent height. For a 2 ft rise on the vent connector for the water heater, read the shaded columns for draft hood–equipped appliances to find that a 3 in. diameter vent connector has a capacity of 37,000 Btu/hr. Therefore, a 3 in. single-wall metal vent connector can be used with the water heater. For a draft hood–equipped furnace with a 3 ft rise, read across the appropriate row to find that a 5 in. diameter vent connector has a maximum capacity of 120,000 Btu/hr (which is too small for the furnace) and a 6 in. diameter vent connector has a maximum vent capacity of 172,000 Btu/hr. Therefore, a 6 in. diameter vent connector should be used with the 150,000 Btu/hr furnace. Because both vent connector horizontal lengths are less than the maximum lengths listed in 13.2.2, the table values can be used without adjustments.

In the common vent capacity portion of Table 13.2(b), find the row associated with a 30 ft vent height and read over to the NAT + NAT portion of the 6 in. diameter column to find a maximum combined capacity of 257,000 Btu/hr. Since the two appliances total only 185,000 Btu/hr, a 6 in. common vent can be used.

F.2.2 Example 5(a): Common Venting a Draft Hood–Equipped Water Heater with a Fan-Assisted Furnace into a Type B Vent. In this case, a 35,000 Btu/hr input draft hood–equipped water heater with a 4 in. diameter draft hood outlet, 2 ft of connector rise, and 4 ft of horizontal length is to be common vented with a 100,000 Btu/hr fan-assisted furnace with a 4 in. diameter flue collar, 3 ft of connector rise, and 6 ft of horizontal length. The common vent consists of a 30 ft height of Type B vent. What are the recommended vent diameters for each connector and the common vent? The installer would like to use a single-wall metal vent connector. See Figure F.2.2.

Solution

Water Heater Vent Connector Diameter. Since the water heater vent connector horizontal length of 4 ft is less than the maximum value listed in Table 13.2(b), the venting table values can be used without adjustments. Using the Vent Connector Capacity portion of Table 13.2(b), read down the Total Vent Height (H) column to 30 ft and read across the 2 ft Connector Rise (R) row to the first Btu/hr rating in the NAT Max column that is equal to or greater than the water heater input rating. The table shows that a 3 in. vent connector has a maximum input rating of 37,000 Btu/hr. Although this rating is greater than the water heater input rating, a 3 in. vent connector is prohibited by 13.2.24. A 4 in. vent connector has a maximum input rating of 67,000 Btu/hr and is equal to the draft hood outlet diameter. A 4 in. vent connector is selected. Since the water heater is equipped with a draft hood, there are no minimum input rating restrictions.

Furnace Vent Connector Diameter. Using the Vent Connector Capacity portion of Table 13.2(b), read down the Total Vent Height (H) column to 30 ft and across the 3 ft Connector Rise (R) row. Because the furnace has a fan-assisted combustion system, find the first FAN Max column with a Btu/hr rating greater than the furnace input rating. The 4 in. vent connector has a maximum input rating of 119,000 Btu/hr and a minimum input rating of 85,000 Btu/hr.

The 100,000 Btu/hr furnace in this example falls within this range, so a 4 in. connector is adequate. Because the furnace vent connector horizontal length of 6 ft is less than the maximum value listed in 13.2.2, the venting table values can be used without adjustment. If the furnace had an input rating of 80,000 Btu/hr, a Type B vent connector would be needed in order to meet the minimum capacity limit.

Common Vent Diameter. The total input to the common vent is 135,000 Btu/hr. Using the Common Vent Capacity portion of Table 13.2(b), read down the Total Vent Height (H) column to 30 ft and across this row to find the smallest vent diameter in the FAN + NAT column that has a Btu/hr rating equal to or greater than 135,000 Btu/hr. The 4 in. common vent has a capacity of 132,000 Btu/hr, and the 5 in. common vent has a capacity of 202,000 Btu/hr. Therefore, the 5 in. common vent should be used in this example.

Summary. In this example, the installer can use a 4 in. diameter, single-wall metal vent connector for the water heater and a 4 in. diameter, single-wall metal vent connector for the furnace. The common vent should be a 5 in. diameter Type B vent.

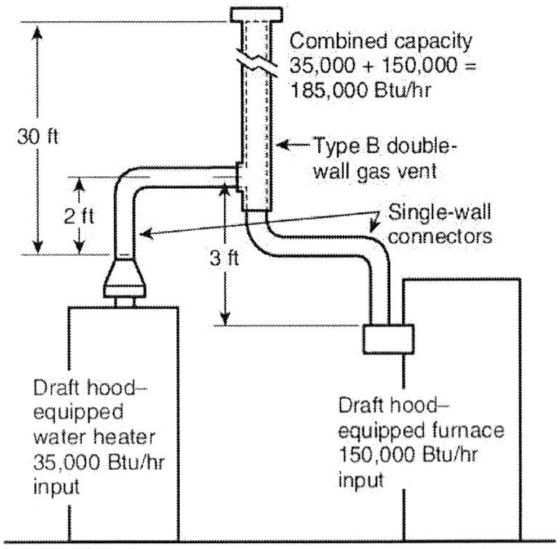

For SI units, 1000 Btu/hr = 0.293 kW, 1 ft = 0.305 m.

FIGURE F.2.1 Common Venting Two Draft Hood–Equipped Appliances — Example 4.

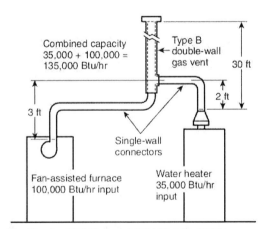

For SI units, 1000 Btu/hr = 0.293 kW, 1 ft = 0.305 m.

FIGURE F.2.2 Common Venting a Draft Hood–Equipped Water Heater with a Fan-Assisted Furnace into a Type B Double-Wall Common Vent — Example 5(a).

F.2.3 Example 5(b): Common Venting into an Interior Masonry Chimney.
In this case, the water heater and fan-assisted furnace of Example 5(a) are to be common-vented into a clay-tile-lined masonry chimney with a 30 ft height. The chimney is not exposed to the outdoors below the roof line. The internal dimensions of the clay tile liner are nominally 8 in. × 12 in. Assuming the same vent connector heights, laterals, and materials found in Example 5(a), what are the recommended vent connector diameters, and is this an acceptable installation?

Solution

Table 13.2(d) is used to size common venting installations involving single-wall connectors into masonry chimneys.

Water Heater Vent Connector Diameter. Using Table 13.2(d), Vent Connector Capacity, read down the Total Vent Height (H) column to 30 ft, and read across the 2 ft Connector Rise (R) row to the first Btu/hr rating in the NAT Max column that is equal to or greater than the water heater input rating. The table shows that a 3 in. vent connector has a maximum input of only 31,000 Btu/hr, while a 4 in. vent connector has a maximum input of 57,000 Btu/hr. A 4 in. vent connector must therefore be used.

Furnace Vent Connector Diameter. Using the Vent Connector Capacity portion of Table 13.2(d), read down the Total Vent Height (H) column to 30 ft and across the 3 ft Connector Rise (R) row. Because the furnace has a fan-assisted combustion system, find the first FAN Max column with a Btu/hr rating greater than the furnace input rating. The 4 in. vent connector has a maximum input rating of 127,000 Btu/hr and a minimum input rating of 95,000 Btu/hr. The 100,000 Btu/hr furnace in this example falls within this range, so a 4 in. connector is adequate.

Masonry Chimney. From Table F.2.3, the Equivalent Area for a Nominal Liner size of 8 in. × 12 in. is 63.6 in.^{2}. Using Table 13.2(d), Common Vent Capacity, read down the FAN + NAT column under the Minimum Internal Area of Chimney value of 63 to the row for 30 ft height to find a capacity value of 739,000 Btu/hr. The combined input rating of the furnace and water heater, 135,000 Btu/hr, is less than the table value, so this is an acceptable installation.

Subsection 13.2.18 requires the common vent area to be no greater than seven times the smallest listed appliance categorized vent area, flue collar area, or draft hood outlet area. Both appliances in this installation have 4 in. diameter outlets. From Table F.2.3, the equivalent area for an inside diameter of 4 in. is 12.2 in.^{2}. Seven times 12.2 equals 85.4, which is greater than 63.6, so this configuration is acceptable.

F.2.4 Example 5(c): Common Venting into an Exterior Masonry Chimney.
In this case, the water heater and fan-assisted furnace of Examples 5(a) and 5(b) are to be common-vented into an exterior masonry chimney. The chimney height, clay-tile-liner dimensions, and vent connector heights and laterals are the same as in Example 5(b). This system is being installed in Charlotte, North Carolina. Does this exterior masonry chimney need to be relined? If so, what corrugated metallic liner size is recommended? What vent connector diameters are recommended? See Table F.2.3 and Figure F.2.4.

Solution

According to 13.2.22, Type B vent connectors are required to be used with exterior masonry chimneys. Use Table 13.2(h) and Table 13.2(i) to size FAN+NAT common venting installations involving Type B double-wall connectors into exterior masonry chimneys.

The local 99 percent winter design temperature needed to use Table 13.2(h) and Table 13.2(i) can be found in *ASHRAE Handbook — Fundamentals*. For Charlotte, North Carolina, this design temperature is 19°F.

Chimney Liner Requirement. As in Example 5(b), use the 63 in.^{2} Internal Area columns for this size clay tile liner. Read down the 63 in.^{2} column of Table 13.2(h) to the 30 ft height row to find that the Combined Appliance Maximum Input is 747,000 Btu/hr. The combined input rating of the appliances in this installation, 135,000 Btu/hr, is less than the maximum value, so this criterion is satisfied. Table 13.2(i), at a 19°F

Table F.2.3 Masonry Chimney Liner Dimensions with Circular Equivalents

Nominal Liner Size (in.)	Inside Dimensions of Liner (in.)	Inside Diameter or Equivalent Diameter (in.)	Equivalent Area (in.^{2})
4 × 8	2½ × 6½	4.0	12.2
		5.0	19.6
		6.0	28.3
		7.0	38.3
8 × 8	6¾ × 6¾	7.4	42.7
		8.0	50.3
8 × 12	6½ × 10½	9.0	63.6
		10.0	78.5
12 × 12	9¾ × 9¾	10.4	83.3
		11.0	95.0
12 × 16	9½ × 13½	11.8	107.5
		12.0	113.0
		14.0	153.9
16 × 16	13¼ × 13¼	14.5	162.9
		15.0	176.7
16 × 20	13 × 17	16.2	206.1
		18.0	254.4
20 × 20	16½ × 16¾	18.2	260.2
		20.0	314.1
20 × 24	16½ × 20½	20.1	314.2
		22.0	380.1
24 × 24	20¼ × 20¼	22.1	380.1
		24.0	452.3
24 × 28	20¼ × 24¼	24.1	456.2
28 × 28	24¼ × 24¼	26.4	543.3
		27.0	572.5
30 × 30	25½ × 25½	27.9	607.0
		30.0	706.8
30 × 36	25½ × 31½	30.9	749.9
		33.0	855.3
36 × 36	31½ × 31½	34.4	929.4
		36.0	1017.9

For SI units, 1 in. = 25.4 mm, 1 in.^{2} = 645 mm^2.

Note: When liner sizes differ dimensionally from those shown in this table, equivalent diameters can be determined from published tables for square and rectangular ducts of equivalent carrying capacity or by other engineering methods.

Design Temperature, and at the same Vent Height and Internal Area used earlier, shows that the minimum allowable input rating of a space-heating appliance is 470,000 Btu/hr. The furnace input rating of 100,000 Btu/hr is less than this minimum value. So this criterion is not satisfied, and an alternative venting design needs to be used, such as a Type B vent shown in Example 5(a) or a listed chimney liner system shown in the remainder of the example.

According to 13.2.20, Table 13.2(a) or Table 13.2(b) is used for sizing corrugated metallic liners in masonry chimneys, with the maximum common vent capacities reduced by 20 percent. This example will be continued assuming Type B vent connectors.

Water Heater Vent Connector Diameter. Using Table 13.2(a), Vent Connector Capacity, read down the Total Vent Height (H) column to 30 ft, and read across the 2 ft Connector Rise (R) row to the first Btu/hour rating in the NAT Max column that is equal to or greater than the water heater input rating. The table shows that a 3 in. vent connector has a maximum capacity of 39,000 Btu/hr. Although this rating is greater than the water heater input rating, a 3 in. vent connector is prohibited by 13.2.24. A 4 in. vent connector has a maximum input rating of 70,000 Btu/hr and is equal to the draft hood outlet diameter. A 4 in. vent connector is selected.

Furnace Vent Connector Diameter. Using Table 13.2(a), Vent Connector Capacity, read down the Total Vent Height (H) column to 30 ft, and read across the 3 ft Connector Rise (R) row to the first Btu/hr rating in the FAN Max column that is equal to or greater than the furnace input rating. The 100,000 Btu/hr furnace in this example falls within this range, so a 4 in. connector is adequate.

Chimney Liner Diameter. The total input to the common vent is 135,000 Btu/hr. Using the Common Vent Capacity portion of Table 13.2(a), read down the Total Vent Height (H) column to 30 ft and across this row to find the smallest vent diameter in the FAN+NAT column that has a Btu/hr rating greater than 135,000 Btu/hr. The 4 in. common vent has a capacity of 138,000 Btu/hr. Reducing the maximum capacity by 20 percent results in a maximum capacity for a 4 in. corrugated liner of 110,000 Btu/hr, less than the total input of 135,000 Btu/hr. So a larger liner is needed. The 5 in. common vent capacity listed in Table 13.2(a) is 210,000 Btu/hr, and after reducing by 20 percent is 168,000 Btu/hr. Therefore, a 5 in. corrugated metal liner should be used in this example.

Single-Wall Connectors. Once it has been established that relining the chimney is necessary, Type B double-wall vent connectors are not specifically required. This example could be redone using Table 13.2(b) for single-wall vent connectors. For this case, the vent connector and liner diameters would be the same as found for Type B double-wall connectors.

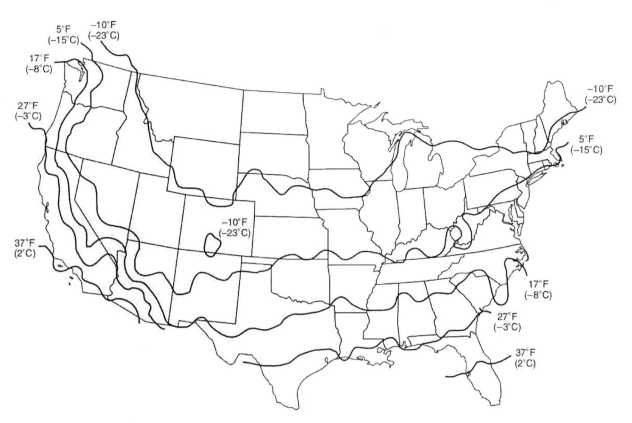

99% Winter Design Temperatures for the Contiguous United States

This map is a necessarily generalized guide to temperatures in the contiguous United States. Temperatures shown for areas such as mountainous regions and large urban centers are not necessarily accurate. The climate data used to develop this map are from the *ASHRAE Handbook—Fundamentals* (Climate Conditions for the United States).

For 99% winter design temperatures in Alaska, consult the *ASHRAE Handbook—Fundamentals*.

99% winter design temperatures for Hawaii are greater than 37°F.

FIGURE F.2.4 Range of Winter Design Temperatures Used in Analyzing Exterior Masonry Chimneys in the United States.

Annex G Recommended Procedure for Safety Inspection of an Existing Appliance Installation

This annex is not a part of the requirements of this NFPA document but is included for informational purposes only.

For SI units, 1 Btu/hr = 0.293 W.

G.1 General. The following procedure is intended as a guide to aid in determining that an appliance is properly installed and is in a safe condition for continued use. Where a gas supplier performs an inspection, their written procedures should be followed.

G.1.1 Application. This procedure is intended for existing residential installations of a furnace, boiler, room heater, water heater, cooking appliance, fireplace appliance, and clothes dryer. This procedure should be performed prior to any attempt to modify the appliance installation or building envelope.

G.1.2 Weatherization Programs. Before a building envelope is to be modified as part of a weatherization program, the existing appliance installation should be inspected in accordance with these procedures. After all unsafe conditions are repaired, and immediately after the weatherization is complete, the appliance inspections in G.5.2 are to be repeated.

G.1.3 Inspection Procedure. The safety of the building occupant and inspector are to be determined as the first step as described in Section G.2. Only after the ambient environment is found to be safe should inspections of gas piping and appliances be undertaken. It is recommended that all inspections described in Sections G.3, G.4, and G.6, where the appliance is in the off mode, be completed and any unsafe conditions repaired or corrected before continuing with inspections of an operating appliance described in Sections G.5 and G.6.

G.1.4 Manufacturer Instructions. Where available, the manufacturer's installation and operating instructions for the installed appliance should be used as part of these inspection procedures to determine if the appliance is installed correctly and is operating properly.

G.1.5 Instruments. The inspection procedures include measuring for fuel gas and carbon monoxide (CO) and will require the use of a combustible gas detector (CGD) and a CO detector. It is recommended that both types of detectors be listed. Prior to any inspection, the detectors should be calibrated or tested in accordance with the manufacturer's instructions. In addition, it is recommended that the detectors have the following minimum specifications:

(1) Gas Detector: The CGD should be capable of indicating the presence of the type of fuel gas for which it is to be used (e.g. natural gas or propane). The combustible gas detector should be capable of the following:
  (a) *PPM:* Numeric display with a parts per million (ppm) scale from 1 ppm to 900 ppm in 1 ppm increments
  (b) *LEL:* Numeric display with a percent lower explosive limit (% LEL) scale from 0 percent to 100 percent in 1 percent increments
  (c) *Audio:* An audio sound feature to locate leaks
(2) CO Detector: The CO detector should be capable of the following functions and have a numeric display scale as follows:
  (a) *PPM:* For measuring ambient room and appliance emissions a display scale in parts per million (ppm) from 0 to 1,000 ppm in 1 ppm increments
  (b) *Alarm:* A sound alarm function where hazardous levels of ambient CO is found (*see Section G.2 for alarm levels*)
  (c) *Air Free:* Capable of converting CO measurements to an air-free level in ppm. Where a CO detector is used without an air-free conversion function, the CO air free can be calculated in accordance with Footnote 3 in Table G.6.

G.2 Occupant and Inspector Safety. Prior to entering a building, the inspector should have both a combustible gas detector (CGD) and CO detector turned on, calibrated, and operating. Immediately upon entering the building, a sample of the ambient atmosphere should be taken. Based on CGD and CO detector readings, the inspector should take the following actions:

(1) Where the CO detector indicates a carbon monoxide level of 70 ppm or greater, the inspector should immediately notify the occupant of the need for themselves and any building occupant to evacuate; the inspector should immediately evacuate and call 911.
(2) Where the CO detector indicates a reading between 30 ppm and 70 ppm, the inspector should advise the occupant that high CO levels have been found and recommend that all possible sources of CO be turned off immediately and windows and doors be opened. Where it appears that the source of CO is a permanently installed appliance, advise the occupant to shut the appliance off and have the appliance serviced by a qualified servicing agent.
(3) Where the CO detector indicates CO below 30 ppm, the inspection can continue. (See U.S. Consumer Product Safety Commission, *Responding to Residential Carbon Monoxide Incidents, Guidelines For Fire and Other Emergency Response Personnel*)
(4) Where the CGD indicates a combustible gas level of 20 percent LEL or greater, the inspector should immediately notify the occupant of the need for themselves and any building occupant to evacuate; the inspector should immediately evacuate and call 911.
(5) Where the CGD indicates a combustible gas level below 20 percent LEL, the inspection can continue.

If during the inspection process it is determined a condition exists that could result in unsafe appliance operation, shut off the appliance and advise the owner of the unsafe condition. Where a gas leak is found that may result in an unsafe condition, advise the owner of the unsafe condition and call the gas supplier to turn off the gas supply. The inspector should not continue a safety inspection on an operating appliance, venting system, and piping system until repairs have been made.

G.3 Gas Piping and Connection Inspections.

G.3.1 Leak Checks. Conduct a test for gas leakage using either a noncorrosive leak detection solution or a CGD confirmed with a leak detection solution.

The preferred method for leak checking is by use of gas leak detection solution applied to all joints. This method provides a reliable visual indication of significant leaks.

The use of a CGD in its audio sensing mode can quickly locate suspect leaks but can be overly sensitive indicating insignificant and false leaks. All suspect leaks found through the use of a CGD should be confirmed using a leak detection solution.

Where gas leakage is confirmed, the owner should be notified that repairs must be made. The inspection should include the following components:

(1) All gas piping fittings located within the appliance space
(2) Appliance connector fittings
(3) Appliance gas valve/regulator housing and connections

G.3.2 Appliance Connector. Verify that the appliance connection type is compliant with Section 9.6. Inspect flexible appliance connections to determine if they are free of cracks, corrosion, and signs of damage. Verify that there are no uncoated copper alloy connectors. Where connectors are determined to be unsafe or where an uncoated copper alloy connector is found, the appliance shutoff valve should be placed in the off position and the owner notified that the connector must be replaced.

G.3.3 Piping Support. Inspect piping to determine that it is adequately supported, that there is no undue stress on the piping, and if there are any improperly capped pipe openings.

G.3.4 Bonding. Verify that the electrical bonding of gas piping is compliant with Section 7.12.

G.4 Inspections to Be Performed with the Appliance Not Operating. The following safety inspection procedures are performed on appliances that are not operating. These inspections are applicable to all appliance installations.

G.4.1 Preparing for Inspection. Shut off all gas and electrical power to the appliances located in the same room being inspected. For gas supply, use the shutoff valve in the supply line or at the manifold serving each appliance. For electrical power, place the circuit breaker in the off position or remove the fuse that serves each appliance. A lock type device or tag should be installed on each gas shutoff valve and at the electrical panel to indicate that the service has been shut off for inspection purposes.

G.4.2 Vent System Size and Installation. Verify that the existing venting system size and installation are compliant with Chapters 12 and 13. The size and installation of venting systems for other than natural draft and Category I appliances should be in compliance with the manufacturer's installation instructions. Inspect the venting system to determine that it is free of blockage, restriction, leakage, corrosion, and other deficiencies that could cause an unsafe condition. Inspect masonry chimneys to determine if they are lined. Inspect plastic venting system to determine that it is free of sagging and it is sloped in an upward direction to the outdoor vent termination.

G.4.3 Combustion Air Supply. Inspect provisions for combustion air as follows:

(1) *Non-Direct Vent Appliances.* Determine that non-direct vent appliance installations are compliant with the combustion air requirements in Section 9.3. Inspect any interior and exterior combustion air openings and any connected combustion air ducts to determine that there is no blockage, restriction, corrosion, or damage. Inspect to determine if horizontal combustion air ducts are sloped upward toward the air supply source.
(2) *Direct Vent Appliances.* Verify that the combustion air supply ducts and pipes are securely fastened to direct vent appliance and determine that there are no separations, blockage, restriction, corrosion, or other damage. Determine that the combustion air source is located in the outdoors or to areas that freely communicate to the outdoors.
(3) *Unvented Appliances.* Verify that the total input of all unvented room heaters and gas-fired refrigerators installed in the same room or rooms that freely communicate with each other does not exceed 20 Btu/hr/ft^3.

G.4.4 Flooded Appliances. Inspect the appliance for signs that the appliance has been damaged by flooding. Signs of flooding include a visible water submerge line on the appliance housing, excessive surface or component rust, deposited debris on internal components, and mildew-like odor. Inform the owner that flood-damaged appliances should be replaced.

G.4.5 Flammable Vapors. Inspect the room/space where the appliance is installed to determine if the area is free of the storage of gasoline or any flammable products such as oil-based solvents, varnishes or adhesives. Where the appliance is installed where flammable products will be stored or used, such as a garage, verify that the appliances burner is a minimum of 18 in. above the floor unless the appliance is listed as flammable vapor ignition–resistant.

G.4.6 Clearances to Combustibles. Inspect the immediate location where the appliance is installed to determine if the area is free of rags, paper, or other combustibles. Verify that the appliance and venting system is compliant with clearances to combustible building components in 9.2.2.

G.4.7 Appliance Components. Inspect internal components by removing access panels or other components for the following:

(1) Inspect burners and crossovers for blockage and corrosion. The presence of soot, debris, and signs of excessive heating could indicate incomplete combustion due to blockage or improper burner adjustments.
(2) Metallic and non-metallic hoses for signs of cracks, splitting, corrosion, and loose connections
(3) Signs of improper or incomplete repairs
(4) Modifications that override controls and safety systems
(5) Electrical wiring for loose connections; cracked, missing, or worn electrical insulation; and indications of excessive heat or electrical shorting. Appliances requiring an external electrical supply should be inspected for proper electrical connection in accordance with *NFPA 70*.

G.4.8 Placing Appliances Back in Operation. Return all inspected appliances and systems to their pre-existing state by reinstalling any removed access panels and components. Turn on the gas supply and electricity to each appliance found in safe condition. Proceed to the operating inspections in Section G.5 through Section G.6.

G.5 Inspections to Be Performed with the Appliance Operating. The following safety inspection procedures are to be performed on appliances that are operating where there are no unsafe conditions or where corrective repairs have been completed.

G.5.1 General Appliance Operation.

(1) *Initial Startup.* Adjust the thermostat or other control device to start the appliance. Verify that the appliance starts up normally and is operating properly.

   Determine that the pilot(s), where provided, is burning properly and that the main burner ignition is satisfactory by interrupting and re-establishing the electrical supply to the appliance in any convenient manner. If the appliance is equipped with a continuous pilot(s), test all pilot safety devices to determine whether they are operating properly by extinguishing the pilot(s) when the main burner(s) is off and determining, after 3 minutes, that the main burner gas does not flow upon a call for heat. If the appliance is not provided with a pilot(s), test for proper operation of the ignition system in accordance with the appliance manufacturer's lighting and operating instructions.
(2) *Flame Appearance.* Visually inspect the flame appearance for proper color and appearance. Visually determine that the main burner gas is burning properly (i.e., no floating, lifting, or flashback). Adjust the primary air shutter as required. If the appliance is equipped with high and low flame controlling or flame modulation, check for proper main burner operation at low flame.
(3) *Appliance Shutdown.* Adjust the thermostat or other control device to shut down the appliance. Verify that the appliance shuts off properly.

G.5.2 Test for Combustion Air and Vent Drafting for Natural Draft and Category I Appliances. Combustion air and vent draft procedures are for natural draft and category I appliances equipped with a draft hood and connected to a natural draft venting system.

(1) *Preparing for Inspection.* Close all exterior building doors and windows and all interior doors between the space in which the appliance is located and other spaces of the building that can be closed. Turn on any clothes dryer. Turn on any exhaust fans, such as range hoods and bathroom exhausts, so they will operate at maximum speed. Do not operate a summer exhaust fan. Close fireplace dampers and any fireplace doors.
(2) *Placing the Appliance in Operation.* Place the appliance being inspected in operation. Adjust the thermostat or control so the appliance will operate continuously.
(3) *Spillage Test.* Verify that all appliances located within the same room are in their standby mode and ready for operation. Follow lighting instructions for each appliance as necessary. Test for spillage at the draft hood relief opening as follows:

   (a) After 5 minutes of main burner operation, check for spillage using smoke.

(b) Immediately after the first check, turn on all other fuel gas burning appliances within the same room so they will operate at their full inputs and repeat the spillage test.
(c) Shut down all appliances to their standby mode and wait for 15 minutes.
(d) Repeat the spillage test steps (a) through (c) on each appliance being inspected.

(4) *Additional Spillage Tests:* Determine if the appliance venting is impacted by other door and air handler settings by performing the following tests:
(a) Set initial test condition in accordance with G.5.2(1).
(b) Place the appliance(s) being inspected in operation. Adjust the thermostat or control so the appliance(s) will operate continuously.
(c) Open the door between the space in which the appliance(s) is located and the rest of the building. After 5 minutes of main burner operation, check for spillage at each appliance using smoke.
(d) Turn on any other central heating or cooling air handler fan that is located outside of the area where the appliances are being inspected. After 5 minutes of main burner operation, check for spillage at each appliance using smoke. The test should be conducted with the door between the space in which the appliance(s) is located and the rest of the building in the open and in the closed position.

(5) Return doors, windows, exhaust fans, fireplace dampers, and any other fuel gas burning appliance to their previous conditions of use.

(6) If spillage occurs during testing, the owner should be notified, be instructed as to which configuration of the home would lessen its impact, and arrange for corrective action by an HVAC or venting professional. Where it is believed that the venting system performance is inadequate, the owner should be notified that alternative vent sizing, design, or configuration is needed in accordance with Chapters 12 and 13. Where it is believed that sufficient combustion air is not available, the owner should be notified that additional combustion air is needed in accordance with Section 9.3.

G.6 Appliance-Specific Inspections. The following appliance-specific inspections are to be performed as part of a complete inspection. These inspections are performed either with the appliance in the off or standby mode (indicated by "*OFF*") or on an appliance that is operating (indicated by "*ON*"). The CO measurements are to be taken only after the appliance is determined to be venting properly. The CO detector should be capable of calculating CO emissions in ppm air free. Table G.6 contains CO thresholds for specific appliances.

G.6.1 Forced Air Furnaces.

(1) *OFF.* Verify that an air filter is installed and that it is not excessively blocked with dust.
(2) *OFF.* Inspect visible portions of the furnace combustion chamber for cracks, ruptures, holes, and corrosion. A heat exchanger leakage test should be conducted.
(3) *ON.* Verify that both the limit and fan controls are operating properly. Limit control operation can be checked by blocking the circulating air inlet or temporarily disconnecting the electrical supply to the blower motor and determining that the limit control acts to shut off the main burner gas.

Table G.6 CO Thresholds

Appliance	Threshold Limit
Central furnace (all categories)	400 ppm[a] air free[b,c]
Floor furnace	400 ppm air free
Gravity furnace	400 ppm air free
Wall furnace	200 ppm air free
Wall furnace (direct vent)	400 ppm air free
Vented room heater	200 ppm air free
Vent-free room heater	200 ppm air free
Boilers (all categories)	400 ppm air free
Water heater	200 ppm air free
Oven/Broiler	225 ppm as measured
Top burner	25 ppm as measured (per burner)
Clothes dryer	400 ppm air free
Refrigerator	25 ppm as measured
Gas log (gas fireplace)	25 ppm as measured in vent
Gas log (installed in wood-burning fireplace)	400 ppm air free in firebox

Notes:
[a] Parts per million
[b] Air-free emission levels are based on a mathematical equation (involving carbon monoxide and oxygen or carbon dioxide readings) to convert an actual diluted flue gas carbon monoxide testing sample to an undiluted air-free flue gas carbon monoxide level utilized in the appliance certification standards. For natural gas or propane, using as-measured CO ppm and O_2 percentage:

[G.6a]
$$CO_{AFppm} = \left(\frac{20.9}{20.9 - O_2}\right) \times CO_{ppm}$$

where:
CO_{AFppm} = Carbon monoxide, air-free ppm
CO_{ppm} = As-measured combustion gas carbon monoxide
O_2 = Percentage of oxygen in combustion gas, as a percentage

[c] An alternate method of calculating the CO air-free when access to an oxygen meter is not available:

[G.6b]
$$CO_{(air-free)} = \frac{UCO_2}{CO_2}(CO)$$

where:
UCO_2 = Ultimate concentration of carbon dioxide for the fuel being burned in percent for natural gas (12.2 percent) and propane (14.0 percent)
CO_2 = Measured concentration of carbon dioxide in combustion products in percent
CO = Measured concentration of carbon monoxide in combustion products in percent

(4) *ON.* Verify that the blower compartment door is installed properly and can be resecured properly if opened. Verify that the blower compartment door safety switch operates properly.
(5) *ON.* Check for flame disturbance before and after blower comes on, which can indicate heat exchanger leaks.
(6) *ON.* Measure the CO in the vent after 5 minutes of main burner operation. The CO should not exceed threshold in Table G.6.

G.6.2 Boilers.

(1) *OFF and ON.* Inspect for evidence of water leaks around boiler and connected piping.
(2) *ON.* Verify that the water pumps are in operating condition. Test low water cutoffs, automatic feed controls, pressure and temperature limit controls, and relief valves in accordance with the manufacturer's recommendations to determine that they are in operating condition.
(3) *ON.* Measure the CO in the vent after 5 minutes of main burner operation. The CO should not exceed threshold in Table G.6.

G.6.3 Water Heaters.

(1) *OFF.* Verify that the pressure-temperature relief valve is in operating condition. Water in the heater should be at operating temperature.
(2) *OFF.* Verify that inspection covers, glass, and gaskets are intact and in place on a flammable vapor ignition resistant (FVIR)–type water heater.
(3) *ON.* Verify that the thermostat is set in accordance with the manufacturer's operating instructions and measure the water temperature at the closest tub or sink to verify that it is no greater than 120°F.
(4) *OFF.* Where required by the local building code in earthquake-prone locations, inspect that the water heater is secured to the wall studs in two locations (high and low) using appropriate metal strapping and bolts.
(5) *ON.* Measure the CO in the vent after 5 minutes of main burner operation. The CO should not exceed threshold in Table G.6.

G.6.4 Cooking Appliances.

(1) *OFF.* Inspect oven cavity and range-top exhaust vent for blockage with aluminum foil or other materials.
(2) *OFF.* Inspect cook top to verify that it is free from a build-up of grease.
(3) *ON.* Measure the CO above each burner and at the oven exhaust vents after 5 minutes of burner operation. The CO should not exceed threshold in Table G.6.

G.6.5 Vented Room Heaters.

(1) *OFF.* For built-in room heaters and wall furnaces, inspect that the burner compartment is free of lint and debris.
(2) *OFF.* Inspect that furnishings and combustible building components are not blocking the heater.
(3) *ON.* Measure the CO in the vent after 5 minutes of main burner operation. The CO should not exceed threshold in Table G.6.

G.6.6 Vent-Free Heaters.

(1) *OFF.* Verify that the heater input is a maximum of 40,000 Btu/hr input, but not more than 10,000 Btu/hr where installed in a bedroom, and 6,000 Btu/hr where installed in a bathroom.
(2) *OFF.* Inspect the ceramic logs provided with gas log–type vent-free heaters to verify that they are located and aligned properly.
(3) *OFF.* Inspect the heater to verify that it is free of excess lint build-up and debris.
(4) *OFF.* Verify that the oxygen depletion safety shutoff system has not been altered or bypassed.
(5) *ON.* Verify that the main burner shuts down within 3 minutes by extinguishing the pilot light. The test is meant to simulate the operation of the oxygen depletion system (ODS).
(6) *ON.* Measure the CO after 5 minutes of main burner operation. The CO should not exceed threshold in Table G.6.

G.6.7 Gas Log Sets and Gas Fireplaces.

(1) *OFF.* For gas logs installed in wood-burning fireplaces equipped with a damper, verify that the fireplace damper is in a fixed open position.
(2) *ON.* Measure the CO in the firebox (log sets installed in wood burning fireplaces or in the vent [gas fireplace]) after 5 minutes of main burner operation. The CO should not exceed threshold in Table G.6.

G.6.8 Gas Clothes Dryer.

(1) *OFF.* Where installed in a closet, verify that a source of make-up air is provided and inspect that any make-up air openings, louvers, and ducts are free of blockage.
(2) *OFF.* Inspect for excess amounts of lint around the dryer and on dryer components. Verify that the lint trap is installed properly and that it does not have holes or tears. Verify that it is in a clean condition.
(3) *OFF.* Inspect visible portions of the exhaust duct and connections for loose fittings and connections, blockage, and signs of corrosion. Verify that the duct termination is not blocked and that it terminates in an outdoor location. Verify that only approved metal vent ducting material is installed (plastic and vinyl materials are not approved for gas dryers).
(4) *ON.* Verify mechanical components, including drum and blower, are operating properly.
(5) *ON.* Operate the clothes dryer and verify that exhaust system is intact and exhaust is exiting the termination.
(6) *ON.* Measure the CO at the exhaust duct or termination after 5 minutes of main burner operation. The CO should not exceed threshold in Table G.6.

Annex H Indoor Combustion Air Calculation Examples

This annex is not a part of the requirements of this NFPA document but is included for informational purposes only.

For SI units, 1 Btu/hr = 0.293 W, 1 ft³ = 0.028 m³, 1 ft = 0.305 m, 1 in. w.c. = 249 Pa.

H.1 New Installation. Determine if the indoor volume is sufficient to supply combustion air for the following new installation example.

Example Installation 1: A 100,000 Btu/hr fan-assisted furnace and a 40,000 Btu/hr draft hood–equipped water heater are being installed in a basement of a new single-family home. The basement measures 25 ft × 40 ft with an 8 ft ceiling.

Solution

(1) *Determine the total required volume:* Because the air infiltration rate is unknown, the standard method to determine combustion air is used to calculate the required volume.

  (a) The combined input for the appliances located in the basement is calculated as follows: 100,000 Btu/hr + 40,000 Btu/hr = 140,000 Btu/hr
  (b) The Standard Method requires that the required volume be determined based on 50 cubic feet per 1000 Btu/hour.
  (c) Using Table A.9.3.2.1, the required volume for a 140,000 Btu/hr combined input is 7000 ft³.

(2) *Determine available volume:* The available volume is the total basement volume:

Available Volume: 25 ft × 40 ft × 8 ft ceiling = 8000 ft³

Conclusion: The installation can use indoor air because the available volume of 8000 ft³ exceeds the total required volume of 7000 ft³. No outdoor air openings are required.

H.2 New Installation, Known Air Infiltration Rate Method. Determine if the indoor volume is sufficient to supply combustion air for the following replacement installation example.

Example Installation 2: A 100,000 Btu/hr fan-assisted furnace and a 40,000 Btu/hr draft hood–equipped water heater are being installed in a new single-family house. It was determined (either by use of the ASHRAE calculation method or blower door test) that the house has 0.65 air changes per hour (ACH). The furnace and water heater are being installed in a 20 ft × 35 ft basement with an 8 ft ceiling height.

Solution

(1) *Determine the required volume:* Because two types of appliances are located in the space — a fan-assisted furnace and a draft hood–equipped water heater — the required volume must be determined for each appliance and then combined to determine the total required volume:

  (a) *Fan-assisted furnace:* For structures for which the air infiltration rate is known, the method shown in 9.3.2.2 permits the use of Equation 9.3.2.2b to determine the required volume for a fan-assisted appliance. Paragraph 9.3.2.2(3) limits the use of the equation to air change rates equal to or less than 0.60 ACH. While the house was determined to have a 0.65 ACH, 0.60 is used to calculate the required volume. Using Equation 9.3.2.2b, the required volume for a 100,000 Btu/hr fan-assisted furnace is calculated as follows:

$$= \frac{15 \text{ ft}^3}{0.60}\left(\frac{100{,}000 \text{ Btu/hr}}{1000 \text{ Btu/hr}}\right) \quad \text{[H.2a]}$$

$$= 2500 \text{ ft}^3$$

Paragraph 9.3.2.2 specifies a lower required volume limitation for fan-assisted appliances at no smaller than 25 ft³ per 1000 Btu/hr. From Table A.9.3.2.2(b), the lower limit is 2500 ft³.

Because the calculated required volume of 2308 ft³ falls below the lower required volume limit, the lower limit of 2500 ft³ must be used as the minimum required volume.

  (b) *Draft hood–equipped water heater:* For structures for which the air infiltration rate is known, the method shown in 9.3.2.2 permits the use Equation 9.3.2.2a to determine the required volume for a draft hood–equipped appliance. Paragraph 9.3.2.2(3) limits the use of the equation to air change rates equal to or less than 0.60 ACH. While the house was determined to have a 0.65 ACH, 0.60 is used to calculate the required volume. Using Equation 9.3.2.2a, the required volume for the 40,000 Btu/hr water heater is calculated as follows:

$$= \frac{21 \text{ ft}^3}{0.60}\left(\frac{40{,}000 \text{ Btu/hr}}{1000 \text{ Btu/hr}}\right) \quad \text{[H.2b]}$$

$$= 1400 \text{ ft}^3$$

Paragraph 9.3.2.2 specifies a lower required volume limitation for appliances other than fan-assisted at no smaller than 35 ft³ per 1000 Btu/hr. From Table A.9.3.2.2(a), the lower limit is 1400 ft³.

Because the calculated required volume of 1292 ft³ falls below the lower required volume limit, the lower limit of 1400 ft³ must be used as the minimum required volume.

  (c) *Total required volume:* Subsection 9.3.2 states that the total required volume of indoor air is the sum of the required volumes for all appliances located in the space:
  Total Required = 2500 ft³ + 1400 ft³ = 3900 ft³

(2) *Determine available volume:* The available volume is determined as follows:

$$(20 \text{ ft} \times 35 \text{ ft}) \times 8 \text{ ft} = 5600 \text{ ft}^3 \quad \text{[H.2c]}$$

Conclusion: The installation can use indoor air because the available volume of 5600 ft³ exceeds the total required volume of 3900 ft³. No outdoor air openings are required.

H.3 New Installation, Known Air Infiltration Rate Method. Determine if the indoor volume is sufficient to supply combustion air for the following replacement installation example.

Example Installation 3: A 100,000 Btu/hr fan-assisted furnace and a 40,000 Btu/hr draft hood–equipped water heater are being installed in a new single-family house. It was determined (either by use of the ASHRAE calculation method or blower door test) that the house has 0.30 air changes per hour (ACH). The furnace and water heater are being installed in a 20 ft × 35 ft basement with an 8 ft ceiling height.

Solution

(1) *Determine the required volume:* Because two types of appliances are located in the space — a fan-assisted furnace and a draft hood–equipped water heater — the required volume must be determined for each appliance and then combined to determine the total required volume:

(a) *Fan-assisted furnace:* For structures for which the air infiltration rate is known, the method shown in 9.3.2.2 permits the use of Equation 9.3.2.2b to determine the required volume for a fan-assisted appliance. Paragraph 9.3.2.2(3) limits the use of the equation to air change rates equal to or less than 0.60 ACH. Because 0.30 ACH is less than 0.60 ACH, 0.30 can be used to calculate the required volume. Using Equation 9.3.2.2b, the required volume for a 100,000 Btu/hr fan-assisted furnace is calculated as follows:

[H.3a]
$$= \frac{15 \text{ ft}^3}{0.30}\left(\frac{100{,}000 \text{ Btu/hr}}{1000 \text{ Btu/hr}}\right)$$
$$= 5000 \text{ ft}^3$$

Paragraph 9.3.2.2 specifies a lower required volume limitation for fan-assisted appliances at no smaller than 25 ft³ per 1000 Btu/hr. From Table A.9.3.2.2(b), the lower limit is 2500 ft³.

Because the calculated required volume of 5000 ft³ is above the lower required volume limit, use this amount as the minimum required volume.

(b) *Draft hood–equipped water heater:* For structures for which the air infiltration rate is known, the method shown in 9.3.2.2 permits the use of Equation 9.3.2.2a to determine the required volume for a draft hood–equipped appliance. Paragraph 9.3.2.2(3) limits the use of the equation to air change rates equal to or less than 0.60 ACH. Because 0.30 ACH is less than 0.60 ACH, 0.30 ACH is used to calculate the required volume. Using Equation 9.3.2.2a, the required volume for the 40,000 Btu/hr water heater is calculated as follows:

[H.3b]
$$= \frac{21 \text{ ft}^3}{0.30}\left(\frac{40{,}000 \text{ Btu/hr}}{1000 \text{ Btu/hr}}\right)$$
$$= 2800 \text{ ft}^3$$

Paragraph 9.3.2.2 specifies a lower required volume limitation for appliances other than fan-assisted at no smaller than 35 ft³ per 1000 Btu/hr. From Table A.9.3.2.2(a), the lower limit is 1400 ft³.

Because the calculated required volume of 2800 ft³ is above the lower required volume limit, use this amount as the minimum required volume.

(c) *Total required volume:* Subsection 9.3.2 states that the total required volume to use indoor air is the sum of the required volumes for all appliances located in the space:
Total Required = 5000 ft³ + 2800 ft³ = 7800 ft³

(2) *Determine available volume:* The available volume is determined as follows:

[H.3c]
$$(20 \text{ ft} \times 35 \text{ ft}) \times 8 \text{ ft} = 5600 \text{ ft}^3$$

Conclusion: The installation cannot use indoor air alone, because the available volume of 5600 ft³ is less than the total required volume of 7800 ft³. Outdoor air openings can be sized in accordance with all air from the outdoors or by use of the combination of indoor/outdoor air method.

Annex I Example of Combination of Indoor and Outdoor Combustion and Ventilation Opening Design

This annex is not a part of the requirements of this NFPA document but is included for informational purposes only.

For SI units, 1 Btu/hr = 0.293 W, 1 ft³ = 0.028 m³, 1 ft = 0.305 m, 1 in. w.c. = 249 Pa.

I.1 Example of Combination Indoor and Outdoor Combustion Air Opening Design. Determine the required combination of indoor and outdoor combustion air opening sizes for the following appliance installation example.

Example Installation: A fan-assisted furnace and a draft hood–equipped water heater with the following inputs are located in a 15 ft × 30 ft basement with an 8 ft ceiling. No additional indoor spaces can be used to help meet the appliance combustion air needs.

Fan-Assisted Furnace Input: 100,000 Btu/hr

Draft Hood–Equipped Water Heater Input: 40,000 Btu/hr

Solution

(1) *Determine the total available room volume:* Appliance room volume: 15 ft × 30 ft with an 8 ft ceiling = 3600 ft³

(2) *Determine the total required volume:* The Standard Method to determine combustion air is used to calculate the required volume. The combined input for the appliances located in the basement is calculated as follows:

[I.1a]
$$100{,}000 \text{ Btu/hr} + 40{,}000 \text{ Btu/hr} = 140{,}000 \text{ Btu/hr}$$

The Standard Method requires that the required volume be determined based on 50 ft³ per 1000 Btu/hr. Using Table A.9.3.2.1, the required volume for a 140,000 Btu/hr combined input is 7000 ft³.

Conclusion: The indoor volume is insufficient to supply combustion air since the total of 3600 ft³ does not meet the required volume of 7000 ft³. Therefore, additional combustion air must be provided from the outdoors.

(3) Determine the ratio of the available volume to the required volume:

$$\frac{3600 \text{ ft}^3}{7000 \text{ ft}^3} = 0.51 \quad [\text{I.1b}]$$

(4) Determine the reduction factor to be used to reduce the full outdoor air opening size to the minimum required based on ratio of indoor spaces:
1.00 - 0.51 (from Step 3) = 0.49

(5) Determine the single outdoor combustion air opening size as though all combustion air is to come from outdoors. In this example, the combustion air opening directly communicates with the outdoors:

$$\frac{140{,}000 \text{ Btu/hr}}{3000 \text{ Btu/in.}^2} = 47 \text{ in.}^2 \quad [\text{I.1c}]$$

(6) Determine the minimum outdoor combustion air opening area:
Outdoor opening area = 0.49 (from Step 4) × 47 in.² = 23 in.²
Paragraph 9.3.4(3)(c) requires the minimum dimension of the air opening should not be less than 3 in.

Annex J Enforcement

This annex is not a part of the requirements of this NFPA document but is included for informational purposes only.

J.1 The following sample ordinance is provided to assist a jurisdiction in the adoption of this code and is not part of this code.

ORDINANCE NO._____

An ordinance of the *[jurisdiction]* adopting the 2021 edition of NFPA 54/ANSI Z223.1, *National Fuel Gas Code*, documents listed in Chapter 2 of that code; prescribing regulations governing conditions hazardous to life and property from fire or explosion; providing for the issuance of permits and collection of fees; repealing Ordinance No._____ of the *[jurisdiction]* and all other ordinances and parts of ordinances in conflict therewith; providing a penalty; providing a severability clause; and providing for publication; and providing an effective date.

BE IT ORDAINED BY THE *[governing body]* OF THE *[jurisdiction]*:

SECTION 1 That the *National Fuel Gas Code* and documents adopted by Chapter 2, three (3) copies of which are on file and are open to inspection by the public in the office of the *[jurisdiction's keeper of records]* of the *[jurisdiction]*, are hereby adopted and incorporated into this ordinance as fully as if set out at length herein, and from the date on which this ordinance shall take effect, the provisions thereof shall be controlling within the limits of the *[jurisdiction]*. The same are hereby adopted as the code of the *[jurisdiction]* for the purpose of prescribing regulations governing conditions hazardous to life and property from fire or explosion and providing for issuance of permits and collection of fees.

SECTION 2 Any person who shall violate any provision of this code or standard hereby adopted or fail to comply therewith; or who shall violate or fail to comply with any order made thereunder; or who shall build in violation of any detailed statement of specifications or plans submitted and approved thereunder; or failed to operate in accordance with any certificate or permit issued thereunder; and from which no appeal has been taken; or who shall fail to comply with such an order as affirmed or modified by or by a court of competent jurisdiction, within the time fixed herein, shall severally for each and every such violation and noncompliance, respectively, be guilty of a misdemeanor, punishable by a fine of not less than $_____ nor more than $_____ or by imprisonment for not less than_____ days nor more than_____ days or by both such fine and imprisonment. The imposition of one penalty for any violation shall not excuse the violation or permit it to continue; and all such persons shall be required to correct or remedy such violations or defects within a reasonable time; and when not otherwise specified the application of the above penalty shall not be held to prevent the enforced removal of prohibited conditions. Each day that prohibited conditions are maintained shall constitute a separate offense.

SECTION 3 Additions, insertions, and changes — that the 2021 edition of NFPA 54/ANSI Z223.1, *National Fuel Gas Code*, is amended and changed in the following respects:

List Amendments

SECTION 4 That ordinance No._____ of *[jurisdiction]* entitled *[fill in the title of the ordinance or ordinances in effect at the present time]* and all other ordinances or parts of ordinances in conflict herewith are hereby repealed.

SECTION 5 That if any section, subsection, sentence, clause, or phrase of this ordinance is, for any reason, held to be invalid or unconstitutional, such decision shall not affect the validity or constitutionality of the remaining portions of this ordinance. The *[governing body]* hereby declares that it would have passed this ordinance, and each section, subsection, clause, or phrase hereof, irrespective of the fact that any one or more sections, subsections, sentences, clauses, and phrases be declared unconstitutional.

SECTION 6 That the *[jurisdiction's keeper of records]* is hereby ordered and directed to cause this ordinance to be published. [NOTE: An additional provision may be required to direct the number of times the ordinance is to be published and to specify that it is to be in a newspaper in general circulation. Posting may also be required.]

SECTION 7 That this ordinance and the rules, regulations, provisions, requirements, orders, and matters established and adopted hereby shall take effect and be in full force and effect *[time period]* from and after the date of its final passage and adoption.

Annex K Informational References

K.1 Referenced Publications. The documents or portions thereof listed in this annex are referenced within the informational sections of this code and are not part of the requirements of this document unless also listed in Chapter 2 for other reasons.

K.1.1 NFPA Publications. National Fire Protection Association, 1 Batterymarch Park, Quincy, MA 02169-7471.

NFPA 56, *Standard for Fire and Explosion Prevention During Cleaning and Purging of Flammable Gas Piping Systems*, 2020 edition.

NFPA 58, *Liquefied Petroleum Gas Code*, 2020 edition.

NFPA 68, *Standard on Explosion Protection by Deflagration Venting*, 2018 edition.

NFPA 70®, National Electrical Code®, 2020 edition.

NFPA 90A, *Standard for the Installation of Air-Conditioning and Ventilating Systems*, 2021 edition.

NFPA 90B, *Standard for the Installation of Warm Air Heating and Air-Conditioning Systems*, 2021 edition.

NFPA 96, *Standard for Ventilation Control and Fire Protection of Commercial Cooking Operations*, 2021 edition.

NFPA 780, *Standard for the Installation of Lightning Protection Systems*, 2020 edition.

National Fuel Gas Code Handbook, 2018 edition.

K.1.2 Other Publications.

K.1.2.1 API Publications. American Petroleum Institute, 1220 L Street, NW, Washington, DC 20005-4070.

API STD 1104, *Welding Pipelines and Related Facilities*, 2013.

K.1.2.2 ASHRAE Publications. ASHRAE, Inc., 1791 Tullie Circle, NE, Atlanta, GA 30329-2305, (404) 636-8400, www.ashrae.org.

ASHRAE Handbook — Fundamentals, 2017.

ASHRAE Handbook — HVAC Systems and Equipment, 2016.

K.1.2.3 ASME Publications. American Society of Mechanical Engineers, Two Park Avenue, New York, NY 10016-5990, (800) 843-2763. www.asme.org

Boiler and Pressure Vessel Code, Section IX and Section IV, 2015.

K.1.2.4 ASTM Publications. ASTM International, 100 Barr Harbor Drive, P.O. Box C700, West Conshohocken, PA 19428-2959, (610) 832-9585. www.astm.org

ASTM D2385, *Test Method for Hydrogen Sulfide and Mercaptan Sulfur in Natural Gas (Cadmium Sulfate — Iodometric Titration Method)*, 1981, reaffirmed 1990 (withdrawn 1995).

ASTM D2420, *Test Method of for Hydrogen Sulfide in Liquefied Petroleum (LP) Gases (Lead Acetate Method)*, 2013, reaffirmed 2018.

K.1.2.5 AWS Publications. American Welding Society, 8669 NW 36 Street, #130, Miami, FL 33166-6672, (800) 443-9353. www.aws.org

AWS B2.1/B2.1M, *Specification for Welding Procedure and Performance Qualification*, 2014.

AWS B2.2/B2.2M, *Specification for Brazing Procedure and Performance Qualification*, 2016.

K.1.2.6 CSA Group Publications. CSA Group, 178 Rexdale Boulevard, Toronto, ON M9W 1R3, Canada, (216) 524-4990. www.csagroup.org

ANSI Z21.13/CSA 4.9, *Gas-Fired Low Pressure Steam and Hot Water Boilers*, 2017.

ANSI Z21.50/CSA 2.22, *Vented Decorative Gas Appliances*, 2019.

ANSI Z21.60/CSA 2.26, *Decorative Gas Appliances for Installation in Solid-Fuel Burning Fireplaces*, 2017.

K.1.2.7 NACE Publications. NACE International, 15835 Park Ten Place, Houston, TX 77084-4906. www.nace.org

NACE SP0169, *Control of External Corrosion on Underground or Submerged Metallic Piping Systems*, 2013.

K.1.2.8 UL Publications. Underwriters Laboratories Inc., 333 Pfingsten Road, Northbrook, IL 60062-2096. www.ul.com

UL 651, *Schedule 40 and 80 Rigid PVC Conduit and Fittings*, 2011, revised 2018.

UL 795, *Commercial-Industrial Gas Heating Equipment*, 2016.

K.1.2.9 US Government Publications. US Government Publishing Office, 732 North Capitol Street, NW, Washington, DC 20401-0001. www.gpo.gov

Responding to Residential Carbon Monoxide Incidents, Guidelines for Fire and Other Emergency Response Personnel, U.S. Consumer Product Safety Commission, July 23, 2002.

K.1.2.10 Other Publications.

Piping Handbook, 2000, New York: McGraw-Hill Book Company.

Project Number 21323, *Validation of Installation Methods for CSST Gas Piping to Mitigate Indirect Lightning Related Damage*, Gas Technology Institute 2015.

K.2 Informational References. The following documents or portions thereof are listed here as informational resources only. They are not a part of the requirements of this document.

K.2.1 NFPA Publications. National Fire Protection Association, 1 Batterymarch Park, Quincy, MA 02169-7471.

NFPA 30, *Flammable and Combustible Liquids Code*, 2021 edition.

NFPA 59, *Utility LP-Gas Plant Code*, 2021 edition.

NFPA 61, *Standard for the Prevention of Fires and Dust Explosions in Agricultural and Food Processing Facilities*, 2020 edition.

NFPA 86, *Standard for Ovens and Furnaces*, 2019 edition.

NFPA 211, *Standard for Chimneys, Fireplaces, Vents, and Solid Fuel–Burning Appliances*, 2019 edition.

NFPA 501A, *Standard for Fire Safety Criteria for Manufactured Home Installations, Sites, and Communities*, 2017 edition.

K.2.2 CSA Group Publications. CSA Group, 178 Rexdale Boulevard, Toronto, ON M9W 1R3, Canada, (216) 524-4990. www.csagroup.org

ANSI/AGA NGV 3.1/CSA 12.3, *Fuel System Components for Compressed Natural Gas Powered Vehicles*, 2014, reaffirmed 2019.

AGA/CSA NGV 1, *Compressed Natural Gas Vehicle (NGV) Fueling Connection Devices*, 2017.

ANSI/CSA FC 1, *Fuel Cell Technologies — Part 3-100: Stationary fuel cell power systems — Safety*, 2014, reaffirmed 2018.

ANSI/CSA NGV 2, *Natural Gas Vehicle Fuel Containers*, 2016.

ANSI/LC 2A, *Direct Gas-Fired Circulating Heaters for Agricultural Animal Confinement Buildings*, 1998, reaffirmed 2015.

ANSI/LC 2, *Direct Gas-Fired Circulating Heaters for Agricultural Animal Confinement Buildings*, 1996, reaffirmed 2015.

ANSI Z21.1/CSA 1.1, *Household Cooking Gas Appliances*, 2018.

ANSI Z21.5.1/CSA 7.1, *Gas Clothes Dryers — Volume I — Type 1 Clothes Dryers*, 2017.

ANSI Z21.5.2/CSA 7.2, *Gas Clothes Dryers — Volume II — Type 2 Clothes Dryers*, 2016.

ANSI Z21.10.1/CSA 4.1, *Gas Water Heaters — Volume I — Storage Water Heaters with Input Ratings of 75,000 Btu per Hour or Less*, 2017.

ANSI Z21.10.3/CSA 4.3, *Gas Water Heaters — Volume III — Storage Water Heaters with Input Ratings above 75,000 Btu per Hour, Circulating and Instantaneous*, 2017.

ANSI Z21.11.2, *Gas-Fired Room Heaters — Volume II — Unvented Room Heaters*, 2016.

ANSI Z21.12, *Draft Hoods*, 1990 reaffirmed 2015.

ANSI Z21.13/CSA 4.9, *Gas-Fired Low-Pressure Steam and Hot Water Boilers*, 2017.

ANSI Z21.15/CSA 9.1, *Manually Operated Gas Valves for Appliances, Appliance Connector Valves, and Hose End Valves*, 2009, reaffirmed 2014.

ANSI Z21.17/CSA 2.7, *Domestic Gas Conversion Burners*, 1998, reaffirmed 2014.

ANSI Z21.18/CSA 6.3, *Gas Appliance Pressure Regulators*, 2007, reaffirmed 2016.

ANSI Z21.19/CSA 1.4, *Refrigerators Using Gas Fuel*, 2014.

ANSI Z21.20/CSA C22.2 — No. 60730-2-5, *Automatic Electrical Controls for Household and Similar Use — Part 2: Particular Requirements for Automatic Burner Ignition Systems and Components*, 2014, reaffirmed 2019.

ANSI Z21.21/CSA 6.5, *Automatic Valves for Gas Appliances*, 2019.

ANSI Z21.22/CSA 4.4, *Relief Valves for Hot Water Supply Systems*, 2015.

ANSI Z21.23, *Gas Appliance Thermostats*, 2010, reaffirmed 2015.

ANSI Z21.24/CSA 6.10, *Connectors for Gas Appliances*, 2015.

ANSI Z21.35/CSA 6.8, *Pilot Gas Filters*, 2005, reaffirmed 2015.

ANSI Z21.40.1/CSA 2.91, *Gas-Fired, Heat Activated Air-Conditioning and Heat Pump Appliances*, 1996, reaffirmed 2017.

ANSI Z21.40.2/CSA 2.92, *Gas-Fired, Work Activated Air-Conditioning and Heat Pump Appliances (Internal Combustion)*, 1996, reaffirmed 2017.

ANSI Z21.40.4/CSA 2.94, *Performance Testing and Rating of Gas-Fired, Air-Conditioning and Heat Pump Appliances*, 1996, reaffirmed 2017.

ANSI Z21.42, *Gas-Fired Illuminating Appliances*, 2013, reaffirmed 2018.

ANSI Z21.47/CSA 2.3, *Gas-Fired Central Furnaces*, 2016.

ANSI Z21.54/CSA 8.4, *Gas Hose Connectors for Portable Outdoor Gas-Fired Appliances*, 2019.

ANSI Z21.56/CSA 4.7, *Gas-Fired Pool Heaters*, 2017.

ANSI Z21.57, *Recreational Vehicle Cooking Gas Appliances*, 2010.

ANSI Z21.58/CSA 1.6, *Outdoor Cooking Gas Appliances*, 2018.

ANSI Z21.60/CSA 2.26, *Decorative Gas Appliances for Installation in Solid-Fuel Burning Fireplaces*, 2017.

ANSI Z21.61, *Gas-Fired Toilets*, 1993, reaffirmed 2013.

ANSI Z21.66/CSA 6.14, *Automatic Vent Damper Devices for Use with Gas-Fired Appliances*, 2015.

ANSI Z21.69/CSA 6.16, *Connectors for Movable Gas Appliances*, 2015.

ANSI Z21.71, *Automatic Intermittent Pilot Ignition Systems for Field Installations*, 1993 reaffirmed 2016.

ANSI Z21.77/CSA 6.23, *Manually-Operated Piezo-Electric Spark Gas Ignition Systems and Components*, 2005, reaffirmed 2015.

ANSI Z21.78/CSA 6.20, *Combination Gas Controls for Gas Appliances*, 2010, reaffirmed 2015.

ANSI Z21.84, *Manually Lighted, Natural Gas Decorative Gas Appliances for Installation in Solid-Fuel Burning Appliances*, 2017.

ANSI Z21.86/CSA 2.32, *Vented Gas-Fired Space Heating Appliances*, 2016.

ANSI Z21.87/CSA 4.6, *Automatic Gas Shutoff Devices for Hot Water Supply Systems*, 2007, reaffirmed 2016.

ANSI Z21.88/CSA 2.33, *Vented Gas Fireplace Heaters*, 2017.

ANSI Z21.91, *Ventless Firebox Enclosures for Gas-Fired Unvented Decorative Room Heaters*, 2017.

ANSI Z83.4/CSA 3.7, *Non-Recirculating Direct Gas-Fired Industrial Air Heaters*, 2017.

ANSI Z83.8/CSA 2.6, *Gas Unit Heaters, Gas Packaged Heaters, Gas Utility Heaters, and Gas-Fired Duct Furnaces*, 2016.

ANSI Z83.11/CSA 1.8, *Gas Food Service Equipment*, 2016.

ANSI Z83.19/CSA 2.35, *Gas-Fired High-Intensity Infrared Heaters*, 2017.

ANSI Z83.20/CSA 2.34, *Gas-Fired tubular and Low-Intensity Infrared Heaters*, 2016.

ANSI Z83.21/CSA C 22.2 No.168, *Commercial Dishwashers*, 2016.

K.2.3 MSS Publications. Manufacturers Standardization Society of the Valve and Fittings Industry, 127 Park Street, NE, Vienna, VA 22180-4602. www.msshq.org

MSS SP-6, *Standard Finishes for Contact Faces of Pipe Flanges and Connecting-End Flanges of Valves and Fittings*, 2017.

ANSI/MSS SP-58, *Pipe Hangers and Supports — Materials, Design and Manufacture*, 2018.

K.2.4 UL Publications. Underwriters Laboratories Inc., 333 Pfingsten Road, Northbrook, IL 60062-2096. www.ul.com

UL 103, *Chimneys, Factory-Built, Residential Type and Building Heating Appliances*, 2010, revised 2017.

UL 441, *Gas Vents*, 2016.

UL 641, *Type L Low-Temperature Venting Systems*, 2010, revised 2018.

UL 1738, *Venting Systems for Gas Burning Appliances, Categories II, III and IV*, 2010, revised 2014.

UL 1777, *Chimney Liners*, 2015, revised 2019.

K.2.5 US Government Publications. US Government Publishing Office, 732 North Capitol Street, NW, Washington, DC 20401-0001. www.gpo.gov

Title 24, Code of Federal Regulations, Part 3280, "*Manufactured Home Construction and Safety Standard.*"

K.3 References for Extracts in Informational Sections. (Reserved)

Index

Copyright © 2020 National Fire Protection Association. All Rights Reserved.

The copyright in this index is separate and distinct from the copyright in the document that it indexes. The licensing provisions set forth for the document are not applicable to this index. This index may not be reproduced in whole or in part by any means without the express written permission of NFPA.

-A-

Aboveground piping, 7.2, A.7.2.5
Access doors and panels, 10.9.4, 10.10.9, 10.25.2.4
Accessible
    Appliances, 9.2.1, 9.4.3, 9.5.1
    Definition, 3.3.1
    Readily (definition), 3.3.1.1
    Valves, 7.8.1, 7.8.2, 7.8.3.1
Agency, qualified, 4.1
    Definition, 3.3.82
Air
    Circulating, *see* Circulating air
    Combustion, *see* Combustion air
    Dilution, *see* Dilution air
    Excess (definition), 3.3.2.3
    Make-up, *see* Make-up air
    Primary, *see* Primary air
    Process, 9.1.7
    Use under pressure, 9.1.5
Air conditioning
    Appliances, 10.2, A.10.2.7
Air ducts, *see* Ducts
Aircraft hangars
    Duct furnaces in, 10.9.8
    Heaters in, 9.1.12, 10.16.5, 10.24.6
Altitude, high, 11.1.2, 13.1.5, 13.2.11
Anchors, pipe, 7.2.6
Anodeless risers, 5.5.4.3
    Definition, 3.3.3
Appliance categorized vent diameter/area, 13.1.9, 13.1.12, 13.1.13, 13.2.18, 13.2.24, F.2.3
    Definition, 3.3.5
Appliances, *see also* Equipment
    Air for combustion and ventilation, *see* Combustion air; Ventilation
    Approval, 9.1.1, A.9.1.1
    Attics, in, 9.5, 12.11.2.2
    Automatically controlled, 10.14.2.2(3), 10.26.7, 12.3.2(5)
        Clearances, Table 10.3.3.2
        Shutoff devices, 10.3.5, 10.3.6, 12.6.5.2, A.12.13.4
        Temperature limit controls, 10.10.3
        Venting, 12.4.4.1
    Carpeting, installation on, 9.2.3
    Categorized vent diameter/area, *see* Vent(s), Sizes
    Clearance to combustible materials, 9.2.2, Table 10.3.3.2
    Combination units, 9.1.19
        Chimneys, 12.6.5.3, 12.6.5.4, A.12.6.5.3
        Venting, Table 12.5.1
    Connections to building piping, 9.6, A.9.6.1.5, A.9.6.3
    Convenience outlets, 9.6.7
    Converted, 9.1.2, 9.1.3
    Counter (gas), *see* Food service appliances
    Decorative, *see* Decorative appliances
    Definition, 3.3.4
    Direct vent, *see* Direct vent appliances
    Electrical systems, 9.7
    Existing, 9.1.22, 12.6.4.1, A.9.1.22, Annex G
    Extra devices or attachments, 9.1.15
    Fan-assisted combustion, *see* Fan-assisted combustion appliances
    Food service, *see* Food service appliances
    Household cooking, *see* Household cooking appliances
    Illuminating, 10.14
    Installation of, Chap. 9
    Instructions
        Installation, 9.1.20, A.9.1.20
        Operating, 11.7
    Louvers, grilles, and screens, 9.3.7, 10.8.5.3, 10.8.7.2, 10.25.2.4
    Low-heat, *see* subhead: Nonresidential low-heat
    Medium-heat, *see* subhead: Nonresidential medium-heat
    Mobile, connections, 9.6.4
    Nonresidential low-heat, 12.6.2.1, Table 12.8.4.4, 12.8.4.6(3), 12.11.2.4, A.12.6.2.1
        Definition, 3.3.4.7
    Nonresidential medium-heat, 12.6.2.2, Table 12.8.4.4, 12.11.2.5, 12.11.14.2
        Definition, 3.3.4.8
    Operation procedures, Chap. 11
    Outdoor
        Cooking appliances, 10.18
            Definition, 3.3.4.9
        Protection of, 9.1.21
    Piping
        Strain on, 9.1.16
    Placing in operation, 8.2.4, 8.3.3
    Portable, connections, 9.6.4
    Pressure regulators, 5.14, 9.1.17
    Protection, *see* Protection
    Purging, 8.2.4, 8.3.3
    On roofs, 9.4
    Shutoff valves, *see* Valves
    Type of gas(es), 9.1.3
    Vented, *see* Vented appliances; Venting; Venting systems
    In well-ventilated spaces, 12.3.4
Applicability of code, 1.1.1, A.1.1.1.1(A)
Approved (definition), 3.2.1, A.3.2.1
Atmospheric pressure, A.12.1
    Definition, 3.3.79.1
Attics, appliances in, 9.5, 12.11.2.2
Authority having jurisdiction (definition), 3.2.2, A.3.2.2
Automatic firechecks, 7.11.1(3), 7.11.6, A.7.11.4, A.7.11.6(1)

INDEX

Definition, 3.3.6
Automatic gas shutoff devices, 5.8.3.1(4), 7.11.5.4, 10.3.6, 10.26.6, A.7.11.5.4, A.12.13.4
Definition, 3.3.27.1
Automatic ignition, *see* Ignition
Automatic valves, *see* Valves
Automatic vent dampers, 12.15, 12.16(3)
Definition, 3.3.7

-B-

Back pressure
Definition, 3.3.79.2
Protection, 5.9
Backfilling, 7.1.2.3
Backfire preventers, *see* Safety blowouts
Baffle, 10.11.3.2(1), 12.14, A.12.14.2
Definition, 3.3.9
Barometric draft regulators, 9.3.1.4, 12.13.4 to 12.13.6, A.12.13.4
Definition, 3.3.84.1.1
Bathroom, installation in, 10.1.2, 10.21.2, A.10.1.2, A.10.21.2
Bedroom, installation in, 10.1.2, 10.21.2, A.10.1.2, A.10.21.2
Bends, pipe, 7.5
Bleeds
Diaphragm-type valves, 9.1.18
Industrial air heaters, 10.8.6
Blowers, mixing, *see* Mixing blowers
Boilers
Central heating, 10.3, A.10.3.7, A.10.3.8.3
  Assembly and installation, 10.3.4
  Clearance, 10.3.3, Table 12.8.4.4
  Cooling units used with, 10.3.10
  Low-water cutoff, 10.3.6, 11.5
  Steam safety and pressure relief valves, 10.3.7, A.10.3.7
  Temperature or pressure limiting devices, 10.3.5
Hot water heating, Table 10.3.3.2, 10.3.5, 10.3.7, 10.3.10.2, A.10.3.7
  Definition, 3.3.10.1
Hot water supply, Table 10.3.3.2, 10.3.5, 10.3.7, A.10.3.7
  Definition, 3.3.10.2
Low pressure, A.10.3.7
  Clearances, 10.3.3.1 to 10.3.3.3
  Definition, 3.3.10.3
  Location, 10.3.2
Steam, Table 10.3.3.2, 10.3.5 to 10.3.7
  Definition, 3.3.10.4
Bonding jumper, 7.12.2.1 to 7.12.2.3
Definition, 3.3.11
Bonding, electrical, 7.12, A.7.12.2 to A.7.12.5
Branch lines, 7.4.1
Branch length pipe sizing method, 6.1.2, A.6.1.2, B.4.2, B.7.3, B.7.4
Definition, 3.3.12
Pressure testing, 8.1.1.4
Breeching, *see* Vent connectors
Broilers
Definition, 3.3.14
Household cooking appliance
  Definition, 3.3.4.6.1

Protection above, 10.17.2
Unit
  Commercial, 10.17.3
  Definition, 3.3.14.1
  Domestic, protection above, 10.17.2
  Open-top, 10.17
Btu (definition), 3.3.15
Buildings
Piping in
  Building structure for, 7.2.3
  Concealed, 7.3
  Connection of appliances and equipment to, 9.6, A.9.6.1.5, A.9.6.3
  Prohibited locations, 7.2.5, A.7.2.5
Piping under, 7.1.6
Structure, 9.1.8
Built-in household cooking units, *see* Household cooking appliances
Burners
Combination gas and oil burners
  Chimneys for, 12.6.5.3, 12.6.5.4, A.12.6.5.3
  Venting system, Table 12.5.1
Definition, 3.3.16
Forced draft, *see* subhead: Power
Gas conversion, 10.5
  Definition, 3.3.16.2
Injection- (Bunsen-type), 9.6.3, A.9.6.3
  Definition, 3.3.16.3
Input adjustment, 11.1, A.11.1.1
Power, 9.3.1.2
  Definition, 3.3.16.5
  Fan-assisted (definition), 3.3.16.5.1
Primary air adjustment, 11.2, A.11.2
In residential garages, 9.1.10.1
Butane, 5.4.5
Bypass valves
Gas line pressure regulators, 5.14
Pool heaters, 10.19.5

-C-

Capping, of outlets, 7.7.2
Carpeting, installation of appliances on, 9.2.3
Casters, for floor-mounted food service appliances, 10.11.6
Central furnaces, *see* Furnaces
Central premix system, 7.11, A.7.11.4 to A.7.11.6(1)
Definition, 3.3.95.1
Chases, vertical, piping in, 7.4, A.7.4.3
Chimneys, Table 12.5.1, 12.6, A.12.6.1.3 to A.12.6.5.3
Cleanouts, 12.6.4.3, 12.6.7
Clothes dryer exhaust duct, 10.4.5.1
Decorative appliance installation, 10.6.3
Definition, 3.3.17
Exterior masonry, Table 13.1(f), Tables 13.2(f) to (i), F.2.4
  Definition, 3.3.17.1
Factory-built, 9.3.8.7, 12.6.1.1, 12.6.2.4, 12.6.6, 12.6.8.2, 12.6.9, 12.11.2.4, 12.11.2.5(4)
  Definition, 3.3.17.2
Gas piping in, 7.2.5, A.7.2.5

Masonry, 9.3.8.7, 12.6.1.3, 12.6.8.1, 12.6.8.2, 12.7.2(3), Table 13.1(c), Table 13.1(d), Table 13.1(f), 13.1.7, 13.2.20, 13.2.23, A.12.6.1.3, A.13.1.7, A.13.2.20, F.2.3
    Definition, 3.3.17.3
Metal, 9.3.8.7, 12.6.1.2, 12.6.8.2
    Definition, 3.3.17.4
Obstructions, 12.16, 13.1.1
Vent connectors, 12.11.1, 12.11.2.4, 12.11.2.5, 12.11.3.3, 12.11.11
Venting system, Table 12.5.1, 12.7.4.4, Table 13(c), Table 13(d), Table 13.1(f), 13.1.7, 13.1.11, Table 13.2(c), Table 13.2(d), Tables 13.2(f) to (i), 13.2.20, 13.2.21, A.13.1.7, A.13.2.20, F.2.3

Circuits, electrical, 7.13, 9.7.3
Circulating air, 10.7.4, 10.9.6, 10.10.4, 10.24.4, 10.25.4
    Definition, 3.3.2.1
Clearances, 9.2.2
    Air-conditioning equipment, indoor installation, 10.2.4
    Boilers, central heating, 10.3.3, Table 12.8.4.4
    Clothes dryers, 10.4.2
    Draft hoods, 12.13.7
    Food service appliances
        Above cooking top, A.10.13.3.1
        Counter appliances, 10.12.2 to 10.12.3
        Floor-mounted, 10.11.2
    Furnaces
        Central, 10.3.3
        For connectors, Table 12.8.4.4
        Duct, 10.9.2
        Floor, 10.10.8
    Gas-fired toilets, 10.23.1
    Heaters
        Industrial air, 10.8.4
        Infrared, 10.16.3
        Pool, 10.19.3
        Unit, 10.24.3
        Water, 10.26.3
    Household cooking appliances, 10.13.3, A.10.13.3.1
    Illuminating appliances, 10.14.1, 10.14.2
    Refrigerators, gas, 10.20.2
    Single-wall metal pipe for vents, 12.8.4.4
    Underground piping, 7.1.1
    Vent connectors, 12.11.5

Clothes dryers
    Definition, 3.3.18
    Installation, 10.4
    Multiple family or public use, 10.4.6.5, 10.4.7
    Type 1, 10.4.2(1), 10.4.3, 10.4.5, 12.3.2(4)
        Definition, 3.3.18.1
    Type 2, 10.4.2(2), 10.4.3, 10.4.6
        Definition, 3.3.18.2
    Venting, 9.3.1.5, 10.4.3 to 10.4.6, 12.3.2(4)

Coal basket, *see* Decorative appliances for installation in vented fireplaces
Code (definition), 3.2.3, A.3.2.3
Code enforcement, Annex J
Combustible gas detector, 8.3.2.2
Combustible gas indicator, 8.3.1.4, A.8.3.1.4

Combustible material
    Clearances to, *see* Clearances
    Definition, 3.3.64.1, A.3.3.64.1
    Food service appliances mounted on/adjacent to, 10.11.3, 10.11.5
    Household cooking appliances mounted on/adjacent to, 10.13.3
    Roof or exterior walls, metal pipe passing through, 12.8.4.5, 12.8.4.6
Combustion (definition), 3.3.19
Combustion air, 9.1.2(1), 9.3, 12.9.2, A.9.3
    Combination indoor and outdoor, 9.3.4, Annex I
    Ducts, 9.3.8
    Engineered installations, 9.3.5
    Floor furnaces, 10.10.4
    Gas fireplaces, vented, 10.7.4
    Indoor, 9.3.2, A.9.3.2.1 to A.9.3.2.3(1)
        Calculation examples, Annex H, Annex I
    Infrared heaters, 10.16.4
    Mechanical supply, 9.3.6
    Outdoor, 9.3.3, A.9.3.3.1(1) to A.9.3.3.2
        Calculation examples, Annex I
    Unit heaters, 10.24.4
    Wall heaters, 10.25.4
Combustion chamber, 8.3.2.1(2), 9.1.18
    Definition, 3.3.20
Combustion products, 10.20.3, 12.9.2
    Definition, 3.3.21
Commercial cooking appliances, *see* Food service appliances
Common vent, *see* Gas vents
Common vent manifolds, *see* Manifolds
Compressed natural gas (CNG) vehicular fuel systems, 10.27
Concealed gas piping
    In buildings, 7.3
    Definition, 3.3.76.1
Condensate (condensation)
    Definition, 3.3.22
    Drain, 12.10
Connections
    Air conditioners, 10.2.3
    Chimney, 12.11.11
    Electrical, 7.14, 9.7.1
    Equipment and appliances, 9.6, A.9.6.1.5, A.9.6.3
    Gas, 5.13.2
        Branch, 7.4.1
        Concealed piping, 7.3.2
        Plastic and metallic piping, 7.1.7.1, 7.1.7.2
    Outdoor open flame decorative appliances, 10.30.2
    Portable and mobile industrial appliances, 9.6.4
Connectors
    Gas hose, to appliances and equipment, 9.6.2
    Vent, *see* Vent connectors
Construction
    Chase, 7.4.2
    Overpressure protection devices, 5.8.4
    Single-wall metal pipe, 12.8.1

Control piping
  Definition, 3.3.76.2
  Overpressure protection devices, 5.8.5
Controls
  Definition, 3.3.23
  Draft, 12.13, 12.16, A.12.13.4
  Duct furnaces, 10.9.5
  Inspections, 11.5
  As obstructions, 12.16
  Safety shutoff devices, *see* Safety shutoff devices
Convenience outlets, *see* Gas convenience outlets
Conversion burners, gas, 10.5
  Definition, 3.3.16.2
Cooking appliances, *see* Food service appliances; Household cooking appliances
Cooling units, *see also* Refrigeration systems
  Boilers, used with, 10.3.10
Copper alloy, 5.5.2.3, 5.5.2.4, 5.5.3.4, 5.5.7.5, 5.5.9.1.3, A.5.5.2.3, A.5.5.3.4, A.7.12.2, B.4.1, G.3.2
  Definition, 3.3.24
Corrosion, protection against, 5.5.2.4, 5.5.2.5, 5.5.3.5, 7.1.3, 7.2.2, 7.3.5.1, 7.3.5.2, 12.6.1.3(3), A.7.1.2.1(B), A.7.1.3, A.7.2.2
Counter appliances, gas, *see* Food service appliances
CSST pipe and fittings, Tables 6.2.1(o) to (s), Tables 6.3.1(h) to (j), 7.2.6.2, 7.2.7, 7.12.2, 7.12.3, Table 8.3.1, 9.6.1(5), A.7.12.2, B.7.2, B.7.4
Cubic feet (cu ft.) of gas (definition), 3.3.25

-D-

Dampers
  Automatically operated vent, 12.15
  Gravity, 10.8.5.3, 10.8.7.2
  Manually operated, 12.14, A.12.14.2
  Obstructions and, 13.1.1
Decorative appliances for installation in vented fireplaces, 9.6.5.1(B), 10.6, Table 12.5.1, A.10.6.2
  Definition, 3.3.4.1
Decorative appliances, outdoor open flame, 10.30
Deep fat fryers, 10.11.2
  Definition, 3.3.4.4.3
Defects, detection of, 5.5.5, 8.1.5
Definitions, Chap. 3
Design pressure
  Allowable pressure drop, 5.3.4, B.7.5, B.7.6
  Definition, 3.3.79.3
  Maximum, 5.4.1, 5.4.4, A.5.4.4(1)
Detectors, leak, 8.1.5
Devices, *see also* Quick-disconnect devices; Safety shutoff devices
  Automatic gas shutoff devices, 10.26.6
    Definition, 3.3.27.1
Dilution air, 9.3.1.1 to 9.3.1.3, 9.3.5, 9.3.7.1
  Definition, 3.3.2.2
Direct gas-fired industrial air heaters
  Air supply, 10.8.5
  Nonrecirculating, 10.8
    Definition, 3.3.56.2
  Prohibited installations, A.10.8.2.3

  Recirculating, A.10.8.2.3
    Definition, 3.3.56.4
  Venting of, 12.7.3(1)(d)
  In well-ventilated spaces, 12.3.4
Direct gas-fired makeup air heaters, venting of, 12.3.2(9)
Direct vent appliances
  Definition, 3.3.4.2
  Venting of, 12.3.5, Table 12.5.1, 12.7.3(1)(d), 12.9.1 Ex., 12.9.2, 12.9.3
Direct vent wall furnaces, *see* Furnaces
Diversity factor, 5.3.2.3 Ex., B.2(5)
  Definition, 3.3.28
Draft controls, 12.13, 12.16, A.12.13.4
Draft hoods, 9.3.1.4
  Central heating boilers and furnaces, Table 10.3.3.2, 10.3.3.6
  Checking the draft, 11.6, A.11.6
  Chimneys, 12.6.1.3 Ex., 12.6.2.3, 12.6.3.1
  Conversion accessories, 13.1.10, 13.2.23
  Definition, 3.3.30
  Duct furnaces, 10.9.2, 10.9.5
  Food service appliances, 10.11.2, 10.12.3
  Pool heaters, 10.19.3
  Unit heaters, 10.24.3(1)
  Vents and venting systems, Table 12.5.1, 12.7.2(4), 12.7.4.1, Table 12.8.4.4, 12.8.4.6, 12.8.5(1), 12.11.2.2, 12.11.2.3, 12.11.3, 12.13, Table 13.1(e), 13.1.2, 13.1.4, 13.1.10, 13.1.11(3), Table 13.2(e), 13.2.12, 13.2.13, 13.2.18, 13.2.22(2), 13.2.23, 13.2.24, A.12.7.4.1, A.12.8.5(1), A.12.11.3, A.12.13.4, Annex F
  Water heaters, 10.26.3
Draft regulators, 12.16 *see also* Barometric draft regulators
  Definition, 3.3.84.1
Draft(s), 9.8.2
  Checking, 11.6, A.11.6
  Definition, 3.3.29
  Mechanical, 12.4.3, 12.7.3(1)(f), 12.7.4.4, 12.9.1, 12.11.4.3
    Definition, 3.3.29.1
  Natural, 9.3.1.2, 12.4.3.4, 12.7.4.1, A.12.7.4.1, G.5.2
    Definition, 3.3.29.2
  Requirements, 12.4.1
Drain, condensation, 12.10
Drip liquids, 4.3.2.1
Drips, 7.6
  Definition, 3.3.31
Dry gas, 7.2.4, 7.6.1
  Definition, 3.3.32
Duct furnaces, *see* Furnaces
Ducts
  Air, 9.3.8, 10.2.4(4), 10.2.6, 10.3.8, 12.4.5, A.10.3.8.3
  Exhaust, 10.4.5, 10.4.6
  Unit heaters, 10.24.5

-E-

Effective ground-fault current path, 7.12.1, 7.12.3
  Definition, 3.3.33
Elbows, 7.5.3, 13.1.3, 13.2.6, 13.2.7
Electrical systems, 7.12 to 7.14, A.7.12.2 to A.7.12.5

Air conditioning equipment, 10.2.8
Gas utilization equipment, 9.7
Ignition and control devices, 9.7.2
Enclosed furnaces, 10.10.12, 10.10.13
Definition, 3.3.45.4
Enforcement of code, 1.5, Annex J
Engineering methods, 4.5, A.4.5(3)
Definition, 3.3.34
Engines, stationary gas, 10.22
Equipment, *see also* Appliances
Added or converted, 9.1.2, 9.1.3
Approval, 9.1.1, A.9.1.1
Bleed lines for diaphragm-type valves, 9.1.18
Combination, 9.1.19
Connections to building piping, 9.6, A.9.6.1.5, A.9.6.3
Definition, 3.3.35
Installation, Chap. 9
Instructions
Installation, 9.1.20, A.9.1.20
Operating, 11.7
Outdoor, protection of, 9.1.21
Placing in operation, 8.2.4, 8.3.3
Equipment shutoff valves, *see* Valves
Equivalency to code, 1.4
Excess air (definition), 3.3.2.3
Excess flow valve (EFV), 5.12
Definition, 3.3.98.3
Exhaust systems, mechanical, *see* Mechanical exhaust systems
Explosion heads (soft heads or rupture discs), 7.11.6(4)
Definition, 3.3.36
Exterior masonry chimneys, *see* Chimneys

-F-

FAN Max, Tables 13.1(a) to (d), 13.1.6, Tables 13.2(a) to (d), 13.2.3(1), 13.2.19.2
Definition, 3.3.37
FAN Min, Tables 13.1(a) to (d), 13.1.1(2), 13.1.6, Tables 13.2(a) to (d), 13.2.1(3), 13.2.3(2), 13.2.19.1
Definition, 3.3.38
Fan-assisted combustion appliances, 9.3.2.2, 13.1.1(2), 13.1.2, 13.1.10, 13.2.3(2), 13.2.23, 13.2.24, Table A.9.3.2.2(b), H.1 to H.3, I.1
Definition, 3.3.4.3
Venting system, 12.7.4.1(2), 12.11.3.1, 12.13.1 Ex., A.12.7.4.1, F.1.2, F.2.2 to F.2.4
Fan-assisted combustion system (definition), 3.3.95.2 *see also* Fan-assisted combustion appliances
Fan-assisted power burners (definition), 3.3.16.5.1
FAN+FAN, Tables 13.2(a) to (d), 13.2.1(3)
Definition, 3.3.39
FAN+NAT, Tables 13.2(a) to (d), Table 13.2(h), Table 13.2(i), 13.2.1(2), 13.2.1(3), 13.2.22(3), 13.2.22(4)
Definition, 3.3.40
Firechecks, *see* Automatic firechecks
Fireplace insert, *see* Decorative appliances for installation in vented fireplaces
Fireplace screens, 10.6.4
Fireplaces, *see also* Decorative appliances for installation in vented fireplaces

Definition, 3.3.41
Gas, *see* Gas fireplaces
Outlets, capping, 7.7.2.2
Shutoff valves, 9.6.5.1(B)
Vent connectors, 12.11.13
Fittings
Appliance and equipment connections, 9.6.1(1), 9.6.1(2)
Concealed piping, 7.3.2
Corrosion, protection against, 7.1.3, 7.3.5.2, A.7.1.3
Gas pipe turns, 7.5
Metallic, 5.5.7, A.5.5.7.1
Overpressure relief device, 5.8.9
Plastic, 5.5.4, 5.5.8, A.5.5.4.2
Used, 5.5.1.2
Workmanship and defects, 5.5.5
Flame arresters, 7.11.2(2)
Definition, 3.3.42
Flammable liquids, handling of, 4.3.2
Flammable vapors, appliances in area of, 9.1.9
Flange gaskets, 5.5.10
Flanges, 5.5.9
Floor furnaces, *see* Furnaces
Floor-mounted equipment
Food service, 10.11, A.10.11.8
Household cooking appliances, 10.13.2, 10.13.3
Floors, piping in, 7.3.5, 12.11.14
Flowmeters, 7.11.2(1)
Flue collars, 12.6.2.3, 12.7.2(4), 13.1.4, 13.1.9
Chimney size, 12.6.3.1(2)
Definition, 3.3.44
Draft control devices, 12.13.3
Draft hood size, 12.13.2.1
Joints, 12.11.6
Multiple, on single appliance, 12.11.3.2
Single-wall metal pipe size, 12.8.5(1), A.12.8.5(1)
Single-wall metal pipe termination, 12.8.3(1)
Vent connector sizing, 12.7.5.3, 12.11.3.6, 13.1.12, 13.1.13, 13.2.24
Vent size, 13.1.2, 13.2.18
Flue gases
Definition, 3.3.49.1
Venting of, 9.1.14
Flues
Appliance
Bleed lines, termination of, 9.1.18(3)
Collars, 13.1.9
Chimney size, 12.6.3.1(2)
Draft control devices, 12.13.3
Draft hood size, 12.13.2.1
Multiple, on single appliance, 12.11.3.2
Single-wall metal pipe size, 12.8.5(1), A.12.8.5(1)
Vent connector sizing, 13.2.24
Vent sizing, 13.1.2, 13.2.24
Definition, 3.3.43.1
Chimney, 10.6.3, 12.6.1.3 Ex., 12.6.3.1(2), 12.6.5, 12.6.5.1, 12.6.8.2, 12.11.4.1, 12.11.4.2, 12.11.11.1, 12.11.13, 13.1.11, 13.2.22, A.12.6.5.3

INDEX

Definition, 3.3.43.2
Food service appliances, *see also* Broilers; Household cooking appliances
　Clearances, *see* Clearances
　Combustible material adjacent to cooking top, 10.11.5
　Connectors, 9.6.1.3
　Counter appliances, 10.12, 12.3.2(7)
　　Definition, 3.3.4.4.2
　Deep fat fryers, 10.11.2
　　Definition, 3.3.4.4.3
　Floor-mounted, 10.11, A.10.11.8
　Kettle, 10.11.2
　　Definition, 3.3.4.4.4
　Oven, baking and roasting, 10.11.2
　　Definition, 3.3.4.4.1
　Range, 12.3.2(1)
　Steam cooker, 10.11.2
　　Definition, 3.3.4.4.5
　Steam generator, 10.11.2
　　Definition, 3.3.4.4.6
　Venting, 12.3.2(1) to (3), 12.3.2(7)
Forced-air furnaces, *see* Furnaces
Forced-draft burners, *see* Burners
Foundations, piping through, 7.1.5
Freezing, protection against, 7.1.4, A.7.1.4
Fuel cell power plants, 10.29
Furnace plenums, 10.2.4(3), 10.2.4(4), 10.2.6, 10.3.3.7, 10.3.8, 12.4.5, A.10.3.8.3
　Definition, 3.3.46
Furnaces
　Central, 10.3, A.10.3.7, A.10.3.8.3
　　Definition, 3.3.45.1
　Clearances, *see* Clearances
　Direct vent, 10.25.2.3, Table G.6
　　Definition, 3.3.45.2
　Duct, 10.9
　　In commercial garages and aircraft hangars, 10.9.8
　　Definition, 3.3.45.3
　　Use with refrigeration systems, 10.9.7, A.10.9.7.3
　Enclosed, 10.10.12, 10.10.13
　　Definition, 3.3.45.4
　Floor, 10.10
　　Definition, 3.3.45.5
　　First floor installation, 10.10.13
　　Upper floor installation, 10.10.12
　Forced-air, Table 10.3.3.2, G.6.1
　　With cooling unit, 10.3.9(1)
　　Definition, 3.3.45.6
　Refrigeration coils and, 10.3.9
　Vented wall, 10.25.2.2, 10.25.2.3, Table 12.5.1, Table G.6, G.6.5
　　Definition, 3.3.45.7
　Wall, 10.25, Table G.6
　　Direct vent, *see* subhead: Direct vent
　　Vented, *see* subhead: Vented wall

-G-

Garages
　Commercial
　　Appliances in, 9.1.11
　　Duct furnaces in, 10.9.8
　　Heaters in, 10.16.5, 10.24.6
　Repair
　　Appliances in, 9.1.11.2
　　Definition, 3.3.47.1
　Residential
　　Appliances in, 9.1.10
　　Definition, 3.3.47.2
Gas appliance pressure regulators, 5.14, 9.1.17
　Definition, 3.3.84.2
　Illuminating appliances, 10.14.5
Gas appliances, *see* Appliances
Gas convenience outlets, 7.7.1.6, 9.6.7
　Definition, 3.3.48
Gas fireplaces, *see also* Decorative appliances for installation in vented fireplaces
　Direct vent, 10.7.2 Ex., 10.7.3(3), Table A.5.3.2.1
　　Definition, 3.3.41.1.1
　Vented, 10.7, A.10.7.2
　　Definition, 3.3.41.1.2
Gas log, *see* Decorative appliances for installation in vented fireplaces
Gas range, 12.3.2(1)
Gas reliefs, 10.8.6
Gas supplier regulations, 1.1.2
Gas utilization equipment, *see* Equipment
Gas vents, 12.7, A.12.7.4.1
　Common, 12.7.5, 12.11.3.5, 12.11.3.6, 13.2.4 to 13.2.10, A.12.7.5.2, Fig. F.1(k), Fig. F.1(l), F.2
　　Definition, 3.3.53.1
　Connectors, *see* Vent connectors
　Definition, 3.3.53, A.3.3.53
　Integral, appliances with, 12.3.6
　Integral, equipment with, Table 12.5.1, 12.7.3(1)(e)
　Multistory design, Fig. F.1(m), Fig. F.1(n)
　Serving equipment on more than one floor, 12.7.5, A.12.7.5.2
　Spaces surrounding, 12.6.8
　Special-type, 12.5.4, 12.6.8
　　Definition, 3.3.53.2
　Type B, Table 12.5.1, 12.6.1.3 Ex., 12.6.3.1, 12.7.1, 12.7.3(2), 12.7.4.1, 12.7.4.2, 12.7.5.3, Table 12.8.4.4, 12.8.4.6(1), 12.11.2.2, 12.11.2.3(1)(a), 12.11.9.2, Table 13.1(a), Table 13.1(b), Table 13.1(e), 13.1.7, 13.1.11, Tables 13.2(a) to (c), Tables 13.2(e) to (i), 13.2.20, 13.2.22, A.12.7.4.1, A.13.1.7, A.13.2.20, Annex F
　　Definition, 3.3.53.3
　Type B-W, Table 12.5.1, 12.7.1, 12.7.2(2), 12.7.3(3)
　　Definition, 3.3.53.4
　Type L, Table 12.5.1, 12.7.3(2), 12.7.4.2, Table 12.8.4.4, 12.11.2.2, 12.11.2.3(1)(a)
　　Definition, 3.3.53.5
　Wall heaters, 10.25.2.2, 10.25.2.3
Gas-fired air conditioners, 10.2.1, A.10.2.7
　Definition, 3.3.50

Gas-fired heat pumps, 10.2.1, A.10.2.7
   Definition, 3.3.51
Gas-mixing machines, 7.10, 7.11.1(1), 7.11.3
   Definition, 3.3.52
   Installation, 7.11.5, A.7.11.5.1, A.7.11.5.4
Gas–air mixtures
   Flammable, 7.11, A.7.11.4 to A.7.11.6(1)
      Operating pressure, maximum, 5.4.2
   Outside the flammable range, 7.10
Gases
   Definition, 3.3.49
   Dry, *see* Dry gas
   Flue
      Definition, 3.3.49.1
      Venting of, 9.1.14
   LP-Gas systems, *see* LP-Gas systems
   Maximum demand, 5.3.1, 5.3.2, A.5.3.1, A.5.3.2
   Purged, discharge of, 8.3.1.3
   Used in appliances, 9.1.3
   Utility
      Definition, 3.3.49.2
      Fixed orifices, flow of gas through, Annex E
   Vent (definition), 3.3.49.3
Gaskets, flange, 5.5.10
Governor, zero, 7.11.4
   Definition, 3.3.104
Gravity, *see* Specific gravity
Gravity furnaces, *see* Furnaces
Grilles, 9.3.7, 10.25.2.4
Grounding electrode, 7.12.2, 7.12.4, A.7.12.2
   Definition, 3.3.55
Grounding, electrical, 7.12, A.7.12.2 to A.7.12.5

-H-

Hangars, *see* Aircraft hangars
Hangers, pipe, 7.2.6
Health care occupancy, 10.21.3(2)
   Definition, 3.3.70.1
Heat pumps, *see* Gas-fired heat pumps
Heat reclaimers, 12.16
Heaters, *see also* Direct gas-fired industrial air heaters; Infrared heaters; Room heaters; Water heaters
   In aircraft hangars, 9.1.12, 10.16.5, 10.24.6
   In commercial garages, 10.16.5, 10.24.6
   Direct gas-fired makeup air, 12.3.2(9)
   Pool, 10.19
      Definition, 3.3.56.3
   Unit, 10.24
      Definition, 3.3.56.5
Heating value (total) (definition), 3.3.57
High altitude, *see* Altitude, high
Hoods
   Draft, *see* Draft hoods
   Ventilating, *see* Ventilating hoods
Hoop stress, 8.1.4.2
   Definition, 3.3.94.1

Hot plates
   Commercial counter appliances, 10.12
      Definition, 3.3.4.4.2
   Domestic
      Definition, 3.3.58.1
      Venting, 12.3.2(3)
Household cooking appliances, 10.13, A.10.13.3.1
   Broilers
      Definition, 3.3.4.6.1
      Protection above, 10.17.2
   Built-in units, 10.13.2, 12.3.2(2), Table A.5.3.2.1
      Definition, 3.3.4.6.2
   Definition, 3.3.4.6
   Floor-mounted, 10.13.2, 10.13.3
   Outdoor, 10.18
      Definition, 3.3.4.9
Hybrid pressure system
   Definition, 3.3.95.3
   Pipe sizing, 6.1.3, B.4.3, B.7.2

-I-

Identification
   Meters, 5.6.5
   Pressure regulators, 5.7.6
Ignition
   Accidental, prevention of, 4.3
   Automatic, 11.4
      Definition, 3.3.59.1
   Electrical, 9.7.2
   Sources, 4.3.1
      Definition, 3.3.59.2
Illuminating appliances, 10.14
Incinerators
   Commercial-industrial, 10.15, 12.3.7
   Venting, 12.3.7, Table 12.5.1
Industrial air heaters, *see* Direct gas-fired industrial air heaters
Infrared heaters, 10.16
   Definition, 3.3.56.1
   Outdoor, 10.31
   Suspended low-intensity tube, 9.6.1.5, A.9.6.1.5
Injection- (Bunsen-type) burners, *see* Burners
Inspections
   Chimneys, 12.6.4
   Draft, 11.6, A.11.6
   Existing installation, Annex G
   Gas piping, 8.1, A.8.1.1 to A.8.1.4.3
   Ignition, automatic, 11.4
   Protective devices, 11.5
   Safety shutoff devices, 11.3
   Vent connectors, 12.11.12
Installations
   Appliances, equipment, and accessories, Chap. 9
   Chimneys, 12.6.1, 12.6.2, A.12.6.1.3, A.12.6.2.1
   Draft hoods and draft controls, 12.7.2(4), 12.13.1 to 12.3.3
   Electrical, 9.7
   Gas piping, 5.1.1, Chap. 7
   Overpressure protection devices, 5.8.4

Pressure relieving/pressure limiting devices, 5.8.4
Roofs, appliances on, 9.4.2
Single-wall metal pipe for vents, 12.8.4, A.12.8.4.1
Specific appliances, Chap. 10

Instructions
Appliance and equipment installation, 9.1.20, A.9.1.20
Manufacturers, 1.1.2
Operating, 11.7

Insulating millboard, 10.11.3.2(2), 10.13.3.1(1)
Definition, 3.3.60

Insulation shield, 12.6.9
Interruption of service, 4.2
Interruption of work, 4.2.2

-J-

Joining methods, 5.5, A.5.5
Joint compounds, thread, see Thread joint compounds
Joints
Flared, 5.5.7.4
Metallic, 5.5.7, A.5.5.7.1
Plastic, 5.5.8, 7.5.2(2), 12.5.3
Tubing, 5.5.7.2, 5.5.7.3
Vent connectors, 12.11.6, 12.11.7

-K-

Kettle, gas-fired, 10.11.2
Definition, 3.3.4.4.4

-L-

Labeled (definition), 3.2.4
Laboratories, shutoff valve for, 7.8.3.3
Leak check, 8.2, A.8.2.3, Annex C
Leak detectors, 8.1.5
Leakage
Check, Annex C
Emergency procedure for, Annex D
Pressure test, 8.1.5.1

Lightning protection, 7.12.5, A.7.12.5
Limit controls, 11.5 see also Temperature limit controls/devices
Definition, 3.3.23.1

Line pressure regulators, 5.7.1, 5.7.2, 5.8.2.1, 5.8.2.5, 5.8.3.1, 5.8.3.2, 6.1.3, Table 6.3.1(c), Table 6.3.1(g), Table 6.3.1(i), Table 6.3.1(l), C.3
Bypass piping, 5.14
Definition, 3.3.84.3
Identification, 5.7.6
Venting, 5.14

Listed (definition), 3.2.5, A.3.2.5
Longest length pipe sizing method, 6.1.1, A.6.1.1, B.4.1, B.7.1
Louvers, 9.3.7, 10.8.5.3, 10.8.7.2
LP-Gas systems, 9.1.4
Fixed orifices, flow of gas through, Table E.1.1(b)
High-pressure gas formula, Table 6.4.2
Leakage check, C.3(2)
Operating pressure, maximum, 5.4.3, 5.4.5
Pipe sizing tables, 6.3, B.3.3
Plastic pipe, use of, 5.5.8(4)

-M-

Main burners
Air supply, 9.3.6.2
Backdraft or fuel spillage, 12.6.5.3, A.12.6.5.3
Dampers or louvers, open, 9.3.7.3, 10.8.5.3, 10.8.7.2, 12.4.4.1
Definition, 3.3.16.4
Draft system operation and, 11.6, 12.4.3.5, A.11.6

Make-up air, 9.3.1.5, 10.4.4
Direct gas-fired makeup air heaters, 12.3.2(9)

Manifolds
Common vent, 9.1.18(5), 12.11.3.5, 12.11.3.6, 13.2.4, Fig. F.1(k)
Definition, 3.3.62.1
Gas, 5.14(7), 9.6.5.3, 12.11.3.2, G.4.1
Definition, 3.3.62.2

Manual reset valves, see Valves, Manual reset
Manufactured homes
Appliances for, 10.28
Definition, 3.3.63

Manufacturer's instructions, 1.1.2
Marking
Gas vents, 12.7.7
Single-wall metallic pipe, 12.8.7

Masonry chimneys, see Chimneys
Material, see Combustible material; Noncombustible material
Maximum working pressure, 8.1.4.2
Definition, 3.3.79.4

Mechanical draft, see Draft(s)
Mechanical exhaust systems, 9.3.1.5, 12.3.2(5), 12.4.4, 12.7.3(1)(f), A.12.4.4
Clothes dryers, 10.4.3, 10.4.5, 10.4.6
Definition, 3.3.95.4

Mechanical venting systems, see Venting systems
Metallic pipe, 5.5.2, A.5.5.2.3 see also Tubing
Appliance and equipment connections, 9.6.1(1), 9.6.1(2)
Connection to plastic piping, 7.1.7.2
Corrosion, protection against, 5.5.2.4, 5.5.2.5, 5.5.3.5, 7.1.3, 7.2.2, 7.3.5.1, 7.3.5.2, A.7.1.2.1(B), A.7.1.3, A.7.2.2
Joints and fittings, 5.5.7, A.5.5.7.1
Low pressure gas pipe sizing tables, B.3.2
Single-wall, for venting, 12.7.2(4), 12.8, Table 12.8.4.4, 12.11.1, 12.11.2.2 Ex., Table 13.1(e), Table 13.2(e), 13.2.25, A.12.8.2 to A.12.8.5(1)
Sizing, Tables 6.2.1(a) to (s), Tables 6.3.1(a) to (j), Table B.6(a), Table B.6(b)
Threads, 5.5.2.4, 5.5.6, A.5.5.6.4
Turns, 7.5.1

Meters, 5.6, A.5.6
Definition, 3.3.65
Leakage check, C.2

Mixing blowers, 7.11.3, 7.11.4, 7.11.5.3, A.7.11.4
Definition, 3.3.66

Multistory installations, 13.2.14 to 13.2.17

-N-

NA, 13.1.1(2), 13.2.1(3)
Definition, 3.3.67

NAT Max, Tables 13.1(a) to (d), 13.1.1(1), 13.1.6, Tables 13.2(a) to (d), 13.2.1(1), 13.2.3(1), 13.2.19.2

Definition, 3.3.68
NAT+NAT, Tables 13.2(a) to (d), Table 13.2(f), Table 13.2(g), 13.2.1(2), 13.2.22(3), 13.2.22(4)
  Definition, 3.3.69
Natural draft, *see* Draft(s)
Natural draft venting systems, *see* Venting systems
Noncombustible material, 4.4, A.4.4
  Definition, 3.3.64.2
  Food service appliances mounted on/adjacent to, 10.11.4
  Thimbles, 12.8.4.5
Nondisplaceable valve member, 9.6.5, 9.6.6.2
  Definition, 3.3.99.1
Notification of interrupted service, 4.2.1

-O-

Occupancy
  Health care, 10.21.3(2)
    Definition, 3.3.70.1
  Residential board and care, 10.21.3(1)
    Definition, 3.3.70.2
Offset, vent, *see* Vent offset
Open flame decorative appliances, outdoor, 10.30
Openings, *see also* Relief openings
  Chimneys, 12.6.5.2
  Combination indoor and outdoor combustion air, 9.3.4, Annex I
  Indoor combustion air, 9.3.2.3, A.9.3.2.3(1)
  Outdoor combustion air, 9.3.3, A.9.3.3.1(1) to A.9.3.3.2
  Pipe, size of, 5.8.9
Operation of appliances, procedures, Chap. 11
Orifices
  Definition, 3.3.71
  Fixed, flow of gas through, Annex E
Outdoor cooking appliances, 10.18
  Definition, 3.3.4.9
Outdoor infrared heaters, 10.31
Outdoor open flame decorative appliances, 10.30
Outlets
  Convenience, *see* Gas convenience outlets
  Piping, 7.7
Outside, installation of piping, 7.2.1 *see also* Underground piping
Ovens, baking and roasting, 10.11.2
  Definition, 3.3.4.4.1
Overpressure protection devices, 5.8
  Piping in vertical chases, 7.4.1
  Setting, 5.8.6
  Unauthorized operation, 5.8.7
Oxygen
  As test medium, 8.1.2
  Use under pressure, 9.1.5

-P-

Parking structures
  Appliances in, 9.1.11.1
  Basement or underground, 9.1.11.1
    Definition, 3.3.73.1
  Definition, 3.3.73
  Enclosed, 9.1.11.1

Definition, 3.3.73.2
Partitions
  Piping in, 7.3.3
  Tubing in, 7.3.4
Pilot, 9.1.18, 9.2.1, 9.7.3, 11.3, G.5.1, G.6.6(5)
  Definition, 3.3.74
Pipe threads, metallic, 5.5.2.4, 5.5.6, A.5.5.6.4 *See also* Thread joint compounds
Pipes and piping, *see also* Piping systems, gas
  Aboveground, 7.2, A.7.2.5
  Bends, 7.5
  Branch, *see* Branch lines
  Buildings, in, *see* Buildings, Piping in
  Clearances, underground piping, 7.1.1
  Concealed
    In buildings, 7.3
    Definition, 3.3.76.1
  Connections, *see* Connections
  Control piping
    Definition, 3.3.76.2
    Overpressure protection devices, 5.8.5
  Defects, 5.5.5, 8.1.5
  Definition, 3.3.75, 3.3.76
  Drips, 7.6
  Equivalent length (definition), 3.3.75.1
  Floors, in, 7.3.5
  Hangers and anchors, 7.2.6
  Identification, multiple meter installations, 5.6.5
  Independent, 10.2.2
  Inspection, testing, and purging, Chap. 8
  Installation, 5.1.1, Chap. 7, 9.6.9
  Joining methods, 5.5, A.5.5
  Materials, 5.5, A.5.5
  Metallic, *see* Metallic pipe
  Outlets, 7.7
  Partitions, in, 7.3.3, 7.3.4
  Plastic, *see* Plastic pipe
  Prohibited devices in, 7.9
  Prohibited locations, 7.2.5, A.7.2.5
  Protection, underground piping, 7.1.2
  Protective coating, 5.5.2.5, 5.5.3.5, 7.2.2, A.7.2.2
  Sediment traps, 7.6.3, 9.6.8
  Sizing and capacities of, 5.3.1, 5.3.3, Chap. 6, A.5.3.1, A.5.3.3, Annex B
    Equations, 6.4, A.6.4.1, A.6.4.2, B.5, B.6
    Methods, 6.1, A.6.1, B.4, B.7.1
    Modification to existing system, B.7.4
    Overpressure relief devices, 5.8.9
    Sizing charts, use of, B.7
  Sloped, 7.2.4
  Strain on, 9.1.16
  Supports, *see* Supports, Pipes and piping
  Turns, 7.5
  Underground, 7.1, A.7.1.3, A.7.1.4
  Used materials, 5.5.1.2
  Valves, 7.8
  In vertical chases, 7.4, A.7.4.3

Workmanship, 5.5.5
Piping systems, gas, Chap. 5
   Addition to existing, 5.1.2
   Bonding and grounding, 7.12, A.7.12.2 to A.7.12.5
   Definition, 3.3.95.6
   Design pressure
      Allowable pressure drop, 5.3.4, B.7.5, B.7.6
      Maximum, 5.4.1, 5.4.4, A.5.4.4(1)
   Flexibility, 5.13
   Gas–air mixtures
      Flammable, 7.11, A.7.11.4 to A.7.11.6(1)
      Outside the flammable range, 7.10
   Interconnections between, 5.2
   Leakage, *see also* Leak check
      Emergency procedure for, Annex D
      Pressure test, 8.1.5.1
   Local conditions, consideration of, 5.13.2
   Materials and joining methods, 5.5, A.5.5
   Operating pressure limitations, 5.4, A.5.4.4(1)
   Placing in operation, purging for, 8.3.1.2, A.8.3.1.2
   Plan, 5.1
   Pressure drop, allowable, 5.3.4, B.7.5, B.7.6
   Pressure testing and inspection, 8.1, A.8.1.1 to A.8.1.4.3
   Purging, 8.3, A.8.3 to A.8.3.2.1
   Removal from service, purging for, 8.3.1.1
   Sizing of, 5.3, 6.2, 6.3, A.5.3.1 to A.5.3.3, Annex B
   Thermal expansion, 5.13
Plastic pipe, 5.5.4, 5.5.8, A.5.5.4.2
   Within chimney flue, 12.6.8
   Connection of, 7.1.7.1, 7.1.7.2
   Sizing, Tables 6.2.1(t) to (x), Tables 6.3.1(k) to (m)
   Tracer wire to locate, 7.1.7.3
   Turns, 7.5.2
   Underground, 7.1.7
   As vent material, 12.5.2, 12.5.3
Plenums (definition), 3.3.77 *see also* Furnace plenums
Point of delivery
   Definition, 3.3.78
Pool heaters, 10.19
   Definition, 3.3.56.3
Power burners, *see* Burners
Pressure
   Atmospheric, A.12.1
      Definition, 3.3.79.1
   Back
      Definition, 3.3.79.2
      Protection, 5.9
   Definition, 3.3.79
   Design, *see* Design pressure
   High pressure gas pipe sizing
      Formula, 6.4.2, A.6.4.2, B.5(1)
      Tables, B.3.5
   Hybrid pressure pipe sizing method, 6.1.3
   Low pressure gas pipe sizing
      Formula for, 6.4.1, A.6.4.1, B.5(2)
      Tables, B.3.2
   Low pressure protection, 5.10, A.5.10

   Maximum working, 8.1.4.2
      Definition, 3.3.79.4
   Operating, limitations on, 5.4, A.5.4.4(1)
   Supply, 5.3.1, 5.3.4, 5.7.1, 5.8.2, 9.1.17
      Definition, 3.3.79.5
Pressure drop
   Allowable, 5.3.4, B.7.5, B.7.6
   Definition, 3.3.80
   Drop per 100 ft pipe sizing method, B.4.4
   Temperature change, calculating drop due to, B.7.5
Pressure limiting devices, 10.3.5, 10.19.4, 10.26.4
   Definition, 3.3.27.2
Pressure regulators, *see* Overpressure protection devices;
   Regulators
Pressure relief devices, 10.3.7, 10.26.6, 11.5, A.10.3.7 *see also*
   Overpressure protection devices
Pressure relief valves, *see* Relief valves
Pressure tests, 8.1, A.8.1.1 to A.8.1.4.3
Primary air, 11.2, A.11.2
   Definition, 3.3.2.4
Process air, 9.1.7
Protection, *see also* Corrosion, protection against; Overpressure
   protection devices
   Appliances and equipment
      Floor furnaces, 10.10.11
      From fumes or gases, 9.1.6, A.9.1.6
      Open-top broiler units, 10.17.2
      Outdoor appliances, 9.1.21
      Physical, 9.1.13
      Pool heaters, 10.19.2
   Back pressure, 5.9
   Control piping, 5.8.5
   Equipment, 9.1.21
   Gas pressure regulators, 5.7.4
   Low-pressure, 5.10, A.5.10
   Meters, gas, 5.6.4
   Piping, underground, 7.1.2, 7.1.3, A.7.1.3
Protective devices, 11.5
Purge/purging, 8.3, 10.8.8, A.8.3 to A.8.3.2.1
   Definition, 3.3.81

-Q-

Qualified agency, 4.1
   Definition, 3.3.82
Quick-disconnect devices, 7.7.1.6, 7.7.2.1 Ex. 2, 9.6.6
   Definition, 3.3.27.3

-R-

Radiant appliances, *see* Decorative appliances for installation in
   vented fireplaces
Ranges, 12.3.2(1)
   Household, separation requirements, Fig. A.10.13.3.1
References, Chap. 2, Annex K
Refrigeration systems
   Boilers used with, 10.3.10
   Coils, 10.2.7, 10.3.9, A.10.2.7
   Duct furnaces used with, 10.9.7, A.10.9.7.3
Refrigerators (using gas fuel), 10.20

Definition, 3.3.83
Venting, 12.3.2(6)
Regulations, gas supplier, 1.1.2
Regulator vents, 5.5.4.2
Definition, 3.3.84.6
Regulators
Draft, *see* Draft regulators
Equipment, 5.7.1
Monitoring, 5.8.3.1(2)
Definition, 3.3.84.4, A.3.3.84.4
Pressure, 1.1.1.1(A), 5.7, 7.4.1, A.1.1.1.1(A), A.5.7 *see also* Gas appliance pressure regulators; Line pressure regulators; Overpressure protection devices
Definition, 3.3.84.5
Gas shutoff valves at, 7.8.1
Pressure testing, 8.1.1.6
Protection of, 5.7.4
Series, 5.8.3.1(3)
Definition, 3.3.84.7
Service, 1.1.1.1(A), 5.2.1, 5.2.2.1, Table 6.3.1(c), Table 6.3.1(g), Table 6.3.1(i), Table 6.3.1(l), 7.8.2, A.1.1.1.1(A)
Definition, 3.3.84.8
Relief openings
Definition, 3.3.85
Industrial air heaters, 10.8.7
Relief valves
Definition, 3.3.98.5
Pressure relief
Definition, 3.3.98.5.1
For steam and hot water boilers, 10.3.7, A.10.3.7
Temperature relief, 10.26.6
Definition, 3.3.98.5.2
Vacuum relief, 10.26.6
Definition, 3.3.98.5.3
Repairs
Gas shutoff prior to, 4.2.2
Pressure testing, after, 8.1.1.3
Residential board and care occupancy, 10.21.3(1)
Definition, 3.3.70.2
Retroactivity of code, 1.3
Risers
Anodeless, 5.5.4.3
Definition, 3.3.3
Corrosion, protection against, 7.3.5.2
Roofs
Appliances on, 9.4
Piping on, 7.2.6.4
Room heaters, 10.21, A.10.21.2
Institutions, installations in, 10.21.3
Prohibited installations, 10.21.2, A.10.21.2
Unvented, 10.21.1.2, 10.21.2, 12.3.2(8), A.10.21.2
Definition, 3.3.56.6
Wall, 10.21.4

-S-

Safety blowouts (backfire preventers), 7.11.1(4), 7.11.6, A.7.11.6(1)
Definition, 3.3.86
Safety inspection, existing appliance installation, Annex G
Safety shutoff devices, 11.3 *see also* Automatic gas shutoff devices; Valves
Definition, 3.3.27.4
Unlisted LP-gas equipment used indoors, 9.1.4
Scope of code, 1.1, A.1.1.1.1(A)
Screens, 9.3.7
Seepage pan, 10.10.10
Separate users, interconnections between, 5.2.1
Service head adapters, 5.5.4.3(2)
Definition, 3.3.87
Service meter assembly, 1.1.1.1(A), A.1.1.1.1(A)
Definition, 3.3.88
Service regulators, *see* Regulators
Service shutoff valves, *see* Valves
Shall (definition), 3.2.6
Shutoff procedure, 4.2.1 *see also* Safety shutoff devices; Valves
Shutoff valves, *see* Valves
Sources of ignition, 4.3.1
Definition, 3.3.59.2
Spaces
Surrounding chimney lining or vent, 12.6.8
Well-ventilated, 12.3.4
Specific gravity
Definition, 3.3.91
Sizing of gas pipe and, B.3.4
Standby fuels, interconnections for, 5.2.2
Steam cooker, 10.11.2
Definition, 3.3.4.4.5
Steam generator, 10.11.2
Definition, 3.3.4.4.6
Steam safety valves, 10.3.7, A.10.3.7
Stress
Definition, 3.3.94
Hoop, 8.1.4.2
Definition, 3.3.94.1
Supports
Chimneys, 12.6.6
Equipment, 9.1.8
Floor furnaces, 10.10.7
Gas vents, 12.7.6
Heaters
Infrared, 10.16.2
Unit, 10.24.2
Meters, gas, 5.6.3
Pipes and piping, 5.13.2, 7.2.1, 7.2.6, 12.8.6
Vent connectors, 12.11.10
Suspended low-intensity infrared tube heaters, 9.6.1.5, A.9.6.1.5
Suspended-type unit heaters, 10.24.3
Switches, electrical supply line, 10.2.8
Systems, *see also* Central premix system; Hybrid pressure system; Mechanical exhaust systems; Piping systems, gas; Venting systems
Fan-assisted combustion system (definition), 3.3.95.2 *see also* Fan-assisted combustion appliances

-T-

Temperature change, calculating pressure drop due to, B.7.5
Temperature limit controls/devices, 10.3.5

Floor furnaces, 10.10.3
Pool heaters, 10.19.4
Water heaters, 10.26.5
Temperature relief valves, 10.26.6
Definition, 3.3.98.5.2
Tensile strength
Definition, 3.3.96
Plastic piping material, 5.5.8(1)
Termination, venting systems, *see* Venting systems
Testing, piping system
Defects, pressure test for, 8.1.5.1
Leakage
Pressure test for detection, 8.1.5.1
System leak check, 8.2, A.8.2.3
Pressure, 8.1, A.8.1.1 to A.8.1.4.3
Thermostats, room temperature, 9.8
Thimbles, 12.8.4.5, 12.8.4.6, 12.11.11.2
Thread joint compounds, 5.5.6.4, A.5.5.6.4
Toilets, gas-fired, 10.23, Table 12.5.1
Traps, sediment, 7.6.3, 9.6.8
Trenches, 7.1.2.2
Tubing
Appliances and equipment connections, 9.6.1(2)
Bonding and grounding, 7.12, A.7.12.2 to A.7.12.5
Corrosion protection, 7.1.3, A.7.1.3
Definition, 3.3.97
Low pressure gas pipe sizing tables, B.3.2
Metallic, 5.5.3, 5.5.7.2, 5.5.7.3, A.5.5.3.4, B.7.3
Partitions, in, 7.3.4
Plastic, 5.5.4, 5.5.8, A.5.5.4.2
Sizing and capacities of, Tables 6.2.1(i) to (s), Table 6.2.1(w), Table 6.2.1(x), Tables 6.3.1(e) to (j), Table 6.3.1(m), B.6, B.7.3
Workmanship and defects, 5.5.5
Type B gas vents, *see* Gas vents
Type B-W gas vents, *see* Gas vents
Type L vents, *see* Gas vents

-U-

Underground piping, 7.1, A.7.1.3, A.7.1.4
Unit broilers, *see* Broilers
Unit heaters, 10.24
Definition, 3.3.56.5
Utility gases
Definition, 3.3.49.2
Fixed orifices, flow of gas through, Annex E

-V-

Vacuum relief valves, 10.26.6
Definition, 3.3.98.5.3
Valve members
Definition, 3.3.99
Nondisplaceable, 9.6.5, 9.6.6.2
Definition, 3.3.99.1
Valves
Accessibility of, 7.8.1, 7.8.3.1, 7.8.3.3
Appliance shutoff, 5.11, 7.7.2.2, 9.6.5, 12.6.5.2

Definition, 3.3.98.1
Gas-mixing machines, 7.11.5.4, A.7.11.5.4
Manual, 7.8, 9.6.5
Automatic, 5.12, 9.7.3
Definition, 3.3.98.2
Bypass
Gas line pressure regulators, 5.14(7)
Pool heaters, 10.19.5
Controlling multiple systems, 7.8.3
Definition, 3.3.98
Diaphragm type, bleed lines for, 9.1.18
Excess flow valve (EFV), 5.12
Definition, 3.3.98.3
Manual main gas control, 7.8.2
Manual reset, 7.11.5.4, A.7.11.5.4
Definition, 3.3.98.4
Mixing blowers, 7.11.4, A.7.11.4
Pressure testing, 8.1.1.6
Relief, *see* Relief valves
Service shutoff, 5.11
Definition, 3.3.98.6
Emergency, 7.8.3.2
Laboratories, 7.8.3.3
Manual, 7.8
For multiple systems, 7.8.3
Tubing systems, 7.3.6
Steam safety, 10.3.7, A.10.3.7
System shutoff, 7.8.1.1, 7.8.1.2, 7.8.4, A.7.8.4
Definition, 3.3.98.7
Used, 5.5.1.2
Vapors, flammable, appliances in area of, 9.1.9
Vehicular fuel systems, compressed natural gas, 10.27
Vent connectors, 12.11, 12.12, A.12.11.3, A.12.11.9
Chimneys, *see* Chimneys
Clearance, 12.11.5
Dampers, 12.14, A.12.14.2
Definition, 3.3.100
Fireplaces, 12.11.13
Inspection, 12.11.12
Joints, 12.11.6, 12.11.7
Length, 12.11.9, A.12.11.9
Location, 12.11.11
Materials, 12.11.2
Maximum length, 13.2.2, 13.2.3
Mechanical draft systems, 12.4.3.4
Obstructions, 12.16
Routing, 13.2.3
Size of, 12.11.3, 13.1.12, 13.1.13, 13.2.4, 13.2.8, A.12.11.3
Slope, 12.11.8
Support, 12.11.10
Through ceilings, floors, or walls, 12.11.14
Toilets, gas-fired, 10.23.3
Two or more appliances, 12.11.3.3 to 12.11.3.6, 12.11.4
Vent dampers, automatic, *see* Automatic vent dampers
Vent gases (definition), 3.3.49.3
Vent offset, 12.7.4.2, 13.1.3, 13.1.7, 13.2.5, 13.2.17, 13.2.20, A.13.2.20, Fig. E.1(1)

Definition, 3.3.101
Vent(s)
  Gas, *see* Gas vents
  Heater, 10.8.6
  Obstructions, 12.16, 13.1.1
  Overpressure protection devices, 5.8.8
  Regulator, 5.5.4.2
  Sizes, 12.7.4, A.12.7.4.1
    Appliance categorized vent diameter/area, *see* Appliance categorized vent diameter/area
    Multiple appliance vents, 13.2, A.13.2.20
    Single appliance vents, 13.1, A.13.1.7
  Toilets, gas-fired, 10.23.3
Vented appliances, Chap. 12
  Category I, Table 12.5.1, 12.6.1.3 Ex., 12.6.3.1, 12.7.4.1, 12.11, Chap. 13, A.12.7.4.1, A.12.11.3, A.12.11.9, Annex F
    Definition, 3.3.4.10.1, A.3.3.4.10.1
  Category II, Table 12.5.1, 12.7.4.3, 12.10.1, 12.12
    Definition, 3.3.4.10.2
  Category III, Table 12.5.1, 12.7.4.3, 12.12
    Definition, 3.3.4.10.3
  Category IV, Table 12.5.1, 12.7.4.3, 12.9.3, 12.10.1, 12.12
    Definition, 3.3.4.10.4
Vented wall furnaces, *see* Furnaces
Ventilating hoods, 10.17.2, 12.3.3, 12.4.4, 12.7.3(1)(g), A.12.3.3, A.12.4.4
Ventilation
  Air for, 9.3, A.9.3, Annex I
  Chase, 7.4.3, A.7.4.3
  Equipment, 9.1.2(1)
  Food service appliances, 10.11.8, A.10.11.8
  Industrial air heaters, 10.8.3.3, 10.8.5
  Infrared heaters, 10.16.4
  Open-top broiler units, 10.17.2, 10.17.3
Venting, Chap. 12
  Definition, 3.3.102
  Equipment not requiring venting, 12.3.2
  Flue gases, 9.1.14
  Pressure regulators, 5.7.5, 7.4.1
Venting systems
  Appliances, 9.1.14
  Connection to, *see* Vent connectors
  Definition, 3.3.95.7, A.3.3.95.7
  Design and construction, 12.4, A.12.4.4
  Equipment, 9.1.2(3)
  Mechanical draft, 12.4.3, 12.6.3.1(4), 12.7.4.4
    Forced, 12.4.3.2, 12.4.3.3, 12.7.3(7), 12.9.1, 12.13.1 Ex.
    Forced (definition), 3.3.95.7.1
    Termination, 12.7.3(1)(f), 12.9.1
    Vent connectors, 12.4.3.4, 12.11.4.3, 12.11.8 Ex.
  Natural draft
    Definition, 3.3.95.5
    Sizing of, 12.7.4.1, A.12.7.4.1
    Testing, G.5.2
  Pool heaters, 10.19.6
  Refrigerators, 10.20.3
  Sizing of
    Appliances equipped with draft hoods or listed for use with Type B vent, Annex F
    Category I appliances, 12.6.3.1, 12.7.4.1, 12.7.4.2, Chap. 13, A.12.7.4.1, Annex F
    Category II, III, and IV appliances, 12.7.4.3
    Chimney venting, 12.6.3.1, 12.7.4.4
  Specification for, 12.3, A.12.3.3
  Termination
    Chimneys, 12.6.2, A.12.6.2.1
    Gas vents, 12.7.3
    Single-wall metal pipe, 12.8.3
    Through the wall, 12.9
  Two or more appliances, single vent, 12.11.3.3 to 12.11.3.6, 12.11.4, 13.2.18
  Type of system to use, 12.5, Table 12.5.1
  Vent offset (definition), 3.3.101
  Vented appliances, *see* Vented appliances

-W-

Wall furnaces, *see* Furnaces
Wall head adapters, 7.1.7.1 Ex.2
  Definition, 3.3.103
Wall room heaters, 10.21.4
Water heaters, 10.26, A.10.26.8
  Antisiphon devices, 10.26.8, A.10.26.8
  Automatic instantaneous type, 10.26.7
  Circulating tank type, 10.26.8, A.10.26.8
  Definition, 3.3.56.7
  Venting, 12.3.2(5), 13.1.11(5), F.2.1 to F.2.4
Weather conditions, 5.13.2
  Floor furnaces and, 10.10.11
  Lightning protection, 7.12.5, A.7.12.5
  Protection against, 7.1.4, A.7.1.4
  Single-wall metal pipe, use of, 12.8.2, A.12.8.2
Work interruptions, 4.2.2

-Z-

Zero governor, 7.11.4
  Definition, 3.3.104